By the Same Author

THE STREETS WERE PAVED WITH GOLD

HARD FEELINGS

Hard Feelings

REPORTING ON POLS, THE PRESS,
PEOPLE, AND THE CITY

Ken Auletta

Random House
New York

c/1980

Some of the articles in this book have been
previously published by the following: *Esquire*,
[MORE] Magazine, The New York *Daily News*, *New York* Magazine,
and *The Village Voice*.

The following articles appeared originally in *The
New Yorker*: Profile of Mayor Koch (Part I) and
Profile of Mayor Koch (Part II).

Grateful acknowledgment is made to the following
for permission to reprint previously published material:

The Village Voice: Four articles by Ken Auletta
are reprinted by permission of The Village Voice.
Copyright © The Village Voice, Inc., 1975/76.

Library of Congress Cataloging in Publication Data
Auletta, Ken.
Hard feelings.
I. Title.
AC8.A783 081 79-3803
ISBN 0-394-50020-2

Manufactured in the United States of America
2 4 6 8 9 7 5 3
First Edition

FOR AMANDA

Acknowledgments

A word of thanks to those who helped coach and, sometimes, coax me. They include: Richard Reeves, Byron Dobell, Milton Glaser, Sheldon Zelaznick, Jack Nessel, Clay Felker, and Walter Bernard of the original *New York* magazine; Tom Morgan, Karen Durbin, Marianne Partridge, Alan Weitz, Judy Daniels and Jack Newfield of *The Village Voice*; William Shawn and William Whitworth of *The New Yorker*; Warren Hoge, formerly of the New York *Post*; Mike O'Neill and Earl King of the New York *Daily News*; and Jason Epstein, my editor at Random House. I might still be a high school dropout were it not for Abe Lass, the caring former principal of Abraham Lincoln High School; and, most of all, a respectful and loving bow to Nettie and Paul Auletta, who taught by example.

These collected pieces are unchanged except for a stray word here or there, the excision of a superfluous sentence or paragraph that would demand needless amplification. No meanings or interpretations have been altered, including several that now seem silly. Postscripts have been appended in the hope of raising questions about journalism in general, and my reporting in particular.

Contents

HARD FEELINGS

Introduction

I became a reporter involuntarily. My candidate for Governor of New York (Howard Samuels), with an assist from his campaign manager (me), was clobbered in the Democratic primary by Hugh Carey. That was 1974, and the mere thought of taking a real job, a job in business, for example, terrified me. My God, what do people in business gossip about—Merrill Lynch? I feared I would lose the sense I enjoyed while working for Samuels or for Robert Kennedy in his 1968 presidential campaign, or as executive director of the New York City Off-Track Betting Corporation in the early seventies, or before that as special assistant to the Undersecretary of the U.S. Commerce Department—that work, somehow, was not *work*. I craved a larger audience than business offered.

So I became a reporter. The pay was lousy. There were no campaign aides to screen calls or type letters. Still, I felt that as a reporter I could affect government policy, could help shape public opinion. I could remain in the thick of a world I liked while avoiding the obsessive concern with how my candidate or government agency looked. No longer would I agonize over what fickle politicians or voters said about my boss. A reporter and columnist is more or less his own boss, freer to say what he thinks. After *selling* someone else, I was about to become a *buyer*.

But first I needed a job. Enter Warren Hoge, who was then metropolitan editor of the New York *Post*. Remembering my brief stint in 1968 as editor and columnist for the now-defunct *Manhattan Tribune*, Hoge took a gamble and invited me to become the *Post*'s chief political correspondent. This was November 1974, and for two weeks my starched sentences appeared in the *Post*. The writing wasn't so hot, but the stories themselves weren't bad. Coincidentally, the day my interview with Governor Carey made "the wood" (the front page), I had an encounter with the *Post*'s publisher (see "Dorothy Schiff: 'Maybe I Am a Silly Person' ") and left the *Post*.

The independence that Mrs. Schiff provided was excessive. My phone did not ring. As a journalist, I was a nobody. Worse, there was the problem of credibility. Reporters tend to be suspicious of anyone who moves directly from politics to journalism. Would I settle old scores? Would I be "objective"? Was reporting just a springboard back to politics for me? Similar questions have haunted others who have made the switch from politics to journalism, including the better-known Bill Moyers, William Safire, and George Will.

For the next eight months or so, I free-lanced, mostly for *The Village Voice,* which paid a princely $100 to $300 per piece. I soon learned that to gain credibility with my new colleagues often meant to lose it with former friends. Looking back, I see that I sometimes went too far to prove my mettle. There were times, for instance, when I may have too zealously criticized my former political allies. It took me a while to calm down and stop trying to prove my journalistic manhood.

In September 1975 I became a staff writer for the *Voice,* producing a weekly "Runnin' Scared" political column and longer pieces. Late that year I also became a contributing editor to *New York* magazine. In January 1977, when Australian publisher Rupert Murdoch purchased *New York* and the *Voice,* more than forty writers and editors, including me, resigned.

That spring I became a writer for *The New Yorker,* a weekly (Sunday) columnist for the New York *Daily News,* and co-host of a weekly interview program on public television (WNET). In March 1979 my first book, *The Streets Were Paved with Gold,* was published.

If there's a better line of work, I don't know of it. I do not have one boss, one beat, or daily deadlines to meet. I enjoy the advantages—the power, the access, the gossip—that I enjoyed in government and politics, but not the disadvantages: too little independence, too many chicken dinners, and an occasional fear of the press.

There are benefits to having been on both sides, not the least of them being the recognition that reporters, like the people we cover, put our pants on one leg at a time. This is the point of a *Village Voice* essay that I wrote May 3, 1976, and might be an appropriate beginning for this collection about my former profession, my current one, and my city:

> I used to be in politics. For the last year or so I've been in journalism. It's often like being in politics.
>
> It is frequently said that politicians and the press are engaged in an adversary relationship. Often they are. But it is surprising how similar the adversaries can be. Politics is sated with prima donnas, headline hunters, ruthless opportunists, thin-skinned cynical egomaniacs; whereas journalism is bursting with prima donnas, headline hunters, ruthless opportunists, thin-skinned cynical egomaniacs.
>
> It was all said in *The Front Page.* And by A. J. Liebling and Evelyn Waugh.
>
> In the wake of the movie *All the President's Men,* it is worth saying again, for that film could lead one to believe that being a journalist is like being Lawrence of Arabia—conquering alien forces, toppling governments. The movie *does* portray the heroic efforts of two great reporters to get their story and check the abuses of governmental power. But less noticed, it also shows that journalists sometimes act like politicians—or, more precisely, like other members of the human race. Woodward and Bernstein were not exactly choir-boys when they shamed a Washington *Post* secretary into enticing an old

boyfriend to providing her a list of all employees working for Richard Nixon's reelection; nor was Bernstein, when, late one night, he pressured a frightened, middle-aged campaign bookkeeper into giving him information; or when he asked the telephone company for confidential phone records. The movie omitted it, but the book candidly related how they (perhaps illegally) badgered grand jurors in order to extract information about Watergate. When politicians do this we usually call them "ruthless" or "opportunistic."

The thought that our behavior can be remotely similar to politicians' offends most journalists, for our job is to *judge* behavior, to judge what is news. We have no choice but to take on a tone of omniscience as we write of the deceit, lies, deals, and scandals of politicians. But, like politicians, we go to the bathroom, sweat, go bald, get fat, want to pay as little in taxes as possible, and sometimes fudge on our expense accounts.

Some journalists are also bigots, assuming that *all* politicans are crooks. I was having a phone conversation with Assemblyman Andrew Stein in mid-January, and to prove to me that he was a good guy, Stein blurted, "John Hess [a *New York Times* investigative reporter] likes me—and he *hates all* politicians." I asked Andy whether he would be offended if John Hess expressed surprise that Andy, unlike *all* Jews, did not have a funny nose?

Yet a John Hess, who has written for [MORE] magazine that the press should be unconcerned about the civil liberties of politicians, is honored as an investigative reporter. Often, he's been a damn good one. But he would not be accorded the same respect were he to walk around blaring that *all* editors are crazy.

It's chic and popular to be antipolitician, and Lord knows, they deserve much of what they get. But it's also a little too glib, and dishonest. Many of the stereotypes we sling at politicians could, with some modifications, be aimed at journalists. Here are some of them:

1. Politicians are "just interested in headlines."

Is the press really so different? Like politicians, reporters strive to get their stories on page one. The first time a story of mine made the *Voice*'s front page, I received a bigger thrill than if my former candidate, Howard Samuels, had landed on page one. Page one can do for a reporter's reputation and livelihood what it does for a politician's "name recognition." And I, like every journalist, want to get back there. David Wise describes the urge in *The Politics of Lying*: "At 7 P.M. on any given day in Washington, the question on the mind of scores of newspaper correspondents is not 'What fresh insights into the endless adventures of government did I bring to my readers today?' but 'Did I make page one?' "

The disease afflicts the best of us. After a lengthy hiatus from daily reporting, Bob Woodward returned to the Washington *Post* in late September 1975 with a bang. His front-page story trumpeted that Howard Hunt was allegedly ordered by the White House to kill columnist Jack Anderson. On October 1 (to keep his story alive?) Woodward followed with: "The Watergate special prosecutor's office has begun an investigation of 'allegations [presumably made by Woodward] that there was a plot to physically injure' " Anderson. The story has not surfaced since. When politicians do that we call it "shooting from the hip."

Like politicians, journalists are subjected to pressures. The politician tries to please his constituents (the voters); a reporter curries favor with his (readers, listeners, viewers, or editors). TV and radio reporters often ask identical questions at press conferences because they want to get on the air as having asked the question that will make news that day; or because they get paid by the number of times they are on the air; or because—like true performers—they wish to create sparks. When Jeff Kamen of WPIX-TV stood up at Ramsey Clark's March 15 press conference and shouted a barrage of the most aggressively dumb questions I've ever heard, he wasn't in the news business. But it made good theater on the ten-o'clock news. JFK sex stories were a hit in *Time* magazine. Front-page headlines in the *Daily News* or *The Village Voice* are designed to sell newspapers. Sometimes they go overboard. When politicians do that we call them "demagogues."

2. Politicians are "ruthless."

Actually, aside from prosecutors, the most ruthless people I know are reporters. Our job is to get a story, and often that means getting a politician. I remember phoning a Bronx judge late one night to ask if he owned a piece of a nursing home. A young boy answered, passing the phone to his nervous father. He had done nothing wrong, he said. He was frightened. So was his wife, who was hovering nearby. The judge mentioned mutual friends, acquaintances, experiences. He told me he had lost money. He sounded like a nice man. Tough shit, Judge. Just give me the facts. Do you own a piece of a nursing home? Period.

Paul O'Dwyer is a fine man. But he's a lousy City Council president. When I worked in politics, he was a friend. When I became a journalist he became just another person to cover. Because the loyalty system is different in politics or in personal relationships. Paul doesn't understand that. He hasn't talked to me in over a year. He probably thinks I'm ruthless, and from his vantage point, he's right.

Certainly Carl Bernstein was ruthless when he told Leonard Downie, Jr., as recorded in his book *The New Muckrakers,* "You act differently with different people. I can get along with a cop or a cabinet officer. You adopt different roles and ploys depending on who you're talking to. You got to know their prejudices and play to them. You got to bullshit some."

Unbeknownst to his callers, James Reston used to tape some of his phone interviews. Dick Reeves has told of reading memos from the top of government officials' desks, arguing that if they didn't want him to see the memos, they should have hidden them. Reporters—like CIA spooks—have been known to get stories by impersonating people: Former Chicago *American* reporter Harry Romanoff reportedly interviewed the mother of murderer Richard Speck by pretending to be her son's attorney. When a politician or government official gives a reporter an important piece of information but ties his hands by first saying it is "off the record," you can be sure that most of us will be able to track down the story. How? By using the information to ask a question of someone else. In that sense, even though we gave our word, nothing is "off the record." Yet when politicians break their word or pledge to the voters, we call them "liars."

3. Politicians are "phonies."

Very often they are. They befriend people they don't like, they smile, wink, slap a back, kiss a baby. They make nice to people. So, to a lesser degree, do journalists. A journalist's sources are the equivalent of a politician's contributors. Reporters, particularly daily reporters, are wary of offending sources who provide valuable information. So reporters sometimes pull their punches in order to get more stories. This is one of Secretary of State Henry Kissinger's secrets. He continues to do the diplomatic press corps the favor of remaining accessible, thereby co-opting reporters like Marvin Kalb of CBS, who treat Kissinger with undue deference.

Journalists who do profiles take pains to put their subjects at ease. Some will ask the more relaxing questions first. Draw them out on topics they enjoy talking about. Don't take notes. Feign sympathy. In an article in [MORE], David Alpern described how *New York Times* reporter Nicholas Gage extracted from Congressman Mario Biaggi confirmation that Biaggi had made a second appearance before a grand jury: "Gage asked first about a number of charges that he knew Biaggi could easily deny. As the congressman began feeling more confident, Gage inquired whether he had been asked about a certain matter at this second grand jury appearance—Gage knew he hadn't— and Biaggi breezily denied it. After several more irrelevant questions, Gage asked again about the second appearance. Yes, there was one, Biaggi replied, but the particular matter Gage had asked about earlier had positively never come up. And that confirmed the second appearance."

Bluffing is one tool in the reporter's arsenal. Granting immunity is another. Many reporters will promise a source immunity (keep his name out of the story) in return for cooperation. Bullying is also used sometimes to threaten an official with negative publicity unless he'll spill the story. The *Times'* Seymour Hersh, one of America's best investigative reporters, is also known for being one of the biggest bullies. Then there are the flatterers. *Time* magazine's Hugh Sidey is the journalistic equivalent of the chief of protocol, making sure that public figures are pleased with the bouquets and soft pillows he places before them.

In addition to the phony reporter, there is the phony story. In 1970, when I was managing Howard Samuels's unsuccessful campaign for governor (I repeated this feat in 1974), a *Daily News* reporter phoned to say that he could not make the trip with Samuels to the Brooklyn beaches but wished to write something. He would call later to find out what had happened. He did, and I told him that the candidate was accompanied by five daughters and one son, ate a hot dog, and got a nice reception. The next day's *News* featured a story of Samuels being mobbed at the beach, reporting what people said to him and even what his daughters said to the multitudes. The reporter made it up. (I've left him nameless—and that's a "political" decision. It might endanger his job.)

4. Politicians worry too much about their "image."

Journalists, like politicians, often worry about their image. Last September's *New York* magazine killed an unflattering cover of President Ford after there were several attempts on his life. The story was pushed back inside the magazine because the editors feared it would look to the public as if *they* were taking a shot at Ford. The story ran in full, so there was no question of censorship. But *New York*'s editors made an essentially "image" decision—just as politicians do when they downplay busing before white Mississippians or hold off a public statement or proposal until the timing is right.

It was an "image" concern of the editors of the Washington *Post*—as the movie reminds us—that they beat the *New York Times* to the Watergate story. When Jack Newfield broke the story of the city's plan to buy Madison Square Garden, a *Times* City Hall reporter—as one journalist who was there remembers it—shouted at his editor, "I'm not going to do that story and chase the *Voice* and Newfield." Image again.

Similarly, most of the press played down the Pike Committee's CIA report because it had appeared first in another paper. Their justification was that there was nothing new in the report. In truth, many reporters covering the CIA beat had a self-interest in playing down that story because they hadn't gotten it.

And Joseph Kraft sounded more like a politician concerned about another pol's image than a syndicated columnist when he reportedly told James Fallows of the *Washington Monthly,* "Anybody who attacked him [Kissinger in 1974] was running the risk of playing into the hands of the hard-liners. A good many of us accepted that line and pulled punches."

5. Politicians are more concerned with "shadow than substance."

Politicians are moved by appearance: The appearance of public support or anger; newspaper editorials, public demonstrations, or calls from political or financial contributors. John Lindsay is often taken as the prototype of the official whose policies were shaped not by "How will it play in Peoria?" but "How will it play in the *New York Times*?" The former mayor did, after all, appoint the Knapp Commission to study police corruption in order to head off a *Times* exposé of police corruption.

The same preoccupation with shadow is common to journalism. Both Terry Sanford and Milton Shapp dropped from this year's presidential derby, complaining that the press ignored the substance of their government proposals and concentrated on the shadow of who was not supporting them. It was hard for the press to take them seriously as presidential candidates. But they have a point in saying the press largely ignored the substance of their ideas. Just as much of the New York press accepted Abe Beame's campaign slogan that he was a fiscal expert. Press accounts of candidate debates invariably stress personality, not issue conflicts. Trying to attract coverage for the release of a serious campaign position paper is like trying to catch cancer.

So, too, the recent release by Daniel Schorr of the Pike Committee report revealed a press corps preoccupied not with the substance of that scathing document but with Schorr's motives. Or as David Ignatius eloquently wrote: "We were all bureaucrats now, more concerned about the threat of leaks than with understanding the vital information they conveyed."

Politicians who behave that way are condemned as "superficial" or "cowards."

6. Politics is full of "conflicts of interest."

It is outrageous that political leaders like Pat Cunningham (state Democratic chairman) or Meade Esposito (Brooklyn Democratic leader) or John Calandra (Bronx Republican leader) trade on their political positions of power to fatten their legal or insurance businesses. Nursing-home owner Bernard Bergman enlisted Assembly Speaker Stanley Steingut, Assembly Majority Leader Al Blumenthal, former secretary to the Governor, Robert Douglass, and Senate Finance Chairman John Marchi less for their brains than for their political connections. Banks place legislators on their boards, lobbyists retain legislators' law firms. The distinction between a politician's public and private interests becomes blurred.

Real or apparent conflicts of interest are not foreign to reporters, however. State Special Prosecutor Maurice Nadjari, testifying before the State Commission of Investigation on January 27, claimed he never leaked a story to the press. That's nonsense. Yet how many reporters who had benefited from these leaks said so? In his book *Conversations with Kennedy,* the Washington *Post* 's Ben Bradlee describes how—torn between his friend (John Kennedy) and his employer (then *Newsweek* magazine)—he sometimes cleared stories with his friend. George Douris, the political editor of the Long Island *Press,* clears the appointment of most Greek-Americans who work in the city administration he covers. Reporters, like politicians, ought to be concerned about even the *appearance* of conflict of interest. John Hess, Jack Newfield, Pete Hamill, Steve Bauman (WNEW-TV), and Geraldo Rivera (WABC-TV) have all written about Andy Stein and his nursing home-probes. They have all written about the appearance of conflict of interest among politicians. They have all also been regular guests at Stein's Southampton estate, eating his food, sipping his expensive wine and pear brandy. Most are good and honest reporters. But when Mayor Lindsay hitched a ride on a Bristol-Myers plane, much of the press correctly chided him for failing to be sensitive to the "appearance" of conflict of interest.

7. Politicians have too many "vested interests."

The press is not always a disinterested observer. It might be interesting to know how many city securities are owned by the media that covered the city's bout to avoid default. (Both the *New York Times* and the *Daily News*, without alerting their readers, invested $500,000 and $100,000, respectively, in city securities.)

Listening to Deputy Police Commissioner Frank McLoughlin talk of the press's insatiable demand for police press cards is incredible. Everyone—semiretired reporters, desk editors, movie critics—wants one as a mark of status. McLoughlin says he has already given out three thousand because he fears to antagonize the press. But now, he says, the press cards are next to "meaningless." The White House complains they don't want to honor them because there are so many that "it is a security risk."

Press license plates—which grant special parking privileges—are in even greater demand. They were designed to allow reporters to drive quickly to breaking news stories. Instead, they often allow reporters and editors to drive to work. When city commissioners or diplomats abuse their parking privileges, the press becomes indignant. Headlines explode with news of "scandal."

The national press corps traveling with a presidential candidate often has a stake in that candidate's reaching the White House. As the candidate moves up, so does the reporter.

Press organizations can also act out of vested interest. When I was executive director of the city's OTB in 1973, a reporter representing the Inner Circle (an organization of City Hall reporters) called. He expressed surprise that my boss, Howard Samuels, had yet to purchase tickets to their annual dinner. Reminding me what an important affair it was—particularly for a man who hoped to be governor—he suggested we purchase a table for $1,000. I felt like I was being shaken down. Since the good wishes of the city press corps were important to

a man running for office, Samuels, at my urging, bought the table. That same
year a city Sanitation Department official was forced to resign and was threatened with legal action after City Hall reporters revealed he had urged his
employees to buy tickets to a political function.

8. Politicians are "egomaniacs," too interested in "saving face."

Lyndon Johnson is the classic example of a politician too proud to admit
his policy (in Vietnam) was wrong. Most lies in politics are not coolly planned
but rather the result of panic, of people blinded by their own egos or desire
not to look bad. It's called trying to protect your ass. It happens in journalism.
As I write this I'm embarrassed. Two week ago I predicted that Pat Cunningham would probably not be reelected state Democratic chairman. Friday, he
was. Five years ago Nicholas Gage wrote a front-page story in the *Times*
predicting City Purchase Commissioner Marvin Gersten would be indicted by
a federal grand jury. He never was, and the *Times* never offered an apology.
When Assembly Majority Leader Al Blumenthal was indicted by nursing-
home Special Prosecutor Joseph Hynes, the *Times* and the *News* editorially
urged that he step down. In the two weeks since his indictment was dismissed,
they—like all of us at the *Voice*—have remained silent.

At 9:27 P.M. on April 6, the night of the Wisconsin primary, ABC-TV,
wanting to be first, rushed on the air with a prediction that Morris Udall had
won. At 10:22 P.M. NBC followed suit. In fact, Carter was the winner. That
same night this writer partook in the self-indulgence that passes for election-
night analysis. Along with writer Jeff Greenfield and the Committee for an
Effective Congress' Russell Hemenway, I appeared on the Barry Gray radio
show from 10 P.M. to midnight. As the returns from the Wisconsin and New
York primaries trickled in, we gave them instant meaning. We tried to sound
informed, but as with ABC and NBC, a lot of it was guesswork. Our opinions
changed every couple of minutes, roughly coinciding with the latest fragments
coming over the wire. One moment we knowingly portrayed Udall as the big
winner. No, it looks like Carter. Or Jackson. Or Humphrey. Then Udall, or
Carter, or Jackson was the big loser.

In the morning papers, most political correspondents filed front-page ana-
lyses offering the readers their instant interpretations. These reporters wrote
their stories at roughly the same hour of night, and, as we did, felt compelled
to tell their readers what it all meant before the dust had settled. Like politicians, we find it hard to keep our mouths shut. The instant consensus was that
the Carter bandwagon had slowed appreciably, that Hubert Humphrey looked
more and more like he might be a deadlocked convention winner—particularly
since Carter would fare poorly in the April 27 Pennsylvania primary. As I
write, it is now the consensus of national political reporters that the Carter
bandwagon is rolling, that he should capture a plurality of the popular vote
in Pennsylvania, and that if he does, a Humphrey candidacy may be dead.
Politicians who blow elections are pegged as "losers."

9. Politicians are "thin-skinned" and "overly sensitive to criticism."

I've always found reporters much more sensitive to criticism than politicians
—in part because they have less experience with it. I remember talking with
my friend Dick Reeves when *Time* magazine was preparing a press-section
profile on him and his book on President Ford. Dick, who can dish it out with
the best of them, was plainly worried. "It may be a bad story," he said.

"They're asking a lot of questions. This guy, Dean Fischer, is asking me questions like 'How much time did you spend with Ford?' " Reeves was genuinely shocked. As was *Times* reporter Steve Weisman when Alex Cockburn's *Voice* column had one small, unflattering reference to him. "I feel like I was punched in the stomach," Weisman said. Steve, whose brilliant City Hall reporting led the *Times* day after day, protested, "I'm not a public figure." Like hell he—we—ain't. In this media age, most reporters have more power over public policy than the average member of the City Council or state legislature. Mayors and governors at least return our phone calls.

As Gay Talese understood early, those who run the *New York Times* are powerful, important people whom the public ought to know more about. Yet Abe Rosenthal, the managing editor of the *Times,* regularly hides from personal profiles. As does Clay Felker, the editor in chief of the *Voice* and *New York* and *New West* magazines. Dorothy Schiff, editor in chief and publisher of the New York *Post,* consented to a magazine profile several years ago only after winning the right to approve each word prior to publication. During the flap caused by his role in leaking the Pike Papers, Daniel Schorr was interviewed by Laurence Stern of the Washington *Post.* "Schorr wandered on and off the record," wrote Bob Kuttner in [MORE], "confirming his role on a background basis but trying to persuade Stern to accept his on-the-record denial that he was the *Voice*'s source." When politicians do this we accuse them of trying to "manipulate" and "manage the news."

10. Politics suffers from "bossism."

Manhattan Democratic County Leader Frank Rossetti has been called "a boss" in *New York Times* editorials. Yet a *Times* editorial endorsement of a Manhattan candidate can deliver more votes than Frank Rossetti's. The New York *Post* frequently cites Brooklyn Democratic County Leader Meade Esposito as a "boss." Yet this February, Mrs. Schiff personally killed an investigative series on supermarkets by reporter Steve Lawrence. Many *Post* reporters believe the reason she did this was her fear of losing supermarket advertising. When asked for on-the-record comments concerning stories affecting their own paper or its management, most reporters act like cautious civil servants and remain silent. The *New York Times* recently combined their separate daily and Sunday departments. One of the reasons, reportedly, was that the *Times* wanted to speak with "one voice." When government officials instruct employees to forward all press inquiries to the press office, reporters have been known to complain of "censorship."

Like political bosses, journalists sometimes abuse their power. We abuse our power when we get angry at some personal affront and set out to *get* a public figure. Truth is, our treatment of politicians is often affected by how cooperative, how personable, a public figure is with us. When he was U.S. Attorney, the press treated Robert Morgenthau as a force for good, in part because he and his office leaked like a Melitta coffeemaker. U.S. Attorney Whitney North Seymour was subjected to generally harsh treatment, in part because he repeatedly lectured and inconvenienced the press, reminding them that leaks were against the law. How much of the general press criticism of the new Woodward-Bernstein book is explained by simple penis envy?

• • •

Do these observations apply to *all* journalists? No. Do they excuse out-rages committed by politicians? No. Do lying and arrogance and conflicts of interest exist to the same degree in journalism as in politics? Of course not. Journalists are judged more on the quality of their work, and by a more discerning audience—their editors and fellow journalists. On the other hand, politicians have more checks on their potential abuse of power than do journalists. In politics, a greater premium is placed on personal loyalty. You do favors for people. IOU's and remembering your friends are part of the glue and currency of politics. In journalism the emphasis is on getting a true story. Personal friendships should not intrude. Politicians are—and should be—held to an even higher standard. They spend public money, swear an oath of office, enter into a public contract when they make pro-mises and seek voter support.

I love being a journalist. I don't miss political dinners, peddling my candidate (whom I admired) as if I were a fish salesman, picking up the papers each night and going to bed happy if my candidate made page one, or with a churning stomach—if he was attacked. It is more satisfying to be judged on what *I* do, to sort out and decide what *I* really think about the substance of a public problem rather than its politics.

Pound for pound there is also more talent in journalism than in politics. Where does one find Murray Kempton's poetic brilliance, or I. F. Stone's integrity? Jimmy Breslin is a bully, but he'll be remembered fifty years from now. So, I hope, will Homer Bigart. Dick Reeves is the most insightful political writer in America. Woodward and Bernstein helped shape the course of history. Gabe Pressman, Sam Roberts, Nora Ephron, Nick Pileggi, David Broder, Leslie Gelb, Mike Royko, Seymour Hersh, Sandy Smith, Donald Barlett and James Steele, Jack Germond, Anthony Lewis, Tim Crouse, George Will, Daniel Schorr, Warren Hoge, Jim Klurfeld, Abe Rosenthal, Dave Shaeffer, James Wieghart, Theodore H. White, Arthur Gelb, Mary McGrory, Mike Wallace, Frank Clines, Steve Weisman, Helen Dudar, Marty Nolan—these are terrific journalists. Thank God we have the *New York Times* to kick around.

But journalism, like politics, is also a public trust. The public relies on our information to make informed judgments. If the "reality" we convey is shaped by our own "politics"—getting on page one, covering our ass, getting back at someone, making nice to a good source—then we don't serve our nonvoting constituents.

It's useful to remember, as I. F. Stone once wrote, that all people are "half-monkey." In his new book, Leonard Downie, Jr., metropolitan editor of the Washington *Post,* has a description of two of America's best report-ers, Woodward and Bernstein. They are, he writes, "persistent, insecure, ambitious, resourceful, and manipulative." That's a pretty fair description of most successful people.

PART I

Profiles

The Mayor: Ed Koch

The New Yorker, September 10 and September 17, 1979

Friends and associates of Mayor Edward I. Koch have noticed that when
the mayor's attention wanders during discussions of the city's fiscal crisis
or some other eye-glazing topic, a sure way to bring him back is to change
the subject to the mayor. The truth is that the mayor finds himself fascinating. With the possible exception of food—Koch loves to eat and to try new
restaurants—his favorite subjects of conversation are himself and his may-
oralty. The mayor discusses himself with a readiness that would be striking
even in the capitals of self-absorption, Hollywood and Washington, but his
pleasure is so undisguised, so childlike, that it seems to charm far more
people than it offends. "Ed likes himself," says Deputy Mayor Philip Toia,
meaning it as a compliment. Corporation counsel Allan Schwartz says,
"The world started when he became mayor." One of the things the mayor
likes about himself is that despite his climb to the top of the ladder, despite
the attention and the power, in his opinion he has remained a regular guy,
hasn't lost the common touch. "I know why I'm popular," he told me not
long ago. "A woman summed it up in a special way on Atlantic Avenue
on Sunday—'Gee, I think you're terrific.' So I asked why. She said, 'Because
of the way you do what you're doing. It's so easy. There's no pomposity.'
I think that's true." Once, when I asked the mayor to assess the blacks'
struggle for civil rights, his answer to this general question was personal:
"First, as you know, I was attacked by some black leaders and newspapers
who would give the impression that not only do I have a conflict going but
I am not popular. Not true. Neither do I have a conflict nor am I unpopular.
Fifty-eight percent of the blacks in the city think I'm doing a very good job."
Edward Costikyan, a Manhattan lawyer, who was co-chairman of Koch's
1977 campaign for mayor and was promised the post of first deputy mayor,
recalls that during all the time they worked together, Koch never once
asked him a personal question—about his family, say. Toia and other
associates have had the same experience. This is not to say that Koch is not
a warm man, good company, unusually candid and accessible. He has many
close friends, particularly for a politician. "I don't think he could have those
friendships if he just had a one-way ego," says David Garth, the media
consultant, who numbers the mayor among his clients. Nevertheless, Koch
is like the Hollywood director in the old anecdote who barks to an associate,

"Enough about me! Let's talk about you. What do you think of me?" When there is no one around for the mayor to discuss himself with, he talks to a tape recorder. He is dictating his diary, with the intention of writing a book about his first term as mayor, whether or not he is reelected.

Some Koch observers think that the constant focus on *me*—the "Hi, how'm I doing?" routine he greets people with—reveals an insecure man straining for approval. His decision, after his election, not to appoint a first deputy mayor is explained as a fear of being overshadowed. "I think there's a basic insecurity there," Costikyan says. "In areas he doesn't feel comfortable in, he doesn't want someone who knows more than he does." Victor Gotbaum, executive director of District Council 37, the city's largest municipal union, believes that during the 1978 labor negotiations Koch kept undermining his own negotiators by demonstrating a lack of trust in them —behavior that Gotbaum regarded as evidence of "an insecurity that overcomes his intelligence." Among those who know the mayor, that is a minority view, and the mayor himself certainly doesn't share it. When asked to describe his weaknesses, Koch says, "I'm really not able to answer that. I'm really quite satisfied with myself. I like myself." One of his closest friends recalls the mayor saying, "You know, David Brown"—a former deputy mayor for policy—"thinks I'm a weak manager. You know, I'm a good manager. He's wrong. I know more about what's going on in this administration than any of them." The friend adds, "He is totally secure. He does not go home at night and wrestle with the notion of how he is performing." Still another slant is offered by an elected official who works closely with Koch. He thinks the mayor is secure with his insecurities. "He is adjusted," this man says, meaning that Koch is comfortable with himself.

Working from his base of self-approval, the mayor is a combative man —with businessmen, labor leaders, politicians, the city bureaucracy, Jews, blacks, Puerto Ricans, and constituents in general. He quotes Manhattan Representative Charles Rangel as saying of him, "You think he's mean to *you*? He's mean to *every*body." The best politics, Koch believes, is the appearance of no politics. In happy support of Rangel's statement, the mayor recounts how he ended special police protection for the spiritual leader of one of Brooklyn's largest Hasidic communities, how he ordered the arrest of blacks who staged a sit-in at City Hall, how he told a minister who jostled him in the Bronx, "Do that again and I put your ass in jail." Others recall his public complaints about the "idiocy" of the state legislature, and his undiplomatic description, at a news conference, of municipal labor: "The labor unions make large contributions to everybody. They don't care if you're Attila the Hun as long as you do what they want."

When Robert Morgenthau was running for district attorney a few years ago and Koch was campaigning with him in front of Bloomingdale's, a member of the Progressive Labor party stuck a megaphone in Koch's ear and shouted, "War criminal! War criminal!"

Koch replied, "—— off!"

Shocked, the young man asked, "Can I repeat that?"

Koch said, "Sure," and the young man announced through his megaphone, "Congressman Koch just told me to —— off!"

The audience of several hundred burst into applause.

Koch has a wonderful memory for slights. When he was a student at the New York University School of Law, he was offended by what he regarded as anti-Semitism on the part of one of his professors. Koch remembers that this professor told the class, "When I went to school, not every son of a shoemaker or butcher or cloakmaker could go." Twenty-two years later Congressman Koch was invited to give the convocation speech at the N.Y.U. School of Law graduation. As he delivered his speech, he spotted his former teacher in the audience and made flattering reference to his ability as a raconteur. The old man beamed. But Koch went on, "I remember one of his little comments twenty-two years ago, when he said to this class of eighty-three people, many of them Jewish, many of them Italian, some of them black, that when he went to school not every son of a shoemaker, butcher, or cloakmaker could go. Well, twenty-two years later that school invited this son of a cloakmaker to come back and give this address." Koch now says, "That gave me a great feeling, I must say. I watched his face. He just shriveled." An elderly Jewish woman, the grandmother of one of the graduates, took the congressman's hand and kissed it, thanking him for "saying that." Koch says, "It was for me very moving. How much crap do people have to take? And isn't it wonderful to be able to hand it out? I don't forget. I get even." Last year Koch got even with Robert Abrams, who was then the borough president of the Bronx and was running for state attorney general. "He had screwed me in 1977," Koch says. "I remember well. He called the day he was endorsing Mario Cuomo. I said, 'Bobby, I can't understand that. You and I have worked together for years.' I said, 'I'm not going to argue, but I think you're making a terrible mistake. And, as you know, the wheel turns.' Then he came to see me when he was running in the primary for attorney general. He asked for my endorsement. I said, 'Bobby, don't you remember I told you the wheel turns? It has turned. No, I won't support you.' After I do that, the slate is clean. I wipe it clean after the wheel has turned." He is now a friend of Abrams.

Koch can recite what someone said or wrote about him, specifying when, and sometimes even what page it was printed on. When I said something to him recently about his extraordinary memory, he recalled the time he ran into the comedian Mel Brooks and his wife, Anne Bancroft, at Maxim's, in Paris. "Remember when we met in the Village at my brownstone?" Brooks inquired. Yes, Koch remembered. It was 1962, and Koch was trying to get signatures on petitions for a futile race he was making for the Assembly. As he knocked at the door, "a monster dog" rushed by, pursued by Brooks and Bancroft. Koch, a stranger, joined in the chase. "That's when Annie and I signed your petition," Brooks reminded Koch. The three of them sat at Maxim's and reminisced. "I didn't say it," Koch told me, "but *he* signed. She didn't. I remember."

What he says he rarely forgives is a "personal insult"—the "vile" rumors of homosexuality he blames Cuomo for spreading in the mayoral race, the "disloyalty" of former Mayor John Lindsay in supporting Koch's congressional opponent after Koch had bravely endorsed Lindsay for mayor, the "lies" about the sincerity of his commitment to civil rights and the death penalty which were propagated by writers for *The Village Voice.* Someone he has found it especially difficult to forgive, for what he regards as "a betrayal," is Queens Representative Benjamin Rosenthal. When Koch and Rosenthal were in Congress together, they were close friends. As mayor, Koch used to invite the Rosenthals to stay overnight at Gracie Mansion. The chief of the city's Washington office, Julian Spirer (whom many at City Hall consider inadequate), was hired with the encouragement of Rosenthal, from whose staff he came. The friendship was poisoned last November, however, when Nat Hentoff, of the *Voice,* wrote a flattering article about Brooklyn Representative Elizabeth Holtzman. Near the end of the article, which appeared on November 27, Hentoff reported that she took exception to Koch's support of the death penalty. He wrote:

> I told her of a conversation I'd had with Congressman Ben Rosenthal this summer [at Cape Cod]. "I'm a good friend of Ed," Rosenthal said, "and I campaigned with him in the mayoralty race. But I was a little troubled one day at an old people's center in Queens when Ed was doing his death plebiscite. You know, 'How many here are for the death penalty?' he says as he raises his own arm. Something must have shown on my face because Ed leaned toward me and whispered through his teeth, 'Listen, this is the only way I can get in.' "

The mayor exploded. On November 27 he dictated this letter to Rosenthal:

> DEAR BEN:
> No one has ever done me as great disservice as you have done if you are accurately reported by Nat Hentoff in this week's Village Voice.
> The comment which you allegedly attribute to me was never made by me. Therefore, what you have done is to give support to those hostile to me who simply could not accept my support of the death penalty. They will now say that my support was hypocritical when, in fact, it was not. And how can I ever convince anyone that I did not say what you purport I said. After all, yours was the testimony of a friend. . . . I also want you to know that you have severely damaged our relationship. Your call this morning indicating that you were sorry you had made a statement capable of such interpretation, but did not believe it had the implications others and myself see, was distressing to me.

If in fact you were not accurately quoted, I would appreciate your advising Nat Hentoff in writing of that and sending me a copy of that letter.

Sincerely,

EDWARD I. KOCH

MAYOR

On November 30 Rosenthal dispatched a letter to the editor of the *Voice,* with a copy to Koch. It read, in part: "Some people apparently feel that my comment implied that Ed Koch was less than totally committed to his support of the death penalty, and was inappropriately using that issue in the mayoral campaign." He said he wanted to "assure" *Voice* readers that Koch gave "his complete intellectual and moral commitment to the death penalty." He went on: "I did believe, however, that the death penalty was an irrelevant issue to raise in the mayoral campaign, and I told Ed so at the time." He concluded by testifying to Koch's "integrity and sincerity," and added: "Nothing has happened to change that opinion." Scrawled on a covering note to Koch was this handwritten message: "I don't want to keep repeating myself—but, I am overwhelmingly regretful about my comments to Hentoff. I will never go to Cape Cod again."

Koch was not swayed. Coolly, he noted that Rosenthal, in his letter to the *Voice,* did not deny saying what Hentoff quoted him as saying. With a lawyer's precision, Koch dissected Rosenthal's predicament: "Either he calls me a liar or he calls himself a liar. Either way, it's unforgivable."

Koch, as Booth Tarkington said of Teddy Roosevelt, enjoys "the fun of hating," and this worries some of his friends. "What bothers me most about him is the depth of his dislikes," says one of his closest out-of-government advisers. "There's a certain unforgivingness toward political enemies that worries me. I think that when you win a campaign you don't have to go to bed with everybody. But I believe you shake hands. He's got to grow out of that. A man who holds public trust can't afford it. You have a greater responsibility. You cannot afford personal feuds when sometime or other you might need a chit for the city. Koch gets even. The Kennedys were the same way. And it's stupid as hell."

Sometimes, however, Koch forgives. Last March, after Lieutenant Governor Mario Cuomo's daughter was mugged for the second time, Koch wrote a personal note expressing sympathy and inviting Cuomo to bury the hatchet over lunch. Koch's anger with Rosenthal, too, was eased to a certain extent when the two men had lunch during a visit to Washington that Koch made late last winter.

Because of his prominent nose and almost bare egg-shaped head, Koch is often described as looking like Frank Perdue, the chicken man. But the patches of hair on each side of Perdue's head lie flat, as if ironed; Koch's hair sticks out, curling like bedsprings. Perdue's face is taut, lined, and colorless; Koch's is puffy and smooth, with a pinkish glow. Whether or not he looks like Perdue, there is no question that the mayor has some of the traits that Perdue attributes to himself on television. Koch is a fussbudget and a stickler for detail. For instance, his mail is screened to a certain extent, of course, but he reads and answers every piece that reaches his desk. "I acknowledge every note," he says. "You know why I do it? Because people don't believe a mayor sees the mail. They think there's this gigantic maw and shredder at City Hall. When we came in, there were thousands of unanswered letters downstairs. My understanding was that the Beame administration's position was not to answer substantive questions, so as not to be on record. Answering my mail is not a fetish. It's purposeful. Besides, it's gracious."

No list of the mayor's personality traits would be complete that did not include tenacity. An example of Koch's willingness to persevere past the point at which others would surrender occurred one August night in 1971, when he was a member of Congress. He had been invited to sit on the dais at an important dinner, and he was eager not to be late. He had flown up from Washington, gone to his Greenwich Village apartment to shave and change, and was hurrying across Washington Square Park on his way to take the Sixth Avenue subway uptown to the Americana Hotel. It was a warm evening, the park was crowded with people, and it was only about six o'clock—early enough so that he would probably have time to circulate among the dinner guests during the cocktail hour. Suddenly, blocking his path, Koch recalls, was "a big black guy—every time I tell the story he gets bigger."

"Give me a quarter!" the man demanded.

"No," Koch responded instinctively.

Whereupon the stranger lifted two ham-size fists and warned, "Give me a quarter, man, or I'm going to beat the hell out of you."

Thoughts raced through Koch's mind: I really should give him a quarter. No, I'm an officer of the law! Koch steeled himself and said, "No. I'm Congressman Koch, and I'm going to have you arrested."

The panhandler looked at Koch as if he were crazy. Apparently unaccustomed to rejection, he dropped his fists, turned, and retreated.

Koch, relieved, hurried a dozen or so steps farther, then stopped. No, I've got to have him arrested, he insisted to himself, scanning the park for a cop. Seeing none, he retraced the route taken by the man, who by this time had collected two quarters from more pliant subjects, had left the park, and was heading up Fifth Avenue. The man noticed the lanky, bald-headed nut he had just met in the park giving chase, and stopped to throw him a menacing stare. But Koch kept coming. Reaching Eighth Street, the man turned toward Broadway, and Koch leaped into the street to flag a passing patrol car. "I'm Congressman Koch," he told the two cops in the patrol car. "I've just been hustled in the park and I want to have the guy arrested. He tried to extort money from me."

"You know how long that will take?" one cop asked.

"Yes, and I don't care," said Koch. "I'm supposed to be on a dais at West

Fifty-third Street at six-thirty and I'd appreciate your rushing it through, but I don't care."

"Get in."

The patrol car sped along Eighth Street and pulled up beside the man.

"I didn't do it!" the man exclaimed as he was surrounded.

"That's him," Koch said.

The cops bundled the man into the back seat. Koch jumped into the front seat, and they drove to the 6th Precinct, in Greenwich Village, where the prisoner became aggressive and boisterous. "You keep that up and I'm gonna take you into the back room," one policeman warned. Koch, a devoted civil libertarian, remembers thinking, *Ya know, I won't stop him*.

After the booking at the precinct house, the panhandler, Koch, and the cops drove down to the Criminal Courts Building, at 100 Centre Street. In the courtroom during the arraignment, as Koch was looking at his watch, the assistant district attorney who was handling the case ambled over to him and said, "Boy, are you lucky! He's pleading guilty to harassment." Harassment is a violation, which is less than a misdemeanor; the guilty plea meant no regular visits to the courtroom.

Koch, standing in front of the bench, said, "Tell the judge, please, I'd like to make a statement."

"You can't make a statement," said the assistant D.A.

"You tell the judge that Congressman Koch would like to make a statement!"

The judge, who had seemed to be asleep, sprang to life. "Oh, by all means," he said.

"Your Honor, I'm here because I'm angry," Koch said, and he went on to outline his concern for the citizens who visit the park and for the obligations of citizenship.

"Oh, yes, it's terrible," the judge responded. He turned to the defendant and said sternly, "If you ever come into my court again . . ." He gave the man a $50 fine.

Not bad, Koch thought. A steep fine.

A Legal Aid attorney pleaded, "Your Honor, my client, who is gainfully employed, does not have the money with him. Can he have a little time to pay?" The defendant was granted three weeks.

Koch was in a hurry to leave the courtroom, as was the defendant. They walked out simultaneously, and Koch recalls, "He sort of smiles at me, this defendant. I couldn't figure out why, but he smiles."

Koch arrived late for the dinner, but he did not forget the incident. He waited three weeks and then wrote to the clerk of the Criminal Court inquiring whether the fine had been paid. For a week, there was no answer. Koch dictated another letter, this time to the administrative judge, David Ross, enclosing a copy of his earlier letter and requesting an answer. Within days Koch received an answer from the clerk of the court: "I'm sorry our response was delayed. We were hoping he would come in and pay the fine.

He did not. We investigated and found that he gave us a false name and address. So we have now issued a warrant for his arrest."

Now Koch understood the defendant's smile. "This is bizarre," he said not long ago. "They don't know who he is. They don't know where he lives. But they've issued a warrant for his arrest." Koch laughs at the incident but not at the controversy it caused. When the encounter received notice in the newspapers, many of Koch's liberal Greenwich Village constituents were outraged. "One thing I'll never forgive you for is arresting that guy," a liberal friend sternly admonished him. "It was vicious to pursue a black man. All he wanted was a quarter."

When I asked Koch not long ago how he dealt with such constituents, he said, "I stood my ground. You call it confrontation. I don't think it is confrontation at all to say, 'Look, that's a lot of crap.' Sure they're gonna yell. But people enjoy it. I enjoy it. My views are not steel-encased. I'm willing to change. But it's the head-on discussion that sets me apart from others."

Still, Koch is just as capable of being evasive as the next politician—as he has been on the issue of rent control. One day several months ago, when Koch was sitting around with his friend Daniel Wolf, the founding editor of *The Village Voice,* I asked him how he squared his belief in the profit motive with his implacable opposition to lifting rent control, which some landlords say prevents them from making a profit. Koch, who pays just $257 a month for his rent-controlled Village apartment, has even opposed a means test for those tenants who might be able to afford a higher rent. Did he really believe his rhetoric, I asked, and if not, wasn't he hypocritical?

"You're right," he blurted. "There are so many inequities under rent control, and I'm going to deal with them in this term."

"You have to understand," said Wolf, "Ed came up through Village politics."

"I didn't say I was perfect," Koch said.

"Some things," Wolf said, "are so explosive . . ."

"You temper some matters," Koch said.

Why was rent control so politically explosive?

"People don't listen to a long explanation," Koch said. "It's not possible, in the course of an election, to discourse on rent control. What is possible is anything you say beyond the barest essentials will be thrown out of context and you'll spend the whole campaign defending. It's just one of those gut issues."

Like capital punishment. The "bare essentials" throughout Koch's 1977 mayoral campaign consisted in asking for a show of hands by those who agreed that murderers should be put to death. Similarly, there was little real discussion of rent control in the campaign, because almost 70 percent of all city apartments are rent-controlled or rent-stabilized.

Koch continued to temper his true views, which were that rent control should be modified. Last February he asked the City Council to extend the current rent-control and rent-stabilization laws for another three years. In April his Planning Commission chairman, Robert F. Wagner, Jr., suggested that rent control may be to blame for abandoned housing. Already, 8 percent of the city's multiple dwellings had been abandoned by private landlords, making City Hall New York's largest owner of residential buildings. In late June, Koch began to match public words with his private convictions, announcing that he planned to submit to the City Council legislation that would permit owners of the city's 400,000 or so rent-controlled apartments to charge higher but still regulated rents. "The price of fuel oil has increased approximately thirty-three percent between April 1978 and April 1979, and has created an intolerable financial pressure on many owners," Koch said.

Koch prides himself on a lack of guile—by which he means, he says, that he doesn't employ "duplicity or artifice." But he adds, "I want to make it clear. I'm not Billy Budd. Billy Budd was a schmuck!" Indeed, Koch can be sly. This quality was evident when he ran against Whitney North Seymour for Congress in 1968. He tells about the race in oral memoirs that were taped for the Oral History Research Office of Columbia University in 1975 and 1976 and are to remain under seal at the university until 1996. Koch has a transcription of them, however, and he recently permitted me to read it and to quote from it. Koch recalls in the memoirs that the Republican nominee asked Koch to accept an impartial arbitration procedure to determine unfair campaign charges.

> I figure, Well, this calls for one-upmanship. So I write back saying, "Your offer does not go far enough. Not only must we have a system whereby we can call for arbitration but no literature can be printed and published before the other has seen it if it mentions the other's name." You have to understand why I did this. I had no intention of ever mentioning his name.

Since Seymour had sponsored ample legislation as a state senator, while Koch had few bills to his credit as a member of the City Council, Koch guessed that Seymour would seek to contrast his legislative record with Koch's. Negotiations got under way with Robert Ruskin, who had served as Seymour's campaign manager in the primary.

"Oh, we're not going to give you our literature in advance," Ruskin protested.

"Only if it has my name on it, remember," said Koch.

"No, we're not going to do that," Ruskin insisted.

> I said, "Well, then I'm going to have to take this up with Seymour. I'm sure his ethics are going to insist on accepting what I consider to be a very reasonable proposal." Seymour gets on the phone, and I said, "Listen, I believe it would be an outrage for you or I to attack one another in an unfair way. I don't expect it to happen, but if [it does] we're left with nothing to do except to

complain after the election. What good is that?" So he concurred. And we signed the letter of agreement that no literature mentioning the other person could be issued in advance of having been approved by the other person as not violating this code of conduct.

Now we're two weeks before the election, and Seymour sends over his literature. I don't have to send mine over, because I don't mention him at all. What is his literature? It's beautifully done—he had a lot of money. It is, as I assumed it would be, a comparison of records in very nice column form.

Seymour, as Koch recalls, boasted of passing a hundred and twenty-five bills and noted that Koch had passed very few; he mentioned his family status—married, two children—and listed Koch as single.

Koch picked up the phone and shouted at Seymour, "This literature isn't fair! You cannot publish it!"

"What do you mean it's unfair?" said Seymour, puzzled.

I say, "What does your hundred and twenty-five bills and my [few] bills have to do with this election? I am not running on the legislation that I enacted. I am running on my community record. You are comparing apples and oranges. I consider that to be unfair. I will not permit you to use that equation. I demand that you have in that literature all of my community services—the tenant groups that I served on *pro bono* and my involvement in saving Washington Square Park." I'd give him a hundred and thirty-seven projects that I'd been involved in to compare with his hundred and twenty-five bills. And I said, "What does your family status have to do with this election? Why should you have in your literature that you're married and you've got two kids and that I'm single? I consider that an outrage. That's got to be removed from the literature." He said, "That's ridiculous." I said, "Well, I demand arbitration." You have to understand: there's no time for arbitration. By the time we have arbitration, the election is over, but he had agreed to it. He begins to scream. I said, "I will not permit this literature, which violates our agreement, to be published. Send it over to the arbitrators."

Seymour said, "There is no time for that. I tell you what we'll do. You write your side of the literature, and we'll print it the way you think you ought to be displayed."

You have to understand what this meant. We took his literature—his column was left unchanged, except I think he removed the family status, but everything else stayed in there—and we wrote my credentials on his literature. So if he had a hundred and twenty-five pieces of legislation, I had a hundred and thirty-seven community projects next to it. On Election Day, I was handing out his literature.

Ed Koch, the second of three children, was born in the Bronx in 1924. His parents, Louis and Joyce Koch, were immigrants from Poland, and the family was very poor. Koch says of his father, "He was the hardest worker I know. Always had two jobs." In the twenties Louis Koch was a partner in a fur business. Joyce Koch worked in the garment industry, and scraped together enough to pay a tutor to teach her to read and write English. When the Depression came, Louis's fur business collapsed, and the family was forced to move with relatives to Newark. Nine of them shared a two-bedroom walk-up apartment at 90 Spruce Street, in a poor neighborhood that, Koch remembers, was about 50 percent black. Louis Koch worked part time in the fur industry, and at night the family, including Ed, aged twelve, went to work at a hat-check concession in Krueger's Auditorium, on Belmont Avenue, which was operated by an uncle. "My uncle, who was not such a nice person, sold this hat-check concession to us on terms that were just onerous," says Koch. "People paid to have their hats and coats checked, and we lived on tips. And this is in the Depression—very tough. First they pay to get in. And then they come and we hat-check. It was very demeaning. It was demeaning to ask people, as we did, 'Don't forget the hat-check boys.' That left a trauma, I must say. To live on the largesse of people is something that I consider demeaning. But I was very good at it. I've always been a very hard worker." Four members of the family worked until two or three o'clock every morning, scrimping and saving for a year until they had enough money to move to a nicer walk-up of their own, at 61 Milford Avenue in Newark.

In 1941 the Koches moved to Ocean Parkway in Brooklyn. Ed Koch began to work his way through City College by selling shoes, but in 1943 he left to join the Army. When he returned, three years later, as a decorated sergeant, Koch moved in with his parents and entered the N.Y.U. School of Law. He graduated in 1948, and embarked on a legal career, continuing to live at home until 1956, when he found himself an apartment in Greenwich Village. There he gravitated to reform Democratic politics, volunteering to work for Adlai Stevenson in 1956 and joining the Village Independent Democrats, a reform club that was then waging an uphill struggle against the New York County and Greenwich Village Democratic establishment led by Carmine De Sapio. Among his passionate VID colleagues, Koch became known as a "hair shirt"—an irritant who insisted on preaching to the already committed, constantly reminding them of their devotion to ending "bossism," patronage, and smoke-filled rooms. Today Koch laughs at his priggishness, yet his favorite words remain judgmental: "vile," "outrage," "betrayed," "richies," "unforgivable," "schmuck."

But Koch was different from most of his fellow reformers: he had a sense of humor. Even his laugh was distinctive: "Heh-eh-eh-eh-eh"—the sound of a car ignition that fails to catch. He was capable of beguiling people with his lack of guile. "When I first saw him I didn't like him," says John Lo Cicero, who is now a friend and one of his aides. "He was campaigning in the street for Mayor Robert Wagner in 1961. Without a loudspeaker he was shouting, and everyone could hear him. I thought he was shrill." A few years later they met, and Koch invited Lo Cicero to join the VID. "You want me to join because I'm Italian," said Lo Cicero, who was well aware that in order to beat De Sapio the club had to recruit Italian-Americans from the South Village, an important source of support for De Sapio's Tamawa Club. Koch, without blinking, replied, "That's right."

The next several years were painful for Koch. In 1960 his mother "died of cancer—a very agonized death," he recalls. "I was not living at home. My father was working. My sister, Pat, was up in Monsey, New York, and had her own two children. My brother lived in New Jersey. I was the only one who had the time. I became the person who would visit my mother every day at the hospital. She was in great pain. It was abdominal cancer. It was a great trauma for everybody." In 1962 Koch experienced his only electoral loss. The VID wanted to contest the renomination of Democratic Assemblyman William Passannante, and urged Koch to be the candidate. Koch recalls that the entire Manhattan Democratic establishment was against him: "I'm the victim. Eddie Costikyan organized it." Costikyan was then the New York County Democratic leader. "I never held it against him because he was very nice to me. But it was a devastating defeat. I got only a third of the vote in the Village, and I got, as I recall, forty percent in the whole Assembly District, and that was because Charlie Kinsolving's area, Murray Hill, supported me heavily. And I said at the time—I actually wept —'I'll never run again. It is a filthy business.' " Koch was particularly upset that Senator Herbert Lehman and Robert Wagner, two pillars of the reform movement, endorsed a regular Democrat: "Coming out against *me*! What a filthy business!" James Lanigan, Koch's reform district leader, also "betrayed us." Koch later got even with Lanigan. "That feeling against him I had for many years I don't have anymore, because I've met him now and he's not in exactly great shape," he explains. "But I remember what I said at the time. He had gotten a job with Chester Bowles, then the ambassador to India, as a counselor at the embassy. When I was asked about that, I said, 'The person who can deliver the Indians into the hands of the Red Chinese is Jim Lanigan.' Heh-eh-eh-eh-eh."

Koch did run again, that same year of 1962—for club president. He won by a margin, he recalls, of 119 to 110. The club elders joined to block Koch. "It was such a narrow victory it really wasn't good for one's personality development," Koch says. The following year he ran again, this time to succeed Lanigan, who had departed for India, as district leader. His opponent was Carmine De Sapio, seeking to bounce back from his defeat two years earlier. Koch won. Two years later he ran for reelection. Many forces allied against Koch, including J. Raymond Jones, the New York County Democratic leader, who called Koch "anti-Italian." Koch confronted the issue head-on, marching down to the South Village, where he was booed. "But he went right in there and took the abuse," says Lo Cicero. "By showing he was unafraid, he showed that it was untrue." It was a bitter contest; at one point Koch refused to shake De Sapio's hand when they met in a TV studio. Again Koch won.

In 1964 Koch went to Mississippi to participate in the civil-rights movement. He intervened when he saw a burly white farmer slapping black youths. "So I go over to the sheriff and say, 'I want to file charges,' " Koch says. "It was like talking to a wall. The sheriff says, 'Blacks on the right, whites on the left.' " The blacks were arrested. As their lawyer, Koch filed a series of countercomplaints against the sheriff and the farmer. An angry mob of vigilantes gathered outside the courthouse, their target being the Jewish lawyer from New York. Koch managed to escape them by slipping out through a side door. But that weekend a group of white civil-rights workers did not escape and were severely beaten. Appalled by the violence, Koch rushed off to Atlantic City, where the Democratic National Convention was in progress, in search of Joseph Rauh, the vice-chairman of Americans for Democratic Action. Rauh was then leading a fight to prevent the seating of the white Mississippi delegation and to replace it with the largely black delegation of the Mississippi Freedom Democratic party. Rauh was too busy to see the Manhattan district leader. Koch persisted until Rauh relented. He wanted to tell Rauh, who represented truth and justice and liberalism to Koch, how the civil-rights workers were brutally beaten.

"What color were the civil-rights workers?" he remembers Rauh asking.

"White," Koch said.

"Can't use it," said Rauh. The case he was trying to build required accounts of brutality against blacks.*

What Koch saw as a double standard within the liberal establishment bothered him—and so did the successful effort by Democratic and Liberal party leaders, in 1964, to deny him the nomination for the State Senate. "I was screwed out of it by a number of district leaders," Koch recalls. "They didn't like me." The following year Democratic district leader Koch bucked those party leaders (though not his Village constituency) when he endorsed John Lindsay, a Republican, for mayor—an endorsement that made page 1 of the *News*. The next year he decided to run for the City Council. Associates warned him that the district was a safe Republican one. He ran anyway, and won. Two years later he wanted the "Silk Stocking" seat in Congress, which had been occupied by Lindsay. "It's not your year," he was told. "It's a Republican seat." Koch won the Democratic primary. Still, he was told, he was the wrong kind of Democrat to win the general election in this affluent district: too bald, too poor, too—well, Jewish.

Koch went on to serve nine years in the House of Representatives, winning his last two contests with 75 percent or better of the vote. As a member of Congress, he worked well with the established powers, being elected secretary of the New York State delegation. But back home he

---

*Rauh, in a letter to *The New Yorker*, denies that he said this and suggests that Koch has a hyperactive imagination. Although he says it is improbable, Rauh concedes he and Koch could both be right. He could have said, "Can't use it"—but only because he says he already had testimony from white civil-rights workers, testimony Koch did not know of.

tangled frequently with the local reform establishment. Like many of his constituents, Koch was an early opponent of the Vietnam war. But unlike many reform leaders, he consistently refused to march in peace parades led by those who waved the Vietcong flag and cheered Vietcong victories. "They hated America," he says. "They were pro-Soviet. I've been there. It's a terrible society. Everybody wants to leave. Open the gates, they'll all come out. Maybe we can have an exchange of population? Heh-eh-eh-eh-eh. I will walk with Communists and Black Panthers, but I will never let them lead me." Bella Abzug and "her savages," as he calls them, attacked Koch as a "Red-baiter." He, in turn, attacked them for opposing the sale of jets to Israel. Koch proudly recalls that in 1964 he was one of two members of the VID to support Robert Kennedy for the Democratic nomination to the Senate. The activists began to call Koch a conservative, which deepened his resentment. Reformers and liberals "never excuse human frailty," he says in his memoirs. "They have absolutes that everybody has to meet, an absolute test. But that changes from day to day. That's the point. It's not 'What did you do yesterday?' No. It's 'What are you doing today?' You may be with them on a hundred issues and then on a single issue you will not be. The others get wiped out. They don't care about that. That is expected. I don't really like them. Whereas with the regulars, loyalty is so important."

Koch believed in loyalty, in Horatio Alger, in the American dream, which worked for him, and in American goodness. Dan Wolf says, "He was shocked by the vehemence of the radicals, by their total hostility to the world he was involved in and believed in. I think he decided then—an emotional thing—he just knew he wouldn't be happy with those people." But his "Rubicon," as Koch calls it, was crossed in Forest Hills in 1971. Koch stunned his liberal constituents by opposing the introduction of a low-income high-rise housing development in this middle-income white community—by addressing a group led by Jerry Birbach, a local loudmouth who became to many a symbol of Northern racism. When Koch returned to his Washington office, he was bombarded by phone calls.

"How can you do this?" he remembers Stanley Geller, a VID leader, saying beseechingly.

"Stanley, the project will destroy the area."

"You can never come out against low-income housing, no matter how big the project is."

"But people will move out."

"I don't care if they move. The Jews in Forest Hills have to pay their dues."

"Stanley, I wish I had a town house like you, a pool like you, or kids in private school. Jews are willing to pay their dues. They're just not willing to pay yours."

Koch says he was hurt. "I was doing what was right in a controversial area and being deserted by friends. It made it possible from that point on not to fear. Now I don't care." But he cared in 1973, when he made a bid for the Democratic nomination for mayor. The effort lasted little more than a month. He failed to raise money, being viewed by the financial establishment as too liberal and by the reform establishment as too conservative.

Koch developed calluses. "I'm sure that as a child he had insecurities," says Dan Wolf, who is perhaps his closest friend and who is now serving as a dollar-a-year City Hall adviser. "He is a man who overcame one weakness at a time. In the old days we used to call it the masculine approach to life. Facing up to your own fears. Now if he's afraid, he'll walk right in." Which is precisely what Koch did in the 1977 race for the Democratic nomination for mayor. The bachelor congressman from Greenwich Village helped overcome his liberal image by vehemently supporting the death penalty, by vowing to crimp the power of municipal labor unions, by sounding like a tough tightwad. Koch came in first in the primary, but because neither he nor Mario Cuomo, who placed second, captured 40 percent of the vote, a runoff election was scheduled for eleven days later. This contest became another Rubicon for Koch. Ugly rumors circulated that he was a homosexual. Koch knew that the rumors could crush him, and he was tense. "You had the posters up and down the streets—'Vote for Cuomo, not the homo' " is how he remembers it. David Garth, Koch's chief strategist, says, "In eighteen years in this business, that was the toughest eleven days I've ever seen a man go through. For the first time I thought there was steel in Ed Koch."

As a local reform leader and member of Congress, Koch was characterized as a liberal. In Congress, he regularly voted for social spending programs; in 1972 he received a 100-percent rating from the liberal Americans for Democratic Action and only a 4-percent rating from the conservative Americans for Constitutional Action. Yet as a candidate for mayor, and now, as mayor, he has sounded less liberal, more like a moderate, and a fiscal conservative.

Pondering the apparent shift in his views recently, Koch said, "There are two reasons for the change. One is that from Washington the perspective is different from what it is here at home. In Washington, you're removed from the problem of meeting your budget constraints. You're dealing with part of the elephant, the part you like the best. You have this huge elephant that people are feeding. And I'm not dumping on the Congress. I had the same perspective when I was in Washington. I was doing the same thing they are doing."

Was it inconsistent for him to parade as a local fiscal conservative and yet demand liberal federal spending programs to assist New York?

"If I were down there now, I'd be much more conservative fiscally," he conceded. "I now know what the problem is to a greater extent. I also know what the voters are telling the people in Washington. It is a conundrum. Congress has to find a balance. No question. There are areas where we're spending too much, and others where we're spending too little. I hope that were I there I'd have the strength to support Carter's spending cuts—most of them, anyway—to a greater extent than I would have before."

It's difficult to force Koch into either a "liberal" or a "conservative" box. He is a liberal when it comes to supporting civil liberties, gay rights, and federal spending for cities; conservative when it comes to cutting the budget, ending poverty-program "rip-offs," opposing preferential treatment, and being deeply suspicious of Soviet motives and therefore favoring a strong national defense. Koch calls himself a "sane liberal." Actually, he's a pragmatist. Like other sixties liberals, he has become skeptical of government, aware of limits, much more concerned with what works. He resembles a good many ex-communicants in reserving his harshest words for those who have remained members of the old church. "Knee-jerk liberals," he calls them, and he says, "I don't believe in half their crap. That government has to become bigger. That government is better if it does more. It's the New Deal out of the thirties—that government solves all problems. I once believed that. I have contempt for government. I should know—I'm in it. When you remove the profit motive, that's what happens. You remove the penalty. There's always someone there to pick up the deficit. Not to hold you accountable. On several occasions kids have come in from the schools to visit me. This one kid said, 'Why doesn't the city have more athletic equipment, and give us bats and mitts?' I said, 'Wait a minute, kid. You look like the type of kid who has a mitt and bat. Why does government have to give them to you? Why not your parents?' " On one occasion Koch said to me, "The good-government groups and social workers destroyed the city for twenty years, and they resent bitterly anyone who wants to come in and reassert the balance and try to get a hold on this." He was referring to welfare. "They do. And they're nice people—all Jewish! Heh-eh-eh-eh-eh. All they want is more, more, more, without controls. I say if it doesn't work, stop it! No. They won't stop anything. More, more."

Koch identifies with the center of the national Democratic party: "If Carter is in the middle of the road, with Kennedy on the left and Jackson" —Senator Henry Jackson—"on the right, I identify then with Carter." He considers Kennedy a friend, though he jokes about how until 1976 Kennedy called him Dick. The senator learned the correct name when Koch wrote to him pledging to support him for President if he ran that year. Koch is proud of his association with the Kennedys. But in 1980, he says, he'll support Carter. "I happen to like and truly support Carter—but, politically, I want him to remember when New York needs him next year that we were helpful. It's like chicken soup. It can't hurt."

Koch's chicken soup, according to a White House aide who works with local and state governments, sways government decisions. "Those who support you early get better treatment," he says. For instance, coaxed by the White House, a reluctant Department of Housing and Urban Development consented to permit the city over the next twelve months to siphon off $52 million of Community Development Block Grant funds—supposedly earmarked for permanent community improvements and the elimination of "slums and blight"—to maintain housing foreclosed by the city after the owners failed to pay their real-property taxes. "That single administrative decision," says the White House aide, "has more fiscal impact on the city than the aggregate of all our other administrative decisions."

Koch is no boy scout about all this. "You can never know whether you got it just on the merits," he says. "But remember, the merits are a judgmental question. There's always the extra added ingredient: Do you have confidence in the person you're dealing with? And: When I needed him, was he there?" The syntax would differ, but George Washington Plunkitt could say it no better.

Three mornings each week Koch rises at six o'clock, slips into yesterday's shorts, socks, shirt, and suit, descends the stairs of Gracie Mansion, and enters a small breakfast room, where he has grapefruit juice and black coffee and reads the late editions of the *Times* and the *News,* comparing them with the early editions he read the night before. At six-thirty he is joined by a police bodyguard, and often by Manhattan City Councilman Henry Stern, an old friend, who accompanied him to Mississippi in 1964 and ultimately persuaded him to endorse Lindsay in 1965. He and Stern are driven in the mayor's Chrysler sedan to the Jack La Lanne gym on Lower Broadway, across from City Hall. Koch is sometimes joined by other government associates. After donning a too-tight Jack La Lanne T-shirt, white shorts, sweat socks, and Adidas sneakers, Koch weighs in. "Two hundred pounds," he will say. "That's my high high. Which is two pounds over my low low." In a garish orange-and-yellow workout room, Koch begins his exercise, under the tutelage of the manager of the gym. First he does a mile on the exercise bicycle, to warm up. Then he does seventeen sit-ups on an incline board, which are followed by seventeen knee-to-chest exercises, another seventeen sit-ups, and another round of seventeen knee-to-chest exercises. By the second set of sit-ups he is puffing, perspiring freely, and beginning to cheat—completing only sixteen sit-ups and allowing his knees to sag. Next come seventeen rounds on the bench press, seventeen shoulder presses on a Universal machine, and seventeen pull-downs. Finally he does eight minutes of running on a treadmill. Then he takes a steam bath and a shower and puts on clean clothes that he has taken with him to the gym.

By a quarter of eight Koch is in his corner office at City Hall. Plopping a bundle of yesterday's shirt, shorts, and socks in a corner, he pulls off his suit jacket, unbuttons his vest, and stands behind the desk that Mayor Fiorello La Guardia once used. Two blocks have been inserted between the top of the desk and its legs to accommodate Koch, who, at six-one, is almost a foot taller than La Guardia. But the desk is now too high. If Koch sits down at it, the top is right under his chin. "I look like a midget," he says. However, when Koch sits in this office it is never at the desk but in a black leather armchair facing a black leather couch and another armchair. Guests gather on those or on one of several burgundy-upholstered Sheraton chairs. The carpet, too, is burgundy, with gold fleurs-de-lis. In one corner is a door that leads to a small kitchen, with a two-burner stove, a small sink, a refrigerator, and a coffeemaker, which labors overtime. A television set stands against one wall of the room. There are four tall windows, which, for security reasons, are bulletproof. Phone consoles with twenty-nine buttons, many connecting Koch directly with members of the administration, stand on a table behind the desk and on a larger table behind his leather armchair. A brooding portrait of La Guardia looms over the couch, as it did during the term of Koch's predecessor. But this room is not without several Koch touches. There is a Matisse nude; a sign on the desk, facing visitors, that reads "If you say it can't be done, you're right. You can't do it"; and a mounted reproduction of a Quotation of the Day by Koch from the *Times*: "Today I'm Italian. Last week I was Polish. And the week before, I was Ukrainian. But everyday I'm Jewish. I love the parades. I go to all of them."

On Wednesdays, at eight, Koch meets with City Council President Carol Bellamy and City Comptroller Harrison J. Goldin. On Fridays, at nine-thirty, they are joined by City Council Majority Leader Thomas Cuite. These meetings are informal; often each participant brings an aide. Many of the mayor's other weekdays begin with his giving dictation to his secretary, Mary Garrigan, a pleasant young woman who worked for Koch in Washington. A morning's correspondence one day last fall included a note to Lewis Rudin, the chairman of the Association for a Better New York, and his wife, Basha, to thank them for sending flowers; a memo to Deputy Mayor David Brown on the city's hiring freeze; a memo to Deputy Mayor Ronay Menschel requesting a follow-up on some matter; a memo to Metropolitan Transportation Authority Chairman Harold Fisher enclosing a newspaper clipping and saying, "If this is accurate, then we're wasting a lot of money"; a letter to a citizen saying, "Yes, I am related to Faye Cohn"; a memo to Deputy Mayor Herbert Sturz answering a memo from him; a memo to Planning Commission Chairman Wagner urging him to answer a letter from Comptroller Goldin; a letter to Representative David Obey, of Wisconsin, inviting him and his wife to stay at Gracie Mansion when they came to New York; and a thank-you note to the news director of WCBS-Radio thanking him for his thank-you note. Koch fusses over his correspondence, first leaning forward on the desk, then pacing back and forth, slowly measuring his words as if they were tablets. He dictates about thirty letters a day to one of his secretaries, refusing to use a tape recorder, which would be more efficient, because he regards recorders as too impersonal. Every Tuesday, at eight, the mayor meets with his cabinet, in City Hall's Blue Room—the ornate chamber where press conferences are held and proclamations read. Currently, cabinet meetings are attended by all the deputy mayors, the heads of several key agencies, and members of the mayor's staff. These meetings, too, are informal. There is usually no written agenda, and those in attendance sit around a long glass-topped table sipping coffee and nibbling on Danish as subway trains rumble underneath their feet and cause the room to shake.

A standard busy-executive item that seems to be missing from Mayor Koch's days is the constantly ringing telephone. Transportation Commissioner Anthony Ameruso says he rarely calls the mayor: "My experience as an agency head is that he gets all kinds of crazy phone calls each day. He doesn't need commissioners calling him all the time." Oddly, Koch does not get "all kinds of crazy phone calls." In fact, he gets fewer than most commissioners get. A review of all incoming calls logged between June 29 and October 17 of 1978—excluding the unlogged calls from members of the administration with direct lines—shows that the mayor received just two hundred and seventy-nine. When weekends and holidays are subtracted from these hundred and eleven days, the mayor averaged about 3.5 calls on each of the seventy-five business days. The highest number, reached on August 3, was eleven. The most frequent callers were Donald Manes, the Queens borough president and Democratic county leader, who made five calls; Bronx Representative Mario Biaggi, five; Senator Daniel Patrick Moynihan, three; Planning Commission Chairman Wagner, three; Meade Esposito, the Brooklyn Democratic leader, three; Mary Perot Nichols, the head of the Municipal Broadcasting System, three; several relatives, three each; A. M. Rosenthal, the executive editor of the *Times*, and Michael O'Neill, the editor of the *News*, two each; Rupert Murdoch, the publisher of the *Post*, two; Municipal Assistance Corporation Chairman Felix Rohatyn, two; and David Garth, two. As was true in previous administrations, calls from average citizens are intercepted by the Mayor's Action Center, which in 1978 received 135,491 inquiries—an increase of 8.3 percent over the last year of the Beame administration.

As a candidate, Koch promised not to be "a ribbon-cutting mayor." He would appoint a deputy mayor for ribbon-cutting, he joked. Inspection of his schedule, however, suggests no dearth of ceremony. Exclusive of unscheduled last-minute meetings, the mayor's private schedule between October 16 and November 28 of 1978 shows, by my count, a hundred and sixty-two governmental meetings; seventy ceremonial, courtesy, or speaking engagements; thirty-one press conferences or briefings; fifteen political functions; seven public appearances, such as walking tours and constitutent hours; two days spent at Yale as a Chubb Fellow; fourteen personal appointments, including two visits to doctors and time out to watch a CBS News show written by Pat Thaler, his sister, who is the director of continuing education at Marymount Manhattan College; and three meetings with lobbyists. By this count, nearly a third of his scheduled appearances were consumed by ceremonial functions. "He is like a kid with the ceremonial stuff," says Wagner, whose father served three terms as mayor. "It's as if Koch didn't quite believe he'd be there and be the center of attention. My father made the same vow not to do the ceremonial stuff, but he found he had to do it. The mayor is expected to be there. It's part of the job." Koch says, "Yes, I'm doing more ribbon-cutting than I thought I would do." That's not to say he doesn't work hard and put in long hours. His last appointment, occasionally over dinner at Gracie Mansion, ends at eleven or so. With no wife or children, Koch has fewer constraints on his time than many politicians have. Like Governor Jerry Brown of California and City Council President Carol Bellamy, he is married to his work. Last Thanksgiving, before sitting down to a Gracie Mansion dinner with his brother and sister and their families at five o'clock, Koch managed to visit the 103rd Police Precinct house, in Jamaica, Queens, to wish the twenty-four cops on duty a happy holiday, and to appear on the Barry Gray radio show on WMCA. The first vacation Koch ever took as mayor, in July of 1978, prompted his staff to organize an office pool to see who could guess the day he would rush home early. He heard about the pool, and to confound the staff, stayed away for four days, as he was scheduled to. He admits that he was miserable being away from the office for so long.

On weekends the mayor goes home to a fourteen-story apartment house a block from Washington Square Park, where he has a three-room apartment. He says he treasures this weekly reminder of his middle-class roots. From here, he can walk across the park to Balducci's and to Murray's Cheese Shop, and can knock at the doors of old friends. Weekends offer solace, a chance to get away. He drives his round-the-clock security detail to distraction, slipping out unnoticed to go shopping alone, take in an afternoon movie, or lunch at an inexpensive new restaurant. Rarely does Koch accept a public appearance on a weekend evening. This time is reserved for his brother's and sister's families and for a dozen or so close friends: Dan Wolf; David Margolis, the president of Colt Industries, and his wife, Bobbie (who was just appointed the city's dollar-a-year official greeter); John and Mary Condon, who are graphic designers; corporation counsel Allan Schwartz; State Supreme Court Justice Leonard Sandler; Councilman Henry Stern; and the restauranteur Peter Aschkenasy (whose wife, Dorothy, works for the mayor as an assistant for special events). Like Koch, his close friends became successes on their own; they were not born to wealth.

If his weekend schedule is still clear on Tuesday or Wednesday, Koch will pick up the phone and invite friends to have dinner (which he cooks) at his apartment or to try an inexpensive restaurant someone has told him about. Koch's cramped apartment is not suitable for elaborate dinner parties. The kitchen is a narrow alley. There is no dining room—indeed, no dining table. But the mayor loves to invite a few guests to sit on a dark-brown leather couch and two facing Barcelona chairs, gathered around the living room's glass-and-chrome coffee table, with plates perched on their laps. In colder months, a white marble fireplace glows. In warmer months, guests gather on a terrace that wraps around the living room and offers an impressive view of Manhattan and dozens of water towers. The living room is painted stark

white and can be flooded with sunlight much of the day, although since
Koch became mayor his security detail has insisted that the shades be half
drawn. A bookcase covers one wall, housing about a hundred and twenty-
five books; a picture of young Edward Koch, as bald as he is today, strumming a guitar; and a David Levine caricature of Koch. The other walls are
hung with several Japanese prints, gifts of Ronay Menschel; a "Koch for
Congress" poster designed by John and Mary Condon, who have done
many of Koch's campaign posters; and a nude painted on a cedar shutter
by an emotionally disturbed thirteen-year-old girl. Underneath the bookcase is a dusty wine rack, mostly empty. Koch, who buys his wine at a store
on Lower Park Avenue, is a cautious shopper, and rarely spends more than
three dollars a bottle.

Koch's staff, excluding deputy mayors and their staffs, is small—fewer
than a dozen principal aides. By comparison, John Lindsay seemed to have
an aide hunched over the shoulder of each commissioner. Many top members of the administration—including deputy mayors, aides, and department heads—are part of an extended family. Some have been with Koch
for years, and are warm personal friends. For the first year of Koch's
administration, Deputy Mayor for Policy David Brown was his closest
government adviser. (Brown resigned last December.) Though Koch
claimed that his seven deputies were co-equal, Brown, who served as Koch's
first congressional chief of staff, was clearly first among equals. He was the
only deputy who had time set aside for him each day on the mayor's
schedule. And like first deputy mayors in the past, Brown was the member
of the administration whom other members went to when they needed an
ally to sell a policy or a personnel change to the mayor, or when they just
wanted to let their hair down and complain. Physically, Brown and Koch
suggested the odd couple. Brown, a lean man with a finely chiseled nose and
carefully parted brown hair that always looks wet, appears younger than
his age, which is forty-two. In general, he has the appearance of Gatsby—
a proper Protestant. Unlike other City Hall colleagues, he rarely strove to
see Koch socially. But there was understanding and feeling between them,
and Koch delighted in boasting to others of Brown's "brilliance." Dan
Wolf, who sits in the office next to Koch's, has been a friend and adviser
since the early sixties, and is the person Koch is most likely to turn to for
personal advice. "I'm the back wall of the handball court" is how Wolf
describes his role. "He likes to talk to me about things he has in mind. I
think he feels he can say anything to me." Special adviser John Lo Cicero,
an outgoing man, has managed several of Koch's campaigns since the
sixties, including the 1977 mayoral victory. He now manages "politics" at
City Hall. Deputy Mayor Ronay Menschel supervised Representative
Koch's Washington office for several years. After she moved to New York,
in 1973, she efficiently supervised both of Koch's offices, in New York and
Washington. Diane Coffey, who first went to work for Koch as a personal

secretary in 1971, has served as the mayor's chief of staff, screening his correspondence and supervising his schedule and his Gracie Mansion living quarters. While she searched for a New York home for her family after Koch was inaugurated as mayor, he let them use his Village apartment during the week, when he was at Gracie Mansion. Maureen Connelly, the first woman ever to serve as mayoral press secretary, is also, at thirty-one, one of the youngest press secretaries. Connelly got to know Koch in 1977, when he was running for mayor and she was working for Garth Associates. As chief of research, she was responsible for fashioning and documenting the "specific" position papers Koch received so much media acclaim for. As press secretary, she has complete access to the mayor, reviews all manner of memorandums reaching his desk, pops in on meetings of her choice, is prized by Koch for having an even better memory than he has, and often serves as his "date" at social functions. (Perhaps because of the increasingly influential role she plays, she is referred to privately by some of Koch's old associates as Madame Nhu.) Corporation counsel Allan Schwartz was formerly Koch's law partner—one reason he can freely interrupt the mayor to tell a joke or protest a course of action. Phillip Trimble, first the mayor's counsel and now a deputy mayor, became an adviser to Koch in the midsixties, when Koch was a councilman. When Trimble moved to Washington to work for Senator J. William Fulbright, he shared Koch's Washington apartment until his wife moved down from New York. The terrace of his Greenwich Village apartment adjoins Koch's. When Trimble was elevated to deputy mayor, his role as counsel was filled by Robert Tierney, who first met Koch at a subway station in 1970, when Koch was running for Congress. He went on to serve as treasurer of Koch's 1972 and 1974 congressional campaigns, and after working as an assistant counsel to Governor Hugh Carey for nearly three and a half years, he joined Koch's staff in April of 1978. Tierney's sister Mary, an aspiring actress, works for Ronay Menschel and often takes the mayor's dictation on weekends. Mary Garrigan, the mayor's personal secretary, has been with him since 1976. She is the only person besides him who has seen the diary Koch is keeping about his first term as mayor; on her own time each weekend she types his dictated musings. Various other members of the City Hall team have also been previously associated with Koch.

The Koch staff does not attract universal acclaim, even from some of its own members. A common complaint is that the staff is disorganized. "The cabinet meetings are ridiculous because there is no rigid agenda," says one deputy mayor. "Surely one of those staff members should take the initiative in setting an agenda." Koch will often give the same assignment to two aides. The way his staff operates is a reflection of the man. He is an open person, very democratic about, for instance, who can attend meetings. When I asked him recently who was invited to attend a special series of breakfast meetings with the Municipal Labor Committee, the umbrella organization of the unions representing the city's workers, Koch replied,

"My cast of characters is whoever is there in the morning." The mayor's approach has its positive aspect: an absence of scheming and of hidden agendas. Once, when a deputy mayor asked for a private meeting to complain about Deputy Mayor Menschel, Koch suddenly interrupted the deputy, excused himself, and left the room. The complainant was baffled—until Koch returned with the accused in tow. "Tell her what you just told me," he said. They would resolve it right there, Koch—confrontation—style. A negative aspect is that this style leads to confusion and time wasted, as everyone strives to get his say. "There are too many people in some of the meetings," says one commissioner, who has a fairly high regard for the Koch staff. "It's embarrassing to discuss one man's job definition in front of other commissioners. There are too many cooks, too many people the mayor wants to keep involved."

Staff confusion is abetted by Koch's impulsive nature. Because he believes so strongly in his own instincts, he is willing to act on impulse, without first discussing a decision. Shortly after he met Allan Schwartz for the first time, in 1964, he invited Schwartz to become his law partner. When he saw Schwartz in late 1977 to ask him to join the city administration, Schwartz surprised the mayor-elect by asking if he needed a corporation counsel. "You got it!" Schwartz remembers Koch responding instantly. Koch offered Deputy Mayor Peter Solomon his post after their first conversation about the job. Solomon says that David Brown told him, "He wasn't supposed to offer you the job, but he liked you." Since a staff's function is to analyze people and subjects in order to protect a mayor—from himself, among others—Koch sometimes drives members of his staff up the wall. "Ed lives from day to day," says Ed Costikyan. "He told me once that when he gets up in the morning he doesn't know where he will end up the day. Someone else controls his agenda—events. He doesn't plan."

The family atmosphere of the Koch staff has its advantages. Because the staff members know Koch, they can often anticipate even his whims. He trusts them, and is therefore not afraid to delegate authority. The situation was quite different in the Beame administration. In his final two years Mayor Beame was surrounded by many people who had been foisted upon him by state and federal fiscal monitors. First Deputy Mayor John Zuccotti and his staff, though they were personally fond of Beame, used to scheme to circumvent him and to force him to make politically unpleasant decisions. In a reversal of traditional roles, Zuccotti usually got the credit when the city made progress; Beame usually got the blame when there were delays. This situation created friction between Beame loyalists, led by Deputy Mayor Stanley Friedman, and Zuccotti loyalists. There is no such split at Koch's City Hall. Instead, Koch suffers the opposite affliction: his people are sometimes too loyal, as befits members of a family. "We all have the same protective relationship and feeling of warmth," says Schwartz, who once shared a partner's desk with Koch. "There is a danger of conceit," one deputy mayor says. "He doesn't have people tough enough to knock him down." Reflecting a not uncommon view, a state official who has worked closely with the last two mayors says of Koch, "He is surrounded by weakness. They're very scared of him. They reflect fear." Ridiculous, counters a longtime Koch friend who heads an agency. "We are overprotective toward Ed." Koch revels in debate, in give-and-take, in a good fight, and the problem, this friend maintains, is not fear but sympathy—sympathy for the enormous pressure on, and pain of, the mayor. There is a natural tendency to defend, to offer warmth, a respite from the rigors of an awful job. Any person needs that; Koch demands it. Several months before Bernard Rome, an old friend of Koch's, was fired as president of the Off-Track Betting Corporation last April, he described his visits to City Hall, saying of Koch, "He pays little attention in our meetings, and I always get the feeling that what he's really interested in is the end of the meeting, when he leans forward, lowers his voice, and asks, 'How'm I doing?' "

A major criticism of the Koch team has centered on the mayor's decision not to appoint a first deputy mayor. To many, the decision has meant that Koch was leaving the reins of his government in the hands of his commissioners. "After a decision is made, it goes to an agency," says Sanitation Commissioner Norman Steisel, who believes that Koch needs a first deputy, "and nobody is really following through to be sure the mayor's expectations are being met." During the mayor's first twelve months the commissioners' biweekly reports were not carefully scrutinized by any member of Koch's staff. Thus, the commissioners and the deputy mayors were free to tell the mayor just what they wanted him to know. There was no one at City Hall going through previous reports or other documents, flagging questions for Koch to ask, or contrasting this month's performance with last month's promise. Commissioners don't tell the mayor what they're "not doing," a commissioner admits. The director of the Office of Operations, who is supposed to watch government, received copies of the reports after, not before, the mayor received his. According to several commissioners, their biweekly reports were never brought up at the regular meetings between their agencies and the Office of Operations. Because the reports are shaped by what the commissioner chooses to impart, cranking them out "becomes *pro forma*, protective, self-serving," a deputy mayor says. Commissioners start fleshing out the reports with filler. For instance, the report submitted on November 2, 1978, by Isaiah Robinson, the chairman of the Human Rights Commission, was devoted mostly to accounts of where he spoke, what fund-raisers or meetings he attended, and what publicity his agency received over the previous two weeks. Anthony Russo, then the director of the Office of Municipal Labor Relations, used to send the mayor a summary of his daily diary, including phone calls made and received. The second paragraph of Fire Commissioner Augustus A. Beekman's September 29 report informed Koch: "On 9/27/78 at 0815 hours, a jogger entered the quarters of Marine Co. 6 at Grand Street and East River and reported the apparent rape of a woman approximately 100 yds. north of quarters."

"I can't say the commissioner form of government is bad," Zuccotti says. "But I don't feel it is appropriate for the difficult things that lie ahead. If you're going to cut the budget by nearly one and a third billion, the mayor has to have a handle on the government. Commissioners don't always provide you with accurate information. They have their own agendas. You say to the commissioner, 'Cut your budget twenty-five percent.' He may try to hide the cuts. And the commissioner's idea of where to cut may not be the same as yours. If you're not on top of it, you leave the choice to somebody else." Koch says that the reason he won't appoint a first deputy is that he wants to communicate to his commissioners that he trusts them. Yet he is so mistrustful of the government bureaucracy that he has installed a new inspector-general program in many of the city's agencies to blow the whistle on waste as well as wrongdoing. Furthermore, the twenty-five inspectors general and two hundred investigators who work under them are instructed to report not just to the agency head but also to Investigation Commissioner Stanley Lupkin.

Felix Rohatyn advances another reason for a first deputy: "I think somebody who is not the mayor should often be the one to say no, in order to be a lightning rod. Also, there are any number of issues that you have to compromise on, and a mayor shouldn't always be compromising." Too much accessibility, Rohatyn adds, removes "the aura of mystery" from a mayor. Moreover, in Koch's case, the absence of a strong first deputy removes a potential check on an impulsive mayor's whims. A state Financial Control Board official worries that "there is no one person to go to in the mayor's absence whom you can rely on and the mayor will go along with —it creates a time lag." Before David Brown left the administration, he assumed several duties that are normally performed by a first deputy, but he says, "I almost never failed to check with Ed before doing something." He would not even schedule meetings without Koch's approval. "Unless Ed sees something as in his interest, you're wasting your time," he says. "You're just going through the motions." When Brown was planning to leave the administration, he pushed Philip Toia as a candidate for first deputy—"at least on the management side." But Brown also appreciated the fact that Koch had "invited some talented deputy mayors to join him without a first deputy," so that suddenly appointing one would be "changing the rules of the game." And, what was more significant, it would mean changing Koch. Brown says that Koch wants to be "the center of the wheel," and adds, "Whether he can work effectively as the center of the wheel remains to be seen."

Most of Koch's deputies and commissioners like reporting directly to the mayor instead of reporting through a first deputy. They are grateful for his accessibility, and they enjoy his company and his good humor. "It's fun to work for Ed Koch," says Police Commissioner Robert McGuire. Transportation Commissioner Anthony Ameruso calculates that he spends more time with Koch than he did with Beame and Zuccotti combined. "The level of personal involvement is a quantum leap over Beame," he says. "Koch is his own first deputy." Lee Oberst, who served as director of the Office of Operations under Beame and for the first ten months of the Koch administration, says, "I love Zuccotti. He is one of the most competent people I have known. But he was a one-man operation. You had to make an appointment two weeks in advance to see him. It was easier to see Beame."

In the final months of the mayoral campaign Koch won points with editorial writers by promising to appoint Costikyan first deputy mayor. Costikyan was a respected figure, a smart, tough man who could serve as a counterweight for what was perceived as the slightly flaky Koch. By late November of 1977, however, Koch had come to feel that the strong-willed Costikyan was treating him like a "dummy." Costikyan says *he* began to feel like a dummy. Costikyan recalls the campaign and Koch's implacable opposition to Westway, the proposed billion-dollar highway and development project along Manhattan's West Side. "I began to realize I didn't have the authority to do anything without checking with him," Costikyan says. "If I did it, he undid it. Westway is a good example. He had devised a good Westway position: He was opposed to it, but he would not lie down to block it. Then he said, 'It will never be built!' A *Times* reporter called me and asked about this. I said, 'Oh, that's just campaign rhetoric.' The reporter called Koch at home, and he called Westway 'an ecological monstrosity.' At that point I started wondering whether I could work with someone like that if I had to check everything." Koch admits that he had been impulsive in offering Costikyan the position. "I didn't understand the full implications of what a first deputy would mean," he says. "Certainly I did not understand that it would mean the mayor would be ceremonial. Heh-eh-eh-eh-eh." When Koch began to think about it, after the election, he came to believe that it was important for the mayor to be the undisputed center of the wheel.

When David Brown announced to the mayor last December that he wished to return to private life, Koch reorganized his team. Brown's title, deputy mayor for policy, was awarded to Herman Badillo, but not Brown's access or clout. Badillo's management functions were parceled out among him: Philip Toia, who became deputy mayor for financial management; Ronay Menschel, who became deputy mayor for administration; and Diane Coffey, who was promoted to chief of staff. Counsel Phillip Trimble was promoted to Menschel's old job—deputy mayor for intergovernmental relations. Robert Tierney moved up to the counsel's post. Deputy Mayors Herbert Sturz and Peter Solomon retained their original titles. Basil Paterson, unhappy with too little to do and uncomfortable with Koch's confrontational approach, had earlier indicated that he was going to vacate his post of deputy mayor for labor relations to become Secretary of State in Albany.

The system still didn't work satisfactorily. Before he left, David Brown had urged Koch to streamline the management of City Hall and the government. The octopus, he had warned, was getting out of control. In succeeding months, similar critiques were offered by press secretary Maureen Connelly and corporation counsel Allan Schwartz, and by David Margolis and Dan Wolf, among others. "I had a sense of the palace guard getting bigger and people becoming overwhelmed with their own positions—each had to have a counsel and a chief of staff," Koch told me recently. "I could feel I was losing a sense of immediacy and intimacy with government. It's like riding in a car close to the ground, where you can feel the pavement. Or riding in a Rolls-Royce. I'm not a Rolls-Royce type." By May of this year Badillo's and Trimble's staffs, for instance, had swelled to twenty-four and forty-four persons, respectively. Koch says he decided last spring to bring to City Hall as deputy mayors two of his favorite commissioners—Housing Commissioner Nathan Leventhal and Planning Commission Chairman Robert Wagner. "But it had to be done at the appropriate time," he says, "and I knew it had to be done in an all-encompassing way. The change had to include my friends as well as my associates."

Early last month Koch suddenly announced those changes. Over the next several months, he said, three deputy mayors would be departing—Badillo, Toia, and Trimble. Two deputies—Ronay Menschel and Herbert Sturz—would remain in the administration, but with lesser titles. Leventhal would be coming to City Hall to "exercise coordinating and supervisory functions" as deputy mayor for operations, and though it was not formally announced, Wagner would become deputy mayor for policy, and when Deputy Mayor Peter Solomon eventually returned to private business, probably for economic development as well. Though Koch said that he still did not believe in having a first deputy, and that his commissioners would continue to have direct access to him, he was granting Leventhal more authority than he had granted Brown (or than Brown was willing to assume). "I still want to know what's going on day to day," he says. "But I want someone to know hour to hour." Typically, and perhaps ominously, the mayor did not precisely define Leventhal's task. Asked to explain his new job as deputy mayor for operations, Leventhal said, "I'm not sure, but my guess is that I'll be responsible for government operations. I'm also going to be in charge of intergovernmental relations and administration—who gets hired, City Hall, the approval of promotions—*I believe.*" In addition to the thirteen agency heads and seven deputy mayors he has now forced out or demoted since becoming mayor in January of 1978, other commissioners will be eased out as part of his reorganization, Koch said. He will reduce the number of deputy mayors from seven to three or perhaps two, will have Ronay Menschel serve as executive administrator, and will change Diane Coffey's title from chief of staff to administrative assistant. Koch said that this represented no demotion for Coffey.

The mayor says that the shakeups involved "the most painful decisions I've made as mayor." He says that it was "excruciating" to meet with and ease out his "two closest friends in government"—Menschel and Trimble.

But Koch came to feel that Menschel did not need a deputy title to perform her role as an executive administrator, and that Trimble, whose advice as counsel he treasured, was like a fish out of water when it came to politics —his principal concern as deputy mayor for intergovernmental relations. Torn between competence and loyalty, Koch, to his credit, chose competence. "I happen to think it was one of the most courageous acts I've ever seen, in public or private life," his friend Margolis says. Koch was somewhat less courageous with Badillo. He had come to admire Badillo's acute intellect, but not the staff he surrounded himself with and not his administrative ability. Koch desired Badillo's resignation, but he told me afterward, "I wouldn't have pushed Herman out. It was clear Herman wanted to go." He said that he would have pushed Menschel and Trimble. Why would he have treated Badillo differently? "Because of his constituency," Koch said —and also because of their "relationship in Congress" and the fact that Badillo had sacrificed a safe congressional seat to join the administration. Two days after this conversation Maureen Connelly phoned me, on Koch's instructions, to say that her boss did not wish to leave a misleading impression: he would have asked for Badillo's resignation if it had not been volunteered.

In his first nineteen months in office Mayor Koch did not focus on improving the delivery of services, as candidate Koch had promised. This is not to say that Koch wasn't on top of the details of his government. "You do get the impression the mayor is in command of the situation," says First Deputy Comptroller Martin Ives. But Koch's personal competence does not necessarily translate into a competent administration. A $13-billion government is not a candy store, or a one-man band. Koch's trademark question—"Hi, how'm I doing?"—is really the wrong question. He should be asking, "Hi, how is the city government doing?" A mayor, even as energetic a mayor as this one, does not clean streets, teach children to read, administer civil-service exams, or actually manage the eighty-odd agencies and departments. Koch may be doing fine with the public or the press, or both, and still not be managing his government well. At the end of his first year he admitted that he was too little involved with the guts of his government. "I'm getting there," he said. "It takes time." He explained that in his first year he was confronted with a succession of crises: he had to produce a four-year financial plan within twenty days of assuming office, recruit a new management team, negotiate new labor contracts, prepare a budget, win loan guarantees from Washington, line up local financing. But Koch's shake-up of his administration last month is a further admission that he has yet to get a handle on the government. Just as former Representative John Lindsay did, Koch has been undergoing on-the-job training as an executive. A member of Congress or a city councilman proposes legislation, issues press releases, attends hearings, and meets with groups, but does not assume responsibility for delivering services, balancing a budget, administering a

government. As a legislator, Koch was accustomed to being, in Felix Rohatyn's words, "a lone cowboy." After nineteen months in office Koch was
still "a lone cowboy." His closest advisers worried that he was trying to do
too much himself. He still insisted on meeting with his scheduling staff. He
fussed over letters. He wasted time, some of it on shooting the breeze with
reporters and regaling them with funny anecdotes, some of which are quite
venomous. "I always like to tweak people if I can," he says in his oral
memoirs, "especially if I don't like them. This is something that's really
vicious in me." He insists on being his administration's primary—sometimes only—lightning rod. One day late last year Ronald Gault, who was
then a special adviser and is now commissioner of the Department of
Employment, was handed a mailgram from the New York Metropolitan
Council of the NAACP denouncing the Koch administration as "callous."
Gault thought that the mailgram required study, and the press office said
that there would be no immediate comment. Since it was already late in the
day and there was no reaction from City Hall, the mailgram was played
down by the press. However, Koch held an impromptu press conference a
few days later to denounce the "outrageous" and "unfair" mailgram. The
mayor can take the heat while he's popular. Presumably, someday he will
not be. The mayor's aides fear that by not husbanding his resources, not
picking and choosing his fights, by insisting on personalizing issues and
taking firm stands, he is collecting enemies who will one day join in ambush-
ing him. What Koch views as a great strength—doing what's "right"—
some of his aides see as a potential flaw.

You judge a good political leader differently from a good manager, Felix
Rohatyn says. A political leader is judged by the image he projects, by
personal acts. Rohatyn gives Koch high marks in this respect. "But in a
manager you look for entirely different things," he observes. "You look not
for the vision of the man but for the kind of organization he surrounds
himself with and the kind of people willing to work for him—and his
willingness to delegate to them." One deputy mayor thinks that there aren't
enough "implementers" among the people Koch has surrounded himself
with during the first nineteen months. "I feel that there are very few people
in this administration who have ever been responsible for managing anything and being respectful of the difficulty of making things happen," this
man says. The management task is compounded by the mayor's feeling that
he is at war with his own government. Koch often speaks like an outsider,
though he is now an insider. There is a tension between his low opinion of
the bureaucracy and his need to win that bureaucracy's cooperation. "You
can't be at war with your own employees," says David Brown. "You might
occupy the agencies but not be able to govern them."

Koch sometimes seems to be at war not only with the bureaucracy but
with the city's entire political-financial-business-labor establishment—a
battle he likes to think he has waged throughout his political career. He is
always on guard, worried that each of these special interests hungers for a

larger piece of the city's shrinking pie. Koch believes in the adversary system—in not getting too close to those who do not share his broader responsibilities to nearly eight million people. "When he became mayor, he came to view us as the enemy," Felix Rohatyn says. "He's declaring war all the time," the labor leader Barry Feinstein says. The hostility and distrust that built up between the mayor and those accustomed to being "partners" of the city's mayors reached a point where some members of the administration began to fear that Koch's ability to govern was being crippled. Koch could get elected without the establishment, but could he govern without it?

Last September, at an Association for a Better New York breakfast, attended by former Mayors Wagner and Lindsay and almost five hundred men and women important in business, banking, the media, and labor, the mayor said that those who had claims on previous mayors had "no claims upon me." Of course, that did not mean they had no "access to me," he continued. "But it does mean that I am able to make every decision on the merits. And that hasn't happened for many, many years." Wagner and Lindsay squirmed. A wave of foot-shuffling and head-turning filled the room. The speech was, Deputy Mayor Solomon told Koch afterward, "a lousy speech." A prominent businessman said a few months later, "Koch had this fantastic opportunity to win over important people. But instead of doing that, of saying we're all here for the same purpose, he went off and criticized previous administrations. When you become mayor, you've got to put down your personal feelings about people and climb above them."

Many people worry that Koch is excessively—needlessly—candid. They complain that a mayor does not have the same freedom to express opinions as a private citizen, or even a member of Congress. "Part of the responsibility of a mayor is to be honest and direct with the voters," Stephen Berger, a former Koch adviser and once the executive director of the State Emergency Financial Control Board, says. "Another part is not to say everything you know or feel at a given moment. There are times when you have to control yourself for the public good, and give yourself the margin to achieve long-range aims. What a mayor says has meanings, echoes. It vibrates out. Everybody takes it seriously. Unlike what a legislator says. And since Ed Koch is popular, what he says is taken more seriously."

There is a constant tension between what the mayor says and what he should say, between being honest and being effective. As Koch says, "What you see is what you get." Unlike many public officials, he utters simple declarative sentences, is not easily intimidated by polls or pressure groups, has a well-developed sense of public service, and maintains wonderfully naïve hopes and expectations of reforming city government and of not being co-opted by the establishment. But while democratic government cannot serve the public if it is beholden to an establishment of special interests, it also cannot dictate to the special interests. It must persuade them. Mayor

Beame, like Wagner before him, was too close to the establishment, and therefore too cautious. Mayor Lindsay, through his first years, was not close enough. A mayor must strike a balance to govern effectively. In his first nineteen months Koch did not strike that balance. He remained, proudly, defiantly, Ed Koch the outsider, the gadfly. Privately, David Brown and others urged Koch to cooperate more with the establishment, and particularly with municipal labor leaders.

On the morning of November 3, 1978, over Danish and coffee in his office, the mayor opened peace negotiations with the Municipal Labor Committee. The meeting was a secret one, mysteriously listed on his schedule as an 8 A.M. "private meeting." Just after 9 A.M., the door to Koch's office was flung open and out walked Victor Gotbaum, chairman of the Municipal Labor Committee; Jack Bigel, consultant to the committee; Barry Feinstein, the committee secretary; and William Scott, deputy to Albert Shanker, who is head of the United Federation of Teachers. I was standing outside the door with Dan Wolf, and after the labor delegation left, the mayor waved Wolf and me into his office. I asked how the meeting had come about. Well, Koch began, MAC Chairman Rohatyn "stupidly" promised the labor-union leaders the right to review the city's budget annually in return for their consent to purchase MAC bonds with employee-pension funds. "He now denies he said it. But he said it," Koch went on. "I told Allan Schwartz there will be no labor veto"—over the city's budget, that is. "If everyone tells you the interest rates will go up, I told Allan, then tell Jack Bigel if they do, there will be more layoffs." Koch would not share his mayoral prerogatives. Bigel, the unions' chief strategist, was accustomed to sharing power. Abe Beame had been a close friend and John Lindsay a political ally. Bigel had had regular access to their office. He had been considered a partner. Now the mayor was a man who insisted that a nonelected leader could not be a full partner. Bigel began to worry that the estrangement had gone far enough. Together, over the course of three years, the unions and the banks and the city and the state and the federal governments—the "partners"—had successfully skirted bankruptcy. That effort could be undermined by misunderstandings and noncommunication. Bigel's central role and his importance as a conduit could also be undermined if he did not enjoy a special relationship with the mayor. So Bigel asked to see Koch, alone. Out of that session the idea for the coffee-and-Danish breakfast was born.

Bigel agreed at the breakfast that the unions would drop their demand for annual budget review. In return, Koch agreed to "wipe the slate clean," he says. "I wanted to show Washington and the country New York was taking a new tack." What of his previous criticism of the bureaucracy and the city workers? "If you want to make a point, as I did, you can't pass every litmus test," he says. "I recognize I wasn't including every point I should." At the breakfast, they agreed to meet regularly to discuss city matters. They also agreed on the content of an open letter from Koch to Gotbaum, dated

November 3, which represented a *mea culpa* of sorts from Koch. He wrote, in part:

> I realize only with the cooperation of the municipal labor leaders and their members can I truly effect all of the reforms necessary to make this the kind of City that will flourish again and provide its residents and workers all that they are entitled to. In the first 10 months this Administration had to take positions and state them forcefully and forthrightly so as to assert the character of the new administration. In the course of these 10 months, I have learned a lot. I have learned that governing the City is not as easy as those outside government think it is. I have learned that municipal labor leaders also recognize their obligations to the City of New York.

David Brown was jubilant. "The mayor was saying he won't go it alone," he said. "It was a policy decision. Ed knows, pointing to 1980, he'll need allies to win more federal help. Ed can get their cooperation now because he is popular. If a drop of blood was spilled, the sharks would form."

Barry Feinstein, president of Teamsters Local 237, was equally jubilant. The meeting was "a clear realization that the mayor can't govern alone," he boasted. "He needs partners. For the first time the mayor is recognizing the requirement to share power." Feinstein appreciates power. Though his local is relatively small—eighteen thousand members—compared with District Council 37 or the United Federation of Teachers, he is considered a powerful leader and negotiator. Feinstein is a burly, outgoing man, in his mid-forties, who chews expensive cigars and believes that those who aspire to the priesthood should not lead unions or enter politics. He helped persuade the Municipal Labor Committee—despite the liberal views of its members—to endorse the reelection in 1978 of conservative Republican state senators. Union leaders might blast Republicans—call the Bronx's Senator John Calandra a "troglodyte," for instance—for the edification of the membership. But this was business. The Republicans, led by Senator Warren Anderson of Binghamton, a man they could talk to, controlled the State Senate. The unions had previously demonstrated that they could sway a majority vote in the Democratic-controlled Assembly: last year Mayor Koch couldn't rouse one Democratic member of the Assembly to sponsor his civil-service-reform proposals. "He got zilch," says Feinstein. "He could have gotten some of it if he'd worked with us." The unions were vulnerable, however, in the more conservative Senate, so after discussions with Anderson, the Municipal Labor Committee made manpower and money—a lot of money—available to Anderson's colleagues. Kent Sanders, one of Anderson's top aides, told a *Times* reporter, "Do you realize we got almost half of the money we raised from unions?" Albert Shanker's teachers' union alone invested more than $60,000 in legislative races. Several Democratic Senate candidates were thus deprived of a significant base of support. The Republicans maintained control of the Senate, and the Municipal Labor

Committee gained, in the words of one of their leaders, "a credit card with Warren Anderson." Feinstein says, "We're all-powerful. We control the work force. We control the dollars that keep this town alive."

As part of the fresh start between Koch and Gotbaum, Koch went to dinner at Victor and Betsy Gotbaum's home, in Brooklyn Heights, on Sunday, November 19. The other guests were Bess Myerson, a co-chairman of Koch's 1977 campaign and his social date for the evening; Lillian Roberts, Gotbaum's deputy; former Family Court Judge Simeon Golar; the writers Michael and Stephanie Harrington; Anne Just, a Vermont state legislator; and two of the Gotbaums' children. Betsy Gotbaum, a good cook and a gracious hostess, pleased Koch by giving him a 1964 bottle of Bordeaux, definitely not of the three-dollar variety. Koch said later, "It was a nice evening. I enjoyed it."

The fresh start lasted for two weeks. After Koch's second meeting with the labor leaders, he told me he was appalled at Gotbaum for criticizing Deputy Mayor Basil Paterson, who, surprisingly, was not at the meeting. Paterson, an old and close friend of Gotbaum's, was the city's chief labor negotiator. That Gotbaum would attack Paterson "shows you how bad he is," Koch told me, and he went on, "He said that when Basil put the give-backs on the table he would have given some back if Basil had not taken them off the table. It shows you how bad Victor's judgment is. In defense of Basil, he took them off after the unions said they wanted an extra one-half-percent raise in return for the give-backs. Now, for him to admit this outrage and refer to Basil as a schmuck is awful. My question is: Would he have had the courage to use that language if Basil were sitting there?"

Nevertheless, Koch refrained from criticizing Gotbaum publicly, and the truce continued, uneasily. The mayor sat with labor leaders to discuss his four-year financial plan and his civil-service-reform package before releasing them publicly. But by midwinter the inevitable conflicts were more visible. The unions felt threatened by Koch's proposed civil-service reforms. Gotbaum opposed Koch's plan to close municipal hospitals and perhaps lay off workers that Gotbaum represented. Most unions resented Koch's confrontational style and what they felt was a preference for making headlines rather than governing. By spring Gotbaum and several colleagues were beginning to whisper about encouraging John Zuccotti or Felix Rohatyn to challenge Koch in the 1981 Democratic primary.

Koch's relations with minority leaders, particularly blacks, have sometimes been even more rancorous than his relations with the municipal unions and the city bureaucracy. Tensions between Koch and blacks developed in the 1977 mayoral campaign, when Koch repeatedly called for the death penalty and denounced "poverty pimps" and "poverticians"—terms that some listeners felt were code words for "blacks." After Koch finished first in the initial primary, however, prominent black leaders flocked to endorse him in the runoff primary against Mario Cuomo. "Ed assured us that the government would reflect properly the makeup of the city," Manhattan Representative Charles Rangel said when he and Basil Paterson and State Senator Carl McCall endorsed Koch. After Koch's victory in the runoff, Rangel, Herman Badillo, and Ed Costikyan were appointed to direct the transition from Beame's administration to Koch's.

It was soon apparent that Koch was as uncomfortable with the black establishment as he was with the white establishment. Tensions rose again when he moved boldly to reorganize the poverty program so as to eliminate the jobs of many middlemen who controlled poverty funds. Since the middlemen were recommended by, or close to, black elected officials, Koch was stepping on toes. Leaders complained that they were not consulted, as Koch had promised they would be, and as they had been in the past. They chafed at Koch's constant criticism of poverty-program "fraud," claiming that he lumped the good and the bad together and created the impression that all poverty programs were "rip-offs." Not so, said Koch, who felt that he could point to some success in dealing with poverty programs. A press release issued last April noted that as a result of restructuring, minority participation in the summer-jobs program increased from 76 percent in 1977 to 92 percent in 1978; the Office of Model Cities was restructured, decreasing the central office staff from two hundred and sixty-two to fourteen and making it possible to shift resources to the field; and the central overhead costs of the Model Cities program were reduced by 94 percent, from $5.1 million to $325,000.

The conflict with black leaders seems to be one part style, one part substance. Mayor Koch is criticized for having a combative personality and for being preoccupied with the middle class at the expense of the poor. Black officials are unaccustomed to white political leaders who treat them as representatives of a special-interest group and refuse to allow blacks to use them as punching bags to placate black voters. Over the years it has not been unusual for black leaders to condemn opponents as "racists"—a charge they have employed as loosely as white politicians employ a term like "irresponsible." White public officials have bridled at the accusation of racism but have usually remained silent. Not Koch. Mayors Wagner and Beame were cautious politicians who rolled with the punches and unfailingly softened the edges of a conflict, searching for a compromise that everyone could live with. Mayor Lindsay walked the streets clamoring for a new "national urban policy" and reminding America of its poor citizens, particularly poor blacks. He was elected with black votes—no small feat for a Republican. And Lindsay was proud to be tagged as "pro-black." Koch is proud to be tagged as "pro-middle class." Revealingly, Koch's fiscal-1980 budget message states that it was prepared "with three principal goals in mind": "to balance the budget," "to reduce our budget gaps in future years," and "to provide for the effective and efficient delivery of services in order to attract and hold business and the middle class." No mention is made of the poor. The mayor wants to send members of the middle class a message that City Hall cares about them, but in the process many minority leaders receive a message of neglect. This feeling is buttressed by Koch's determination to treat everyone alike and, as one of his black advisers observes, by his tendency to "personalize" criticism. Koch is offended by double standards, perhaps as much as he is by racism. What lingers in his mind about Mississippi and his visit there in 1964 is not the racism and violence directed against civil-rights workers, though he was obviously moved enough to go and lend his help. He remembers most vividly what he regards as the hypocrisy of a liberal like Joseph Rauh, of the ADA, who on learning that it was white, not black, civil-rights workers who had been beaten, allegedly said, "Can't use it." "That was a trauma for me," says Koch. "I never forgot it."

Koch is not one to turn the other cheek. One of his louder feuds has been with Herbert Daughtry, of Brooklyn, a black minister. It began in June of 1978 after Arthur Miller, a black businessman and civic leader in Crown Heights, was choked to death by policemen under mysterious circumstances. The police subdued Miller after an altercation and were alleged to have accidentally strangled him with their nightsticks. The black community was enraged and suspicious. A grand jury was impaneled. Daughtry's Brooklyn-based organization, the Black United Front, wrote to the mayor urging a meeting. The group also forwarded a copy of its "agenda," including demands that "all police officers at the scene of Arthur Miller's death be suspended immediately and remain suspended until a thorough investigation of the murder be expedited and the killer or killers be brought to justice"; that "three Black psychiatrists be appointed to examine all police officers involved"; that "the entire investigation, including psychiatric findings, be made public"; that "a screening board be set up to evaluate the files of policemen who are to begin assignment in all Black communities and that the Black United Front be part of the selection process"; that the 77th Precinct have "immediate changes" and the "staffing pattern be altered to represent 50% Black and Hispanic policemen"; that, because of "frequent allegations" of assaults by the Crown Heights Jewish Community Patrol, an organization of Hasidic Jews, "all federal money" to this organization should be "discontinued"; and that "the practice of regularly closing off of service roads on the Jewish Sabbath and other special Hasidic days be stopped immediately."

Clearly, white police officers and Jews—perhaps most white citizens—would feel threatened by this agenda. A reader of the Bill of Rights might conclude that the agenda, if it were adopted, would violate the rights of privacy and due process, among others. For many years City Hall had been the recipient of fevered agendas and demands. Most had been ignored. Mayor Koch, however, took this one seriously. He dictated a three-page response, picking apart the agenda and asserting, "Your demand that officers involved in the Miller case be examined by three Black psychiatrists not only violates the spirit of the civil-rights movement but is racist in character."

Why did the mayor himself respond?

"Because I have a rule to answer every letter I get. It's a compulsion," Koch says.

The conflict heated up. A few weeks later Daughtry dispatched a three-page retort charging that City Hall was pro-Jewish. He complained of "Jewish fund-raising," of Jewish "savages," of "Hasidic arrogance and contempt," and of "people who are guilty of the crimes that the Hasidim have perpetrated," and he stated that "most Black people wonder how you and other Jewish people would react . . . ," and so on. Substitute "black" for Jewish "savages," and it is easy to imagine the screams of "racism" at such stereotyping. Enraged, Koch wrote back calling the letter "abusive" and concluding, "I see no point in a further exchange of letters."

Daughtry's letter confirmed Koch's darkest fears—struck a raw nerve. "I'm very conscious of being Jewish," says Koch. He is also conscious of, and threatened by, what he considers widespread black anti-Semitism. As a member of Congress, he seethed at black colleagues who voted against aid for Israel; he feared that their votes were an expression of their hostility to Jews. In his oral memoirs of 1975 and 1976, Koch reveals his innermost feelings and fears about race relations:

> I find the black community very anti-Semitic. I don't care what the American Jewish Congress or the B'nai B'rith will issue by way of polls showing that the black community is not. I think that's pure bull. . . . They'd like to believe that. My experience with blacks is that they're basically anti-Semitic. Now, I want to be fair about it. I think whites are basically anti-black. . . . But the difference is: it is recognized as morally reprehensible, something you have to control.

For Koch, as for all moralists, issues tend to be clear-cut; if it is wrong for whites to stereotype blacks, it is wrong for blacks to stereotype whites. Koch's views, unlike those of many liberals, are not clouded by compassion for the descendants of slaves, the victims of racism. He accepts no excuses, brooks no insults, applies but one standard. That one standard leads him to oppose preferential-treatment programs as "reverse discrimination." The goal of the civil-rights movement, he says, should be for blacks "to be treated like whites." He is disdainful of welfare cheats and probably wonders why more people do not struggle to escape poverty, as the Koch family did. To most liberals, all poor blacks are victims; to Koch, some are villains. For instance, he thinks that some criminal violence is caused by black racism rather than by poverty. For a Greenwich Village reformer, Koch says some surprising things in his memoirs. In discussing racial balance in the public schools, he says:

Why don't I believe in [imposed] racial balance in the schools? Because it doesn't work, because it destroys the public-school system. People who were sending their kids to the public schools—white middle-class people—take them out if they can afford it. And the only people who are left there are the poor, Boston being the best illustration.

Liberal theory, he believes, often doesn't work, because it ignores reality. He quotes former Harlem district leader Hilda Stokely as saying in the late 1960s:

"We're not interested in having our black kids sit next to your white kids on a bench in the school. What we're interested in is equal schools, equal education. That's what we want." And I said to her, "But, Hilda, what you're saying is terrible. You're saying separate but equal, and the Supreme Court says there can't be such a thing as separate but equal." And she said, looking at me rather directly, "I wouldn't tell a Jew how to bake a bagel," which I think sums it up. She knew more then than we knew then and that we're learning.

Koch's views crystallized and began to surface when he opposed low-income high-rise housing in the middle-income community of Forest Hills. His liberal friends were enraged, he recalls:

"Don't you want people to mix—everybody should be homogenized." I said, "No, I don't believe that at all." I said, "Would Chinatown be Chinatown if instead of it being occupied by the Chinese we made certain that since they're only one percent of the population in the city of New York or even less, on every block there be ninety-nine other people to every one Chinese? It would be ridiculous. Would Little Italy be Little Italy? . . . Is Riverdale a ghetto because it's primarily middle-class Jewish? Ridiculous."

Like many of us, Koch holds racial views that are contradictory. On the one hand, he believes that most people, deep down, are racists. On the other hand, he claims that the conflict is one of class, not race: "I believe that people of like life style have very little problem in living together. It's people of different life styles who have a problem of living together." The class, or economic, interpretation, however, does not explain the clash between poor whites and poor blacks in Mississippi, the clash between lower-middle-class Italians and blacks in Coney Island, or, more recently, the firebombing of black middle-class homes in middle-class Yonkers, Queens, and Staten Island. His views regarding affirmative action are also inconsistent. On the one hand, he says city policies should be color-blind. On the other hand, last November he publicly urged the City Council (in vain) to appoint a black or a Puerto Rican to fill the vacant Bronx Borough presidency. After the New York Regional Board of the Anti-Defamation League took him to task for this recommendation, Koch wrote to the League on November 17: "Council members are going to take many factors into consideration, and though you probably disagree with me, I think that it is reasonable for them to take into consideration the fact that no black or Puerto Rican presently sits on the Board of Estimate." At a November 3 commissioners' meeting, Koch declared, "I sent to everyone a memo that we have so few Hispanics in government. The statistics are deplorable. . . . You have to reach out and seek to bring in blacks and Hispanics." Regarding affirmative action, Koch is as guilty of placard-thinking as he believes liberals are. What he really seems to be against are words like "affirmative action" and "quotas," and not the policy of affirmative action. Does such a policy mean that blacks would have jobs reserved for them? Of course. Koch understood that when he held open one post of deputy mayor for a black (Basil Paterson) and the post of chairman of the Human Rights Commission for a Puerto Rican woman (Patria Nieto-Ortiz).

Minority leaders, recognizing that there is sometimes a discrepancy between Koch's bellicose words and his policies, feel that he is often posing for votes, and he may be. Their concerns would be eased if the mayor were less preoccupied with the middle class or were surrounded by more blacks. Koch has no close black friends to help him reach out to leaders, to assure them of his good faith. Nor has he done as well as he promised in staffing his administration with blacks. In the campaign, Koch said that he would have more blacks in his administration than the combined total of the last three mayors, but figures compiled by Ronald Gault's staff show that as of last March, Koch fell far short of that total. He had appointed blacks to 18.4 percent of the top-level positions—deputy mayors, commissioners, administrators, directors, and deputy commissioners or administrators. In the three prior administrations, the percentages for blacks were: Wagner, 4.9; Lindsay, 10.5; and Beame, 12.1. (As for Hispanics and women, Koch says that he made no specific promises in the campaign. But the percentages for Hispanics are: Wagner, 2.5; Lindsay, 3.8; Beame, 7.3; and Koch, 5.1. For women: Wagner, 9.9; Lindsay, 17.1; Beame, 15.3; and Koch, 18.4.)

Those blacks whom Koch has surrounded himself with have increased the communication chasm between the mayor and the city's black leaders. Former Deputy Mayor for Human Services Haskell Ward and Department of Employment Commissioner Ronald Gault, who have been the mayor's principal black advisers, come from a Ford Foundation background rather than a political one. Ward, who until he announced his resignation last month was Koch's closest black adviser, was identified with dismantling the poverty program. He was seen by many black leaders as Koch's man, not theirs—but then, that was what Koch preferred. Former Deputy Mayor Basil Paterson, who had deep political roots in the black community, chose not to serve as Koch's black adviser, and until he left the administration, concentrated instead on labor relations. Ward and, to a lesser extent, Gault are strangers—non-backslapping professionals, with whom politicians are reluctant to swap confidences or discuss a political problem. In previous administrations, members of the black community always had their "own man at City Hall"—someone they had worked with and recommended. Thus, with regard to appointments, Koch is seen as changing the rules of the game.

Many black leaders don't fathom Koch. They are accustomed to charging, not being charged with, "racism"; when they hear of a white politician barking "Shut up!" to a black one—as the mayor is reported to have done to black Brooklyn Councilwoman Mary Pinkett—visions of plantations and slavery enter their minds. "Koch treats everyone alike," Ronald Gault explains. "That's a weakness as well as a strength, because people who don't know him perceive it as anti-them—particularly minority groups. The mayor is thin-skinned. He doesn't pretend to be anything else. You scream at him, he'll scream back." As the mayor cut the city's budget and threatened to close four of the city's seventeen hospitals which serve the poor, the screaming on both sides intensified. And Koch's enjoyment of a good fight, his tendency to personalize, his determination to treat everyone alike, his belief that most blacks are anti-Semitic, and perhaps a lack of compassion on his part joined to create discord between Koch and black leaders.

Koch, a politician sensitive to the public's mood on the death penalty and rent control, for instance, refused to treat his estrangement from black leaders as a political problem. During his first year Koch resisted advice to lower his voice, refused to deny himself the pleasure of snapping back at critics, black or white. Early this year a group of black ministers withdrew an invitation to the mayor to attend a celebration of Martin Luther King, Jr.,'s birthday on January 15. The ministers claimed they "could not guarantee the mayor's safe passage in Harlem" because of his "racist policies." Koch lashed back. Calling someone a racist "is as gross a crime as racism itself," Koch said on a local radio program. "What is that minister saying —that white people should not come to Harlem?" What would happen, he went on, if a white neighborhood leader declared, " 'So-and-So, a black person, may not come into this neighborhood'? We would denounce that as racist. This particular clergyman can get away with it and not an editorial denounces him."

The mayor's logic is unassailable; his political judgment is not. By speaking out so forcefully, he may have kept the controversy alive and convinced other black leaders, however falsely, that he was interested only in scoring points with white middle-class voters. Charges of "racism" blossomed. State Senator Vander L. Beatty, of Brooklyn, who is chairman of the Black and Puerto Rican Legislative Caucus in the state legislature, initiated a petition drive for the mayor's recall. Though Beatty had little visible support, Koch began to recognize a political problem. "I am the victim of racism," he told Lee Dembart of the *Times.* "But if the single black newspaper in town runs these terrible, unfair, racist stories about me, I don't know that I'll have the avenues to make it clear. Sooner or later, the big lie overcomes."

The mayor began to make peace overtures. "We have to try harder," he told me. He vainly urged the state to increase welfare grants, which are frozen at 1972 cost-of-living levels. He held private meetings with black leaders. His State of the City Message last February 1 called for "an end to the rhetoric, the posturing, the harmful language of confrontation." As he had done with city labor leaders, the mayor was offering a modest *mea culpa.* But some differences with minority leaders, as with the unions, cannot be soothed with words. Profound policy differences will continue to separate Koch from many black leaders. His version of reality is different from theirs, and candor compels him not to hide the fact. The black leaders believe that budget cuts fall disproportionately on the poor; Koch claims that 60 percent of the city budget is earmarked for the poor. Blacks want more government services; Koch, seeking to balance the budget, talks of fewer. Blacks complain that Koch is too concerned about the middle class; Koch says that without a stable middle class, there will be no one to pay for the services the blacks want. These differing versions of reality sprang into bold relief last January 8, when local branches of the NAACP warned that efforts to close municipal hospitals could create civil disorder. A day later the Committee of Interns and Residents, the union that represents all of the more than two thousand interns and residents in the municipal hospitals, asserted that poor people would die if hospitals were closed. In a statement, the committee also declared: "We say city hospitals provide jobs for New Yorkers." Koch had denied that the closings would endanger the health of the poor. And preoccupied with his budget deficit and mindful that middlemen sometimes use the poor to justify their own jobs, the mayor said, "Hospitals are not for employment purposes. They're for sick people. Hospitals are not supposed to be make-work projects."

A glorious Saturday afternoon last autumn. Gracie Mansion's spacious lawn, which slopes down toward the East River, is lush. Squirrels run across the green carpet and scamper up trees covered with orange leaves. The bright sun glazes the river, which is still except for an occasional tugboat floating by. The blue sky is streaked with silver bullets that twist in graceful arcs as they rise from La Guardia Airport. It is a perfect day for a walking tour, which is what Mayor Edward I. Koch has planned for the afternoon. Inside Gracie Mansion, Maureen Connelly, his press secretary, shows me the second-floor living quarters. A few feet past the head of the stairs, we enter a suite that was home for Koch's predecessor, Mayor Abraham Beame, and his wife, Mary. In a sitting room are facing antique love seats that Mary Beame upholstered in cut velvet. Between the love seats, a gaudy chandelier hangs so low that tall visitors must duck it. The mayor, Miss Connelly says, spends little time in the sitting room, and he spends even less time in the adjoining bedroom. Everything in this bedroom is in miniature, as if it had been built to order for the five-foot-two-inch former mayor. There is a tiny rocker, two frail dollhouse-like wooden chairs, a desk built close to the floor, and a small dresser with a mirror that reaches to my chest. The walls are covered with bright-yellow wallpaper sprouting irises, tulips, and carnations.

The contrast with Koch's bedroom, at the other end of the floor, is striking. There, three abstract paintings hang on stark-white walls. The floor, bare except for a somber Oriental rug, is littered with dirty black socks crumpled into balls, early editions of the *Times* and the *News,* which Koch carefully inspects each night, and a pair of wingtip shoes. A platform bed is unmade: brown-and-black-striped sheets on top of a green thermal blanket and quilt are heaped into a mound. A large black-and-white papier-mâché Pee Wee rabbit rests on the floor next to the bed, which faces a twenty-one-inch television set. On a white mantelpiece rests a picture of the mayor's sister, Pat Thaler, with her husband and their three children. There is a stereo set, including a tape deck, on which Koch plays his favorites from the sixties—Simon and Garfunkel, Judy Collins, "Man of La Mancha." White shelves built into the wall hold more records than books. Koch's favorite book, he once told me, is Merle Miller's *Plain Speaking*, a biography of Harry Truman. "I'm not someone—and I regret it—who reads a great deal," Koch says. "I'm talking about outside of government papers, which I read a lot of. I suppose one of the things I don't have enough of is a historical perspective on what's taking place. Mine is more educated instinct." There are two other rooms on this floor—a sparsely furnished room with a desk, where Koch sometimes works, and a guest bedroom.

The mayor is ready to depart. He is accompanied by his old friend Daniel Wolf. The mayor gets into the front seat of his Chrysler, and Wolf and I sit in the back. Today Koch plans two surprise appearances in Queens. "I like to go back to places I campaigned in extensively," he says. "I have a good recollection of how I was received then, and I like to compare it with now." Such visits afford him an opportunity to learn what is on the public's mind and, not incidentally, to sample neighborhood food. Koch particularly enjoys visiting middle-class communities. He identifies with the residents—with their work ethic, their close family ties, their sense of loyalty, their patriotism, and their struggle to escape poverty. He sees a different challenge from the one that confronted Mayor Robert Wagner and, particularly, Mayor John Lindsay, in the sixties. They wanted to communicate concern for the poor, to give them hope, to keep the streets cool. Koch wants to communicate concern for the middle class, and to give *them* hope. The sixties were focused on social problems; the seventies are focused on economics. Lindsay worried about integrating neighborhoods, Koch worries about preserving their tax base. "I happen to have as middle-class values as anyone," he declares as his car passes through Jackson Heights, Queens.

"You couldn't fit in in Jackson Heights," Wolf says.

Koch agrees. Turning around in the seat, he says that it would be "too dull."

The mayor, aware that he sounded condescending, explains what he meant. "Jackson Heights is the heart of the city. It's a stable community, composed of hard-working taxpayers. I absolutely love them. But it would be phony for me to say that given the choice between living in Manhattan and living in Jackson Heights at a lower rent, I'd take the lower rent. I'd pay the higher rent. Manhattan is the most exciting part of an exciting town. But I feel I identify with the people of Jackson Heights."

The mayor's car stops on Queens Boulevard, in Forest Hills, and Koch, hands stuffed in the pockets of his brown-checked sports jacket, strides past the stores on Seventy-first Avenue. On the corner, Assemblyman Alan Hevesi, broom in hand, heads a contingent of civic leaders in an effort "to raise everyone's consciousness to clean Forest Hills," he says.

The mayor stops to applaud their efforts, and as he does so a crowd gathers. "Hi, how'm I doing?" he asks his audience, which is middle class and mostly white. A burst of applause is the answer.

"You should be running now for mayor," says Hevesi.

"It will be better in three years," says Koch, and he proceeds to turn the gathering into a Hyde Park forum.

"I am committed to helping the middle class," he says.

A car horn blares.

"Give that guy a ticket!" Koch says, and the crowd roars.

"What about kids smoking on the corner?" asks a young man.

"But isn't that the woman's responsibility?" Koch asks. "The mayor can't take over Mama and Papa's responsibility."

Koch then asks his audience, "Am I doin' okay?"

"I get your letters," says a woman who identifies herself as Paula Newberry. "He's written to me three times," she explains to me. Each time she had written to complain that her apartment at 10 Holder Place was "illegally taken off rent control." "I am pleased with him," she tells me.

So is Bessie Joffe, who volunteers, "I am just an admiring citizen, but I'm telling you he's doing a great job."

The mayor heads east, followed by a pack of citizens.

"Excuse me," a middle-aged woman says, grabbing his arm. "I'm Italian, not Jewish. You're the best."

A man in a passing car shouts, "Hey, Ed. How ya doin'?"

Koch could not be happier. There is energy, support, approval—vindication—to be found in the affection of these people. He stops to ask, "If there was one thing you wanted me to do, what would it be?"—and he listens intently to the responses, instructing an aide, who had met us in Forest Hills, to take notes. Occasionally he himself scrawls a reminder on a small white memo pad.

"Terrific job, Mr. Mayor!" calls out seventy-two-year-old Ellwood Weinreich of Forest Hills.

Why "terrific," I ask him.

"Because he's trying hard," Weinreich says. "He's not up for reelection now, yet he's doing things like this."

"Where should we eat?" Koch asks. After prolonged discussion he settles on the Stratton Restaurant on Queens Boulevard, which has a glass-enclosed sidewalk café.

The next stop is South Jamaica, Queens, a predominantly black low- and middle-income community. The mayor's car stops at Jamaica Avenue and 162nd Street, and Koch darts across the street to shake hands with several people waiting for a bus. Like Queens Boulevard in Forest Hills, this is a commercial strip. The major differences between Jamaica Avenue and Queens Boulevard are that here there are more bargain centers, more street peddlers, more garbage hugging the curb, more black faces. The greeting is nearly as warm as it was in Forest Hills. "He's doing a beautiful job," says Mary Chambers, a black woman, flashing a big smile toward Koch.

Koch is less well known here, however. He approaches Panagrotis Treskas, a Greek national who sells hot dogs and soda from a cart. Grabbing the startled peddler by the hand, Koch asks, "Do you know who I am?"

Treskas peers blankly into the stranger's face. Several seconds elapse. "From the telephone company?" Treskas finally blurts. The stranger shakes his head. Treskas is worried now. Out comes the laminated license from the City Department of Health. "Here, here"—he shoves it in front of the stranger to prove that his business is legal.

As the mayor walks along, a crowd forms. Thelma Moore, a homeowner, complains, "It's Saturday, and they still haven't picked up the garbage. That's not unusual." But she doesn't blame the mayor: "Just because the garbage doesn't get picked up, I can't just dislike him for that."

As he strolls among the shoppers, Koch inquires, "Was Mayor Beame here? Was Mayor Lindsay here?"

Instead of responding to that question, a woman asks one of her own: "What about York College?"—a reference to a proposal that a campus be built in Jamaica to replace the rented facilities that the college now occupies.

The cost, Koch says, would be $140 million over the long term and $80 million in the short term. "It comes out of your taxes. I'm not gonna permit your tax dollars to be wasted."

The crowd swells, encircling Koch, who is standing beside a licensed jewelry display case belonging to John Darthard, a black man in his mid-thirties who served in the Army and spent a couple of years in college. Darthard offers the opinion that a campus for York College would have education value, and Koch disagrees, maintaining that Queens College already serves the black community of Jamaica. The York campus is not needed, and in any case, cannot be afforded, he says. Koch and his staff have, without announcing it, decided against the proposal.

"I peddled at Queens College for three years," says Darthard. "After a period of two years they took my concession away. No reason. People of a Jewish origin were allowed to continue." There would be no discrimination against blacks if a York campus were built and they had their own college, he says.

"The question is: Where do we put your money?" Koch responds in a mellow voice. His own answer is clear: enrollment at the City University, of which Queens College is a part, is declining, and it makes no sense to divert scarce resources to the construction of new colleges when the old colleges are unfilled. To Koch, York College is primarily a resource-and-budget question. To Darthard, York College is obviously a means of ensuring nondiscrimination and perhaps the economic rejuvenation of South Jamaica.

A young woman asks the mayor why the financial assistance granted minority students in the City University's SEEK (Search for Education, Elevation, and Knowledge) program is so meager.

"Oh, come on," Koch says, perhaps recalling his own days of poverty, when there was no SEEK program. "You get from SEEK an allowance, right?"

"A hundred dollars every three weeks," she says.

"And other students do not get an allowance unless they go through the program," Koch says. "The reason you are in the program is that you need tutorial help."

"No. Financial help!" she says.

"Did you know we're graduating students with an eighth-grade education?" Koch says. "We have a limited amount of money in New York."

The young woman did not budge, and neither did Koch. He could sense that this audience was unsympathetic to his argument, but he says the same things in black neighborhoods that he says in white neighborhoods. He believes that people respect a politician who tells them what he really thinks, even if it's not what they want to hear. Many black leaders have made it clear that they are not charmed by the blunt-talking mayor. Polls suggest that he is somewhat more popular with black citizens than with their leaders, though his simmering feud with black leaders has affected his popularity. John Darthard, who disagrees with Koch about York College, is a fan: "I think he's great. He comes across as an individualist. I think he's truly, honestly concerned. Look, it's a big job."

A Monday with the mayor shortly before last Election Day. Koch is meeting with City Council President Carol Bellamy, Comptroller Harrison Goldin, and members of the Bellamy and Goldin staffs at 8 A.M. It is an informal session. The mayor asks Goldin, who is running for state comptroller, how he expects to fare.

"I think I'll win by five points," Goldin says.

"Eight," says Goldin's executive assistant, Richard Wells. (Privately,

Koch predicted that Goldin would lose by 5 percent; he lost by just over 3 percent.)

Koch wonders if everyone has read Governor Hugh Carey's answer to a question in that morning's papers. When Carey was asked to explain why he was not doing better in the polls, he replied, "My personality."

"Wasn't that terrific?" says the mayor.

Bellamy and Koch laugh about how they took a back seat to Carey at the previous day's marathon race, permitting the candidate to present the awards. "No greater love hath any man than to give up giving the awards," Koch says.

Briefly they discuss the next year's projected budget gap and a story in the morning papers about the arrest of a city councilwoman and a state senator who staged a sit-in at a Crown Heights firehouse to protest its closing. The mayor, who prides himself on having one standard of justice, approved their arrest.

The meeting ends at eight-twenty, and Koch heads for his desk, where he hovers over a stack of memos and reports. He dictates personal responses to several invitations to public or private events. From his inside coat pocket Koch pulls his small white pad on which he scrawls reminders. Going down the list, he sends a memo to Parks Commissioner Gordon Davis: "I am told that the Washington Square Park lavatories are in dreadful shape. If that is true, would you have that corrected?"

At nine o'clock Koch pauses in his dictation for a meeting with Frank Costello, the conservative Democratic candidate for the 35th Assembly District seat in northwest Queens. The candidate needs a picture with the mayor. It would have been unthinkable for a candidate from this predominantly middle-class and Catholic community to seek John Lindsay's endorsement, or even Congressman Koch's. Both Mayor Lindsay and Congressman Koch were too liberal. It is a measure of Koch's current popularity and his shedding of his former liberal image that Costello now journeys to City Hall. To put it another way, because Koch is not viewed as a liberal he is more popular. New Yorkers relate to Koch for many reasons, not the least of which is that he speaks his mind. "He communicates with the electorate like no other human being I know," says Victor Gotbaum, the executive director of District Council 37, the city's largest municipal labor union, and Koch's frequent adversary. "He's in Bay Ridge and he's in Queens. He talks very down-to-earth language." Like many citizens, Koch appears to be angry with government. He is an incumbent who acts like an anti-incumbent. "Ed asks the simple, down-to-earth, 'stupid' questions," says Dan Wolf admiringly. "Like 'Why not arrest them?'" Koch communicates a sense that the banks, the business community, the unions, the political-party mechanism—his so-called "partners"—did not elect him. Dirty streets, union or poverty-program or business rip-offs—which many politicians come to accept as normal—Koch regards as outrageous. He can be priggish and self-righteous, but he is not a cynic. And

Koch is popular among many white New Yorkers, particularly Catholics, because he is unpopular among black leaders. "He is currently in a position of much greater strength than John Lindsay was in his first year or Abe Beame was in his," says former First Deputy Mayor John Zuccotti.

At nine-twenty Dan Wolf wanders in. Koch hands him a newspaper feature story recounting how the mayor approved the arrest of the two public officials at the Crown Heights firehouse. Pleased with the story himself, he asks Wolf's opinion of it. Wolf reads it, and says he likes it.

Wolf—who is sixty-four, married, has two teen-age children, and lives in Greenwich Village—met Koch in the early sixties, when Koch was president of the Village Independent Democrats, and now he is considered Koch's closest friend, an extra set of eyes and ears. He can attend any City Hall meeting he chooses. He receives photocopies of all the biweekly reports from the heads of city agencies. Among the mayor's youthful aides, Wolf stands out as more a contemporary of Koch's, and he has the skills of a master psychologist—a requirement for any editor of *The Village Voice.* As a skeptical journalistic outsider, he reinforces Koch's anti-establishment instincts. "I find his best quality is taking positions," Wolf says of the mayor. "Being clear on positions. Not being diplomatic. Those things I like. I once said to him, 'Ed, I'm not good for you. The qualities I value in you are the ones others don't like.' He laughed. Most people warn him to be careful, to control himself, to not be himself. But the best of Ed is being himself. That's one reason he likes me. He likes that advice."

Others don't. Some of the mayor's advisers feel that Wolf encourages Koch's worst tendencies—impulsiveness, belligerence, an enjoyment of confrontations, a hostility to government and the establishment. Wolf pleads guilty. He is a stationary target. Yet anyone, in or out of government, who tries to loosen the bond between Wolf and Koch gets nowhere. Wolf sits in an office next door to the mayor's, but he has no fixed responsibility and isn't responsible for organizing or running a department. He is nearly impregnable. No bureaucratic foe can claim Wolf did not do his job. He does not have to please those who work in City Hall or outside. He has to please only one constituent—the mayor.

At a quarter of ten Maureen Connelly enters with his schedule. "How much junk has snuck into the schedule?" Koch asks. Miss Connelly asks if they should schedule visits to city agencies, and reminds the mayor that the reason they're not scheduled is that he keeps canceling them. "I'd rather go at the last minute," Koch says, suspicious that his troops will shine their boots if they know he's coming.

Meade Esposito, the Brooklyn Democratic leader, calls. Koch reaches for the phone, and smiling broadly, says, "You don't mind that we arrested two of your elected officials?"

Esposito says he would like to meet with Koch and his political aide, John Lo Cicero. Could they come to Esposito's mother's house for "meatballs" on Sunday afternoon, November 5?

"Terrific!" Koch says.

But Esposito has another piece of business. Is there a way to avoid withdrawing the police patrol car that has been assigned for some months now to protect the Lubavitcher Rebbe Menachem M. Schneerson, the spiritual leader of one of Brooklyn's largest Hasidic communities?

"The cop car is going on October twenty-eighth," Koch declares.

Deputy Mayor David Brown, Sanitation Commissioner Norman Steisel, John Lo Cicero, and Robert Tierney, another aide, arrive to discuss possible ways of speeding up the delivery of new sanitation trucks. The phone rings. It is Republican State Senator John Marchi of Staten Island. Marchi is widely respected for his decency and for the fair manner in which he chairs the powerful Senate Finance Committee. He is returning Koch's call.

"John," says the mayor, "I've been importuned to have a picture taken with your opponent. Is that okay? You know how I feel about you."

Marchi says he understands.

"I just want you to know," the mayor concludes. "I think you are the best."

The sanitation meeting resumes. Commissioner Steisel says he has only eight hundred and fifty trucks operating on each shift and needs a thousand. A hundred and ninety collection trucks that have been ordered will not arrive until spring. (Several months later Steisel said that delivery time had been cut in half, from twenty-four months to twelve, and that the trucks arrived on time.) To survive the winter, Steisel wants permission to hire extra mechanics to repair existing trucks.

"Is the city ordering the wrong trucks?" Koch asks.

"We could have bought better trucks," the commissioner admits, "but we can't cut off the order."

Koch asks why it takes twenty-four months to get a truck.

"Because there is no central person goosing them along, and the trucks are made special," says Steisel.

"Since it takes so long to get an order, why don't we order the same trucks as Chicago and other cities?" Koch asks.

Each city insists on its own "models," Steisel says. At least, some of the new trucks are larger. That means bigger loads and, he notes, harder work for the men. "We're trying to talk about it not as loads a day but as route extensions," he cautions, "though the reality is that the men have to work harder." To "sell" them, he needs the cooperation of the Uniformed Sanitationmen's Association. That won't be easy to get, he says. The union is split. Just the other night the president of the union, Edward Ostrowski, found himself in a fistfight with a union rival. The mayor shakes his head in disbelief. To sell the new routes, Steisel says, he may have to agree to rehire two hundred laid-off sanitation workers.

At noon the mayor leaves City Hall with Dan Wolf and Maureen Connelly for a lunch uptown with staff and executives of WCBS-TV. The mayor's lunch hour is often reserved for press appointments—"my filter" to the public, he calls the press. (Lunch is also a time to collect information and meet interesting people. The writer Theodore H. White and his wife, Beatrice, were recently surprised to receive an invitation to lunch with Koch at City Hall. They went, and were charmed to find that he simply wanted to exchange ideas.)

The mayor returns to City Hall for a brief courtesy meeting at two-forty-five with Stella Hackel, the director of the Bureau of the Mint, and Deputy Mayor Herman Badillo. Just after three the chairman of the state's Metropolitan Transportation Authority, Harold Fisher, comes in, trailed by Deputy Mayor Brown, Planning Commission Chairman Robert F. Wagner, Jr., Wolf, and Tierney. A big bear of a man, Fisher is, at the age of sixty-eight, one of New York's premier power brokers. His power derives from his raising money for candidates and volunteering his legal services to them. Fisher was an early supporter of Representative Hugh Carey for governor, and Governor Carey appointed him to his current part-time post. He serves as treasurer of the Brooklyn Democratic County Committee. Though his friend Carey endorsed Mario Cuomo for mayor in 1977, Fisher stood by his old friend Abe Beame. When Beame lost, Fisher chose Koch over Cuomo, yet retained his ties to Carey. Moreover, though he is an organization Democrat, he is close to many Republicans; he served as attorney for State Assembly Speaker Perry Duryea, a Republican, when Duryea was indicted in 1973 for violating the state election law—a law that had been written by Fisher himself when he was serving as counsel to former State Assembly Speaker Anthony Travia, a Democrat. One would expect that Fisher and Koch would not click. Fisher is the consummate insider, a Democrat who considers reformers more of a menace than Republicans, a man who refused to give up his law practice to serve as MTA chairman. But Koch likes Harold Fisher—likes his sense of loyalty, his directness, the warmth he shows friends. Koch "can turn on to anyone who's warm," Dan Wolf explains. The advantage of this personal approach is that the city, for the first time since its Transit Authority was taken under the state MTA's umbrella, exercises a veto over the MTA's city policies through Koch's friend Fisher. The disadvantage is that Koch is not free to criticize MTA mismanagement. A major Koch weakness, says one commissioner, whom Koch calls a superstar, is that "he makes judgments based on the instinct he has for the person presenting the information rather than on the information itself."

Fisher is accompanied to City Hall by aides, but he asks them to wait outside while he first has a private conversation with the mayor and his team to learn their agenda, to avoid staff clashes, and to reduce the chances for press leaks. (They remained outside throughout the meeting.) The purpose of this meeting is to discuss the Queens By-pass plan, an ambitious proposal for the construction of new subway lines and connections that would ease congestion and expand service to outlying sections of Queens. It would permit Long Island Rail Road commuters to by-pass the Jamaica station and come directly into Manhattan. Eighty percent of the construction costs would be borne by the federal government.

Koch says that the plan is "a waste of money."

Fisher is not so sure. "My problem with making that decision today," he tells the mayor, "is that we could get that four hundred to five hundred million dollars today"—from the federal government. If the city does not go forward with the by-pass, there will be no federal funds. Fisher wants to avoid making a decision today; one method of delay is the scheduling of public hearings, but he wants to avoid public hearings, too.

Planning Commission Chairman Wagner agrees that hearings are unnecessary. He would like to use the federal funds to renovate existing subway lines, not to build new ones.

If we can stall for a year, says Fisher, we buy time to learn if the city can trade in the funds.

But if we don't go forward on the by-pass, says Deputy Mayor Brown, how does the MTA achieve the goal of transporting Long Island commuters directly into Manhattan?

"The Long Island Rail Road will be a disaster from here on in without massive amounts of money," Fisher says, and he adds that such amounts will not be available. He complains that his predecessors built new cars but forgot to build maintenance shops. "They shouldn't have built those cars. They should have built old-style cars. Right now those cars cost seven hundred and fifty thousand dollars each, and we need two hundred cars. If we don't eliminate the Jamaica bottleneck and bring the Long Island Rail Road into Grand Central Station, the Long Island Rail Road will be a disaster."

Brown wonders if it would not be a mistake to leap at federal dollars just because they are available. Maybe there are better ways to spend the money.

"I think the by-pass is a necessity," Fisher says. Nevertheless, he turns to Koch and assures him that this is just "an informal meeting."

Koch sums up: First, it's agreed that at the moment it appears that the city could not get the money unless it decides to go forward with the Queens By-pass. Second, a decision should be deferred for a year, if possible. Third, if the facts do not warrant the by-pass, it's important that "we use this year to develop other options."

Fine, says Fisher. "But if we can't get that final money any other way, we should take it."

Brown says again that he is not sure; he warns that over a period of time the by-pass would commit City Hall to spend matching funds it does not have. Besides, he cautions, federal money is *our* money. "We can't just say we got some money, let's spend it."

"Are you saying we should not do it because we may have to spend seventeen million in 1988?" Fisher asks, incredulously.

No, says Brown. "I'm questioning it. We started and never finished some subways."

"Other areas will be looking to grab the dough," Fisher warns. "Otherwise, it will go down the drain."

"Let's sum up," Koch says. "What do we do so that we don't prejudice the five hundred million?"

"We have to figure out something we're gonna say," Fisher says. "I have to talk to the fellas who go to Washington. First, we have to say we're not ready for hearings. We have to study it more first. We just have to figure out how to say we're conducting studies, talking to the LIRR—any damn thing!"

"The mayor needs an answer if he is asked why it's taking so long," Brown says.

Fisher suggests that they say there is a clash between the city's Highways Bureau and the MTA over the cost of the by-pass. "Therefore, we have a right to say it needs further study."

"Why not have the Department of Transportation study it?" Brown says. They have "some money" for studies.

"Great!" Fisher says.

(Thus, a "study" was born. An April 1979 report on "Capital Needs and Priorities for the City of New York," prepared by the City Planning Commission, notes, "In October 1978 Mayor Koch and MTA Chairman Fisher agreed to engage a consultant to undertake a comprehensive review of all rail alternatives in the Queens corridor. This study, now in its early stages, is scheduled to provide . . .")

The meeting ends at three-forty. Five minutes later Deputy Mayor Brown returns for his daily appointment with the mayor. The first item on his list is to urge Koch to call Governor Carey directly concerning the prospective appointment of Comer Coppie, Budget Director of Washington, D.C., as executive director of the state's Financial Control Board. Brown says that Robert Morgado, the governor's chief of staff, is not responding to pressure, because the governor is concerned that he will be criticized for making a long-term appointment before an election. Koch agrees to call Carey. (That City Hall has a hand in the selection of the executive director suggests how much the Control Board's role has changed since its creation in September of 1975. To assure investors that Mayor Beame no longer ran City Hall alone, the executive director was appointed solely by the governor. When the Koch administration asked to amend the Control Board legislation last year, Governor Carey readily agreed. Governor Carey's relationship with Koch, unlike his relationship with Beame, is marked by mutual respect; and in any case, Carey, on the eve of a state election, was eager to escape the firing line. When the amendment passed, the word "Emergency" was deleted from the Control Board's title—a projected $2-billion budget gap by fiscal 1982 presumably did not qualify as an emergency—and the mayor now shared with the governor the power of appointing the executive director, who would oversee the city's contracts and budget. The prisoner was to appoint his warden.)

Just after five Koch gets into his car and heads uptown with Ronald Gault, one of his black advisers, for a scheduled walking tour of East Harlem. At the corner of 102nd Street and Third Avenue, the car stops and the mayor is greeted by leaders of the Third Avenue Merchants' Association of East Harlem. In the riots and looting that took place during the blackout in the summer of 1977, many stores in East Harlem were vandalized. Most of the stores have reopened, without government assistance. But, the mayor is told by David Acosta, the owner of El Barrio Cleaners and the president of the association, many of their customers have fled this predominantly Hispanic and black neighborhood. Acosta claims that in the last four years 80 percent of the housing on East 103rd Street has been vacated. The manager of the McDonald's at 103rd Street complains that business has been off 25 percent since the blackout. Outside his store, the sidewalk is blanketed with beer cans, bottles, empty egg cartons, crumpled paper bags. There is only one city refuse basket on the block, and it has overflowed. "This is terrible," Koch declares, asserting that "lousy sanitation service" is the most frequent complaint he receives in both poor and affluent neighborhoods. Turning to an aide, Koch orders him to make sure that refuse baskets are placed along this part of Third Avenue within forty-eight hours.

On Third Avenue, some friendly students gather around the mayor. A student at Hunter College asks why students are not eligible for half-fare subway and bus rides.

"Why should we pay for you?" asks Koch.

"We can't afford it," she says.

"When I was in school I worked my way through," the mayor responds.

Striding through the Johnson Houses, a public-housing project, Koch inspects a stretch of neat gardens kept by residents. It is growing dark, and as he approaches Lexington Avenue and 105th Street a stench of wine and urine is in the air. Across the street a menacing-looking group of young men and women, drinking beer and loudly banging drums, glare at the mayor and his contingent. "They're not angry," says Ronald Gault. "They're showing off."

A drunken middle-aged man shouts, "Now for another three years we'll wait for a politician to come by and tell us how poor we live!"

The mayor visits the Otto Chicas Company, a store on East 115th Street that sells religious articles; he promises Chicas and his son Roland that the Buildings Department will not be allowed to bulldoze an abandoned building the Chicases recently bought and intend to restore. The department "should kiss your feet" for restoring a building, says the mayor, shaking his head in disbelief that one of his agencies has actually planned to raze this building.

Several blocks away, at 24 East 116th Street, Koch stops to visit a fourteen-apartment brownstone that was recently rehabilitated by Angel Colón, a thirty-nine-year-old entrepreneur. The lobby features painted murals donated by a local artist who was eager to display his work. The electric wiring in the building was installed by a neighbor. "He rents one of my stores, and we made a deal where I pay later," Colón says. Music is piped into the lobby. Two guards are employed at the minimum wage to patrol from 8 P.M. to 6 A.M. Colón shows the mayor a neat one-bedroom apartment with a brick fireplace. The rent, he says, is $175 a month. The entire building was renovated for $11,000. Unbelievable, says the mayor, and he goes on to explain that it costs the city three times that sum to rehabilitate a building. "This was a thrilling experience," Koch says as he gets back into his car after warmly embracing Colón. To rebuild New York, he says, "you've got to get the private sector—people like Colón."

At 7 P.M. the mayor's car pulls into the driveway at Gracie Mansion. Waiting in the living room for the mayor are Senator Daniel Patrick Moynihan; Deputy Mayors David Brown and Philip Toia; Maureen Connelly; David Margolis, a businessman who is a friend and adviser of the mayor's; and Richard Ravitch, a businessman who in August of 1978 quietly resigned from the Board of Directors of the Municipal Assistance Corporation to devote more time to his private business and because he believed MAC was selling securities that might not be creditworthy. Moynihan heard about this meeting from Ravitch and asked Koch if he might attend. For more than a year Ravitch has been warning anyone who would listen that New York may be slipping irrevocably toward involuntary bankruptcy. He told this to members of the Carter administration and to friends like Moynihan and Victor Gotbaum. After Ravitch expressed his fears to Brown, Brown asked Koch if he would set aside three hours at the Mansion to hear Ravitch make his case. The mayor did.

Over cocktails, Ravitch begins his presentation by warning Koch that the federal and state governments are setting him up as "the fall guy." Criticism of Koch's tepid budget-cutting efforts is already beginning to surface, he says. He agrees that Koch has not cut deep enough, but says, "Part of my view of the fiscal crisis is that the mayor does not have the power to cure it all by himself." He does not believe that the city, alone, can make up a cumulative budget deficit over the next three years of more than $2 billion. And this staggering sum does not include the cost to the city of a 1980 labor settlement, conservatively pegged at $600 million over two years. Ravitch briefly reviews the history of the city's fiscal crisis, beginning with the banks' refusal in early 1975 to sell city securities. The original objective of MAC, when it was created, in June of 1975, was "dishonest, because it was really saying, 'How do we kid the public into buying securities?' " he says. "The more honest question would have been 'How do we make the city creditworthy?' The approach was basically cosmetic." He says that he turned down an offer from the governor in the fall of 1975 to become the first executive director of the Financial Control Board, in part because he didn't think that the board's approach would work. He says that the city then succeeded in avoiding bankruptcy partly "because the federal government provided the city with substantial new aid." But city expenditures simply rose to sponge up that new aid. The city won a reprieve when the federal government approved a $2.3-billion seasonal loan program in 1975. Another reprieve was granted in 1978 when the Carter administration and the Congress approved federal loan guarantees, only after New York promised, he says, "to do in the next four years what it had not done in the last three." The federal government, he says, extended a hand for "political" reasons; employee-pension funds risked $3.8 billion in purchasing city and MAC securities not because it was a good investment but because "bankruptcy would be worse and they gained leverage over labor negotiations"; the banks rolled over notes because they feared that bankruptcy would unleash note- and bond-holder suits charging them with fraud. In summary, he says, "the city has been able to avoid bankruptcy to date because people extended credit for noneconomic reasons."

Dinner is announced. The mayor, suit jacket off and vest unbuttoned, leads his guests into the chandeliered dining room, where three servants hover over a rectangular table draped with a white linen cloth and set with china plates, fine crystal, and decanters of wine. Ravitch is assigned a seat directly in the middle of the table, facing Koch. Sometime in 1980, Ravitch says, "absent substantial state or federal aid or other relief, there is dim prospect the city will be able to balance its budget—and there is little chance the responsibility for that will be pinned on anybody but you." Ravitch is looking directly at Koch. He goes on to say that bankruptcy would be "a disaster for this city," and that to avoid it "the partners"—the banks, the unions, and the state and federal governments—must be induced to make further "give-ups," further "sacrifices." The financial community has to reduce its interest rates, he says; the union pension funds must accept lower interest rates on their future purchases of city and MAC securities, and the unions must surrender some of their fringe benefits; the federal and state governments must increase their aid. And the mayor must tell the public "the unvarnished truth"—that the fiscal crisis is far from over. "My bottom line," Ravitch concludes, "is that I think we have a year now in which you have a chance to figure out what to do."

The mayor, his head braced on his fist, nods.

"I'm sorry this is boring," Ravitch says.

"No, it's not boring," Koch answers. He scans the table and invites questions and comments.

Senator Moynihan recounts a recent conversation with the President. Without additional federal assistance, he told Carter, it was likely that New York would be forced into bankruptcy. The President was shocked, perhaps because just two and a half months before, in front of City Hall, Moynihan and others profusely thanked Carter for "saving" New York with federal loan guarantees. Moynihan's sense of the congressional mood was bleak.

"I am convinced," Koch says, "we are not able to go back any time in the future for more federal assistance."

Toia, who is deputy mayor for finance, offers another perspective on federal retrenchment. "Somewhere along the way, we've lost the message," he says. "Blumenthal"—Secretary of the Treasury W. Michael Blumenthal —"signed off on a hundred million more in federal aid, and we've only got twenty-three million. We'll be lucky to maintain our current levels of federal aid." The Koch four-year financial plan, introduced last January, assumed an increase of $100 million in federal support, and Toia and Koch believe that the federal government "reneged" on a promise. (Blumenthal did "sign off on" Koch's four-year plan, certifying that the plan, including federal-aid projections, was "reasonable." But Blumenthal later reminded City Hall that he did not have the power to make promises for the Congress, which cut federal aid. Nor could he predict altered economic and political circumstances.)

"The question facing New York is: Which group of taxpayers is going to pay for this insolvency?" says Ravitch. "The city? The federal government? The state? Bondholders? Or city workers?" The mayor can "begin to confront the public, the President, and the governor with the problem," he says. Or the mayor can wait until the 1980 presidential campaign, when the city will have more political leverage. "There is something to be said for this strategy," he adds.

"There is nothing to be said for that strategy," says Moynihan, the tiny veins in his nose and cheeks reddened. "It is deception."

Ravitch says that since Koch is at the peak of his popularity, now is the time for the mayor to spend his credibility with the public and his partners and act.

Brown is not so sure. Speaking for the first time, he says that the weakness of the Ravitch position is that the mayor cannot "command his allies" because he does not control them. But, he admits, "if we don't get out in front of them, they will have you for dinner."

Ravitch concurs. They'll claim that "you're unwilling to take on the problem," he says.

The first priority, says Maureen Connelly, is for Koch to make deeper cuts in his budget. If he fails to do that, he will lack the credibility to demand sacrifices from his partners.

Ravitch disagrees. The mayor can't put his "piece on the table without extracting from the others, too," he says. "Koch will have to use the threat of bankruptcy as his ultimate weapon."

Toia returns to the question of federal aid. It's true that there will be no large increase in federal aid in coming years, he says. Nevertheless, the city and the state can ally themselves with others in pressing the federal government to assume, for instance, more of the welfare-cost burden. This they should do.

Brown returns to the contradictions. On the one hand, he says, Koch has been willing to make tough decisions and is an optimist who has brought new spirit to the city and the government. On the other hand, Koch's optimism doesn't square with the facts: "A grim view of the city is needed in order to take a leadership role." But Koch's view is far from grim. He has regularly boasted of the city's "renaissance." Brown points out to Koch that if he accepts the thrust of the Ravitch thesis, he must alter his public position, because "the rhetorical curve is getting away from the fiscal curve."

"It is not just a question of tone," Connelly says, apparently feeling that Ravitch flirts with too neat—too idealistic—a solution. She does not believe that all the parties have the same interests; it is naïve to suppose they do.

"There is an appearance of disagreement here," says Ravitch, "and I'm not sure there *is* disagreement."

There is the *reality* of disagreement, Koch says, speaking for only the third time. "Margolis is saying the city has to do what it has to do and then go to the other parties. Ravitch is saying we're all in this together and suggesting we say to each, 'This is what you have to do.' "

Ravitch disagrees, saying that he is not in favor of deferring cuts. His point is that the city cannot cut enough and will need help from the partners.

But that wasn't his point earlier, when he urged the mayor to play poker and not show his cards before the others did. Koch, who has a talent for peeling arguments down to their core, has put his finger on the essential difference.

The mayor invites his guests to adjourn to the living room. Over cordials, Moynihan asks him to state his own views. "It is not helpful for me to speak at this moment," Koch says. "There is no disagreement. I'm prepared to do those things that are necessary." The gap confronting City Hall in fiscal 1981, he says, is not $1 billion, because two-thirds of that sum will be met by state and federal aid. (Ravitch argued that this assumption was unrealistic.) The mayor says he wants to strike a balance between his responsibility to tell the truth and his responsibility to inspire confidence. "It's really like legionnaires' disease," he explains, referring to the summer of 1978, when there were fears that an epidemic had broken out in New York. "We acted without creating panic. Our approach was straightforward and low-key. And that's what we'll do" with the fiscal crisis. In the tension between his twin responsibilities, however, Koch leaves little doubt that he comes down on the side of inspiring confidence and optimism. "I think people are not thinking of whether to move or stay but whether to move back to the city," he concludes.

Now Ravitch exposes a basic disagreement. He does not believe that Koch's optimism squares with the facts. Studies show that more people are fleeing the city than are returning to it. What is most worrisome is that the city is losing the wrong people—middle-income blacks and Hispanics as well as whites—and is being left with too many poor people and a dwindling tax base to support them. "It's never pleasant to sound like a Cassandra," Ravitch says. "A lot of it"—the business renaissance of Manhattan—"is due to a devaluation of the dollar. The assessed value of city real estate has gone down more than a billion and a half dollars since 1976."

New York is losing political muscle as well as its housing stock. Moynihan says that the 1980 federal census will result in the loss of four New York members of Congress. "That's not all bad," he jokes. "I can imagine losing four congressmen and having a better delegation."

Everyone laughs, and then there is a moment of silence. Koch glances at his watch. It is nearly ten o'clock. He says, "Well, I think we've had an extraordinary evening. I'm very appreciative that you made a presentation. It leaves a great deal of food for thought. I don't know what the options are. I am committed to doing whatever needs to be done. I don't flinch from that. I'm an optimist by nature. This is all the down side. We've yet to hear the up side: increased revenues. I'm hopeful we'll increase revenues. So the long and short of it is that I'll do what I have to do."

A few minutes later, in the car on his way to make a presentation to the American Image Awards Dinner of the Men's Fashion Association of America, at the New York Hilton, Koch says of the dinner, "The intensity was extraordinary. The first thing is, this was not something new. What it does is accelerate the response we have to make. The one thing new is Ravitch's feeling that they're setting me up. Let me tell you why I don't think they're consciously doing it. For what? Why destroy me? I'm not convinced of duplicity. But I am convinced of the need to reiterate that solving the problem is dependent on all the partners' doing what they promised to do." The major disagreement to surface, he says, was one of timing. "Ravitch is saying we should not begin to make cuts until we establish a quid pro quo, and if we don't we will go into bankruptcy. David Margolis' position is to do what we have to do and then extract from the others, either through threats of bankruptcy or through labor negotiations." Koch implies that he sides with Margolis.

During his first year in office, the mayor seemed to side with neither Margolis nor Ravitch. He came closer to siding with former Mayor Beame's incrementalist approach. As Maureen Connelly reminded him, he, like Beame, had made no program cuts and had not altered fundamentally the broad range of services provided by the city government. Like Beame, he had nibbled at the budget, relying on wage freezes, attrition, and across-the-board reductions. Criticism of Koch's caution came, most significantly, from the federal government. A private memorandum sent to President Carter by three of his domestic advisers last December slipped into the hands of the press and into public view in early January. The memo stated that the city's "budget outlook is deteriorating, as projected deficits have been revised steadily upward since last spring." The advisers complained that the mayor had backed off from his planned 1979 service cutbacks and 4-percent attrition rate: "In our view, the mayor's failure to implement these cuts in 1979 was a mistake, and his failure to do so has deepened the post-1979 deficits." They charged that Koch, like Beame, had relied on one-shot revenues and increased federal aid. The crunch would come in eighteen months, they wrote. Until then, the city could get by. By delaying painful decisions, they said, Koch was angling to guarantee that "the crisis will peak at the beginning" of fiscal 1981—that is, in the summer and fall of 1980, a presidential election year. Thus, "the administration's political problem is evident," the memo said. "The dynamics of New York politics are such that local parties are almost certain to blame 'the 1980 fiscal crisis' on the administration." Accordingly, Carter's advisers suggested that the federal government should press to "accelerate city expenditure reductions and increased state aid in order to modify the present back-ended nature of the plan."

When stories about the memo appeared, first in the *News* and then in the *Times,* the mayor, after receiving a series of soothing calls from Washington, simply told the press he had not yet read the memo. "The federal administration would like us to do more," he said. "In fact, we have done more." Eager to cool the controversy, one of the advisers who had written the critical memo offered public praise of the mayor's leadership. As had often been true through the first three and a half years of the fiscal crisis, the "partners" were eager to avoid a public split. All agreed that bankruptcy would be a disaster, and that avoiding it required cooperation. Like mountain climbers connected to the same lifeline, they might quarrel at night, but by day they inched forward together, one step at a time.

Koch's close friend Margolis was quoted in the semimonthly *Fiscal Observer* of November 16 as saying of the budget-cutting, "He's not doing as much as I would like," whereupon Koch dispatched the following letter, dated November 22: "Dear David, I read your comments in *The Fiscal Observer.* They are indisputable and I will try to deal with the issues raised. Sincerely, Ed." The letter implicitly acknowledged that Koch agreed with the White House. But there were other pressures. Commissioners clamored for more resources. And deeper budget cuts, he feared, would rupture the lifeline to the municipal unions. To city workers, cutbacks are not abstract budget numbers but lost jobs and real pain. The unions strenuously opposed layoffs, pushing Koch to press the federal partner for more aid instead. Each time the mayor mentioned layoffs, as he did last December, when he promised "modest" layoffs, union leaders complained bitterly. Barry Feinstein, the president of Teamsters Local 237, called the mayor's words "reprehensible" and said they "could lead to a total breakdown in the relationship with my union." Committed as he is to avoiding bankruptcy, Koch could not tolerate that. Employee-pension funds, which are effectively controlled by municipal-union leaders, are now the city's principal bankers. On past occasions the unions have threatened: no cooperation, no loans. Koch could counter by threatening bankruptcy, but that would be an empty gesture, since his partners know that he believes bankruptcy unthinkable. "Leaving the social costs aside," the White House memo warned the President, "the fact that the municipal unions are both the city's bankers and the recipients of the cutbacks will make the achievement of the 1981 mark extremely difficult, to the point where serious discussion of the bankruptcy option is possible."

The thrust of the federal government's effort has been to press Koch to press the unions and the local banks for more sacrifices, and Governor Carey for more state aid; the local partners have responded by urging Koch to join with them in pressing Washington for more help. "The real villain is what happened in Washington," Victor Gotbaum said early this year. He and others wanted Koch to threaten to tell President Carter to drop dead in 1980 unless he came through with more federal aid. Put enough political pressure on Carter and he will cave in, they asserted. This, Ravitch warned, was "fairy-godmother talk." He said that Carter probably couldn't persuade the Congress to go along with more aid even if he tried.

In his first year Koch chose to follow cautious budget-cutting advice and incautious political advice. His natural optimism and his propensity for living one day at a time probably contributed to this decision. He has faith in Ed Koch. He believes that in a jam he will do what has to be done. Unlike Beame, he takes pride in and enjoys making tough political decisions. But, also unlike Beame, he feels insecure dealing with budgets and finance, and this partly accounts for his caution. During the transit labor negotiations in the spring of 1978 the mayor memorized and privately rehearsed to a commissioner the figures in the proposed settlement. He was, the commissioner recalls, "like a schoolboy trying to get comfortable with the numbers." He "absolutely glazes over" on budgetary matters, Deputy Mayor Peter Solomon admits. During a briefing on November 6, 1978, with the mayor, Deputy Mayor Toia, and others, Budget Director James Brigham handed the mayor four memos. One of these outlined the city's cash-flow projections for capital projects. After allowing several minutes for the mayor to read the memos, Brigham read the key paragraphs aloud, as if to a child. In this meeting, as in others concerning budgets or finance, Koch did not take charge or ask basic questions, the way he often does in meetings. Instead, he nodded and frequently said "Okay." As Brigham came to an explanation of how the city had failed to spend all the capital-budget dollars it was supposed to, Toia interrupted to say, "Let's stop here, so we're sure you fully understand what we're saying here. The last sentence says . . ." Koch had not noticed that in the first three months of the 1979 fiscal year capital expenditures were $33 million below projections; that is, Mayor Koch's delinquency in capital spending was 10 percent worse than the Beame record that Candidate Koch had criticized. (The capital budget, which is financed by long-term borrowing, is devoted to improving the city's physical plant, such as streets and bridges; underspending in this budget means that the city is not renewing its capital facilities. The expense budget, which is financed by current revenues, is devoted to current expenses, such as labor and supplies; underspending in this budget has the desirable effect of building a surplus.)

When Koch is asked about his discomfort with numbers, he responds, "I have to rely on my financial team. I think it's a pretty good one. I never said I was a financial genius." Because he is not a financial genius, he is less self-reliant than he likes to be and than some of his advisers and associates wish he were. There is a widespread feeling, shared by Margolis and others, that in Koch's first nineteen months his fiscal team was weak. Like the mayor, Toia and Brigham spent the first year getting to know their jobs— the numbers, what had to be done. The public paid for their inexperience in the 1978 labor negotiations. As the negotiations began, the mayor loudly proclaimed that it was his intention to win sixty-one "give-backs" from the unions, totaling about $300 million in fringe benefits. While budget aides told Koch that the cupboard was bare, experienced union negotiators, assisted by Allen Brawer, a former staff assistant to the city's budget director, began unearthing underspending in the expense budget. The more they found, the higher their demands rose. In the end, the new mayor retreated, agreeing to drop all his give-back demands and assenting to an 8-percent wage increase over two years, plus a $750 annual cost-of-living bonus. Compared with previous city labor settlements or with those in private industry, this was a modest package. Compared with Mayor Koch's rhetoric, and considering the huge budget gap that the city must close by 1982, it was an extravagant one which would cost the city almost a billion additional dollars over three years. Koch explains that budget officials assured him there was no money. "They weren't lying," says the mayor. "The reason was that in the past the less you told the mayor the less chance he would make a mistake." Norman Steisel, who was first deputy budget director during the labor negotiations, disagrees: "To say we hid dollars from him is not fair." But Steisel admits that budget officials tried to protect the new mayor. "That was part of it. The guy had only been in office twenty days. I guess we assumed he knew the complexities of the budget better than he did."

The new Koch administration, like the Lindsay administration in 1966, was not prepared for negotiations with a skillful, experienced opponent. "He gave the unions back things the city should not have given back," says John Zuccotti, who was first deputy mayor in the Beame administration. "He also settled for more than he had to—at least two hundred million more over two years. That's not going to help the city in the 1980 negotiations." Edward Costikyan, Koch's original choice for first deputy mayor, is more troubled by Koch's weak grasp of the budget. A mayor can't delegate responsibility for budgets and finance, he says. "That's not delegating. That's abdicating. Delegating is saying, 'Okay, here are my guidelines. Go do it.' The biggest part of delegating is checking. I don't think he's managed the city's finances. That's his Achilles' heel." Ironically, despite

Koch's resistance to having a first deputy, his own unsure grasp of finances in effect made Toia and Brigham first deputies.

The mayor and his budget team presented a new four-year financial plan to the public last January. The mayor explained that approximately $1 billion of recurring expenditures had to be cut from the budget over the next three years, and he said that these cost reductions would be achieved primarily through attrition. The work force would be reduced by about six thousand in fiscal 1980. There would be a reduction in city services, the closing of some municipal hospitals, work-rule changes, the elimination of several departments, and extensive management improvements. The cuts that the mayor proposed were deeper than had been made the first year, but not nearly as deep as David Margolis urged or the voters had been led to expect when they elected Koch. More drastic cuts were outlined in what was called a "contingency program." These would come, Koch warned, if the state failed to increase aid by $200 million (most observers believe that the state will not fail to) and the federal government failed to increase aid by $100 million (most believe that it will fail to).

City Council President Carol Bellamy called Koch "overly optimistic" for delaying cuts in the hope of claiming more federal aid from a Congress and a President pledged to reduce aid. Comptroller Harrison Goldin said that the actual budget gap could reach $1.6 billion—55 percent more than Koch claimed. In making this estimate, Goldin said, he assumed that there would be another 8-percent wage settlement in 1980 (which would cost $425 million), that oil prices would increase by 50 percent or more, that a national recession was approaching, that the cost of goods and services would continue to rise, and that there would be reductions in federal aid.

In April, when Koch formally presented his budget for the 1980 fiscal year, projected deficits for future years were below earlier forecasts. Instead of a gap of $889 million in fiscal 1981, the figure was halved to $406 million. Koch could point cheerfully to 1978 as the first year in the last nine when the number of private-sector jobs in New York increased; to expanding local revenues (partly a result of inflation); to record tourism; and to a decrease (despite inflation) of 1 percent—$170 million—in the size of the city's 1980 budget. He was also aware that a quiet policy of deliberate underspending of the expense budget was building a cushion. Underspending partly accounted for a statutory surplus of about $200 million in fiscal 1979. The mayor felt so confident about the city's fiscal prospects that he proposed to expand the city's work force. If Armageddon was to come, clearly fiscal 1980 was not the year.

But a June 7 review of the 1980 budget, prepared by Special Deputy Comptroller Sidney Schwartz for the state's Financial Control Board, clashed with the mayor's optimism. The review said that the budget contained only $34 million in net expenditure reductions, or 22 percent of the reductions Koch proposed in January. City-funded spending, the review noted, had increased by $130 million over Koch's January estimates. The biggest change between the January four-year plan and Koch's April budget came in Koch's budget-cutting proposals. In January, 25 percent of the total budget actions necessary to balance the city's books by 1982 were planned for 1980. In April, only 11 percent were.

A June 11 analysis of Koch's April budget by the state Municipal Assistance Corporation was equally critical. This report pointed out that although Koch promised to shrink the city's work force by 1982, he nevertheless proposed to stop the attrition clock during the whole of 1980. Since attrition has been the city's chief budget-cutting tool, MAC worried that Koch was discarding his primary weapon. MAC charged that by taking this tack, Koch was forgoing $65 million in savings this year and a cumulative total of $300 million by fiscal 1982.

Koch's budget message itself acknowledged that there were ominous signs for future years. Koch projected budget deficits of $793 million in 1982 and $814 million in 1983. And these deficits included just $431 million for new labor contracts. Though the mayor hailed his "balanced" 1980 budget, he acknowledged that it was only "technically" or "legally" balanced, and that achieving it was possible only because state law still allowed New York to put $285 million worth of expense-budget items in the capital budget. Moreover, since the state also permits the city a two-year lag in funding its pension liabilities, which resulted in a savings of $115 million, the proposed 1980 "balanced" budget is really $400 million in deficit. It is not clear how Koch will close gaps in succeeding years. What does seem clear is that the real budget crunch for the city will probably not come until fiscal 1982—somewhat later than the White House and Ravitch feared and somewhat earlier than the mayor, who will be running for reelection that year, could desire. City Hall currently projects the fiscal-1982 gap to be $830 million. Assuming the same 8-percent two-year pay increase negotiated in 1978—"I believe we'll be very fortunate if we can hold it at eight percent," says Koch, mindful that inflation is rising faster—MAC estimated the gap at more than $1 billion. Clearly, this mayor, like his predecessor, was moving slowly, hoping that additional aid would materialize and that city revenues would increase. And though the state's Financial Control Board and the federal monitors may have been profoundly uneasy, they officially approved Koch's 1980 budget and the city's four-year financial plan.

A few thoughts about garbage: The mayor has scheduled a discussion of the Sanitation Department with former City Council President Paul Screvane, Sanitation Commissioner Norman Steisel, and Robert Tierney. Screvane was a sanitation worker for twenty-eight years, and rose to become commissioner in the late 1950s. Now in private business, Screvane requested this meeting to offer his help and to express concern about the low morale in his former department. If morale were good, he tells Koch, worker productivity would increase by 25 percent. Koch recounts his shock at finding that many of the city's forty sanitation garages were without private toilet stalls, hot water, or heat. Immediately, the mayor ordered repairs. What else, he asks Screvane, can he do to boost morale? "Pat them on the back," suggests Screvane. Koch admits that in his first year he did attack the work force, because he wanted to convey his dissatisfaction. But now that he has made the point, he says, the message will shift. Personally signed notes from Koch have been put in employee paycheck envelopes; he has gone out of his way to praise and publicize outstanding workers; he has polled workers and solicited their advice.

Screvane also blames faulty equipment for the low morale. The city shouldn't buy sanitation trucks all at once, he says. One time Mayor Lindsay ordered five hundred new trucks at once. After eight years—the average life of a truck—many broke down simultaneously. The city should stagger the purchases, he advises. Steisel agrees, but notes that 40 percent of his equipment is more than eight years old, and that it takes fully twenty-four months to order and receive a new truck. (On another day Operations Director Lee Oberst explains to me that to order a truck requires thirteen steps, including approval from the Office of Management and Budget, the City Council, the Department of Purchase, the corporation counsel, and the Financial Control Board. Because of the delays involved, the original price of the trucks rises. "So we must either reduce the number of trucks or ask for new money," Oberst says, sighing. "If we ask for new money, we have to go back to the Office of Management and Budget"—the first of the thirteen steps.) Steisel says that he has ordered new trucks but that there is no immediate solution to the problem. On any given day a fourth of his department's sixteen hundred collection trucks break down.

The number-one service problem on the public's mind, says Koch, is "lousy sanitation service"—grime, not crime, in the streets. The public's perception of declining sanitation service is matched by those objective measurements available to the city. Project Scorecard, a rating system originally devised by the Fund for the City of New York, a small private foundation, in cooperation with the city, compared the cleanliness of city streets in September of 1978 with that of September of 1974. The percentage of acceptably clean streets in Manhattan fell from sixty-six to forty-four; in the Bronx, from sixty-three to fifty-two; in Brooklyn, from seventy to fifty-four; in Queens, from eighty-eight to seventy-eight; and in Staten Island, from ninety-five to eighty. City streets, it was also found, were dirtier near the end of Koch's first year than they were in Beame's last year: 39.7 percent were dirty in October of 1978 as opposed to 31.9 percent the previous year. And sanitation services continue to decline. Koch reported last month that half of all city streets are now rated as dirty, and that none of the fifty-eight sanitation districts in the five boroughs have appreciably improved service in the past year. (The major problem, Koch told me later, is "the need to get more loads per day out of each sanitation worker," and he added, "It's my guess that they're not working a full day." The mayor's surmise was supported by a recent *News* investigation. The reporter Alex

Michelini quoted an Office of Operations study of sanitation collection crews in Staten Island which showed that the city could get at least two hours, fifty-six minutes more productive time from each sanitationman through stricter supervision and the use of relay trucks. Michelini wrote that sanitationmen were averaging sixteen days' sick leave annually, and that on some days as many as 7.5 percent of the seventy-five hundred members of the department were out sick.) Computer printouts kept by the Office of Operations show that the average three-man sanitation crew collects less than two truckloads of garbage a day—not three loads, which is the target figure. The mayor confronts Screvane with this problem: How do we get three loads a day?

It used to be, says Screvane, that the men called it a day when their work load was complete. But under former Mayor William O'Dwyer the workday was set at eight hours; the goal became punching the clock rather than completing an assignment.

Steisel observes that in some areas of the city three loads a day is not possible, because the distance to the dumps is too great—something that the computer printouts don't reveal. (Lee Oberst says that to solve this problem the city should imitate Flint, Michigan, which has huge transfer trucks cart the garbage to the dump.)

The meeting ends with Koch thanking Screvane for his advice.

Several days later, in Commissioner Steisel's wood-paneled, gymnasium-size office on Worth Street, behind City Hall, I ask Steisel about using two-man rather than three-man crews—a policy that has long been favored by city officials and, though it is not explicitly prohibited in the contracts, has long and successfully been resisted by the sanitation union.

Steisel says that he plans to introduce larger, side-loading, two-man trucks "in low-density residential areas to start," and to reroute his fleet. Just those two steps, he claims, "could save at least twenty million dollars and as much as forty million." Moving deliberately, Steisel has devised a series of targets to improve his department's performance. He knows he is Koch's designated miracle worker. "If Steisel can't do it, no one can," the mayor says of Steisel, a thirty-seven-year-old commissioner he transferred from the post of first deputy budget director last October to replace a Beame-administration holdover. Steisel wants to move cautiously. He does not disagree with Oberst, who says that the city's basic service-delivery problem stems from its "monopolistic" nature. "There is no competition. We have to stimulate artificial competitive tools," Steisel says. Steisel believes that management accountability and productivity measurements are among such tools. The first few months on the job he spent concentrating on improving management—decentralizing decision-making, reorganizing the supervisory structure of the department, and easing civil-service strictures in order to have more flexibility in assigning foremen and assistant foremen.

But Steisel has been wary of an approach that has long been advocated by reformers: contracting out certain sanitation districts to private carters, and thereby creating direct competition between private and city carters to determine which can deliver services cheaper. This practice has been adopted by such cities as Montreal, Minneapolis, New Orleans, and Kansas City, Missouri. Steisel responds to this idea cautiously, saying, "It's something we have to study"—which is how sanitation commissioners and mayors have responded for more than ten years. Steisel also says he wants to study "gain-sharing"—an incentive system whereby city sanitation workers would agree to deliver services for a fixed but reduced price, with the public and the workers sharing the savings. The 1978 sanitation-union contract contained a provision that called for a study of gain-sharing. And so did the 1976 contract before it.

Steisel's claims that competition and gain-sharing require further study arouse suspicions that, like his predecessors, he is playing to the wrong audience—not to the public, which receives poor service, but to the bureaucracy, which delivers it. Steisel aggressively defends the need for caution. The replacement of antiquated equipment takes time, he says; the city cannot contract out sanitation districts until management has devised "performance standards" and a set of goals to measure the competition. And most important, he says, he must first address "the basic underlying problem in the department"—low morale. Sanitation workers feel picked on, abused. "There is also the problem that I don't even know how to talk about without appearing condescending," he says. "I think a lot of the workers are humiliated because of the way society views garbage. Garbagemen deal with dirt, and dirt is dirty. Nobody blames the cop if there are not enough cops on the street. The anger is directed at a different level. In sanitation, the anger is directed at the worker."

A somewhat different sanitation-service perspective is offered by Richard Doviken, superintendent of Sanitation District 1 in Manhattan. His district is one of fifty-eight sanitation districts in New York City; it runs south from Eighteenth Street to the tip of Manhattan and from the Hudson River, on the west, to Lafayette Street, on the east. Doviken works in a cell-like turn-of-the-century office on the second floor of a garage on West Street at Canal. His desk faces a wall of maps. A dirty window behind the desk looks out on the collapsed West Side Highway and rotting abandoned piers. Seated behind his desk, wearing a forest-green uniform with gold shoulder leaves, Doviken, who has been a sanitation worker for twenty-five years, brushes aside the morale problem. "I can understand it, but I don't feel it," he says. "If I did, I'd give away the store every day. It may be a dirty job, but the money's clean." His major concern is faulty equipment. Though his district is rated among the more productive ones, between 18 and 30 percent of his equipment is out of commission on any given day. He has only one mechanic and one CETA (federal Comprehensive Employment and Training Act) greaser to repair a total of twenty-two trucks. "If we could supply better equipment, the job would be much easier for the men," he says.

"They can be on four different pieces of equipment a day. If we could give them good, safe equipment, their morale would be up." With adequate equipment, his two daily shifts—the day shift averaging about fifty men and the night shift about fifteen men—could meet their cleanup schedule of two loads a day, covering each block a minimum of three times a week. Without it, they cannot.

How does he feel about two-man crews?

"They make no sense at all," he says. "One less man means less tonnage. The maximum you can expect one man to pick up is seven tons a day. And a sanitationman burns out in thirteen years."

Doviken's district is densely populated. Couldn't two-man crews work in less densely populated, less commercial districts?

"They do in Florida," he says. "There, garbage collection is private." He doesn't believe that private collection will be introduced here, because of union opposition.

But would he favor it?

"If the city gave it out to commercials, if it had the right management, it could be worked," he says. "You'd get better equipment. You wouldn't have the tremendous size of the five boroughs if it were localized. If they went to competitive bidding, you'd have more accountability. Far more." He favors the concept, but sees practical stumbling blocks. Under the current citywide system, when one district suffers a disproportionate number of truck breakdowns another district lends trucks and men. Today Doviken has sent seventeen men to Staten Island and seven trucks to other districts. He worries that if districts were in competition with each other, this citywide sharing would not be possible. Another problem with contracting out, he says, is that certain department activities—snow removal, for instance—might not appeal to the private contractor, interested in maximum profits. Give the private firms the better jobs, he fears, and city sanitation services are bound to appear less efficient.

Would gain-sharing work?

"In this particular district, if they were to pay by tonnage, you'd see an upswing in tonnage," he says. "But in Staten Island you couldn't. There, the men have to go house-to-house." Thus, within the department the accident of assignment would determine the size of the worker's bonus. A similar problem is that if gain-sharing were tried in other city departments, it would reward the inefficiently run departments and penalize those that were well managed. The well-run departments would have little leeway to generate productivity savings for the workers to share—the Fire Department being a good example—but the inefficient department could offer a bonanza to workers. This potential built-in unfairness could arouse jealousies among departments and cause problems for the city when it negotiates labor contracts.

There is also a political problem. For instance, Barry Feinstein, whose union represents Housing Authority workers, has been told by city officials that savings of $5 million to $8 million could be achieved if larger containers were used to remove garbage from housing projects. However, since larger, more easily removed containers represent what Feinstein calls "a change in the terms and work conditions of my contract," he would demand discussions and at least half of the productivity savings. Under gain-sharing or productivity bonuses, presumably the sanitation union would demand at least as much. If the two unions could somehow resolve their conflict, from the workers' point of view garbage collection would be easier, and workers would profit from it. But from the taxpayers' or the city's point of view the termination of a wasteful practice might result in no dollar savings. Also, from the taxpayers' point of view there is a policy question: Should public employees be paid extra for doing what they are supposed to do?

Many city officials, confronting a fiscal crisis for the foreseeable future, believe that more layoffs of workers will be required—layoffs that Doviken and the union leaders regard as counterproductive. "In this period in America the more people you lay off, the less productivity you get per man," Doviken says. "It's a psychological problem. For years my district had a hundred and ninety men. Now we're down to a hundred and nineteen. My people think they're doing the work of the hundred and ninety men. They're not. We have dirtier streets. Fewer trucks. Yet because they go over the same streets, they believe they're doing the work of the men laid off."

Doviken is convinced that service can be improved. Productivity would rise if he were given more flexibility as a manager, he maintains, and if the civil-service system were reformed. "The seniority system protects the non-worker as well as the hard worker," he explains. "You have to qualify the man even though he's not qualified." Layoffs must be based on seniority, not on performance. Choice shifts are awarded to the men on the basis of seniority, and this means that a manager cannot reward or punish. "I don't harass a man. That's about the only reward I can give," Doviken says. He also blames the public: "More service is not always the answer to maintaining cleaner streets and sidewalks. There's got to be civic pride. The generation we're living in allows materials to be used and disposed of." A refrigerator, says Doviken, comes in a huge crate with shock-absorber bumpers, a reinforced top and bottom, stuffing inside, baling wire, and "all this ends up on city streets." City streets become junk yards. "Why do people abandon cars?" he asks. "I'm up to ten or fifteen a week. They could trade them in or sell them for junk. Why don't they? I don't know. This is the way we live."

Can a mayor make a difference?

"In all my twenty-some-odd years," observes Doviken, "the only mayor I've ever met was Wagner—in Bermuda, where I was vacationing." He would like to see the mayor focus on changing the sanitation-union contract, which he feels ties management's hands. He remains skeptical about the productivity-measurement system that was introduced late in the Beame administration, the use of which has been expanded by Koch.

"Those are good management tools," he says. "But I break my back here, and anyone who evaluates my work has to say, 'He's doing worse.' I haven't had a sanitation inspector from Canal Street south to the Battery in months. We had retirements and new promotions. So we're working short." In addition, quantifying output can mean overlooking quality: "The minute I pick up something off my route, I leave a street of garbage. Then the district manager calls. Then my 'productivity' goes down. I get letters of complaint. I see the handwriting on the wall. I'm frustrated this way every day."

Not for long, however. This career civil servant—who unconsciously refers to the city government as "they"—will soon retire from his $28,300 city job and move from Staten Island to New Port Richey, Florida.

One floor below, among the workers in Doviken's garage, the view is different, though no less pessimistic. The men are as angry at the public as the public is at them.

"The morale stinks," declares Jimmy Quirk, a union shop steward on the night shift with thirteen years on the job. "No one ever tells us we do a good job. Look, we're only human. When we go into a restaurant, people look at us like we're goofing off." To avoid scenes, Quirk now orders his coffee to go.

"We're mostly high-school graduates," says one worker defensively. "We're not dumb."

Coming off the day shift on this numbingly cold winter day, workers mill around in the dark concrete locker room. They all have complaints to make, the foremost being their aging garage, which so shocked Mayor Koch on a visit that he immediately ordered repairs. The lockers are too narrow for the men's heavy clothing. "I got a locker the Police Department threw out," complains Quirk. The locker room is frigid, and the light from bare ceiling bulbs hardly reaches the floor. Next door, in the makeshift wash-up room, there is one sink for the hundred and nineteen men. Less than half of the garage is heated.

Upstairs, a smaller locker room doubles as the garage toilet. A hot-water faucet handle in one of five sinks spins but nothing comes out. Of a total of four toilets, only two work. Since there are a few female CETA workers at the garage, the men assigned to the smaller locker room have to vacate it when the women use the toilet. Nothing personal, say the men, but it bugs them that a private lavatory was recently constructed for the women. It angers them that these inexperienced CETA workers take home only twenty dollars a week less than they do. That the CETA workers are black doesn't help.

Surroundings are just one of many complaints. The negotiated 4-percent pay raise that was to start last October 1 was not received until around the first of the year. And the fiscal crisis jeopardized one of the great attractions of a government job—security.

Then, there is the lousy equipment. "We want to do a day's work," explains Quirk. "But we can't if the equipment breaks down. And when it does, who do they blame? They blame us." The workers, not without reason, blame previous city administrations, which borrowed from the capital budget to fund the expense budget, leaving less money to spend on trucks, spare parts, and garage renovation.

Nor has management ever consulted the workers on the equipment they are to operate. "The guy who designed our truck has to be seven feet tall," complains Pat Rizzo, a ten-year veteran who is the day shift's shop steward. The cabin door is so high that the driver "can't see a small car or a person," he says.

Two-man crews?

"No!" shouts a worker. "We got heavy baskets. There's a safety factor. Who helps you if you get tangled in the truck?" His co-workers nod, pointing out that the driver, in the cabin of a noisy truck, can't hear cries for help.

Contracting out?

"The privates can't handle it," claims Christopher Cerio, a burly man with a thick mustache. "They think it's just house stops. We have to clean catch basins and empty the litter baskets." In New York, private carters usually make bulk pickups from commercial customers. The city workers have to go between cars and lift many more individual cans. But their prime worry about contracting out, and also about gain-sharing, says Cerio, is layoffs: "It's like saying you could save half a million dollars but you have to lay guys off."

No, the way to improve productivity, the men suggest, is to end their fear of being laid off. They would also like a regular five-day week and an occasional pat on the back. They share Doviken's concern that measurements of productivity only quantify their work. Because the collection schedule has been reduced since the advent of the fiscal crisis, says Pat Rizzo, wire baskets and garbage cans often overflow and spill on the street. "If we were to stop and pick up everything, we wouldn't do thirty percent of the route," he says. "They tell you we're supposed to do that, yet if we don't finish the route, there is a complaint against us."

Many of these men work very hard. John Dalton, a ten-year veteran, and his crew collected thirteen tons of garbage today. "A private carter can do no better than these men," says Doviken, scanning the day's productivity charts. Abstract productivity schemes don't always take into account the reality of these men, their fears, their anger.

But apparently the Koch administration is succeeding with the work force better than many union leaders claim. "Koch is a pretty good man," says Quirk.

Rizzo says, "He's doing the best he can under the fiscal crisis. I thought at first he was sort of hostile. I think now he's trying to work with the department. He ordered equipment. He visited some garages."

Commissioner Steisel has won praise for sending an open letter to the men soliciting their suggestions on how to improve service. "It was the first time," says a grateful Quirk. "He seems to want to find out what the problems are. It gives you a sense that at least the boss cares about you."

One morning late in 1978 the mayor discusses the future of the South Bronx with Deputy Mayor Herman Badillo, Deputy Mayor Peter Solomon, Planning Commission Chairman Robert Wagner, Housing Commissioner Nathan Leventhal, and Edward Logue, the director of the South Bronx Development Office.

What is important to note, Badillo says, is that neighborhoods are living organisms, capable of unpredictable growth as well as contraction. The West Side of Manhattan is still changing, as is demonstrated by the new shops springing up along Columbus Avenue. If the West Side could come back, so can the South Bronx.

But, cautions the mayor, the devastation in the South Bronx dwarfs that in Manhattan, where it is also easier to attract private investment. His main concern, he says, is that the federal government not renege on its commitment, which began when President Carter, on an overcast day in October of 1977, stood among the mountains of rubble on deserted Charlotte Street and announced his intention of forging a partnership to rebuild the South Bronx. It would become a "showcase" for the nation, Carter promised. First the Beame administration, then the Koch administration rushed to accept the President's generosity. Together, the city and federal governments would rebuild an area that had been compared to a desolate moonscape. The price tag of $1.5 billion in federal, city, and private funds which was originally agreed to is, according to a ranking federal urban official and a city commissioner, about one-tenth of the sum needed to truly rebuild the South Bronx. Understandably, city leaders press the federal government to provide new, additional funds for the South Bronx. They do not want to siphon scarce resources from other neighborhoods. To do so would invite protest from four of the five borough presidents, who sit on the Board of Estimate and must approve the South Bronx plan; moreover, to drain money from still marginal areas like South Jamaica, in Queens, or Bushwick, in Brooklyn, might speed the decline of those areas. Together, city and federal officials have worked for more than a year to shape a plan to rebuild the South Bronx. They have quibbled over details and personalities, and each side has always tried to induce the other to sweeten the pot of money. "The problem," says Koch, "is that every time we talk to the feds about more money they say, 'Well, we didn't say that.'" If they back off or insist on larger amounts of city funds, warns the mayor, he will summon the press, denounce the federal government, and walk away from the entire effort.

Of course, "the problem" with the South Bronx effort is not whether the federal or the city government is reneging on a few million dollars. The problem is less political than fiscal: available resources do not match the promises made. There is scant prospect that any combination of government and private resources will be available to rebuild the entire South Bronx. The fundamental question is whether the vast effort and the limited resources should be spent there or elsewhere. It is Badillo's contention that to allow the South Bronx to continue to deteriorate is an outrage—another broken promise—and that poor people fleeing the South Bronx will move into and hasten the decline of other neighborhoods. This, he charges, is a policy of "planned shrinkage." Badillo's focus is on what should be. His opponents, led by Wagner, tend to focus on what is: on the reality of the area's already shrinking population, on what they see as the need to make choices.

To build 27,500 subsidized housing units in the South Bronx, as proposed in the original South Bronx plan, would, Leventhal says, divert citywide housing funds. A quarter of all federal Section 8 rent-subsidy money for the entire city is routed to the South Bronx. "So we shouldn't be out publicly saying it will have no effect," Leventhal cautions. He also warns that in 1980 the federal government plans to reduce Section 8 subsidies.

They wouldn't dare, Koch says. President Carter "won't want to be embarrassed" as the 1980 election nears. Carter may own the bank but New York has a large political account.

Logue, responding to a suggestion from Wagner that the entire effort be reevaluated in six months, suggests twelve or eighteen months as a more appropriate test period.

Fifteen months, Koch declares. At that point, "we can judge whether our goals are achievable" and whether the federal government has met its commitments.

"Fifteen months coincides with the 1980 campaign," Logue says.

"Right," says the mayor, smiling.

On a Saturday morning in December, Mayor Koch goes to Bushwick, Brooklyn, to conduct one of his so-called constituent hours, during which members of the community can bring their questions and complaints to the mayor and his aides. Bushwick, which was once a stable middle-class community, has been ravaged by fires and housing abandonment in recent years; most of its citizens now are black or Hispanic and are very poor. Among the mayor's advisers, there has been concern that Koch's visit could provoke an incident. The meeting is held in the gymnasium of a public school, and several hundred citizens are in attendance, seated on folding chairs facing a row of bridge tables, behind which sit the mayor and several members of his administration. "Only one problem per customer," Koch jokes to the citizens, who fill out cards, draw numbers, and trickle up for an audience with the mayor or some other city official.

The meeting lasts two hours, and Koch or members of his administration talk to two hundred and fifty-two people. As this count is blared over a loudspeaker in the gym, John Lo Cicero hurries over to whisper in the mayor's ear. Three thousand Hasidic Jews are rioting in Borough Park, he says. They have taken over the 66th Precinct police station. First Deputy Police Commissioner Joseph Hoffman is on his way to the precinct. Instinctively, Koch says he should join Hoffman. Lo Cicero urges him not to go —advice seconded by all the advisers gathered around the mayor except Dan Wolf. He thinks that Koch should go. Koch accepts Wolf's recommendation.

Koch, Wolf, and two reporters squeeze into the back seat of the mayor's car. Lo Cicero jumps in up front. "How did they take over the police station?" Koch asks. Information is scanty, Lo Cicero says. "So now it will give grist for blacks to do the same," Koch says to Wolf as Lo Cicero gets James Meehan, the Police Department's chief of patrol, on the car telephone.

Meehan, who is at the station house, reports that between forty and fifty cops were injured when citizens stormed it a few hours earlier. With the arrival of reinforcements, he says, the police have reclaimed the station house, but it is now surrounded by perhaps three thousand Hasidic Jews.

The mayor tells Meehan that he is on his way but wishes to speak to Hoffman before appearing at the station house.

A few minutes later Hoffman calls and clears the visit.

"Everybody thought there'd be rioting and picketing in Bushwick," Koch says when he gets off the phone. "Who would have thought there'd be rioting here?" Unlike Bushwick, Borough Park is a predominantly middle-income Jewish enclave, with rows of one- and two-family houses. In recent years there has been occasional tension as poor Hispanics have moved into the neighborhood, but for the most part it remains a quiet residential community with a low crime rate.

The mayor's car stops in front of a barricaded street a block from the besieged station house. Chief Meehan is waiting, and pokes his head through the car window to brief Koch. A phalanx of plainclothesmen and uniformed policemen escorts Koch and his party to the rear of the station house. The station house is a tiny moated castle surrounded by a raging ocean of people, all white, many wearing black fur hats and long earlocks that flow into beards. "How come you came?" the first Hasid to notice the mayor on the street shouts bitterly. "It's only Jews they're beating up!" As word spreads that Koch is here, Hasidim pour toward the rear entrance, but the mayor's party is moving very fast. As the mayor is whisked in through the rear door, the swelling crowd begins chanting, "Liberal! Liberal! Liberal!"

The station house is ankle-deep in debris—parking-ticket and arrest forms, pieces of broken chairs, overturned file cabinets, shards of glass from the front window, loose bricks that were thrown through the windows, and twisted wires from a broken computer terminal. Beckoning the mayor to a small room, Hoffman gives him a lawyer-style description of what happened. Irving Sussman, an elderly Orthodox Jew, was walking home alone from the Bobover Synagogue late Friday night when he was stabbed and left to die not far from a street corner. Word of his death spread, and by late morning residents had begun to mass in front of the station house to protest inadequate police protection. A delegation of community leaders, including Assemblyman Samuel Hirsch, entered the station house to talk with police officials, and was followed by more people. Before long, fighting broke out inside the station house, leaving thirty-eight policemen and four civilians injured. "The issue has now become police brutality," Hoffman says. After reiterating the community's alarm about inadequate police protection, Hoffman informs Koch that before the riot the Police Department's Neighborhood Stabilization Unit was scheduled to add forty extra officers to the precinct—temporarily—over the next several weeks, in a normal rotation.

"Want to go out?" asks Hoffman.

"Sure," says Koch. But before he does, several community leaders are allowed to brief him on their concerns. Then, forming a wedge, the police help push Koch toward the front door, facing Sixteenth Avenue and a mass of hostile faces; the police nervously surround the mayor on the front steps of the station house, just a few feet from chanting members of the Jewish Defense League, a group of radical activists. Hearing both jeers and cheers, Koch focuses first on the JDL jeers. "In every community, there is a meshugana!" Koch bellows into a bullhorn. He is trying to soften the crowd with humor, and half succeeds. Puzzled, the cops look at each other and laugh. As Koch shouts that four civilians and thirty-eight policemen were hurt, boos and hisses drown his words. The crowd doesn't believe him. Koch promises an investigation, and, more significant, "beefed-up patrols." He is using the information provided by Hoffman without explaining that the Neighborhood Stabilization Unit is a temporary arrangement and was scheduled before the death of Irving Sussman. Jerking his hand to signify that Koch is pulling a fast one, a nearby cop whispers to another cop, "There's no one here to beef up with."

The mayor remains outside only a few moments, then retreats to the muster room, where he is engulfed by the press. "I want everybody to know I am very supportive of the Police Department," Koch begins.

"They should be locked up," growls a cop standing just beyond the knot of reporters. Looking about at the carpet of debris, he shakes his head and says, "What *is* this?" The shock is setting in. Along the walls, cops cluster and grouse. *Our station house was invaded. Cops were injured in our own station house.* Sworn to protect the public, these cops had to be protected from the public by reinforcements. As the mayor is escorted out through the rear door, he passes these men, one of whom mutters, "It's a shame he has to go out the back door."

"Fellas, you're doing a good job," the mayor declares while rushing out of the building. Outside, he is greeted by a throng of angry Hasidim. "How'm I doing?" the ebullient mayor calls out, not waiting for a reply, as a wall of policemen hurries him to the car. The faster the mayor strides, the faster the crowd follows, and it surrounds the car seconds after Koch has closed the door. Sitting directly behind the driver, Koch rolls down the rear window, calmly leans forward, and waves. "Bye-bye," he says. "Bye-bye."

"Enough!" Dan Wolf gasps, his head between his palms, as the car pulls away.

"You act as if you'd just been to a bar mitzvah," I say to Koch.

"No, saying 'Bye-bye' has a calming influence," the mayor says, adding that "levity" defuses tense situations. Those packed in the car are uneasy, perhaps a little frightened. Not Koch. "What a great life," he chirps as the car speeds off to Maimonides Medical Center.

Koch wants to visit four Orthodox Jews who were reportedly hurt in the clash with police, including Rabbi Edgar Gluck, who is a member of the Mayor's Community Liaison unit, and Assemblyman Hirsch. On entering the hospital's emergency room, the mayor is greeted by friends and family of the injured with the depressing news that one of the four injured men has died of cardiac arrest. Shaken, Koch goes to a tiny first-aid room to meet with Gluck, Hirsch, and an acquaintance of Hirsch's, who was also injured. Gluck was struck on the skull with a nightstick. Hirsch's injuries are obvious. Blood cakes his white shirt. A nasty gash crosses his forehead, his upper lip is swollen, and his face is scratched. The acquaintance required eight stitches to close a head wound.

Towering over Hirsch and Gluck—both diminutive men—as they stand to receive him, Koch asks Hirsch to describe what happened.

Citizens did enter the station house and behave in a disorderly manner, Hirsch admits. But they did not riot. Hirsch says he rushed into an adjoining room, where the police were milling, and pleaded with them not to retaliate by barging out of the room swinging clubs. He promised to get the citizens to leave peacefully. "The cops didn't pay any attention," he says in a calm voice. "They came out of the room. The cops, as soon as they were jostled, started clubbing people. One guy in particular did the clubbing."

"Got his name?" the mayor asks.

Hirsch knows the face and the blond hair, that's all. "As I held his club, he punched me in the mouth," continues the assemblyman. "Then he clubbed me." Hirsch collapsed and was carried outside by friends, and his head wound was bandaged by a paramedic. Hirsch says he regained his strength and returned to the station house and "the cops started jostling me —they were really nasty."

The mayor beseeches Hirsch to sit down. Politely but firmly, he refuses. It is hard for anyone watching Hirsch not to be impressed. He does not raise his voice, does not moan or whine or adopt melodramatic poses or call attention to his injuries. There seems to be no bitterness. "Mr. Mayor, I've got a lot of faith in you," he says, looking up at Koch. "I'm a politician, like any other. But believe me, the situation could have been defused. The problem is deep-rooted. Part of the problem is that the police are under-staffed in that area. Friday night, there are no private cars in use because of the Sabbath. We can't take a taxi. We can't take our own cars." He wants more cops shifted from day patrol to Friday-night patrol. He dismisses reports that thirty-eight policemen were injured in the melee. And he warns that if the Police Department is solely responsible for investigating what happened, there may be a cover-up.

"Will there be an investigation?" a *News* reporter asks.

"Without passing judgment on events, there is no question there has to be an intensive investigation," says Koch. "Did the police take sufficient measures to deal with the situation in a nonviolent way? Both Assemblyman Hirsch and Rabbi Gluck say the police used excessive force." On the other hand, Koch adds, the city must look into the allegations made by policemen on the scene.

The mayor's response is even-handed, but he has clearly been moved by the assemblyman's tranquil posture and thoughtful words. "You are a good man," he says, touching Hirsch's shoulder as he leaves.

"I can return the compliment five times," says Hirsch.

As the mayor is walking to his car, a woman on the street yells, "I sent you a letter!" The letter, she tells Koch, urged him to prevent paroled prisoners from returning to stable neighborhoods.

"You want a Devil's Island?" Koch demands as he is surrounded by friends and relatives of the injured. All talking at once, they begin to tell him about the rocks and insults thrown by the police, but mostly about their fear of criminals.

"One at a time—I can't hear," Koch says. "There are only six thousand police on patrol throughout the city on any given day. They can't all be in Borough Park." He does not wait for them to respond but takes advantage of the momentary silence to ask, "Anyway, aside from this, am I doing all right?"

The question is as jarring and out of sync here as it was outside the station house. It seems less a deliberate effort to humor or calm the crowd than a reflexive self-indulgence, and his audience does not immediately respond.

The car heads for Manhattan, and the mayor reaches for the phone to talk to First Deputy Police Commissioner Hoffman. Koch is worried that pent-up police emotions might explode. "You are not going to move them off the street if they demonstrate peacefully?" he asks Hoffman. Reassured, he urges Hoffman to visit the hospital. "Get a statement from the three of them . . . Hirsch was an extremely persuasive witness, and he says he can identify the cop . . . No, I'm not prejudging. But why don't you go over there yourself." With only four civilians injured, he goes on, "there can't be thirty-eight injured cops."

"Sixty-two is the latest number," says Hoffman.

"Sixty-two cops! Do you believe it?"

"No," says Hoffman.

"Neither do I."

How can the police be responsible for investigating themselves? Koch rejected this notion when—in 1966, during his campaign for a seat on the City Council—he supported the unsuccessful effort to create a Civilian Review Board to investigate charges of police brutality. "I have to depend on McGuire," he says now, referring to Police Commissioner Robert McGuire. The car pulls up in front of his Village apartment building at 4:25 P.M., and the mayor announces that he plans to spend his free Saturday evening doing nothing but sleeping.

But his phone does not let him rest. Among the many callers tonight is Ronald Gault. All day long, Gault says, black leaders have been calling him to ask why no Jewish leaders were arrested for taking over a police station house, while black Councilwoman Mary Pinkett was arrested for staging a firehouse sit-in. Why was the mayor "apologetic" to a mob that had damaged a police station? Would Koch have been as "conciliatory" if the faces had been black rather than white? And Gault tells the mayor, "The street question is about how the police reacted. There would have been fifty civilians dead if the same thing happened in the black community." This was not Gault's view, but it was the view of his callers. They worried about a double standard for blacks and whites, a worry that Gault shared before calling Koch.

Koch tells Gault that "the police are going to investigate and if they can identify people, we're going to prosecute."

Gault says he is satisfied. Others are not. They remain troubled about an apparent double standard; troubled that Koch pacified a mob with a misleading promise of more police protection; troubled by Koch's curious reverie in the face of adversity.

The following Monday the Borough Park station house looks very different from the way it did Saturday. The floor has been swept clean, notices have been reposted on the bulletin board, and precinct cops are nonchalantly joking. Milton Schwartz, assistant chief of police and commanding officer of the Brooklyn South Area, informs a handful of reporters that sixty-two police officers were injured on Saturday. Eyebrows jump, and Chief Schwartz explains that the number is high because cops are required to report any injury, even a bruise. If the injury recurs and there has been no earlier report, he says, they may not be eligible for disability benefits.

Saturday's anger seems spent. "I have no complaints against the mayor or the police commissioner," says George Summerhill, an eleven-year veteran of the force who lives in Staten Island and serves as one of three Patrolmen's Benevolent Association delegates from the Borough Park precinct. "They backed us all the way." But the basic problem remains: "We need more cops. We used to go a whole week with one or two radio runs. Now we get fifteen to eighteen in one night." Summerhill can understand the frustrations of citizens who stormed the station house: "They want more police on the street. They're entitled to have them."

Among these men, as among the sanitation workers I have talked to, Mayor Koch seems popular. They are willing to overlook his campaign promises to get them to work harder and sacrifice lucrative fringe benefits. "My personal opinion is that Mayor Koch is doing a good job," says Alfred Dahl, a fifteen-year veteran and also a PBA delegate. "I don't agree with everything. I don't appreciate his gay-rights position. But he's got guts. Got to give him credit for it. I think it takes quite a lot of guts to come to the station house in front of people of his own faith. Other mayors would show up two days later, or be interviewed at home."

Summerhill is pleased that "Koch won't bend to certain political groups." He particularly appreciated what he saw as Koch's refusal to be pushed around by militant black leaders, and he approved of Koch's refusal to pick more Jewish cops to placate Borough Park.

True, cops got bigger raises under Mayor Lindsay, but, says Dahl, Lindsay didn't communicate support and sympathy for cops, and Koch does.

"The mayor has shown sensitivity for working police officers," says George Douris, director of public relations for the PBA. Among policemen, as among sanitation workers, the feeling that their bosses respect and support them is crucial.

Leaning on the front desk, Summerhill explains that layoffs have sapped morale. A job that he and others sought for security is no longer secure. The men worry about more layoffs, about Koch's commitment to shrink the force through continued attrition. They don't like that. But at least they like the vibes coming from police brass. "The police commissioner seems to be backing the men," says Summerhill. Chief Schwartz "is a good man because he backs his men," he continues. "He's fair. He's tough. He cares about the men. That's the big thing."

Police Commissioner Robert McGuire thinks that the mayor deserves credit for improved morale. "You can't kid cops. Cops know he's straight. Know he's a tough guy. He's gone to the funerals. He's cried. That's not lost on the cops. They know he's not a phony."

The Police Department was a special target of Koch when he was running for mayor. He complained about the small number of cops on patrol, about lavish contract benefits, about work rules that prevented the efficient deployment of the police. Koch claimed that the city didn't have to hire more cops to increase the number on patrol. He promised greater civilianization, improved management, crackdowns on abusers of sick leave, and more one-man patrol cars in low-crime districts. Koch and Commissioner McGuire have made efforts to fulfill these promises. Koch has been less successful in fulfilling a promise to improve the productivity of each cop. Like all uniformed employees, a cop receives twenty-seven working days' vacation after three years; and, in return for a few extra minutes a day of paperwork and "briefing time," he also receives what are called chart days — extra days off. In the 1978 labor negotiations, Koch agreed to increase the number of chart days. Patrolmen were awarded six additional chart days, bringing their total to eighteen. Typical figures for the department's 2,300 sergeants range from four to ten additional chart days, bringing their total to between twelve and twenty-eight. The 806 lieutenants won from four to six additional chart days, bringing their total to between eight and fourteen. Like all uniformed employees, cops also receive one day of personal leave for "whatever reason," and unlimited sick leave (averaging about thirteen days annually). Thus, the average police officer is off about sixty days a year in addition to the standard two days off each week. In effect, most police officers work a four-day week. The Financial Control Board reported that as a result of the 1978 negotiations, policemen would work fewer "productive hours." If, for instance, all police sergeants were reduced to eight chart days off, Special Deputy Comptroller Sidney Schwartz once calculated, this single action would be the equivalent of adding 256 sergeants to the force. Improving police coverage does not necessarily require spending more money.

From the taxpayers' point of view, reducing the number of days off makes sense. From the cops' point of view, it does not. "They keep wanting to cut us, but they don't give us compensation," complains Summerhill. "I deal with psychos, men with guns and knives. We handle many jobs. There's lots of stress on this job. Guys have heart attacks. The average age of cops is thirty-eight. Running up on roofs after burglars is tough for a thirty-eight-year-old cop. Studies show the men need time off from their jobs. You work holidays. Last year and the year before, I worked Thanksgiving, Christmas, New Year's Eve, and New Year's Day. I couldn't get a day off because of the lack of manpower. Everybody else was out enjoying the holidays. Okay, it's my job."

Still, it is not surprising that citizens tend to feel cheated. They are paying more and receiving less. The mayor's budget message of last April said, "We acknowledge that there may be a reduction in patrol services during the year." And though candidate Koch promised a dramatic improvement in the number of cops on street patrol each day, his own Management Report of August 1978 acknowledged that there were 151 fewer cops on patrol on an average day in fiscal 1978 (including the first six months of the Koch administration) than there were the year before; the figures were 6,636 and 6,787, respectively. In July of this year the average daily patrol force was 6,091, or 545 fewer cops than were deployed in the last month of the Beame administration. Further manpower losses are projected for next year.

The loss is mirrored in Borough Park, a low-crime precinct. Although the Police Department will not, for security reasons, disclose the number of cops patrolling streets on any one shift, it is known that last winter 135 cops and two civilians were assigned to the 66th Precinct. At one time the precinct had 210 cops. Divide 135 cops into three daily shifts, take into account days off, vacations, sick days, court appearances, and clerical work, and between fifteen and twenty officers are left patrolling Borough Park's streets during each shift. Privately, police officials agree that this arithmetic is correct. It is not surprising that residents sense little police presence. On this point, Borough Park citizens and cops agree.

They differ over what happened that Saturday in Borough Park. The citizens complain that they were the victims of a police riot; the police counter that they were the victims of lawlessness incited by a few troublemakers. The chief culprit, the precinct cops maintain, was Assemblyman Hirsch. They charge that he resisted their entreaties, sneered at them, gave the order to storm the station house. Some weeks after the incident Hirsch and two others were arrested for assault. The mayor was stunned, as I was. It was hard to believe that any case could be made against the man we saw, caked with blood, speaking so thoughtfully, in the hospital. But Koch said he reserved judgment and would let the courts determine Hirsch's guilt or innocence. And Hirsch, who had called the mayor a good man "five times," was now furious at his former ally, and was debating with himself whether to sign a petition—being circulated by State Senator Vander Beatty—urging the right of the public to recall a mayor. Koch often says that in politics it is inevitable that "the wheel turns." It had turned once again.

Notes from a cabinet meeting last fall: The meeting begins at eight o'clock in the Blue Room of City Hall. Nineteen members of the administration—fourteen white men, two black men, two white women, one Puerto Rican man—gather around an oblong conference table, sipping coffee or tea and nibbling Danish. Most cabinet meetings are free-form. They are attended by the deputy mayors, various commissioners and department heads, and some members of the mayor's staff. There is rarely a prepared agenda, and participants say what's on their minds. This cabinet meeting has more of an agenda than most. After a brief status report from the mayor on the week's developments, Deputy Mayor Brown distributes copies of a memo listing Koch's 1977 campaign and 1978 governmental promises for new initiatives. It was only natural, Brown says, that the focus of the administration's first year was on cutting the budget. What he hopes to do today, however, is to shift the focus of its attention to "positive programs." What new initiatives could City Hall encourage that would not drain limited resources? Briefly, Brown outlines the memo and then gives the others a few moments to read it.

John Lo Cicero, the mayor's political adviser, is the first to speak. The administration promised to improve services, to make an economic-development effort, to stabilize middle-income neighborhoods, he says, and "we've done all that."

"Even God couldn't do that!" snaps Koch. The question, Koch says, is how, given meager resources, New York is to embark on new programs. "How do we stabilize the middle class? That's the first thing, maybe, we could talk about."

"How do we define the middle class?" asks Dan Wolf.

Retaining whites in the city, says Deputy Mayor Philip Toia, who lives in a turn-of-the-century Victorian house in a racially integrated Flatbush neighborhood.

"By the way," says Herbert Rickman, special assistant to the mayor, whose responsibilities include liaison work with organized Jewish groups, "the middle class does not yet feel this administration has fully addressed it."

Deputy Mayor Herman Badillo suggests that they should focus on working to maintain one- and two-family homes in middle-class areas. He says that a mortgage-insurance program would help shore up these homes. Badillo is not the most popular figure in this room. He addresses his remarks directly to the mayor, and rarely looks around the room when he speaks. Sixteen men in the room have their suit jackets draped over their chairs or at least unbuttoned. Badillo's sharply tailored charcoal-gray pin-striped suit jacket remains buttoned, and he sits erect in his chair as he says, "As you know, I'm a CPA. What I'm suggesting is that there be greater mayoral involvement. If the mayor doesn't claim credit, you can be sure the borough presidents will."

"If the perception of your administration is that it is focused solely on the middle class, it will be to your detriment," Corporation counsel Allan Schwartz says to Koch. The mayor must also focus on the problems of the poor and "convey to people that there is a renaissance."

An issue that cuts across income and racial lines, suggests Deputy Mayor Basil Paterson, is poor sanitation service. "No matter what else we do, that is a service that affects everyone." Therefore, the mayor should target sanitation and strive to improve it dramatically. That would be visible proof that government works for rich and poor, black and white.

Planning Commission Chairman Wagner suggests that no matter how they slice the city budget pie or what services they concentrate on, the overriding reality is that the pie is smaller. The city has only $2.3 billion in capital funds to spend over the next three fiscal years. "That's not very much money," he says. "Take Staten Island alone. They want sewers. That's two billion dollars right there." In the short run, he agrees with Paterson. Having cleaner streets is *do-able*. But *desirable* goals may no longer by *do-able*. The reality of budget scarcity haunts city policymakers no matter which way they turn—as does their inability to always spend money effectively. The decline of the South Bronx is but one example. Potholes in streets are another.

(Similar dilemmas face city policymakers in housing. Last April, Wagner's Planning Commission issued a twenty-five-page report that dealt, in part, with housing abandoned by landlords. City Hall, the commission noted, had involuntarily become the landlord of more than 10,000 multiple dwellings—8 percent of all such buildings in the city. By September of 1980 City Hall will own more than 16,000—13 percent. Unless drastic policy decisions are made, city officials estimate, by 1981 City Hall will have become the landlord for a population—400,000—exceeding that of all but about thirty cities. The city collects no property taxes from most of these buildings, and according to the Housing Department, collects less than 40 percent of the rent. In addition, the current city budget allotted $35 million to provide fuel and utilities for these properties. And 34 percent—$82 million—of the city's federal Community Development funds, a large part of which is supposed to be earmarked for rehabilitation, is being diverted to this maintenance effort. The city, Koch and Wagner complained, could no longer afford to be "the landlord of last resort." One solution, said Wagner, would be to ease rent control and other regulations that prevent private landlords from making a profit. Coupled with anti-redlining strictures, such a policy change might address the causes of housing abandonment. But, Wagner conceded, it would not address the problem of poor tenants who cannot afford to pay higher rent. A housing subsidy to bridge the gap between what the landlord needs in order to maintain the building and earn a profit and what the tenant can afford to pay would be one solution. But the city can't afford a subsidy, and the federal government says it can't, either. Koch described another "solution" to me in April: "If we cannot restructure the whole thing and get out of the rent business, and we're still left next year with these large numbers of properties, we're going to vastly reduce our commitment to providing services to these buildings. No other city does. What they do is simply tell tenants, 'You don't like it, get another apartment.' " Here the problem is not fiscal but political. Could the mayor turn his back on such large numbers of citizens, many of them poor? Would other elected officials, whose concurrence would be required, go along?)

The mayor believes that city voters are realistic. He recaps for the cabinet an incident that occurred over the weekend, when he was touring Corona, Queens. "Anybody want to pay more taxes?" he asked the knot of people gathering about him. "Then I went into my little tirade: 'You want a library? You have to cut something else.' People accept that."

Budget Director James Brigham chimes in to offer another perspective on reality. Seventy percent of the city's personnel costs (excluding pensions) paid for out of locally raised funds are concentrated in four agencies—police, fire, sanitation, and education—"so we have to get smaller in those agencies," he says. The rub is that those are the services most crucial to middle-income residents. Cut them and you risk encouraging the flight of more middle-income residents. Don't cut them and you risk bankruptcy.

"The optimum strategy would be to target communities that are fringe communities, those about to tip," says adviser Ronald Gault.

Unavoidably, the city must pick and choose those things it can do, says Deputy Mayor Herbert Sturz. What it chooses should be highly visible—like cleaning up Times Square or providing more wire-mesh trash baskets.

"I don't want to call them gimmicks," he says, "but we need producible stuff."

Badillo cautions that a citywide policy may not work, because each neighborhood has different priorities and concerns. A "targeted" approach is called for. He says that in the one-family area where he lives—Riverdale —sanitation is not the primary concern.

The conversation meanders for an hour. The cabinet members have not yet grappled with David Brown's memo. Nor have they defined what they mean by the middle class. They have seesawed between improved services for the middle class and improved services for everyone, between the need to raise the expectations of the middle class and the fear of raising them too much, between hopes for new programs and fears that these cannot be afforded.

At ten minutes after nine the mayor announces, "I have to go to the bathroom." The cabinet takes a five-minute break.

Dan Wolf whispers to me, "What I find interesting is the emphasis on the middle class here. A few years ago people would have jumped on you for even using the term." It was thought by many to be a code word for "racism."

"I think this meeting is very helpful," Koch remarks when the session resumes. The mayor is pleased when people—members of his team—feel involved.

David Brown, who has said nothing since opening the meeting, is clearly exasperated. "One point of this exercise was to show the things the mayor was already committed to," he remarks. "What are we doing on the positive side? I don't think we should forget that. Maybe it means picking a few things people want, and doing them."

As the meeting draws to a close, one member of the cabinet asks if there isn't a danger that in touting new programs, City Hall will undermine public belief in the fiscal crisis.

Yes, Brown says. But the mayor should at least identify several new program initiatives. We cannot afford to fail to inspire hope, Brown says. We cannot allow the impression that "New York is a sinking ship."

Koch smiles and says, "I think of it as a light canoe making its way downriver."

SECOND THOUGHTS

While preparing this profile I tried to be neither a participant (new journalism) nor a spectator (the old). The writer tried not to tell readers what to think, and at the same time, not to confuse them with an on-the-one-hand, on-the-other account. The writer served as one part tour guide, one part judge, pointing to various landmarks, striving to separate truth from falsehood. The approach succeeds only if the reader believes the reporter has mastered the information and is fair. Readers are left to draw their own conclusions.

How readers respond to Koch depends in large measure on what they value. Some readers were put off by Koch's self-absorption, pettiness, hostility to the establishment, strained relationship with black leaders, or his occasional ineptness in matters of government as opposed to politics. Others were impressed by his candor, hard work, brains, his independence of the establishment, or his lack of cynicism. Some readers thought I tried to paint a sympathetic picture of Koch; others, that I succeeded in portraying him as a fool.

Although the consensus of his friends was that he emerged sympathetically, Mayor Koch was displeased. During the five or so months we spent together, Koch often predicted he might have to read the profile at least three times before he could appreciate it. No, Mr. Mayor, I would say. Read it three times—and wait five years. We would laugh together, but Koch was uneasy. The night before the first installment appeared in *The New Yorker,* I treated Koch to dinner at Garguilo's Restaurant in Coney Island. It was my way of saying thanks to someone who was more open and accessible than any public figure I had ever covered. It was also—I half-joked— perhaps the last time he would speak to me. As we said goodnight that Tuesday, I handed Koch a proof copy of the magazine, which he and his press secretary read together in the back seat of the mayor's car returning to Manhattan. The next afternoon press secretary Maureen Connelly phoned to talk about the first installment. The mayor, who happened to wander into her office, got on the phone and coolly complained that he came across as an egomaniac.

His reaction, no doubt, was prompted by the profile's lead: "Friends and associates of Mayor Edward I. Koch have noticed that when the mayor's attention wanders during discussions of the city's fiscal crisis or some other eye-glazing topic, a sure way to bring him back is to change the subject to the mayor." For Koch, the profile went downhill from there. Ironically, this was not my original lead. The manuscript began with the anecdote of Congressman Koch being mugged in Washington Square Park. My editor at *The New Yorker,* Bill Whitworth, thought it a serviceable lead, but suggested that there was a better lead later on in the manuscript. What struck him after he read the manuscript, he said, was Koch's often endearing self-absorption. It accounted for his personal charm and his governmental flaws. Why not hit the reader right between the eyes with it? I'm glad I took the advice.

From *The New Yorker,* I learned other things, too. My first sentence originally read: ". . . a sure way to *lure* him back is to change the subject to the mayor." At *The New Yorker,* manuscripts are edited and then circulated as galleys, with authors jealously inspecting each suggested change. One of the first I noticed was that the word *lure* had been replaced by *bring.* I immediately scratched it out, substituting *lure.* Surely it was a more colorful word. Back came the second set of galleys, and once again, *lure* was replaced by *bring.* Who was doing this? Bill said it was William Shawn, the long-time editor of the magazine, who inspects each galley and page proof word for word and who, by my calculation, unbelievably read and reread the profile no fewer than four times (once in manuscript, twice in galleys, and at least once in page proofs). Why did Mr. Shawn persistently change the word? I asked. Because, Mr. Auletta, Mr. Shawn would say in his polite and formal way, *lure* is an evocative word, distracting the reader from the punch line of the sentence. *Bring,* however, does not stand out or cause the reader to pause before reaching the punch line. The sky lit up.

Another lesson had to do with my tendency, a common one among my colleagues, to hunt for substitutes for the verb *said*—exclaimed, exhorted, noted, declared, admonished, stated, huffed. After I had changed many of the *saids* back to exclaimed, exhorted, noted, declared, etc., in the second galleys, an exasperated Whitworth tried to make his point by explaining that there was no substitute for the word *the.* Like the verb *said,* he continued, *the* was a background word which blends into any sentence no matter how many times it appears. Litter your copy with substitutes, he said, and the sentences become stilted.

The mayor's associates had more serious journalistic complaints. Sure, they had the standard gripes about interpretation and the selection of material and whether I should have given more weight to Koch's favorable aspects, told a negative anecdote differently, and so on. But they expressed subtler concerns. One Koch adviser said that the unusual access the mayor permitted—over the course of five months I was allowed to attend almost any mayoral meeting, study Koch's unpublished memoirs, his mayoral correspondence, incoming telephone log, biweekly reports from commissioners—gave me a distorted picture of Koch. He suspected that all the time we spent together, the sometimes venomous Koch I saw, the prankster, the time-waster, was really a man going overboard to impress a journalist he happened to like and who was preparing a profile for an important publication. That may be true. Perhaps, sometimes, I was witnessing a performance without knowing it. On the other hand, perhaps the public regularly witnesses a performance without knowing it.

It could also be that the mayor, an engagingly open, candid man, was too open and accessible. The press does not have a First Amendment right to squat in the mayor's office taking notes. Sometimes the presence of a reporter prompts advisers either to show off or to restrain themselves. Throughout the dinner with Senator Moynihan at Gracie Mansion, for instance, I felt that had I not been there, Moynihan would have figuratively grabbed Koch by the lapels to shake home his concerns about the city's budget. Later, Moynihan implied as much to me. Perhaps the mayor would have spoken more. On other occasions—cabinet meetings, for instance—I had the sense that advisers might have tailored their words to suit the press. They were showboating.

While I was thankful to Koch for being so open, sometimes I felt he was too open. I tried to appear nonchalant, but still I couldn't believe he would let me sit and take notes throughout the sensitive dinner meeting at Gracie Mansion, or that, after many requests, he finally relented and permitted me to read his sealed memoirs. Most public officials are too secretive, unlike Koch. But politicians and the press are meant to be in an adversary relationship. Reporters lust to record things public officials consider not just embarrassing but premature and incomplete. Politicians are under no obligation to volunteer negative information, to respond immediately to every news flash, to short-circuit deliberations, to spend too much time explaining and too little *doing.* The public interest sometimes requires governmental privacy.

The mayor also complained that it was unfair of me to quote a passage on black anti-Semitism from the heretofore unpublished memoirs he tape-recorded in 1975–1976, without at least granting him an opportunity to clarify or update what he had said then. And what he said then was: "My experience with blacks is that they're basically anti-Semitic. Now, I want to be fair about it. I think whites are basically anti-black. . . ." Knowing that the quote was potentially explosive, that Koch when he was a congressman had been loose with his words and might have been even more so because the memoirs were under seal until 1996, shouldn't I have been more judicious? Or, as Koch suggested, didn't I owe it to someone who had been so generous with me, to alert and allow him "to refine or reject" it. Koch felt abused.

Maybe I should have gone back to the mayor to update the quote. The reason I did not was that we had spoken many times about race relations. I was convinced the memoirs accurately conveyed his true feelings and fears, as well as his fondness for stark, simplistic exclamations. I also feared that an updated quote, permitting Koch to soften what he had said, would serve his interests more than the readers'. After all, I was convinced Koch really believed what he said in the memoirs. Moreover, Koch's comments opened the door to a fuller explanation of the reasons for his tense relations with many black leaders. To have withheld the information because it was potentially explosive would have been on balance, it seems to me, more a political than a journalistic act.

Like any politician, I, too, wanted the best of both worlds: to write something that would interest readers and yet be agreeable to Koch. Still, as much time as I spent with Koch, I knew one day I'd sit at the typewriter and tell the truth, at least as I saw it. The reporter's audience is the reader, not the person he is profiling. The politician's audience is more diverse, consisting of voters, fellow politicians, history, and the press. Reporters are only part of a politican's audience. Maybe Koch forgot that when he permitted me to read his memoirs.

Publication of Koch's comments about black anti-Semitism generated several stories that dominated the local press for days. The controversy both pleased and repelled me. It caused more people to read the profile. It also helped push the mayor out of his cocoon to initiate a series of meetings with black leaders, to begin to respond more sensitively to their concerns. But the quote was also used by his enemies to bludgeon Koch as a "racist," which he is not. And while I liked the attention, it was unsettling to see my 60,000-word profile reduced to a 400-word story about anti-Semitism. Because it was controversial, it was considered news. True, what Koch said was important. But I prefer to believe that the real news in the profile was what was said about the mayor's government; about his personality and character and how these shaped the way he governed. Such an analysis, admittedly, does not lend itself to thirty-second radio reports or four-hundred-word stories.

Finally, though I strove not to draw a bottom line for the reader, freeing him to sort through the contradictory evidence and form his opinion of Koch, such a strategy conceals what the writer thinks of Koch. For the record, I like and respect him—with reservations, of course.

Roy Cohn:
The Legal Executioner

Esquire, December 5, 1978

Don't mess with Roy Cohn.

The "21" once did. The restaurant spa of the rich and powerful used to seat Roy in Siberia, upstairs in a corner with the tourists. One day Roy called and made a reservation for four at 8 P.M. Purposely arriving ten minutes early, he was brusquely led to his usual far nook. Promptly at 8 P.M. the Duke and Duchess of Windsor entered the room. "Ten captains stood up," as Roy remembers it, and tried to steer the Duke and Duchess to a choice table. From the corner of the room, Roy waved to his dinner guests. They waved back, pulling away from the captains to join their friend. "Please, Mr. Cohn," the captains beseeched him. "Allow us to give you a more comfortable table." He wouldn't hear of it. "Roy loved it," recalls his boyhood friend William Fugazy. "He fixed them. That was his way of showing them. Now he gets the good tables."

Today Roy is holding court at one of his favorite "21" tables, against the wall facing the entrance, where everyone can see him. Captains hover nearby, snapping to light his thick Cuban cigar. A red phone is placed to his right. His legal clients are sprinkled throughout the wood-beamed room. Roy Cohn has reason to be pleased—he has survived more crises than Richard Nixon. In the early fifties he was the arrogant red-baiting counsel to Senator Joseph McCarthy, the twenty-six-year-old who threatened "to wreck the Army" if favored treatment was not granted his friend David Schine—Bonnie, Bonnie and Clyde, is how Lillian Hellman referred to Cohn, Schine and McCarthy. In the sixties he was indicted four times (the first case ended in a mistrial) and always acquitted. He has suffered several judicial reprimands for unethical conduct, had his wrists slapped in civil cases, and been ordered to make restitution. In the seventies he has been indicted for violating Illinois banking laws; the Internal Revenue Service has audited his income-tax returns for the last nineteen years and seized some of his assets. He has been the target of criticism and innuendo about his ethics, his finances, his personal life. He has even been accused of conspiring to murder a young man. Roy Cohn, some say, is the personification of evil.

Actually, Roy Cohn personifies the problems of the law. Of all the attributes of a good lawyer, cynicism is certainly among the foremost. How else could one weave a defense for a client who is guilty? Like mock UN assemblies for college kids, one day you argue the Soviet Union's position; the next, the United States'. What you say has little to do with what you believe. In fact, convictions can get in the way. You're an advocate, not a judge. Your interest is form, not content—the process. Surprising the prosecution, entertaining the jury, flattering the judge, leaking information to the press, figuring out angles, coaching testimony, unearthing sympathetic witnesses, feigning anger or sorrow—they're all part of the game. Roy just plays the game harder, tougher, makes up his own rules. "He does what he has to to win," observes a former associate, comparing him to Richard Nixon's favorite football coach. "It's the George Allen school of law. He'll pull out some plays every now and then that aren't in the book." This has earned Roy considerable notoriety.

The notoriety hasn't hurt a bit. At fifty-one he has seen his law firm, Saxe, Bacon & Bolan, expand rapidly. Its town house office at 39 East Sixty-eighth Street is bursting with forty-two employees, including twelve lawyers. They have just rented an additional floor at 667 Madison Avenue. Clients include Newhouse newspapers and Condé Nast magazines; the Catholic Archdiocese of New York; the Ford Model Agency; Studio 54; Potamkin Cadillac, Baron di Portanova; the biggest names in New York real estate, including Lefrak, Helmsley, Trump; Louis Wolfson, owner of Affirmed; Warren Avis, as in rent a car; Peter Widener and his sister Tootie, a Main Line Pennsylvania family with coal, rail, and racetrack interests; Jerry Finkelstein, a New York businessman; John Schlesinger, a British investor in South Africa; Carmine "Lilo" Galante, the reputed boss of bosses; "Fat Tony" Salerno; Nicholas "Cockeyed Nick" Rattenni; Thomas and Joseph Gambino, sons of the late Carlo; and a string of hoods; Nathan's Famous; Luca Buccellati, the jeweler; Congressman Mario Biaggi; Mrs. Charles Allen, Jr., wife of the chairman of Allen & Company. He has counseled his friend George Steinbrenner, owner of the Yankees. As a favor to his friend Halston, Roy advised Bianca how to handle Mick. He was to be Onassis' divorce attorney against Jackie.

The more publicity Roy generates, the more clients he attracts. Just recently he exploded on the front pages, bringing a stockholder suit against Henry Ford, charging that Ford accepted bribes and siphoned company funds for his personal living expenses. He made the evening news when he appeared, without fee, as the attorney for J. Wallace LaPrade, former head of the FBI's New York office, who was fighting Justice Department charges involving his role in illegal bugging and break-ins. Unlike most lawyers, he is not press-shy. "I'm a ham," he boasts. When gossip columnist Liz Smith reported that Roy was representing Christina Ford in her divorce action against Henry, Christina issued a denial, which Smith duly printed. "Then I had a correspondence with him," says Smith, "where he said he was representing her." She believes Roy leaked the original column item to her through a friend for publicity. Cohn denies it, admitting only that he had met with Christina. He promised to produce the Liz Smith letter to disprove her claim, but never did. No matter. "The more you say he's a ruthless bastard," chuckles his law partner Stanley Friedman, "the more it helps." Has publicity, much of it negative, helped? "All of this has done me a lot of good, there's no question about it," admits Cohn. "I'd be a liar if I denied it. It's given me a reputation for being tough, a reputation for being a winner." A former assistant U.S. attorney who still believes Roy should be behind bars puts it another way: "He's the only person I've ever known as a prosecutor who enjoyed being indicted. He enjoys the limelight."

The publicity almost guarantees that Roy's phone calls will be returned. "I can get attention, no question about it," says Cohn. "They know my name. The usual response is 'What did I do?' " His standard technique is to dispatch a threatening letter on behalf of a client—"Hey, mister. This is now the eleventh hour before the monster strikes!" is how Roy puts it.

"Roy symbolizes viciousness in protecting a client or going after someone who needs viciousness to right a wrong," says Bill Fugazy. He fights his cases as if they were his own. It is war. If he feels his adversary has been unfair, it is war to the death. No white flags. No Mr. Nice Guy. Prospective clients who want to kill their husband, torture a business partner, break the government's legs, hire Roy Cohn. He is a legal executioner—the toughest, meanest, loyalest, vilest, and one of the most brilliant lawyers in America. He is not a very nice man.

Once when a husband tried to pull a fast one and ordered two moving vans to sneak up to collect furniture at 7 A.M., his hysterical wife called Roy. "What should I do?" she screamed. "Sit tight," he calmed her. "I'll call the cops." He had the husband thrown in jail. "I must have had fifty men call me over the years and ask, 'We hear Roy Cohn is going to represent my wife. Would you make sure he doesn't rough us up?' " says Fugazy. "The mere sending of a letter from Roy Cohn has saved us a lot of money," says builder Donald Trump. "When people know that Roy is involved, they'd rather not get involved in the lawsuits and everything else that's involved." Publishers, TV networks, editors are accustomed to receiving preemptory phone calls or threatening letters from Cohn, and cringe at the court costs of taking him on.

Cohn is a unique kind of bully—fearless. During the Army-McCarthy hearings in 1954 he lunged at and tried to punch his co-counsel, Robert Kennedy. Considering Cohn's lack of agility—at a recent Yankee game when everyone in the box ducked to avoid third baseman Graig Nettles chasing a foul ball, Roy stood up and got punched in the neck—he is fortunate people interceded before he could swing at Kennedy. "I know that if I were in a fight," says publicist Howard Rubenstein, who has his own collection of influential clients, "I'd want Roy Cohn in my corner. I've seen people in divorce fights say, 'Oh my God, it's Roy Cohn.' It's like in the Wild West, when one of the hired gunmen with forty notches in his gun strides into the bar and everyone ducks or says, 'I better get out of here.' He's not the Lone Ranger in a white suit. His reputation as a bad guy willing to stand up and fight helps him."

To his clients, Roy is like a faith healer. "He's almost a mother's helper," says builder Sam Lefrak. "He doesn't tell you he's going to lose, like most lawyers." When the federal government was suing the Trump organization for discriminating against minorities in their housing projects, Donald Trump searched for a lawyer. "They all said, 'You have a good case, but it's a sticky thing,' " remembers Trump. Then he met Cohn for the first time at a party, explained his predicament, and was thrilled when Roy instantly declared, "Oh, you'll win hands down!" Sitting beside him at "21," Republican socialite Sheila Mosler, whose divorce he is handling, exclaims, "To me, he's like a brother."

Looking at Cohn closely, one is not surprised that "21" would shove him in a corner. Hooded, bloodshot eyes give him the appearance of a convict. A deep scar wiggles like a river down the center of a thick nose. Lines streak from either side of the nose to the mouth, which he lubricates with lizardlike strokes from his tongue. Short hair hugs his head, which is balding on top. The hairline is neatly shaved to form an arch above his ears, extending down and around the entire back of his head. Two thin red lines curve around each of Roy's ears, the result, he admits, of cosmetic surgery to correct "bags" and "heavy lines." He looks like a killer. Except for the body and the deportment. He's only five feet eight inches tall, 144 pounds. The suit he is wearing this day is dark blue, slightly tucked at the waist, with a faint stripe. A modest paisley tie fades into a nondescript striped shirt. His mannerisms—the licking of the lips, the waving wrists—are effete.

Roy waves to Leo van Munching, the head of Heineken; Victor Potamkin; Donald Trump; and a procession of friends who flit by. He has always made powerful friends. At the age of ten he was introduced by his father, Al Cohn, a respected Bronx and then New York State supreme court judge, to FDR. Roy, who began speaking at political rallies at the age of nine, promptly informed the President he agreed with his court-packing schemes. When Roy was a teen-ager, Dora and Al Cohn insisted that their chubby —and only—son attend their dinner parties with Ed Flynn, Carmine De Sapio, and other movers and shakers. "It was extraordinary," recalls a Democrat who attended regularly, "to see ten grown-up couples and then sit next to a fifteen-year-old. Roy was always on the scene. He fit right in." Says Neil Walsh, a boyhood friend, "When he was sixteen, he was forty." Four of his closest childhood friends—Generoso Pope, Jr., Si Newhouse, Jr., Richard Berlin, and Bill Fugazy—are today, respectively, owner and publisher of the *National Enquirer,* chairman of the Condé Nast publications and part owner of the Newhouse communications empire, president of the Hearst Corporation, and owner of one of the world's premier travel and limousine services. For twenty years Roy exchanged Christmas gifts with FBI Director J. Edgar Hoover. Bernard Baruch testified as a character witness at his first trial. Gossip columnists Walter Winchell and Leonard Lyons, who did not speak to each other, showered Roy with praise, as did George Sokolsky.

Hanging out at "21," the Stork Club, and the Latin Quarter, Roy met all kinds of people. In the mid-fifties the owner of the Latin Quarter approached him in Miami. "I have a daughter who's a great admirer of yours. She'd like to meet you," the father told him. So, together, they walked over to meet the daughter. "Barbara, I told Roy you were a great admirer of his and wanted to meet him."

"I said I would like to meet him. I didn't say I admired him," Barbara Walters admonished her father.

The conversation went downhill from there. Intrigued, Roy called her the next day for a date. On their first date, not surprisingly, Roy took her to the Bronx County Democratic dinner. Later, on the way home, Barbara broke the news: she was engaged. "So get married," Roy snapped. They did not see each other for three years. Barbara was working with William Safire in public relations for the Tex McCrary agency; Roy was practicing law. But Roy had obviously made an impression. His phone operator announced one morning, "Miss Walters from Tex McCrary is calling." As Roy recalls it, he huffed, " 'Well, if Miss Walters from Tex McCrary is calling, let her talk to my secretary.' Two days later I'm playing golf with Si Newhouse, and on the tenth tee, it got to me. I said, 'God, I wonder if that was *Barbara Walters*'? So I ran off and called her." They started going out. The family thought they would get married, as once they thought he would marry a girl named Joan Glickman. Instead, Barbara became another of Roy's good friends.

By parlaying his friendships and brains, Roy is today a powerful man. Even when he was considered a pariah, after returning from Washington in the fifties, he was always seen at the Hampshire House parties of Edwin Weisl, Lyndon Johnson's attorney and a partner in Simpson Thacher & Bartlett; with the Newhouses, the Berlins, the Fugazys, the William F. Buckleys. Through innocence by association, he regained respectability. When Democratic party chief Carmine De Sapio sought the editorial support of the Newhouse newspapers for candidates in Queens or Syracuse, he'd call Roy. As salesmen drop their calling cards, Roy is always volunteering, "Anytime you need help, just call on me." The Catholic Archdiocese, led by his friend Cardinal Spellman, received Roy's free legal counsel, including his help in the school-prayer case.

The Cardinal was given Roy's yacht for a ten-day holiday in St. Thomas and for charitable boat rides. Roy also helped raise money. Every year he would buy a table or tickets to Democratic, Republican, and Conservative party dinners. Though not much of a political giver himself, he raises money through his clients. He serves, for instance, as one of eight on a New York steering committee to collect money for the citywide Democratic party. At Roy's instigation, the late Lewis Rosenstiel, founder and chairman of

Schenley and a client, gave $2.5 million to Cardinal Cooke for the Cardinal Spellman Foundation and $1 million to christen the Hoover (J. Edgar) Foundation. Roy knows how to flatter friends. "I was sitting next to Rosenstiel once at the annual Al Smith dinner," recalls a New York pol. "He was just sitting there, looking around. Suddenly he stood up and saluted Roy Cohn, calling him 'field commander.' Roy stopped and saluted Rosenstiel, calling him 'supreme commander.' It was unbelievable."

Former Mayor Beame was a friend of Al Cohn's and came to rely on his son for advice. Stanley Friedman, Roy's new law partner, was deputy mayor under Beame, and with Roy's prodding, sought and won the post of Bronx Democratic chairman. The Brooklyn leader, Meade Esposito, turns to him for free legal advice, sending elected officials in trouble with the law to Roy for help. He represented Manhattan Republican chairman Vincent Albano in a divorce proceeding. When you're in trouble, Roy is a comforting presence. Not only is he supremely confident; he's living proof you can escape just about anything. But don't cross him. State Liquor Authority chairman Michael Roth, leading a posse of policemen, closed the disco Studio 54, a client, one night for operating without a liquor license. Cohn didn't forget. "In the spring of 1978, when the state Conservative party was about to nominate Roth for attorney general, Roy called me and was really irate," says state chairman J. Daniel Mahoney. The party went ahead and nominated Roth; and Roy went ahead and engineered that party's first statewide primary, supporting David Caplan. Roth, who also had the Republican nomination, was forced to divert an estimated $40,000 and precious time scouring the state to find the 114,000 registered Conservatives. Roth won, narrowly. But he's haunted by the memory of Cohn. "It was like chivalry," he says. "A personal insult must be avenged."

Parties also add to Cohn's power. Given at Studio 54, the East Sixty-eighth Street town house, or his three-and-one-half-acre estate in Greenwich, Connecticut, they attract a chorus line of judges, mayors, elected and party officials, monsignors and priests, publishers, gossip columnists, writers, models, actors, landlords, businessmen, celebrities. "I used to be wary of Roy, but then I went to one of his parties, and the people I saw there were all respectable," says builder and Association for a Better New York chairman Lewis Rudin. "He seems to know everybody," chimes a new friend, New York's Deputy Mayor Herman Badillo. "A good lawyer," clucks client Sam Lefrak, "must keep a line of communication open to political people. You must have a relationship. You can't just walk in. You got to know the judges. You got to know the clerks. You got to know the procedures."

Steve Rubell, co-owner of Studio 54, admits he's gotten some grief because of Roy. He met and was accosted by Lillian Hellman in California: "How can you have Roy Cohn represent you? He ruined people's lives." But Steve, like many of Roy's other friends, dismisses that as ancient history: "Look, I did crazy things when I was fifteen years old." Besides, Hellman has only seen Roy Cohn the monster. His friends see something else. At Roy's spring birthday party, held at comedian Joey Adams's home, Barbara Walters, David Edelstein, chief judge of the U.S. District Court, Baron di Portanova, TV host Stanley Siegel, gossip columnists Earl Wilson and Virginia Graham, and Donald Trump all stood up and toasted Roy. "When you're down and out, you can count on him" was their refrain. Afterward Roy got to display his gracious side. "I gave him a party at Studio 54," Rubell says. "He invited one hundred fifty people. Three thousand to four thousand showed up. Margaret Trudeau showed up. Everyone! I had a cake made of Roy with a halo around his head. This big cake was on a stand. Then Margaret Trudeau went and sat on it."

On purpose?

"No. Margaret Trudeau doesn't do anything on purpose—even think. But Roy went up to her and said, 'You weren't supposed to do that now. Do it later.' Instead of making her feel like an idiot, he made her feel comfortable. He's very gracious."

Roy was certainly gracious to Charles Allen, Jr., chairman of Allen & Company. While Rubell was sprawled on a couch in the middle of Studio 54's dance floor, brooms sweeping clean the confetti and debris from the night before, a messenger appeared with a hand-delivered letter from Roy, tersely commanding "a membership card today (unlaminated okay) for Charles Allen, Jr." It seems that Mr. Allen couldn't get into Studio 54 one night and thought to call his wife's divorce attorney for assistance. Roy favors his friends with parties and VIP treatment at Studio 54 and passes to Yankee games. When President Carter's inflation czar, Robert Strauss, the former Democratic national chairman, wanted his wife to see Studio 54, he arranged it through Roy. "Between Studio 54 and the Yankees, I feel like a ticket agent," says Roy, not quite complaining.

Yes, sitting here at his favorite "21" table, Roy has reason to be content, to feel mellow. But he is combative, expounding on some favorite topics: "stuffed shirts" and Wall Street law firms. The bar association: "a bunch of unctuous power brokers." Welfare: "No politician has the guts to tackle welfare fraud." Andrew Young: "a racist." In many ways Roy hasn't changed since the fifties. He still talks of "the Iron Curtain" and worries that Russia and China will "bury the hatchet because their goal is the same: the Communization of the world." The future: "I believe there's going to be a Communist world someday." Roy swaps confidential tidbits about some of his clients, asking that the reporter keep it off the record, of course. It is titillating stuff to hear of the armistice Roy negotiated between a well-known man and his wife. They now share separate quarters of the same apartment, separate phone numbers, separate lovers, and they never, but never, talk to each other. Presumably, such morsels are the favors Roy bequeaths his gossip-columnist friends.

It is 4 P.M. The room is empty, save for the waiters polishing plates for dinner and reassuring Roy that he may stay as long as he wishes. It's time, however, to go to court. But first Sheldon Tannen, an owner of "21," asks if he may please steal a moment of Roy's time to discuss a personal matter.

Outside, a white Chevrolet and driver are waiting—a temporary substitute for Roy's customary black Rolls-Royce—to take him to the state supreme court's appellate division. Al Cohn's picture, like that of other past judges, adorns the wall of the courthouse, and Roy is one proud son: "He had everything I don't have. He could control his temper. He didn't hate people's guts. The funny thing is that his reputation is enhanced because of me."

The courtroom is not unlike a church. Thick stained-glass windows reach to the ceiling, which arches into a dome decorated with the names of former justices, including Al Cohn's, and peaks into a blue-and-green stained-glass centerpiece. Frescoes grace the walls. The five appellate judges sit behind a curved, elevated, and elaborately carved mahogany bench. Kneeling before them is the conference table, divided by a portable lectern, where opposing lawyers sit. Behind them and to either side are wooden benches, arranged like pews, for spectators. There is a flutter among the few spectators as Roy enters. He is a celebrity, a showman. It doesn't matter who his client is—today he is arguing an appeal for Fred Trippe, whom Roy did not represent when he was convicted of falsifying the records of his methadone-testing laboratory and bilking the city of thousands.

A legend has grown up about Roy Cohn's courtroom appearances. Judges and others marvel that he can speak for hours without notes and has total recall, including the ability to recite the page number of testimony given months before. It is said by many that he will lie, cheat, invent facts, smoke with bullying rage, or ooze with charm—whatever is required. Says one of his Columbia Law School classmates who loathes him, "There is a feeling in the legal profession that he is a formidable adversary not because he's a brilliant lawyer but because he will stop at nothing." Dick Schaap, the WNBC sportscaster, encountered Cohn in a divorce proceeding with Schaap's wife, whom Roy is representing. "My wife would point at me and say, 'He's a liberal, Roy. He hates your guts!'" recalls Schaap. Which was true. He remembers walking into Cohn's office and spying a picture of Roy whispering into Senator McCarthy's ear. Schaap fumed. Yet he found himself surprised that Roy acted like "a stand-up comic. His timing was perfect. He was charming." What about his reputation as a killer? "It hasn't gotten that far yet," he says. "I may not be laughing long."

"His ability as a public speaker is probably the best in the business," certifies James LaRossa, who enjoys a reputation as one of the best criminal lawyers in the business. But, says a prominent attorney who has worked beside Roy in cases, "I could make a great trial lawyer out of him. He is spread too thin. He's really not a good trial lawyer because he doesn't have time to do the homework, and it shows in his cross-examination of witnesses." Sometimes it shows in his briefs. In the Henry Ford class action

suit, Roy wildly charged that a "Morris" Taubman received inside information about a Detroit land deal from his friend Henry Ford. The man's
correct name is A. Alfred Taubman. The papers also charged that Ford
gifted model-agency business to the Leslie Fargo Agency, where Kathleen
DuRoss, "a person in a close personal relationship with the defendant,
Ford, has an interest." The owner of the agency signed an affidavit swearing
that DuRoss has never owned an interest in her business.

Cohn's fabled self-assurance is on display today. Without notes he plucks
from his memory the page number of past testimony, marshals his arguments precisely, pausing only to step back, to slide his arms behind his back,
and pace before the justices. When Roy is finished, Assistant D.A. Jerrold
Tannenbaum, his adversary, rises. "Your Honor!" he booms, voice throb-
bing. "There is no way this court can determine this appeal if the record
is falsified." Roy sits motionless, staring straight ahead, arms folded, intently biting his cheek. As soon as his young foe pauses, Roy leaps from his
chair, never once taking his eyes from the judges, nudging, almost pushing
Tannenbaum from the podium. "I think he owes this court an apology!"
he barks. But there is no conviction in Roy's voice. He is used to being
attacked. What other lawyers would consider a blight on their integrity,
Roy considers perfectly normal. When Henry Ford's attorneys documented
in open court the times Roy's ethics have been questioned by judges, Roy
shrugged it off. "He actually thinks it's normal to be reprimanded by a
judge," says one of Ford's shocked attorneys.

What this attorney doesn't understand is that to Roy the courtroom is
not a forum where gentlemanly adversaries gather. It is a battlefield, an
arena where his enemies, he believes, try to *kill* him. The story of his trials,
or at least his four New York trials, are recounted in *A Fool for a Client,*
a book Roy wrote in 1971.

In the *United Dye* case, in 1964, Cohn was tried by then U.S. Attorney
Robert Morgenthau with the support of Attorney General Robert
Kennedy. The grand jury indictment charged that Roy sought to obstruct
justice in order to prevent the indictment of four men in a stock-swindle
scheme and then perjured himself by denying it. Roy retorted that Kennedy
and Morgenthau were engaged in a "vendetta"—Kennedy because Roy got
the job he wanted as counsel to McCarthy; Morgenthau because he resented
Roy's charges that his father, the former Secretary of the Treasury, naïvely
allowed Communists to work in and undermine his agency and the United
States. The case ended in a mistrial when one juror's father died. When
retried, Roy was acquitted.

Cohn's second and third indictments from the Morgenthau office came
within two months of each other in 1968 and early 1969. The third indictment was tried first. In the *Fifth Avenue Coach Lines* case, Roy was charged
with bribery, conspiracy, extortion, and blackmail for allegedly bribing a
city appraiser to help his client, Fifth Avenue Coach, snare a higher award

in a pending condemnation trial. The trial contributed to the Cohn legend when his attorney, Joseph E. Brill, was felled by a heart attack. It tells you something about Roy's Machiavellian reputation that there are those who believe the heart attack was feigned so Roy could offer his own summation. The advantage of defending himself was clear: Since Roy had not been called as a witness in the trial, he was now free to offer his own testimony without being cross-examined. For two days, without a note, Roy delivered an eloquent seven-hour summation, ending with a protestation of love for America. Tears streamed down Roy's and the jurors' cheeks. Then the jury was sequestered to deliberate.

During his first trial, when the jury sent in some questions for the judge, it looked bad for Roy, remembers his friend Neil Walsh. "But Roy insisted we all go to Lüchow's for dinner. It was like a funeral. Even Roy's attorney said, 'Roy, you got to admit it looks bad.' But Roy said, 'F_____ it! We'll win on appeal.' " Now, as the jury gathered and Roy's close friends huddled and bit their nails, the defendant rushed off to catch the opening-night performance of a new play, *The Mundy Scheme,* directed by and starring two men who once befriended Roy's beloved mother. Again, Cohn was acquitted.

The third trial came in 1971 and was a spin-off from the *Fifth Avenue Coach Lines* case. Cohn was accused of bribery, conspiracy, and filing false reports with the Securities and Exchange Commission (SEC). Each of the trials featured former business associates testifying against Cohn in return for guilty pleas and their freedom. Again, Cohn was judged innocent. To this day, a former prosecutor believes he was guilty in each case. But he believes Roy is today almost immune from prosecution—the theory being three strikes and you're out.

Morgenthau and his former assistants tend to be defensive about their prosecution, with reason. Cohn was the victim of some of the same vicious techniques he once employed as a young prosecutor and aide to McCarthy. During the 1964 trial Cohn's mail and that of his attorney was intercepted, earning Morgenthau a loud and well-deserved rebuke from the American Civil Liberties Union. Stories about Cohn were leaked to the press on the eve of the trials before jurors were selected. According to Irving Younger, a former assistant U.S. attorney under Morgenthau who penned a confessional for *Commentary* magazine in 1976, Kennedy and Morgenthau personally assigned him full time to "get" Cohn.

They failed to "get" Cohn but succeeded in granting him an aura of invincibility, respectability, and even sympathy. As Sidney Zion, then a legal-affairs reporter for the *Times,* wrote at the time:

> In liberal salons during the dear old days, the free-association game was a cinch: Say the name Roy Cohn and the response was a chorus of Joe McCarthy-witchhunt-vendetta-trial by headline.
> In conservative watering places these days, the free-association game is a

cinch: Say the name Bob Morgenthau and the response is a chorus of Roy Cohn-witchhunt-vendetta-trial by headline.

Thus do the ironies abound as time and positions change, as prosecutors become defendants, friends become informers, and informers become friends.

Can it be true that in the final months of the sixties, Roy M. Cohn is carrying the banner for civil liberties in the Southern District of New York?

Is it possible that United States Attorney Robert M. Morgenthau . . . has become Joe McCarthy in order to get Roy Cohn?

But there were other charges and judgments against Cohn, ones where the issue remained his, rather than the prosecutor's, behavior. In the civil case *SEC* v. *Fifth Avenue Coach Lines, Inc.* (1968), the court declared, "Cohn benefited from the use of Fifth's money to pay the loans made to him by" other directors and sought to "cover up" the participation of two directors in approving questionable schemes. The court enjoined him from violating the securities laws, a warning rap on the knuckles. Roy appealed the decision and lost. Legal standards have changed. "Today, a similar warning," says SEC attorney Ted Sonde, who participated in the original case, "would be grounds for dismissal from the bar in most states." Roy remembers the decision more modestly: "They dismissed every charge against me except one: I had been negligent in failing to submit something for board of directors approval."

In January 1970 Cohn and three other men were criminally indicted by a Chicago grand jury for violating Illinois banking laws. Working through Defiance Industries Incorporated, it was charged they connived secretly to gain control of more than 15 percent of the stock of two Illinois banks. In a related civil suit, Cohn and his co-defendants were also accused of using the banks for their own purposes, including the cashing of a $50,000 check by Cohn's law firm against a nonexistent checking account. Those charges, remarkably similar to a suit Roy would later lodge against Henry Ford, declared that Cohn used the banks for his own benefit in "total disregard of the well-being of Guaranty, its minority stockholders, and its depositors." The criminal charges were eventually dropped.

In *United States* v. *Johansson* (1971), the federal government sought to collect back taxes from the proceeds of the third Floyd Patterson-Ingemar Johansson heavyweight championship fight, which Roy promoted as a one-third owner of Feature Sports Incorporated. The lower court held Cohn responsible for the back taxes. On appeal, the higher court found Cohn and his partner Tom Bolan guilty of ignoring the lower court: We "cannot escape a conclusion that both Bolan and Cohn were directly and personally responsible for causing Feature Sports Incorporated to violate the court's orders."

In another confrontation with Illinois banking laws, this time a civil case, in 1973 Illinois Circuit Court Judge Daniel Covelli ordered Cohn and one of his former partners to pay $1.6 million to Louis E. Corrington, former president of the Mercantile National Bank of Chicago. When Cohn failed to appear in court, the judge ruled he had defaulted and awarded the full claim to Corrington. "Eventually," Roy says, "the suit was dismissed."

In *In re: Estate of Rosenstiel* (1976), Cohn was accused of tricking his eighty-four-year-old client Lewis Rosenstiel to change his will when he was dying in a Florida hospital. The will change was significant, since it would have made Cohn a trustee and executor of the $75-million estate and would have elevated two of Roy's clients—Rosenstiel's granddaughter, Cathy, and her husband, James Finkelstein (son of Roy's client and friend Jerry)—to become trustees of the estate. Dade County probate judge Frank B. Dowling, in a bristling twelve-page opinion, concluded: "Roy M. Cohn misrepresented to the decedent, Lewis S. Rosenstiel, the nature, content and purpose of the document he offered to Mr. Rosenstiel for execution." Cohn, he found, misled his nearly senile client by professing that the document he signed with a shaky hand would save one of his five ex-wives from prison. The court voided the amended will. Roy vowed to appeal.

Cohn blames "the local establishment" for this setback. He also counterattacks Rosenstiel's tax lawyer, Maurice Greenbaum, who pressed the challenge against Roy. Greenbaum, he claims, sneaked into the hospital room while Rosenstiel "was in a coma and put a pen in his hand and had him sign an X to a piece of paper, which divested him of substantial assets out of his estate." ("A purely diversionary tactic," says Greenbaum of Cohn's counterattack.) In other words, if Cohn was guilty, so was Greenbaum. The thrust of Roy's defense was not that his ethics were beyond reproach but that Greenbaum's were no better. It was the same tack he took when criticizing Vice-President Spiro Agnew's 1973 resignation for accepting bribes. "How could one of this decade's shrewdest leaders make a dumb mistake such as you did in quitting and accepting a criminal conviction?" read his open letter to Agnew in the *New York Times.* "Alger Hiss and Daniel Ellsberg can still argue their innocence. You no longer can." That Agnew was guilty did not offend Roy. What did was that he admitted it. Despite his threat to appeal the Rosenstiel decision, Roy never did.

In still another clash with the Florida courts, *SEC* v. *Pied Piper Yacht Charters Corp.* (1976), Cohn and his law firm were charged with civil contempt for breaching their fiduciary responsibility as agents for a $210,000 escrow fund when they substituted a bond for money in the account. Judge Edmund L. Palmieri said Cohn's denial of knowledge about the terms of the escrow account were "not credible," since he had negotiated the terms himself. The judge denounced Cohn and said he was guilty "of obfuscation by bold assertions of half-truths and untruths" and that he listened to his testimony "with surprise bordering on stupefaction." The case was dismissed—"with prejudice"—when Cohn and his associates replenished the escrow account. Roy says that the judge was prejudiced: "Every time we walk into the courtroom . . . I think his blood pressure goes up by about one hundred points." He also claims the SEC had granted written permission for what he did with the escrow account. Actually, attorney Michael Harris, of the SEC's New York office, did initial a letter from Roy. But the court found Harris "did not read the enclosed bond" forwarded by Cohn and "was never advised of the true nature of the bond proposed to be substituted. The Court accepts Harris' testimony that he initialed the letter as a courtesy." Besides, the judge intoned, only the court, not the SEC, was empowered to grant approval.

Roy's Florida battles are mere skirmishes when placed alongside his war with Internal Revenue. "Without question," he admits, "I hold the world's record for having been audited by the IRS." They have been auditing his returns for the last nineteen years and claim, says Roy, that he owes the government $1.4 million in back taxes. "Forget about it," says Cohn. "I don't even have a bank account. Everything I get, the IRS grabs." They seized his Keogh retirement plan and even a $60 checking account. The IRS is engaged "in a vendetta," he asserts. Nevertheless, he concedes, "I paid in the last two years a couple of hundred thousand dollars in back taxes." Actually, he paid almost $300,000.

The IRS is not the only creditor chasing Roy Cohn. From January 1970 to December 1977, no less than twenty-eight judgments were filed against Roy in Manhattan's state supreme court. In fourteen separate cases, judges ordered him to pay the state of New York a total of $71,392.61. In three separate judgments, he was ordered to pay the city $9,328.10. Dunhill Tailors, oil credit-card companies, a locksmith, a mechanic, a photo-offset company, a stationery store and office-supply company, temporary office workers, travel agencies, and storage companies have all filed claims against Cohn. In seeking payment, these smaller creditors must retain attorneys or bill collectors. It gets pretty expensive, particularly since Roy relishes a fight. For a relatively small bill, it's often not worth the trouble. Rather than pursue Roy, a Manhattan button store swallowed a $60 bill. Asked about these unpaid bills, Roy says that during his nine-year legal battle in New York, monies and energy were diverted to survival, "and there was a total lack of attention to other things." Again counterpunching, he says he was "a sitting duck" for predators and was hit "with a bunch of phony judgments." Today, however, "ninety to ninety-five percent of the legitimate obligations are all cleaned up," he says.

And, finally, the father of a dead young man thinks Roy "could have" plotted to murder his son. The charge relates to the mysterious sinking on the night of June 22, 1973, of the ninety-seven-foot *Defiance,* off the Florida coast. The yacht, once owned by publisher Malcolm Forbes, was leased for years by the Cohn firm from Pied Piper Yacht Charters Corporation. Though chartered and used by others, many considered it Roy's yacht.

Before the boat left the West Palm Beach Marina for New York, a number of suspicious things occurred. The local sheriff and Coast Guard had begun investigating reports that the boat was soon to be scuttled. The captain, claiming the *Defiance* was unseaworthy, refused to take her helm unless she was repaired. The owners refused, and he resigned. He was replaced by David Vogel, owner of a police record in three states, who had served time in the federal prison at Lewisburg. A member of the four-man crew, twenty-one-year-old Charles Martensen, confided to his father his foreboding that the boat was unseaworthy and might never make it to New York. Nevertheless, the boat left the marina. That night a fire broke out, and the *Defiance* went to rest on the ocean's floor. Captain Vogel and two other members of the crew jumped overboard and survived. Charles Martensen did not. According to Captain Vogel, the last person to see him alive, Charles probably got trapped in the galley while trying to silence the roaring flames.

Charles's father, L. T. Martensen, accepted the sinking as an accident—until Captain Vogel called to offer condolences. In describing the events, Vogel said that Charles and he were in the galley together when they suddenly noticed the engine room's bulkhead glowing a bright red. The senior Martensen, a former Navy man and an engineer by training, thanked the captain for his call and went to bed. At 4 A.M., he recalls, "The lights went on. Wait a minute. Bulkheads don't glow red!" Then he began to relive the conversation, convincing himself that Vogel sounded as if he had rehearsed his eyewitness account. Alarmed, Martensen went to the FBI and spent a good part of the next few years sleuthing the case, writing letters, talking to salvage experts, interviewing the crew. On July 11, 1973, he secretly taped this phone conversation with crew member Gary Tedder:

MARTENSEN: Do you have any suspicion that the fire was not started accidentally?
TEDDER: Yeah, I do. That's why I want to go up and see the FBI. . . . The FBI asked me if I thought the boat was sabotaged. I think it was.

In a letter to the Justice Department, Martensen wrote: "I am convinced that Vogel murdered Charles Martensen by gunshot prior to the arson of the vessel." He urged them to salvage the boat in order to inspect "the skeletal remains of Charley." He said it would cost about $100,000. The FBI did not salvage the boat, but it did conduct an investigation. "I must conclude," Assistant Attorney General Richard L. Thornburgh wrote Martensen on April 5, 1976, "that we have not developed such evidence as would demonstrate criminal activity with respect to either the sinking of the Yacht *Defiance* or the presumed death of your son, Charles Martensen."

The father, who speaks more softly but is no less tenacious than Cohn, remains unconvinced. On a recent visit to New York from his Michigan home, he calmly said, "I do think Cohn told them to scuttle the boat. I have no question about that." Did he believe Cohn gave the order to get rid of his suspicious son? "He could have." The motive? The $200,000 insurance policy on the yacht.

"He thinks I murdered his son?" Roy exclaimed when told of Martensen's comments. "Let's look at it this way: A, I didn't own the boat; B, I didn't get the insurance; C, the statement is an outrageous falsehood; Four, how am I going to get angry at a man who lost his son? . . . You got to feel terrible about it. I'm certainly not going to get into a name-calling contest or a criminal lawsuit against a father who lost his son. All I can tell you is that I understand his bitter feelings, and if he read someplace that I gave a party on the boat or it was my boat, even though I never met his son, never heard of his son, never hired his son, never saw his son in my entire life, and never had any insurance come to me, directly or indirectly, I'm still not a bit angry at a man who reacts emotionally. . . . Wow, when you lose a son. I couldn't be sorrier for him and for what happened."

The truth of what happened to the *Defiance* may or may not be under seventy-five feet of water. Certainly there is no evidence that I know of to charge Cohn with murder or with ordering the boat scuttled. But what of the $200,000 insurance policy? It was paid to a dummy corporation set up by Pied Piper Yacht Charters, owners of the boat—the same company whose escrow account Roy manipulated. According to court papers, part of the insurance money was dispersed to pay off the yacht's mortgage; another $15,875 went to Cohn's law firm for legal fees; another $7,100 went to the law firm as reimbursement for personal property lost on the boat; and $7,950 was paid to Cohn directly for lost property. Confronted with this information, which contradicted his earlier claims, Roy says simply, "This is possible. I'm not sure whether we were paid by the insurance company or by Pied Piper."

Roy lives comfortably, though one could never tell from his cramped ground-floor office at Saxe, Bacon & Bolan. Its walls are filled with autographed pictures, plaques, and press clippings. The gallery includes Roy whispering to McCarthy; Roy with Reggie Jackson—"To Roy, Cosell says you're wearing a piece"; Roy with a halo on the cover of an old *Esquire*; Roy on the front page of the second section of the *Times*—"Roy Cohn, at Fifty-one, Enjoys Prosperity and Controversy" reads the headline. J. Edgar Hoover, Cardinal Cooke, an American Legion plaque, and a photograph of Al Cohn are among the other items on display. Below the pictures is a small flowered couch. A desk perhaps four feet in length, its surface clean except for two piles of papers, a phone, and three flowers perched in a glass of water, is where Roy works. The desk faces a dark mirrored wall.

Cohn used to occupy the far more spacious office on the town house's fifth floor, the one with a cathedral ceiling, bar, greenhouse, where the secretary works, an outdoor patio and adjoining apartment, complete with kitchen, living room, fireplace, and loft bedroom. But Roy gave the office to Stanley Friedman when he joined the firm in early 1978. Friedman, who sports monogrammed eyeglasses, is quite comfortable there. Roy—from all accounts a generous man—is perfectly content in the basement. He spends little time in the office anyway. Meetings with clients are held in the living room on the first floor. The most striking piece of furniture in the room is Dora Cohn's former grand piano, on top of which rest autographed pictures of Ronald Reagan; Cardinal Spellman and Roy together on the *Defiance*; William F. Buckley; former Senator Everett Dirksen; and Roy's favorite aunt, Libby Marcus. The windows face East Sixty-eighth Street. Adjoining this room is a dark sitting room that opens into a drab olive-green dining room. The table is covered with a cloth and surrounded by four chairs that rest on a stained and wrinkled green-and-blue area rug with dirty white ruffles. A stark, somber Lester Johnson painting looms over the entire room. Not very cheerful, is it? I ask Roy's handsome young administrative aide Vincent Millard, an aspiring actor. "He's very glum," says Vincent. A swinging door opens to the kitchen. On the next floor there is a bedroom where Roy sleeps when in town.

After changing from his blue, vested suit, Roy appears wearing a camel's-hair sports jacket; bright orange-green-and-blue-striped shirt; fire-engine-red knitted tie with matching red woolen socks; and tassled Gucci loafers. His outfit for the Yankee game. But first he must stop and have a drink with Altemur Kilic, Turkey's deputy representative to the United Nations. The Rolls, with cocoa-brown leather seats and the RMC license plate, waits outside the Pen & Pencil restaurant. The ambassador is a large man whose only apparent flair is a goatee and mustache. He is not a smooth man capable of genuine diplomatic charm. Nor is Roy, who is too intense. But Roy is shielded by his celebrity. He orders a glass of champagne on the rocks, a side shot of Stolichnaya vodka, and half a lemon. Popping a tiny white pill from a silver box into his cocktail, Roy commences a monologue for the attentive ambassador about America's "fantastic habit of supporting our enemies and opposing our allies . . . The Panama Canal treaty was a sellout and a signal to the rest of the world that we're a bunch of patsies . . . When American leaders lose confidence in the country's goodness, forget about it . . . Here we are screaming about human rights in South Africa—the same week we give the red-carpet treatment to the Soviet Union!"

The ambassador says nothing. When Roy finishes and is about to leave, the Turk asks, "Isn't it impossible to get into Studio 54?"

"No, it's easy," Roy says. "You can go anytime you want. We represent them." The bald ambassador, who knew, blurts, "Thank you very much."

"No problem," says Roy, telling the ambassador of the time he was dining at Windows on the World with Barbara Walters and her mother, and the bouncer from Studio 54 tracked him down by phone. "We have a guy here who says he's the president of Cyprus. What should we do?" Roy asked a couple of questions, then said, "Let him in." The Turkish ambassador would never have to suffer that indignity.

• • •

As the Rolls aims for Yankee Stadium, in the Bronx, Roy is asked about his friends. "God, I have so many good friends," he answers. "I could name you fifty people." Or more. The first thing many think of when the name Roy Cohn is mentioned is *McCarthy* or even *evil.* But ask that same question of many who know him and they answer *friendship* or *loyalty.* Carmine De Sapio may no longer be leader of Tammany Hall or the Democratic party, but he still gets invited to Roy's parties. Monsignor Gustav J. Schultheiss may no longer be secretary to a cardinal, but on his seventieth birthday, recently, Roy surprised him with a party. When Abe Beame was denied his party's renomination for mayor and left City Hall, Roy continued to invite him to parties. "I hated to see Abe Beame at Roy's last birthday party," remembers Rubell. "No one was talking to him. Abe was just walking around. Mary Beame was at a table by herself. Well, Roy sat down for one hour at his own party and talked to them. He even took Mary Beame on a tour of his house. He understood their pain."

With notable exceptions—welfare mothers, for instance—Roy identifies with victims. "You'll talk to dozens of people who were on the balls of their ass and you'll find that Roy took their case gratis," says partner Friedman. "The reason is simple. He has gone through the trials and tribulations of being a victim. He knows what it is to stand alone. When he's a friend, he's a friend for life." His law firm, like his friends and clients, is part of an extended family. Tom Bolan, his partner for twenty years, allows Roy to sign his name to documents and stashes some of Roy's intemperate letters in a drawer "to cool." The firm's president, John Lang, is married to Rita, daughter of Vina Murphy, the Cohn family's former maid. The Cohns helped finance John's law-school education, as Roy now provides a paralegal job with the firm for John, Jr. Several of the firm's employees have been there for a quarter of a century, and Roy is fiercely loyal to them. "When I had my three trials, they were all there seven days and seven nights a week," he declares.

"To accept a client," says Roy, "I either have to like the client or feel they are getting a rough deal. The same kind of rough deal I got. I have to develop an equation, a community of interest with the client." Steve Rubell is a client Roy likes. "I speak to Roy about every day," Rubell says. "I call him. He calls me and asks, 'Is everything okay?' I think he thinks I'm a vulnerable person. He thinks I'm too soft." Roy's boyhood friends remain his adult friends. He takes pride in his seven godsons, contributing to their trust funds. "It is," says a disparaging former prosecutor, "right out of *Grease.* Roy never grew up. He has kept his high-school friends. When we were young, there was that same intensity of friendships Roy has today."

Like his friends, Roy's weight also remains fixed. He stays a trim 144 pounds by doing two hundred daily sit-ups and water-skiing every day but four over the last three months on Long Island Sound. Those little white pills in the silver box are saccharine tablets. Food is not important, and Roy has been known to forget to order in restaurants, preferring to pick, with his hands, at the plates of friends.

His life style is not as rooted as his friends or his weight. Roy is always jetting about the world on business. Rarely does he stay in any one place very long. He vacations each year with clients on the island of Mykonos, with the di Portanovas in Acapulco, on British investor Schlesinger's boat in the South of France. Life changed when his mother died. After returning from Washington in the mid-fifties, he lived at 1165 Park Avenue with his parents. When Al Cohn died in 1959, Roy remained devoted to his mother, sharing the apartment and enjoying the breakfasts she made for him each morning before she died in 1967. "His life style changed completely when his mother died," thinks Bill Fugazy. "Roy was closest to his mother. She gave stability to his life. There was a lot of entertaining at home. His father and mother were two superb human beings. Now Roy spends time in Europe. He flies over for a day." He relaxes at Studio 54, Yankee games, or luncheons with socialites.

Roy's liberal, jet-setting life style doesn't square with his conservative politics. It is just one of many contradictions. He hates "stuffed shirts" yet befriends and represents several of that species. He can be a cold-hearted executioner—and a warm-hearted friend. He blasts "canaries" like Joe Valachi and John Dean who rat on their friends but has no sympathy for Dashiell Hammett, who refused to finger his Communist friends for the House Un-American Activities Committee. His heroes include such conservative icons as J. Edgar Hoover, William F. Buckley, Barry Goldwater, and Douglas MacArthur, yet his claimed friends include such liberals as Paul O'Dwyer, Herman Badillo, and Fred Friendly, producer of the Edward R. Murrow special that did so much to defang Senator McCarthy. He abhors "Nazi-like tactics" of law-enforcement officials who prosecuted him, professes support for the American Civil Liberties Union and those defendants' rights promulgated by the Warren Court—yet blindly supports FBI officials who used such tactics and violated those rights. He is a self-proclaimed "cynic" who nevertheless calls many of his cases "causes." He enjoys a near-photographic memory yet has a curious propensity to forget important facts.

To discuss some of these contradictions, the afternoon after the Yankees won their game, Roy allows me to join him on the town house's patio. The "lousy weather bureau," as he calls it, had predicted rain, so he canceled water-skiing and a late swim in his heated Greenwich pool. But now the sun is shining, so he removes the camel's-hair sports jacket and powder-blue LaCoste shirt, revealing solid arms and shoulders and an even bronze tan, front and back. "Just wait a second," he asks, grabbing a deck chair and pushing it into a corner facing the sun, spinning the top of a jar of specially prepared suntan cream and rubbing liberal doses on his face, neck, and shoulders.

Just as Roy closes his eyes, the phone rings. "Tell the judge that's fine," he thanks federal judge John Cannella's law clerk. Roy is seeking to goose along a new trial motion for former Congressman Frank Brasco, who served a prison sentence for conspiring to accept payoffs from mobsters and who is a personal favorite of Brooklyn leader Meade Esposito. Roy is shepherding the case as a favor to his friend Meade, as he handled George Steinbrenner's appeal to baseball commissioner Bowie Kuhn when the Yankee owner was suspended because of a criminal conviction.

Is it true that the IRS has a lien on all his earnings? "I'm not really clear on that," he surprisingly answers. "I don't think they have a lien on any of my earnings." Handed a twenty-two-page court document—Notice of Tax Lien—from the IRS, itemizing two decades of back taxes owed by Cohn and his firm, he leafs through it and blithely declares, "This is a routine thing. It's no big deal." A big deal, he says, would be if IRS had placed him under "a jeopardy assessment, which means they grab everything you have." Is the reason they do not grab everything because he owns nothing? Not the house in Connecticut or New York, not the shirt off his back or the red-white-and-blue socks with stars he now has on his feet? Is it true that he expenses everything to his firm to avoid the tax collector?

Ridiculous, he responds. His answer is only half true. Roy says his salary ranges between $75,000 and $100,000 annually from the law firm—not a lot for a man who brings in an estimated $1.5 million in legal business each year. "We have an enormous overhead," Roy explains. "And I have no need for it." One reason they have a tremendous overhead is Roy's expenses. Besides owning the town house—technically owned by the 39 East Sixty-eighth Street Corporation—the firm pays part of the rent for Roy's Greenwich house, owns the three cars Roy uses—the 1957 Rolls, a deep-green 1952 Bentley with white upholstery and license plate *ROY C,* a 1978 white Cadillac convertible—and pays for his phones and most of his meals. Were his expenses $100,000 a year? Roy says that's way too low but refuses to provide a figure. A former associate claims they are between $300,000 and $400,000. "My life is ninety-nine percent intertwined with my clients. My social life is intertwined with my clients," says Roy. "My life is ninety-nine-percent business."

The law firm, incorporated three years ago, also carries more than a $1-million life insurance policy on Roy and has just introduced a profit-sharing plan for its members. In addition to his salary and profit-sharing, Roy's arrangement with the firm permits him to retain any business "I try outside of New York and Connecticut" and any earnings from writings, including a book on divorce he hopes to finish soon. Business investments, he says, are limited to Florida real estate. As for incidentals: "I pay for my clothes. I pay for food." Isn't it true that by relying so heavily on expenses, he is slipping the IRS? "I don't know. Partly," he admits. Then why is Roy any different from Henry Ford, whom he accuses of using corporate funds for his personal benefit? "The expenses they pay for Henry Ford were his personal expenses," he says. "The only thing the company pays for me is for entertaining and retaining business." And for using the car to take him to Yankee games.

This is not chiseling in Roy's mind. He knows he is not a greedy man. Even as a boy he would plop money on a desk and anyone who wanted it could take it. He forgets to bill clients; is generous to his godchildren and law associates. Unlike many prominent men, he notices and is kind to doormen, chauffeurs, little people. But Roy feels government was and is out to screw him. They persecute him. Cost him a lot of money and heartache. Besides, it is a contest, a battle of wits. Roy pictures himself as the populist, the little guy taking on the establishment. He is incapable of making a connection between what he does and what he accused Henry Ford of because Ford is a big shot, a country-club type, a guy born with a silver spoon in his mouth. Even though Roy was born to wealth—the Marcus family owned businesses that evolved into Van Heusen clothes—and benefited from connections, he sees himself as a victim. Even when he was counsel to McCarthy and compelling a fair number of people to cower, including President Eisenhower and the Republican and Democratic party establishments, Roy saw himself and McCarthy as victims. *They* got him and McCarthy in the fifties. *They* tried to get him in the sixties. And now he is getting back. Justice—western style.

Roy's concept of loyalty is not unlike that of a mob chieftain. "From the standpoint of my own personal moral code, I can think of no circumstances under which I would testify against a friend," he says, pushing back the chair to stay in the sun, which is sinking behind the roof. "Life is too short."

What if the friend did something wrong?

"What, selling heroin? I wouldn't represent someone who I believe sold heroin . . . The moral judgment I make is that I will not handle the hard-drug case; except if the person is guilty, I will negotiate the plea whereby the person admits his guilt and goes in and pleads guilty."

Let's say you were Frank Serpico and your buddy on the police force was on the take. The Knapp Commission investigating police corruption asks you about it. What do you say?

"And this was a very good friend of mine?" says Roy. "I'd quit. I'd quit the police force."

But you can't quit the human race. What would you say to the commission?

"I'd do everything I could to avoid—er, I wouldn't lie under any circumstances. But I'd do everything I could, within the bounds of legal propriety, not to hurt someone whose friendship I had accepted."

Even if they had committed a dishonorable act?

"Well, when you get down to the question of a dishonorable act . . . unless it's something heinous, like the killing of a cop or an innocent person or hard drugs or something like that, I don't consider myself a one-man ombudsman."

Isn't that a cynical attitude?

"Yes, I'm very cynical, there's no question about it. That's why I was cynical about Watergate. I mean, I've seen this stuff all around in every political situation for years and years. And it's another thing that engendered a degree of sympathy on my part for a guy like Nixon, who was born in a log cabin. Because I know that the alternative political campaign costs enormous amounts of money. Cash contributions exist, I suppose. Always will, I suppose. And when you pillory a guy who never had anything and worked his way up . . . you're sort of leaving the world to the Rockefellers and the Kennedys, whose acts of theft are barred by the statute of limitations. So I am a cynic."

But wasn't Nixon deficient in character?

"Not only character but deficient in judgment. I mean, that he kept those tapes, which they didn't have to make in the first place, is a little bit off. What was the deficiency in Nixon's character? You mean the fact that he didn't turn in Mitchell and Haldeman and Ehrlichman? Did President Eisenhower turn in Sherman Adams? Did Lyndon Johnson turn in Bobby Baker? Did Jack Kennedy turn in Judge Morrissey? Yes, I am a cynic . . . I think Nixon's deficiencies were magnified out of proportion, particularly by comparison with the up until then accepted norm. Does Carter have deficiencies because he spent three months taking a totally indefensible position in supporting Bert Lance and coming out with nonsensical statements like 'Everybody in America overdraws,' when you were talking about an overdraft of almost half a million dollars on a noninterest-paying basis —which anybody else would go away for five years if they did something like that? So I just don't see where Nixon's character deficiencies dwarf those of his predecessors or successors."

Using his feet, Roy jams the chair against the doorway to catch the final moments of the sun's rays. Except for his face, shade blankets his entire body. Conceding that past Presidents employed dirty tricks and, in effect, covered for their friends, as Carter did for Lance, Roy is asked whether the American public doesn't have a right to expect higher ethical standards from its Presidents.

"It apparently doesn't work very well, does it? Because Nixon's successor is Carter. Do you see a real difference between Bert Lance and . . ."

But, Roy, Carter blindly defended his friend, he didn't engage in a criminal cover-up, did he?

". . . It may be a matter of gradation."

It's a grubby world, Roy thinks. With the exception of his extended family of friends and associates, it's all a jungle out there. "The reason I love dogs," he says, "is that you know they're sincere." Roy's life-sharing experiences with the outside world teach that it is composed of hostile forces —the Rosenbergs and other spies when he was a young prosecutor; Communists and dupes when he was with McCarthy; the federal government when he was brought to trial in the sixties. His life has been consumed by controversy, fights, feuds. The attacks against Roy Cohn by his enemies have sometimes been no less vicious than his. Therefore: Everyone lies, smears, covers up, protects his friends. The rules of the game don't count as much as winning, which explains the ease Roy has in describing how he would have defended President Nixon:

"Oh, it would have been a cinch," he responds. "Get rid of the tapes. I mean, that takes exactly five minutes. You know, very simple: Did you have a legal requirement to make tapes in the first place? No, it was just my idea, you know, for historical purposes, so on and so forth. So since you weren't required to make them in the first place and there's nothing which requires you to keep them, get rid of them."

How would you answer the charge that you are destroying evidence?

"Because at that point it wasn't evidence. At that point they weren't under subpoena or anything else." Roy gave similar advice to a political client who, he says, "had done something embarrassing and kept a detailed account of it in a diary." Roy told him to "burn it," deep-six it. If the prosecutor asked about the diary? "The answer is yes," he quickly retorted. "But on advice of counsel, I got rid of it. Why'd you get rid of it? Because my counsel said I was under no legal obligation to keep the diary, and that the diary was subject to misinterpretation . . ."

Does he represent people he knows are guilty?

"Not really. Not really. I think I'd be the worst person in the world to represent somebody I believe was *morally guilty.* In other words, you can take the Salerno tax case. It was an expenditures case proving, you know, he spent this much money. Here's a fella who was a gambler. I suppose ninety-eight percent of gamblers . . . don't file income taxes. Period. Tony Salerno never misfiled an income tax in his life. He paid more taxes than any President of the United States."

Do you believe he paid taxes on all his earnings?

"I don't know. But I'll tell you, frankly, no gambler knows what his exact earnings are. Knowing Tony Salerno, I would think he couldn't. I would think the best he could do is estimate. He's very heavy into sports betting and stuff like that, and I don't think he'd actually know."

But except in Las Vegas, sports betting and bookmaking are illegal.

"He, er, wasn't charged with sports betting."

You just said he was "into sports betting." It's illegal.

"So it's illegal. . . . You mean it's illegal for me to bet on a game?"

Most gambling in this country is controlled by organized crime. The profits from this business are poured into such activities as drugs, infiltration of legitimate businesses, shylocking. And Tony Salerno? According to Joseph Veyvoda, chief of Organized Crime Control for the New York City Police Department, Salerno is a kingpin of organized crime: "He goes into more than gambling. He's into loan-sharking and taking over legitimate businesses. He's damn close to the top." Sure, everyone deserves a legal defense, even Tony Salerno. But Roy and our most prominent criminal lawyers, while parroting this truth, choose to ignore another: Their fees are made possible by extortion, drugs, murder.

The sun disappears, and so does Roy. Cooperative, perhaps enjoying the game, he invites me to join him for breakfast the next morning. Every day he is in New York, Cohn holds court in the town house's dining room. Elvira, his cook of fourteen years, prepares the same breakfast every day —a lump of cream cheese or farmer cheese, three strips of well-done bacon, and an iced tea with lemon. Members of the firm appear to review office business with Roy, who is dressed informally. Usually he dons a bright-gold silk robe. On this morning, he is resplendent in a pink cotton shirt open at the neck, chocolate-brown twill slacks, and loafers. A phone, with Steinbrenner on the other end, is cradled to his ear. First they discuss a legal matter. Then Ron Guidry. Everyone, including Billy Martin, is second-guessing whether manager Bob Lemon should have altered the pitching rotation to save Guidry for a possible play-off game with Boston. Roy just asks questions.

Young associates trickle in. They do not look like Wall Street lawyers. Their suits tend toward plaids; their shirts, to patterns and darker colors; their ties leap at you. Several speak with the rich accents of New York's streets and wear pinkie rings. Roy is proud that he is the only Ivy League (Columbia) lawyer in the firm. He says he won't hire any, since they "lack common sense" and the "toughness" that comes from kids who struggled and worked their way through school. They pepper Roy with questions about legal maneuvers, drafts of letters to people they are about to sue. He fields them like a shortstop, shooting back answers and flicking his hands up and down as if they were flapping fans attached to his wrists. What should be done, asks one of the attorneys, about producer Jon Peters, who did not give their client, photographer Rebecca Blake, sufficient photo credits in his movie *Eyes of Laura Mars*? "What can we do to break his balls?" Roy shoots back.

Don't mess with Roy Cohn.

This is quintessential Cohn. Be tough, always attack. Don't apologize, except for what he calls "technical" mistakes—style, not substance. Like his admitted mistake of appearing "arrogant" and "smart-alecky" before the Army-McCarthy hearings in 1954, when questioned about his threat "to wreck the Army" if they did not give favored treatment to his buddy David Schine. Ditto his criticism of Spiro Agnew's resignation. Or Richard Nixon's. Or the questions raised in court about his legal ethics. Or his current defense of J. Wallace LaPrade and FBI officials who broke the law —"Nothing these men did was not well-intentioned," he says. The focus is on form, not content.

But is Roy Cohn so different from other lawyers, including those who enjoy wrinkling their noses at him? In one sense he is. Roy is more extreme, less wary of overstepping moral boundaries, crasser, less refined, and more candid. On the other hand, his cynicism is taught in the most respectable law schools. Lawyers are supposed to be essentially amoral; advocates, not judges; to represent a client, not the truth; to create a reasonable doubt, even if you have none; to turn a trick for a fee—doing whatever is necessary, short of breaking the law yourself, to protect a client.

That otherwise distinguished jurist Oliver Wendell Holmes wrote: "For my own part, I often doubt whether it would not be a gain if every word of moral significance could be banished from the law altogether."

Edward Bennett Williams, whom Roy and others consider the *finest trial lawyer* in America, seemed to agree in Jimmy Hoffa's 1957 bribery trial. The government had a strong case, and a potent witness, John Cheasty, who testified that Hoffa offered riches if he would join a congressional investigating committee and smuggle him confidential memos. As Hoffa's defense attorney, Williams's task was to undermine Cheasty's credibility. He succeeded in black Washington, D.C., where eight of the twelve jurors were black, by smearing Cheasty as anti-black, accusing him of once trying to bust up the Alabama bus boycott. As Williams knew, even if true, the accusations were irrelevant to the trial. But, as he cynically suspected, they would not be deemed irrelevant by the jurors. Nor would the surprise appearance of Joe Louis as a character witness. Hoffa was acquitted. Roy pulled similar tricks with Catholic jurors in his trials, inviting Ned Spellman, nephew of the cardinal, to be a character witness. Every time a lawyer advises his client to preface his testimony with "To the best of my knowledge" or some other hedge, as likely as not he is being true to Holmes's accepted wisdom.

As Mr. J. P. Morgan once harrumphed, "I do not want a lawyer to tell me what I cannot do. I hire him to tell me how to do what I want to do." In China, no such questions are asked. Disgusted with lawyers who defended dynastic landlords, China has simply banned the domestic practice of law.

Whatever complaints or judgments are registered against Cohn, no bar association has ever banned him. Evil he may be, but as Roy reminds visitors, he is a member in good standing. Like an outlaw, Roy may have some notches in his gun, but no one has dared ask him to leave town.

SECOND THOUGHTS

Writer Tom Morgan once told me that when he worked on a Cohn profile for *Esquire* in the mid-sixties, he found himself sitting and staring at the typewriter for twenty-four straight hours. He had done his reporting, organized his information, outlined his piece. Yet he kept heaving pages into the wastebasket. Tom had writer's block. He had difficulty purging the hatred he felt for Cohn. Exhausted, he lumbered off to see *Hiroshima Mon Amour.* Somehow this beautiful and harrowing movie calmed him. Returning to the typewriter, Tom banged out a tough but fair profile, one that to this day holds up well.

Tom Morgan understood that with a controversial character like Cohn, it is too easy to kick him in the balls. Cohn-haters would cheer, Cohn-lovers would boo. And few would read it because they'd either heard it all before or because they didn't trust the reporter. The notion of trust is worth a word because it is central to a journalist's work. We get people to cooperate with us in gathering news or, more important, in doing a profile, because we gain their trust. If Roy Cohn or Ed Koch thought I set out to "do a hatchet job," I would have learned much less about them. So trust is important to the process of gathering information. But it is also crucial to the final product. With non-polemic writing, readers should trust the reporter, have confidence that he or she is not scoring ideological points, holding back information, twisting facts.

People like Roy Cohn present an interesting journalistic challenge. I took pleasure, frankly, struggling to escape the contempt I felt for Cohn, trying to see Cohn as he saw himself, as friends saw him. My starting question was not What do I think of Roy Cohn? but rather, What is Roy Cohn like? My starting assumption was that anyone who would take several months to profile is too complex to be rendered as a cardboard cut-out character. If a writer wishes to sketch cartoons or proselytize, he should write comic books or seek public office. Exhortation is boring; explanation rarely is. Or as Samuel Johnson admonished critics some centuries ago: "Don't *attitudinize.*" Although I did not set out to *get* Roy Cohn, I also did not wish to write an antiseptically "balanced" profile. Unavoidably, Cohn emerged as more than a monster.

Some readers told me they found themselves liking the Cohn I described; others hated him. Again, readers seize and retain those facts or qualities that matter most to them. A couple of successful businessmen said they came away respecting Cohn's ruthlessness and amorality, which they thought practical. Other readers were repelled by his ethical blindness or his past association with Joseph McCarthy. Some appreciated his loyalty to friends; others detested his disloyalty to values. The most common praise was that the profile was "fair"; the most common criticism, that it was "too fair."

On balance, I think I wrote it the right way. But I do have doubts. The flaw in so detached an approach is that in striving to be fair, to paint a complex portrait, one which places the subject rather than the writer at center stage, I may not have communicated adequately what a truly awful man Roy Cohn is. The accumulation of positive as well as negative evidence may tend to work to the disadvantage of someone you basically respect (Mayor Koch) and to the advantage of someone you don't (like Roy Cohn).

Accept the premise of a rounded profile, of explaining the subject's view of himself—the notion that a good profile, unlike a good short column, should have texture and space to escape a single, sharp point of view—and Cohn can't emerge all bad. He becomes more appealing simply because readers are surprised to find that he has *any* virtues at all. The sum of the parts is greater than the whole.

Some further ironies: I thought the overall effect of the profile—reviewing the multiple court judgments against Cohn, his failure to pay bills, his sloppy legal work, his lack of an intellectual or ethical anchor, the money he receives to defend mobsters, his lust to "kill" adversaries—was devastating. Some readers did not agree. I was reproached by friends for failing to *get* Cohn. Several victims of McCarthyism complained that I should have printed innuendo about Cohn's personal life; in effect, should have pulled a Cohn on Cohn.

Finally, the attention was good for Cohn's law practice. Most citizens of this republic would be personally mortified and professionally damaged by such publicity. Not Cohn. As I noted in the profile, he is a paid "killer." The nastier he appears, the greater his attraction to clients wishing to punish someone. When the issue of the magazine appeared, Cohn dispatched his Rolls-Royce to *Esquire* to collect a bundle of copies. One of his partners phoned me to say thanks. An old friend called to ask if I would intercede and ask Cohn to represent him in a nasty litigation against a punk-rock group he managed. Liz Smith, the gossip columnist, reported that Cohn was stalking about the Beverly Hills Hotel denouncing the profile as "a hatchet job."

A few weeks later I received an invitation to attend Cohn's annual birthday party at Studio 54. I skipped it, but concluded that Cohn was not upset. I wish he were.

The Last Angry Principal

New York, May 3, 1976

Long Island City High School, in Queens, has changed little since it opened in 1905. Unlike many city high schools, its walls are unmarred by graffiti, its windowpanes are intact, its 3,018 students file through the corridors in an orderly fashion, ask permission to go to the bathroom, dress neatly, and keep their mouths shut.

This is Dr. Howard Hurwitz's school. A short, bald, paunchy, dogmatic, arbitrary, intelligent, concerned, conservative, tough man, Hurwitz has ruled this school for the past ten years. And the stable, predominantly working-class Catholic and Greek community, which is struggling to retain its neighborhood and values, wants his reign to continue.

"This is like school was twenty-five years ago," enthusiastically exclaims one parent, Janet Adler. The principal tries to keep it that way. In 1970 the Board of Education asked him to distribute a students'-rights handbook. Hurwitz refused. In 1973 the board asked him to distribute an ethnic census. Hurwitz refused. Last year he refused to allow a student to publish an article on students' rights in the school newspaper because he thought it inaccurate and irresponsible. And this year he became the first New York City high-school principal ever to be suspended when he defied the Board of Education and refused to readmit to his school a seventeen-year-old girl he considered "disruptive." When the board won a court order to evict Hurwitz from the school, a clear majority of the school's parents and students, rising to his defense, barricaded and closed the school.

It is Thursday morning, March 25, and outside Long Island City High School several hundred parents and students—most of them white—remain from the larger group which had demonstrated in support of Dr. Hurwitz. Their voices are worn thin from shouting all morning. "You want to know the story here?" says Eileen Hinden. "My son Steven doesn't mind giving up a little freedom for a lot of security." A crowd forms. "Without Dr. Hurwitz this place would be a jungle," says Debbie Cannizzaro, a senior. "My uncle used to get beat up here. Hurwitz came in and now you can walk in the school and be safe."

A sign addressed to Board of Education Chancellor Irving Anker is perched atop the school's spiked fence: ANKER SIT ON IT. Directly across from that sign is the main entrance to the school. Like border guards, a delegation of parents carefully check my press credentials before granting passage down the corridor that leads to the principal's office. To the right is a large coffee urn and homemade sandwiches and cake for the parents who have guarded the school, in shifts, for three days and nights. To the left, a large bench is jammed in front of a door, with maybe thirty parents parked in front of it.

"We don't want to let him out of the building," explains Jeannette Pfeiffer, vice-president of the Ditmars Community Association. Her daughter recently graduated.

"He stands for discipline in the school. If this is allowed to happen here, what will happen to other schools?" asks Janet Adler. "This has become a cause. The middle-class community is finally standing up. We pay all the taxes. It's our school."

Inside the principal's office, gathered around a low kindergarten table, sit a priest, several community leaders, parents, students, former students, and Dr. Hurwitz. The drapes are drawn; the bare black couch where Hurwitz has slept for two nights is in one corner. In another is a bottle of Barolo wine, a pot of hot coffee, some cake. The walls are littered with eleven framed newspaper clippings—AMERICA'S TOUGHEST PRINCIPAL screams one headline—artwork, and separate and unanimous New York State Senate and Assembly resolutions commending Dr. Hurwitz.

Dr. Hurwitz is staring at a lump of cottage cheese, dried lettuce, and rye toast—his lunch. Two young girls enter the office to tell of the recent meeting of QUALICAP, the local community-action agency whose education affiliate, the Education Action Program, is defending the young girl Hurwitz suspended.

"I'll explain what's going on," says Dr. Hurwitz.

"Eat first. Eat," pleads senior cheerleader Rosemary Monaco.

"QUALICAP's been trying to get me dismissed for years," continues Hurwitz, poking with his fork at the cottage cheese. "I suspended the girl because she was disruptive. Then the superintendent gave me an order to bring her back. I said, 'You can't give me that order.' Suppose I was at My Lai and the lieutenant ordered me to shoot people? As luck would have it, it happens to be a black girl." (Ten percent of his students are black; 19 percent are Hispanic.)

Dr. Hurwitz is becoming more expansive: "This girl became so threatening and so abusive that I couldn't run the school with her here."

His secretary, Eva Stern, sticks her head into the room to tell Dr. Hurwitz that he has another press call. Father Fahy, assistant pastor of St. Patrick's Church, picks up the conversation: "The issue is the right of students to have an education. Parents really think it's their last stand."

"This is it," says Rosemary Monaco. "If you have a disruptive person, it's hard to get your point out. In junior high school I was afraid. Now I forget what it was like, after four years here."

Dr. Hurwitz hangs up the phone and picks up the conversation: "I feel it's impossible to run a school from this office. The kids have got to know you. You've got to be in the boys' toilet four to six times a day. I walk around with my recording device and dictate maybe twenty memos a day. I give my teachers three days, maybe one day, to answer. I have my Xeroxed copy, and if I don't get an answer, I send them my copy and I write 'Well?' Then I get an answer." He is smiling now, that tight-lipped smile that looks as if he's making a face.

Nettie Hurwitz is on the phone from home. She tells her husband she is worried. "My pension isn't jeopardized!" he bellows back at her. WINS Radio is on the other line, wanting to conduct an interview. Dr. Hurwitz speaks of the suspended girl as having "severe emotional problems."

"I'm going to put a hundred thousand dollars on the line," he tells his interviewer, "and I want it matched by the Civil Liberties Union. That's a standing offer. I want it matched"—he whacks the desk. "In cash, not in city bonds. Let them say this is a model student. I'll go for two hundred thousand dollars. I'm willing to go five hundred thousand in cash. Model student? My God!"

That night, after extended negotiations with Board of Education officials, City Councilman Peter Vallone, executive chairman of the Astoria Civic Association, reports that a compromise has been reached and the school can open Friday morning. "The board gets to say that Dr. Hurwitz is under suspension," explains Vallone, "and Hurwitz gets the satisfaction that he's still in school. The girl comes back and gets protection."

"You got a pass?" Hurwitz calls out to a student at eight o'clock Friday morning. His hands are on his hips and he is in the hall watching as his students quietly file by on their way to class. But Dr. Hurwitz is being watched as well. WABC-TV and its cameras are there; the *New York Times*, the *Daily News*, WHN. Dr. Hurwitz jogs back to his office to take a call from Danny Meenan of WMCA Radio. Suddenly he is shouting and slams the phone down. "No more calls," he commands Mrs. Stern.

"Where's Gerry?" Hurwitz asks, darting from his office toward Gerry Nozilo, a member of the Astoria Civic Association, who is by the main entrance. "Anker denies any agreement's been made," Hurwitz tells him. "You better get in touch with Vallone."

They retreat to the principal's office, where Gerry gets on the phone to round up "the troops," as he calls them. Dr. Hurwitz is seated at the conference table, softly saying what a disciplined, orderly community this is, that the Mafia used to be very big here and that many of its second- and third-generation families have now gone legitimate. But its power remains. If Irving Anker presses this community, Hurwitz warns, they'll kill him. Gerry darts for the door, pausing to say, "Okay, I have to round up the troops. If Anker closes this school, he's through." Dr. Hurwitz looks at me knowingly.

He goes back outside to patrol the corridor. Passing students, teachers, and parents offer their warm congratulations. "This is nothing short of insanity, to destroy this education program to get Hurwitz," Hurwitz says to a group of reporters. Doug Johnson of WABC-TV returns from phoning the Board of Education and reports that as far as they are concerned the original agreement holds. At 9 A.M. Dr. Hurwitz goes to his office to receive a phone call. Five minutes later he comes back out and says, "It looks good. It looks like a minor misunderstanding."

By Tuesday of the following week Dr. Hurwitz had received a tall stack of letters from people all around the country—letters from scared teachers, fellow principals, elementary-school children, former students, concerned parents.

In them the words *courage* and *discipline* are repeated often. Isabel Diguisto sent him a telegram: HOLD THE FORT, LAST OUTPOST OF CIVILIZATION. A pained father from Oceanside, Long Island, wrote that his son "would be alive today" if his Boardman Junior High School principal had had the guts to suspend the "punk" who beat his son. Most black parents probably think of the white middle class as the establishment. It is startling to read letter after letter from white middle-class people who perceive themselves as powerless and as bucking the "establishment."

Aware that the press had studiously avoided interviewing the girl (the New York *Post*'s James Wechsler and, later, *The Village Voice*'s Nat Hentoff would come to be exceptions), I asked to speak with her. Miss Bernice Lyons, executive director of QUALICAP, directed me to the office of Elaine Keith, director of its Education Action Program. Unlike Miss Lyons, Miss Keith (a white woman) had met Hurwitz. She entered his school in late 1970, accompanying a parent whose son was about to be expelled. Dr. Hurwitz immediately had her arrested for trespassing. (She was convicted, but the case was dismissed on appeal.)

Miss Keith was having lunch at the Galaxy, a restaurant near the school. I entered the restaurant with some impressions of the young girl and the incident which had led to her suspension. She had received forty-three citations of school misbehavior over a three-year period. Eva Stern, secretary to Dr. Hurwitz, had explained that the climactic incident took place in the teachers' room. "She had a heated argument with Miss Young, not me, about *Ebony* magazine," said Mrs. Stern. "She asked me who the hell did I think I was, asking her for her pass. It wasn't what she said, it was the way she said it. The way she yelled and screamed." Miss Wilhelmina Young, an assistant principal—who is black—recalled the incident slightly differently. She was passing the teachers' room and saw that the girl and Mrs. Stern were having words, so she intervened and told the girl to put the magazine away. What did the girl say? "Nothing," said Miss Young. Was the girl aggressive? "No, no. But I knew from the tone of what her response was that it was important to intervene." Miss Young further explained that "I see her two periods a day" and "she can be disruptive in that she does not follow orders . . . she'll shrug her shoulders at you, roll her eyes. You say, 'Sit up,' and she'll take her time."

Mrs. Laura Goldner, the school's assistant principal, acknowledged that the girl was not violent, but said, "There have been instances of insubordination." The dean of girls, Sallie Shulman, said that she and the other two deans had repeated difficulties with her. Sometimes the girl was "adorable," she said, and other times "she refused to answer my call slips." Carl Berlin, executive assistant to the Queens High School superintendent, has studied her official school record and said she was neither a violent nor a threatening person, though she was not a model student.

Of the fifteen or so black students interviewed, perhaps half thought the incident was racially motivated; the rest did not. None of the fifty or so white students thought it was.

Clearly, the girl was not an extreme child. Why then, Dean Shulman was asked, did the school take the extreme step of suspending her from school? "We consider a child to be a severe problem if he doesn't follow the rules of common decency," she replied. "I was standing at the front door this morning and a boy walked in with a hat on. I asked him to take it off. It sets a tone. Youngsters in this school ask permission to go to the bathroom. In the lunchroom when everyone leaves they pick up their lunch and throw their garbage away."

The girl, a pretty, light-skinned seventeen-year-old with a big dimple and an even bigger smile, was having lunch at the Galaxy with six white women from the Education Action Program. She is not quite five-feet-one, though she looks taller because of a full, neat Afro. She sports a dark-blue gauze jacket, navy-blue shirt, clean dungarees, and Earth shoes. Thin silver looped earrings reached down, almost touching the handsome white stones that curled around her neck. Was this the monster who one parent had warned "carries a knife"?

She was scheduled to graduate in three months, she said, hoping to go on to New York Community College to study to become a dental technician. She is one of six children—one of her older brothers would later stop by the Action center just to see that his kid sister was okay. Right now she was doing fine, munching on a hamburger and French fries.

What caused the incident that led to her suspension? She said that in February she had volunteered to pick up the mail for her home-economics teacher, Mrs. Rita Bassuck. On March 3 "I had to wait for the other monitor to put the mail in the boxes. It was in the general office. *Ebony* magazine was lying on the desk and while waiting I started browsing through it. The secretary, Mrs. Stern, asked me to put it down. She told me if I wanted to read *Ebony,* I should go to the library and read it there. I put it down. I didn't say anything to her. I then went to the teachers' box and picked up the mail. She stopped me and asked me who I was. I told her who I was and what my homeroom was. Neither of us shouted. I just left. The next day I was back in the office picking up the mail and, um, she asked me did I have permission to be in the teachers' mailbox? I told her yeah. So she wanted to see my pass. I didn't have any pass with me. I explained that she could call Mrs. Bassuck and she would explain. She said she was going to call Miss Young [the assistant principal]. I told her to call Mrs. Bassuck, and I left." She said no voices were raised.

"The next day," she continued, "the dean of girls [Mrs. Shulman] came to get me. She told me to follow her to Dr. Hurwitz's office. When I sat down he said, 'I have here a number of things you've been doing in school. You've got to control your temper. You're being expelled by the superintendent. . . .' I asked him why he was suspending me. He said I was being kicked out and he wouldn't discuss it with me, he'd discuss it with my mother."

Was this her first run-in at the school? No, she responded. "I had a couple of incidents." Was she wrong? "Most of the time," she said. "Mostly because I was late for classes."

Was this incident racially motivated? She paused and thought, then said, "No, I think he'd do it to anybody. He doesn't care what color you are."

Howard Hurwitz, who has lived in the same Tudor-style Jamaica, Queens, house for twenty years and has sat on the same eighteenth-century English couch for thirty-four, putters about in an ancient round-collared, saddle-stitched navy-blue shirt and bruised brown penny loafers. "There's no contemporary furniture in this house," announced Nettie Hurwitz, his wife of thirty-four years, as her Howard relaxed at home one recent night and talked about the past.

He graduated from Brooklyn College in 1936, earned an M.A. from Columbia University in 1937 and a Ph.D. in political science from Columbia in 1943. He was a teacher in city schools from 1938 to 1953, then an assistant principal for thirteen years at Manual Training and Jamaica high schools. In 1966 he became the principal at Long Island City. He has written eleven books, including *An Encyclopedic Dictionary of American History,* as well as countless articles and pamphlets. Most of these are aimed at puncturing what he feels is the permissive attitude rampant in schools and society.

He thinks of the past more fondly. "I was in the fifth grade with Mrs. Sheppard," he recalled. "I always got an 'A' for deportment. I sat in front of the teacher. Well, I was sitting there with my hands clasped and someone dropped a pencil. So Mrs. Sheppard walked over and cracked *me* in the face. I didn't say anything. I figured if she hit me, there must be some reason. I got home at the end of the day and said, 'Mom, I got slapped by Mrs. Sheppard and I don't know why.' . . . I think the reason I did not get upset was that I loved her. She was beautiful. She dressed nice. In those days the teachers dressed nicely. *You can put that down.* The tone of schools has changed."

But Howard Hurwitz hasn't changed. He attacks the idea that schools are and must be a reflection of society, and dismisses the idea that people

are mere products of their environment. "I'm not an economic determin-
ist," he states. "I believe that with the right leadership our school system
would not have been ruined. . . . There isn't a school system in the United
States of America that I couldn't straighten out, given a nucleus of good
teachers. Could I take over any school in New York if I were a younger
man? You bet I could.

"What would I do if I were principal of the worst high school?" he asks.
"First I would establish my authority. I would learn from the deans who
the most serious offenders were. I would interview them in my office, notify
the parents, and suspend them. I would call the captain of the precinct and
have him over for lunch. I would not, except under extreme circumstances,
arrest a student. I would suspend perhaps twenty students. I could then
straighten out the rest." What of the students' right to a high-school education? He makes a face: "The Hurwitz philosophy is that no child should
remain in the school system who is disruptive."

Society's definition of the disruptive child may have changed, but not
Howard Hurwitz's: "A disruptive child is anyone who interferes with the
education of others. Period. It could range from knifing someone to whis-
tling . . . Where you don't have order you do not have learning." He
condemns the now-common view that kids—black, Puerto Rican, Italo-
American—respond better if taught by one of their own. "You've got to find
a good strong man regardless of color. I didn't have a Jewish teacher as a
kid. I never thought about it. My mother certainly didn't go down and say,
'We need a Jewish teacher for my Howard.' "

He plunges into his favorite topic—the bureaucrats at the Board of
Education who he feels have destroyed the school system. "In the old days
when I was a teacher," he remembers, "you had to establish your authority.
There are not too many teachers like that now, so you have to have principals behind the teacher, since there is no superintendent behind the principal. We have the weakest group of high-school superintendents in the
history of the school system. Can you imagine an Irving Anker, with the
charisma of a rabbit—put that in quotes—running the largest school system
in the world?"

"The problem with Hurwitz is that he's a little sick," states Deputy
Chancellor Bernard Gifford. Board of Education President Isaiah Robinson
has publicly compared him to Hitler. Even one of Hurwitz's most prominent local supporters privately worries that "Howard could be dangerous.
One thing bothers me more than lawlessness, and that's too much law. You
don't have a crime problem in the Soviet Union because they shoot you. He
once told a kid he'd suspend him for slouching in his seat in the auditorium."

Hurwitz picks at his chicken. Nettie urges him to eat. Instead, he remi-
nisces about a principal he once admired: a tough disciplinarian who motivated his brightest students to new heights and into Harvard. But this

principal ignored all but the smartest students, he said. "He never had my heart. He never had my retarded son."

Donald, his son, is now thirty-two. He is, according to a 1973 book by his father, "a high-grade moron." Donald has lived with his mother and father all these years. And though his mother sometimes wanted to give up and even send Donald off to an institution, Howard Hurwitz drove his only child the way he now drives his students.

"Donald has never been capable of the kind of reasoning—the gathering of facts and the weighing of alternatives—that is essential to making sound decisions," his father wrote in *Donald: The Man Who Remains a Boy.* "It would have been easy to give in to his pleas. Although he has divided us momentarily, we have exercised firm control—but we have not been despots, benevolent or otherwise. It is simply that we deeply believe we cannot substitute his judgment for ours in basic decisions affecting his health, education, job, and social life."

So Howard Hurwitz pushed his son to be bar-mitzvahed and to speak before a packed audience for the first time in his life, to attend school with normal children, to get and keep menial jobs, first in a printing plant and then at W. T. Grant's, and to view these as challenging opportunities. If Donald is ever to marry, writes his father, he will marry "a normal girl."

Howard Hurwitz claims that his son remains the central event in his life: "I think I never would have had, with my personality, the patience for slow learners that I have." Abraham Zamichow, chairman of the English department at Long Island City High School, thinks Donald's effect on his father is broader: "His overall philosophy represents an intellectual standard that has been eroded throughout the country. We now say that certain people who come to us are disadvantaged or weak. Other educators have in many ways reinforced this. Now many parents are complaining that because of this we short-change their kids. In too many schools the student comes in and can't read and we say, 'Okay. Sit down and look at the pictures.' "

Donald is permitted to look at pictures on television. But he is pushed and prodded by his father to work and practice hard. Tonight Donald sat in his room, and as his parents beamed, he read effortlessly from one of his many physical-fitness books. "He reads better than ninety percent of high-school graduates," says his father proudly.

Howard Hurwitz drives his teachers as hard as he does his students or his son. "I'll address the faculty meeting," he says, "and there is no such thing as the slightest commotion or disturbance when I speak. It's just something I expect—even in these days of declining professionalism." He looks warily upon the teachers' union and what he feels are teachers' declining commitment to professionalism and their growing commitment to wage and benefit increases (many believe that the Council of Supervisors and Administrators—the principals' union, of which Hurwitz is an officer —is as guilty of protecting incompetents).

Hurwitz grows almost apoplectic when he thinks of teachers who take long weekends. The worst case he can remember took place last November: "A teacher came to me and said he had plans for Christmas in Florida. He said to me, 'I know how strongly you feel about extending vacations, and I wouldn't ask, but it's imperative.' He said he'd like to take two days off. I said, 'The answer is no, but convince me. What is it?' You know, I get a headache when I think about what he said. The fact that I didn't kill him proves I'm compassionate! So help me, he said the reason he had to go down to Florida was that he owned two condominiums and had to put the curtains up or he could not rent!" Dr. Hurwitz's eyes widened and he slowly lifted himself from the table. " *'What'd you say, you crazy son of a bitch?'* I shouted. I told him, 'When you come back I'm not letting you back in school.' He didn't go."

While Hurwitz is tough on his teachers, he recalls with particular displeasure one of his first principals: "He was an arch-conservative and I was a liberal. He had no heart. I wrote a weekly article for this publication and every week I would send him a copy. He never acknowledged them. One day I went to see him and asked if he found them worthwhile. He said, 'I didn't agree with a word you wrote, and it's worthless.' That was his way of treating a young teacher. I have some left-wing teachers, but I'll never criticize their political views." Would he try to censor the substance of what they teach so as to conform to his more rigid views? Never, he says. As long as their attendance is good and they work hard, he is satisfied.

Dr. Hurwitz, the historian, has few personal heroes. Among them are Justices Louis Brandeis and Benjamin Cardozo. Both were, in his words, "minority justices whose views triumphed." George Washington "had guts" because he led a people, one-third of whose citizens supported the British. Abraham Lincoln is admired because he was "a man who suffered in his personal life." He admired Franklin Delano Roosevelt until he learned, among other evils, that Roosevelt cheated on his wife.

Like his heroes Brandeis and Cardozo, Howard Hurwitz believes his time may have come, that his minority position may soon become the majority position. "Let them send back to the school a student I have judged to be disruptive," he warns the Board of Education, "and I shall be insubordinate again." He reflected for a moment, and added, "You want to know something? I don't think they ever will." (Hurwitz acts unaware that he has compromised and the girl has been returned to his school.) "I think the people would rise up and the schools would be closed and the legislature would remove Anker."

This is not a modest view, but Howard Hurwitz would be the last to suggest he is a modest man. After dinner, as he sipped his hot tea and nibbled on the delicious banana-nut cake his wife had baked, I asked him to describe his weaknesses. For perhaps a full minute there was silence.

"That's a fair question," he said, continuing to ponder it.

"I can tell you he doesn't know where his socks are." Nettie laughed.

More silence. "I know I have weaknesses. People don't like me."

"They're jealous of his accomplishments," interrupted his wife.

"People aren't jealous of sixty-year-olds," he corrected her. "Let's say a fault is when I have told a teacher something twice and that teacher continues something that is unprofessional. I can be very searing. And I know, in a sense, that I'm taking advantage of the teacher. I mean, when I go over you, you don't come up for air. I admit I give teachers a tongue-lashing— but I wouldn't mind if the mayor of New York listened." Then why is it a fault? "Because you should not talk to a professional that way.

"In a sense," mused Howard Hurwitz, "I'm living in the past. I'm imposing old values that have passed."

Nelson Rockefeller:
Guile Under Pressure

The Village Voice, September 8, 1975

It was a normal campaign week for Vice-President Nelson Rockefeller. On Tuesday and Wednesday he cheerfully humbled himself before a gathering of conservative Southern Republicans, denying he was now or had ever been a *liberal.* On Thursday the campaign headed north to New York City, where Rockefeller testified under oath before the Moreland Act Commission on Nursing Homes, denying, in effect, that he had been governor for fifteen years while the nursing-home scandal spread. The week ended upstate, where Rockefeller testified before a grand jury investigating the Attica prison uprising, presumably denying that he was a cold-hearted *conservative.*

Rockefeller's nimble performance recalled other highlights of a dazzling career: the solemn campaign promises of 1962 and 1966 not to raise state taxes—followed in 1963 and 1967 by tax hikes; his March 21, 1968, pledge not to run for President—followed by his April 30, 1968, declaration of candidacy; his 1972 and 1973 Watergate silence—followed by his 1974 call for a government "that places enduring moral principle over immediate political advantage; or his current effusions that Ronald Reagan and Howard (Bo) Callaway are "great guys."

Another "great guy," Morris Abram, chairman of the Moreland Nursing Home Commission, came to the hearing room at 14 Vesey Street last Thursday set for a Rockefeller performance of great bravado. For days he and his staff prepared for this encounter. They had decided that Abram, who was closer to Rockefeller in age and Sam Ervin in Southern accent and courtly manner, should alone conduct the interrogation. They became students of Rockefeller's various techniques, and of his opponents' mistakes.

The Senate had made a mistake in its vice-presidential confirmation hearings, insisted one source close to the commission: "There were too many people asking too many questions on too many subjects." Abram was aware of the way Rockefeller had disarmed the senators by anticipating their questions with statements of filibuster length, by oozing charm, by uttering graceful *mea culpas.* He was also steeled for the intimidating brusqueness Rockefeller displayed toward lawyers for the McKay Commission, which investigated the Attica revolt.

Abram expected no *mea culpas* today. His commission had conducted a dress rehearsal the day before, and Abram scrawled pages of questions on yellow legal pads. Members of his family sat nervously in the audience. His staff had carefully prepared and collected incriminating state documents and were cued to hand copies to the former governor and the press simultaneously.

Rockefeller had obviously done no such preparations. Fresh from two full days in the Deep South, he brought with him four attorneys, a press secretary, several advance men, a delegation of Secret Service men, and the praise of George Wallace. Plus neat rows of marked yellow folders, some stuffed in a small suitcase carted by a female attorney. Unlike Abram, he had clearly not read and reviewed all the documents. "He was not well prepared," a commission member would say later, after almost five hours of sparring with Rockefeller. "Unfortunately," he added ruefully, "he is naturally well prepared."

Rockefeller didn't have to be well prepared. He has his act down pat. Unlike Abram, he knows that politics is theater, more form than substance. While the commission was looking to unearth the truth, he was looking to avoid a headline seriously damaging to his campaign to retain the vice-presidency.

He knows that politicians are very different from journalists. Journalists assume their readers remember every word and story they have written; politicians, who skip from role to role, simply assume their public forgets everything they say.

Morris Abram relentlessly chased Nelson Rockefeller. He carefully established that Rockefeller could have saved millions of taxpayer dollars if as governor he had hired the auditors requested by his own Health Department. "I think there is merit in what you say," Rockefeller reluctantly conceded. He showed that during the Rockefeller administration nonprofit nursing homes built by the state often cost twice as much per bed as that of proprietary homes. The former governor carefully admitted he was "not as clearly aware of this as you've stated today." Rockefeller's November 6, 1969, promise that building nursing homes would cost the public "absolutely nothing" was a promise, Rockefeller acknowledged, that was "excessive." Abram proved Rockefeller was guilty of the same mismanagement Rockefeller accused Mayor John Lindsay of— demonstrating that the state lacked a plan when it suddenly discharged patients from state mental hospitals in 1968.

When he appeared before the U.S. Senate for his confirmation hearings in November 1974, Rockefeller advertised his apologies. He was sorry for the gifts to former employees. He was sorry for the clandestine financing of a negative book about his 1970 Democratic gubernatorial opponent.

There was nothing new in this technique. Rockefeller has played humble when he wanted something. When he wanted to run for reelection in 1966 but polls showed that his voice and face were unpopular, he willingly sacrificed himself and substituted goldfish and actors in his campaign commercials. But all he wanted today was to avoid a headline that would startle people outside New York. When he conceded points to Abram, it was always in subdued, dull language. "You have no regrets?" one reporter asked him at the lunch break. "No," he replied. "I must say I did my best."

Rockefeller displayed a dazzling array of acts. He was alternately: Funny. Bored. Impatient. Angry. Sincere. Incredulous. Hostile. Charming. He was a *teacher,* scolding the commission for "oversimplifying"; a *philosopher,* providing homilies on "individual responsibility" and the meaning of "democracy"; a *preacher,* warning them "you cannot legislate honesty"; a *barrister,* throwing his opponent off guard by challenging his words— preferring "delegated" to "shunted aside," "look into" to "intervene"; a *host,* acting as if he had invited them to the hearing and rewarding his guests with "I think that your commission is offering tremendous service"; a *dissembler,* vividly recalling that he and Samuel Hausman did not discuss Bernard Bergman at a forty-five-minute meeting on May 4, 1973, but unable to remember what it was they discussed.

As Nixon proclaimed he was too busy bringing peace to the world to fret over details of his reelection, so Rockefeller professed that as governor he left his appointees free to get involved in "operational details" while he "concentrated on policy and the future." Pitching his voice to the conservative audience outside the hearing room, he berated citizens who shunted their parents off to nursing homes. "One of the things we have to do," he puffed, "is take more responsibility." Yet he ducked responsibility for state nursing-home decisions made by people under his command.

As Patrick Buchanan admonished the Senate Watergate committee, so Rockefeller sought to admonish the commission of his political innocence. Unlike Buchanan, he refused to describe how politics really worked. Instead he pretended he was as politically innocent as he said the commission was. He expressed shock and denied there was "political influence" in his administration. Rather than acknowledging that his chief of staff, T. Norman Hurd, met with Bernard Bergman nine times because Rockefeller's chief Jewish adviser, Samuel Hausman, cautioned it was critical to capture "the Jewish vote," Rockefeller chose to continue Hurd's fairy tale that he was just performing an "ombudsman" role, same as he would for an ordinary citizen.

Instead of telling the truth and educating the public that government cannot be divorced from politics, that doing favors for people is often central to winning political support—and the real question is often one of degree—Rockefeller borrowed some prissy Common Cause slogans. "I didn't operate government on the basis of politics but of what was best for the public," Rockefeller declared at one point in response to Abram.

But peering through the many acts and faces, last Thursday the essential Rockefeller was on display. New York's nursing-home scandal—like another reelection campaign—was taken in stride as just another obstacle to overcome; Rockefeller had little feeling, little sense of the old victims. Most people—except those he needs—had become as inanimate to him as one of his famous buildings or his miles of concrete roads.

Nursing homes had become an "issue," just another opponent. He could not recognize the victims without recognizing his own complicity. And so he said that "seventy to eighty percent of nursing homes are fine"; bedsores are not necessarily a sign of nursing-home "abuse," since "bedsores develop in people's homes." When Abram said that Hurd had met regularly with Bernard Bergman, whom Rockefeller's own state Public Health Council had condemned as "deceptive," the former governor retorted, "It's the end product that counts." Nine meetings don't count. All that counts is that Rockefeller's time and political ass were spared.

At one point in the hearing, Abram showed that "old people often got caught" in the dispute between local governments and the state, each refusing to pay for patient care. Rockefeller smugly replied, "This happens very often in a democracy."

One of the most difficult—and important—things to decipher in politics is a candidate's instincts. Many governmental decisions, particularly executive decisions, are made quickly, without briefing papers or deliberation. It is more important to know what a candidate's instincts are than what is contained in some position paper. When Barry Goldwater was asked in the early sixties why he refused to support most civil-rights legislation, he responded, "You cannot legislate love or brotherhood." True. But his answer also revealed that in his gut he favored property rights over social or human rights. When Morris Abram painted a picture of the thievery behind wretched nursing homes, Rockefeller cautioned, "You cannot legislate honesty." That, too, is true. But, as noted, you can audit nursing homes.

Part of former Mayor Wagner's success in politics was attributable to people who constantly underestimated him; part of Nelson Rockefeller's success is due to people who constantly overestimate him. For years the press assumed and wrote that his reelection was certain. His wealth, his staff, his social distance could prove intimidating. Before Thursday's hearing, a source close to the commission spoke of Rockefeller as "a master," "very skillful, very well prepared." After the hearing, the same person said he was not surprised by Rockefeller's "skillful performance . . . I felt he had done a strong job in defending himself, and while you still have to quarrel with the man . . . when you apply a descriptive word to what he did, it is not pejorative."

In executive session before the commission, Samuel Hausman had testified that he did not bring up nursing homes in talking with "the governor," as he referred to Rockefeller. Yet he explained that he often talked with Governor Wilson about his problems. Why Wilson and not Rockefeller? he was asked. "Because he's a plainer man," he said.

Thursday's hearing ended as it had begun, with Rockefeller walking to the platform and shaking hands and offering a little personal touch to each commission member. He and the chairman chatted about the United Negro College Fund dinner in October that Abram will chair and where Rockefeller will be the principal speaker. He asked commission member Peter Berle how his mother was. One by one he gripped the hand of each commissioner and staff member. Then he darted back across the table, seeking another staff member because "I didn't say good-by to her."

The host was thanking everyone for coming. "He's turned the whole thing into a victory," privately marveled one reporter. "Do you think this was a waste of your time?" inquired another. "No," smiled the Vice-President, "I think the commission's work is important." Alternately he would wink, lift his eyebrows in unison, smile, squeeze a familiar reporter's arm. He bounded over to a platform to appear live on Channel 13, where he escaped Bob Ansen's serious questions by repeatedly thanking and congratulating him on "the important" work they do.

On the way back he spied Miss Bonnie Butler, a young commission staffer who this day served as a messenger depositing a succession of embarrassing documents with the former governor. He gently squeezed her by both arms and winked. "You were the one bright, attractive note today," he said. Miss Butler blushed.

About to depart, the former governor decided to accommodate the press and answer more questions. "Do you feel in any way this was useful today?" he was asked. Rockefeller smiled, winked, lifted his eyebrows, but did not answer. No one noticed. "Has the appearance here affected your 1976 campaign?" quickly asked a reporter. "I have no campaign," replied Rockefeller. The talk shifted to other things. To the Middle East. The city's fiscal crisis. "Thank you, Mr. Vice-President" rang out a voice. "Thank you for your patience," the Vice-President replied to the press.

Jack Hamilton, the commission's public-relations counsel, congratulated him. A reporter reached over to Hugh Morrow, the Vice-President's press secretary, and exclaimed, "He's an expert." Morrow beamed as his boss stopped to shake the hands of several cops who stood outside the hearing room.

Then the Vice-President bounced down the flight of marble stairs, heading a parade of staffers and Secret Service men. He thanked another cop, walked over and patted the arms and hands of the women at the switchboard desk, the cop at the inside door, the four young girls beside the front entrance. He said "Thanks for the job you're doing" to the helmeted cop at the curb beside his Lincoln limousine, pressed closer, reached out and touched the people crowding the sidewalk, waved and blew kisses to citizens across the street, recognized and said hello to a rabbi, and shouted to no one in particular as he entered his car, "This is still a great city. The greatest."

He was off to another campaign stop. This time, the grand jury.

Hubert Horatio Humphrey:
Defender of the Faith

New York, March 15, 1976

"It now appeared to him fitting and necessary, in order to win a greater amount of honor for himself and serve his country at the same time, to become a knight-errant and roam the world on horseback, in a suit of armor . . ."

—Cervantes, *Don Quixote*

The knight-errant of American liberalism, Hubert Horatio Humphrey, journeyed to the main ballroom of the Americana Hotel one recent Sunday, as he did to Newark two nights before, to honor a member of Congress. On the surface, nothing had changed. Humphrey spoke for fifty-three minutes —eleven of which he spent on introductions—regaling his audience with odds and ends from his scrapbook of old speeches.

In fact, much had changed. Liberalism—that old-time religion—was now in disrepute. Liberals had lied and mismanaged city monies and created administrative monsters out of programs like Medicaid. Busing wasn't working. "Law and order" was no longer just a conservative slogan. In 1976 the Democrats' leading presidential candidates and governors had abandoned the church. Ford was in the White House, Reagan on the hustings, and the problems of poor people on the back burner. There should have been little for this gathering of New York Democrats to cheer about.

Enter Hubert Humphrey, defender of the faith, here to reassure this congregation of liberals that they have not been wrong, that humility in the pursuit of social justice is no virtue. "Get yourselves together and get ready, because we're going to bring on the dynamo," warned Brooklyn Congresswoman Shirley Chisholm.

Manhattan Borough President Percy Sutton introduced him as "a man who has not just come to the cause." Humphrey bounded for the stage, accompanied by the cheers of Herman Badillo, Bella Abzug, Charles Rangel, Paul O'Dwyer, and a pat on the back from Brooklyn Democratic chief Meade Esposito.

"Sometimes I wonder whether those who sometimes speak for us really know what this party's about" was Humphrey's opening salvo at the seven-minute mark, just prior to another four-minute digression in which he blessed Shirley Chisholm's "heart." Eventually, Humphrey came back to his main point, back to the unnamed Democratic presidential candidates and governors who, like rats, were attacking traditional liberalism.

"I think we can and will win this election because we prove that the party of Franklin Roosevelt and Harry Truman and Adlai Stevenson and John Kennedy and Lyndon Johnson still cares. . . .

"Ronald Reagan is setting the rules for this campaign. Less is good. Government is too big. . . . Well, I'll tell you, I'm not about to fall for it. . . ." Humphrey was getting into the old rhythm, whacking the podium first with his right hand, then with his left, one minute ridiculing Reagan as "the midnight Romeo of the desert," the next, those "pseudo-intellectuals" (Governor Jerry Brown, presumably) who "peddle" that "less is more."

"I am not ashamed to tell you I am a New Dealer," Humphrey said, his voice rising. "I want to warn you, my friends, that when people turn their back on our family, your heritage . . . you will lose, and deservedly so. . . . There are some people today who are running against Washington [presumably Jimmy Carter]. They are not positive. I'll tell you, they say federal programs don't work. But if you put an arsonist [a Republican] in charge of these programs, of course you'll have a fire. . . . The 'less government' theme is just a code word for neglect, a code word for ignoring our cities. . . . Neglect of our cities is a new form of racism.

"I'm waiting for someone on the national scene to outline a program of what our cities ought to be." He banged the podium top again, and again, reminding his audience of John Kennedy's promise to land a man on the moon before the close of the sixties. "We made up our mind to do it and we didn't ask the costs. . . . Today what we need again is a voice like Roosevelt's saying that we have nothing to fear but fear itself. . . ."

Most of his enthusiastic audience seemed to believe him, as many would not have in 1968. In that year U.S. Senate candidate Paul O'Dwyer, passionately against the Vietnam war, refused to embrace Humphrey's presidential candidacy. Tonight O'Dwyer sat directly across from Humphrey at the head table and they chatted amiably. In 1972 George McGovern bitterly blamed Humphrey for affixing the "radical" tag on him in the California primary. This year, says a senior member of his staff, "McGovern likes him and thinks he's a big-hearted, smart, likable guy." In 1970 Earl Craig, Jr., challenged Humphrey in a Minnesota Senate primary race. This year he endorsed him for President. Mark Green, a former Ralph Nader associate and current Ramsey Clark campaign manager, summarizes the common ailment: "I'm soft on Hubert Humphrey."

So are a lot of other present and former liberal activists. Their reasons can be gleaned from Humphrey's speech. He never mentioned Vietnam. The prime issue was no longer foreign policy, but the economy. Liberal activists have also changed. They are more practical. "The people who got into politics in 1968 or 1972 have fewer illusions about politics," thinks McGovern's press secretary, Alan Baron. Humphrey has been punished for his sins. And at a time when liberals are confused over their presidential candidates, as well as their own ideas, and are drifting into unfamiliar pessimism, old Hubert just bounces back to reassure and rekindle their lost optimism.

In the process, Humphrey intends to win "a greater amount of honor" not just for liberalism, but for himself. Hubert Humphrey—as he has in four of the last five presidential campaigns—is running for President. You learn this not from a formal announcement. It is in the flirtatious tease he treated his audience to Sunday night: "Before I forget, I am a candidate . . . [Pause] I'm a candidate for the U.S. Senate." It is on the lapels of several of his Washington staffers who wear tiny gold HHH pins. It is in the regional meetings of the Joint Economic Committee, which Humphrey chairs, and which has given him a statesmanlike platform to address the Democrats' number-one issue, unemployment, in some of its number-one cities—Chicago, Atlanta, Boston, Los Angeles, New York. It is in his invitation to twenty or so New York Democrats to visit his hotel suite late Sunday night, in the way he privately disparages the current candidates as "ponies, not horses." Eugene McKenna, who headed Humphrey's New York staff in 1972, now says he is "running a boiler-room operation" to "keep track of who is filing for convention delegates and who they are and where they're going to be."

The Humphrey people are counting on Jackson to falter, and on labor —and perhaps Humphrey—to stop Carter. A lot of Democrats, including Hubert Humphrey, plainly don't fancy Carter. The political problem for Humphrey is that he had hoped to remain above the fray and to be everyone's second choice at a deadlocked convention. But if Humphrey waits too long, Carter might walk off with the nomination, the liberals might coalesce around Udall, or labor might jump on a post-Massachusetts Jackson bandwagon. Yet if Humphrey plunges into the race, he becomes everyone's target.

Right now Humphrey can still act the elder statesman. Democrats who peg Carter, probably correctly, as an opportunist for, among other sins, embracing Lester Maddox in 1970, forget it was Humphrey's arms that were hugging Maddox in 1967. Fibbing about one's humble background is not foreign to Humphrey. As Carter claims he is a peanut farmer when, in fact, he is a major peanut warehouser, so Humphrey used to imply he was raised in poverty in Doland, South Dakota, when in reality he hails from a prosperous family. The Democrats Humphrey says are waffling on busing in 1976 are only doing what Humphrey did in Florida in 1972. And those he thinks are retreating from liberalism are merely following the old liberal master who, addressing the U.S. Chamber of Commerce on May 1, 1968, assured his listeners he was no longer a fiery liberal. "Some say, 'You've changed, Mr. Humphrey,'" he said, "and indeed I have. Of course I've changed. And I hope for the better."

Polls show that Humphrey is popular among Democrats; certainly he is among party leaders. But that may not be enough in a year when the voters, unlike their leaders, may be tired of both liberalism and the familiar. If that is true, then the knight-errant, once again, is tilting at windmills.

Jimmy Carter's Courtiers

The Village Voice, June 28, 1976

In many ways, Washington, D.C., is a smaller, more provincial town than Plains, Georgia. Its one industry—politics—is preoccupied with ulcerating questions about this Jimmy Carter fella. Do they *really* want to return square dancing to the White House? And who are these "rednecks" from Georgia, *anyway*?

One learns a lot about Jimmy Carter by spending time with the "rednecks" around him. After spending three weeks—on the road with the candidate, at campaign headquarters in Atlanta, in Plains, and in Washington—the surface differences between the Carter campaign and most others leap at you. No Carter staffer ever began a sentence with "Frankly" or "Let me be perfectly honest." Rarely did they ask that their words be placed "off the record." In New York or Washington, a reporter struggles through a blizzard of "Franklys" and often gets the truth only after first promising his source immunity from direct quotation.

The Carter campaign also looks different. Jackets, shirts, and ties have been replaced by open-necked sport shirts, coffee by Coke. People seem to move slower, talk slower, hold fewer meetings. "There's not a lot of sitting and talking," says political director Landon Butler. Issue task-force coordinator Orin Kramer, who has worked in Northern campaigns, suggests, "People in this campaign don't have typical political personalities, they're not manically political."

Running a national campaign out of Atlanta, rather than Washington, is also different. And important to its success. It underlined the campaign's anti-establishment, anti-Washington theme, and helped strengthen the campaign's Southern base. Working out of Georgia "has almost given me a built-in staff," Carter declared the morning after his big Ohio victory while standing on the dusty railroad loading platform attached to his Plains campaign headquarters. Atlanta guaranteed a steady supply of volunteers. Not to mention money. More than 20 percent of the approximately $6 million raised nationally (exclusive of federal funds) was raised in Georgia. Of the 683 people who reside in Plains, an astonishing total of roughly 550 have contributed money.

Atlanta also permitted some of the key people in the campaign to donate more time. This includes the adviser generally considered closest to Carter,

Atlanta attorney Charles Kirbo, as well as campaign treasurer Robert Lipshutz, whose law firm houses the campaign's first team. The media guru, Gerald Rafshoon, runs an advertising agency just blocks from the head-quarters.

The campaign is also different in that the candidate truly delegates his authority. Richard Nixon's 1960 campaign manager, Robert Finch, com-plained after their narrow defeat that they would have won had Nixon spent less time trying to be the campaign manager. Lyndon Johnson was a notori-ously bad delegator of details. Because he presided over a squabbling court, George McGovern was forced to involve himself in decisions better left to others. Similarly, one week Gerald Ford is pushed by hawkish advisers to take the gloves off and attack Reagan, the next he is convinced by the doves to play presidential. The battles between Scoop Jackson's Senate and cam-paign staff flared into open warfare before the Pennsylvania primary. Lloyd Bentsen fired his campaign manager. Birch Bayh removed his. Fred Harris didn't need one. Jerry Brown's staff often acted as the supporting cast in *One Flew Over the Cuckoo's Nest.* Morris Udall's campaign changed cam-paign managers as the Chinese change foreign ministers.

When I heard Carter say, while standing not long ago in the rotunda of Newark's City Hall, that he didn't know what states his schedule would take him to the following week because his staff had not told him, I didn't believe him.

But now I do. On the night of the last primaries, a smiling Carter stood before a packed press conference in downtown Atlanta and again deflected a question about his schedule. "Mr. Jordan"—he broadly beamed at his campaign manager—"will I remain in Georgia the rest of the week?"

The reason Carter can comfortably delegate this kind of power is because he is not surrounded by strangers, as is true for most national candidates. The people closest to Carter have worked with him for a long time, from five to fourteen years, and many of them have not worked for any other political candidate. They're unified by mutual trust and by a common admiration for the candidate. "The people who are implementing this cam-paign act as if they were each one finger of Jimmy Carter's hand," says Barry Jagoda, a thirty-two-year-old former Emmy award-winning producer for CBS News who now serves as Carter's TV adviser. "If Carter were running the campaign he'd be doing the same thing. They're all an extension of him. . . . What's interesting is how much freedom each has in his own area."

In short, Carter, unlike most legislators who run for executive office, is used to delegating authority. But the degree to which his campaign is decentralized is unusual. In effect, the campaign has at least three campaign managers. Unlike most campaign managers, Hamilton Jordan does not oversee the press, issues, or advertising. Like his candidate, he did not see Rafshoon's commercials until after they were on the air. In most cam-paigns, reporters seeking an authoritative answer will call the campaign

manager. In this campaign, talking to press secretary Jody Powell is sufficient.

"Take me and Jody," explains Jordan. "Jody is the closest to Jimmy
because he travels with him all the time. I defer completely to him on issues
and the press. At the same time he defers to me on organization and strategy
things. Jimmy has a good deal of faith in our collective ability to run the
campaign. . . . A lot of it comes from working together a long time. We are
a loose group of people who jointly make up decisions. I could, if I wanted
to, override Jody on an issue decision or Rafshoon on the media. I have that
authority. But I don't use it."

When a campaign is decentralized at the top level, it's usually because
people are competing and the candidate fears stepping in to resolve it.
Tensions swell, spill over, and poison the rest of the staff. But competition
and feuding don't seem to haunt the Carter campaign. An important reason
is that people's jobs are carefully defined. In a Kennedy campaign two
people were usually doing one job. The Kennedys believed, as did FDR, in
creative conflict. Sometimes that can be destructive. "In the McGovern
campaign," recalls Carter's finance chairman, Morris Dees, who was deeply
involved in that effort, "everyone was running around like a bull in heat."

"We've all worked together," explains adviser Kirbo, looking out the
window from his twenty-fifth-floor downtown law office. "They like each
other and each one has a place. They were just boys when they started in
1966. I've seen them grow and mature, and I'm proud of them. And Jimmy
is, too. . . . They're more like brothers."

Some think they're too close. "The people who run that campaign have
been together a long time," says Ms. Bebe Smith, a native Georgian who
was McGovern's state coordinator in 1972 and who quit the Carter campaign last October. "I felt, when I was there, that they didn't tolerate
outsiders well." But that view was not shared by any of the important
"outsiders" I talked to. "This is the most open campaign I've ever seen,"
says Orin Kramer.

Congressman Andrew Young, an early and important black supporter,
calls the campaign "a cause, a movement. It was an impossible dream that's
come true. The average campaign is full of opportunists that want something." Frank Moore, the campaign's congressional liaison, puts it somewhat differently. As Hamilton Jordan placed his boots on the desk and
chuckled appreciatively, Moore expressed both the campaign's good humor
and latent bitterness when he said, "These guys remind me of when the
hunting season opens. When it gets closer to the deer season they go out
and get their boots, go get their shells, polish their guns. That's what the
guys in Washington are like. When the campaigns start they go hunting for
candidates."

The Carter campaign has also been successful because these people, like
the Vietcong, traveled light, outflanked their foes, believed in their cause,
and built popular support. They simply did a better job than the competi-

tion. They started their activities for the July New York convention last February. A coordinator, James Gammill, was picked and given his assignment. He moved to New York in May. In February the Udall campaign was assigned the Roosevelt Hotel for the convention. As of early June, no one from the Udall staff had ever contacted the hotel by phone or in person.

A big difference between this campaign and most is the way its people talk about their candidate. Campaign operatives often wind up working for themselves. They come to harbor a certain contempt for their candidate. Sure, they "respect" him, agree with his stands "on the issues," even "like" him. But he's always "putting his foot in his mouth," "taking too long to decide," "screwing up." The candidate has to be protected from himself. The most extreme case is the way Haldeman and Ehrlichman kept things from Nixon, including drink. Frank Mankiewicz, Gary Hart, and Gordon Weil were always scheming, in 1972, how to manipulate weak George McGovern. President Ford's advisers struggle trying to make him appear presidential.

The truth is that many of our politicians are weak people, without a clue or even concern as to who they are. The process they partake in helps induce that confusion. For they are continually being defined by what other people think of them—the voters, their county or legislative leaders, interest groups, or their staffs.

With all his flaws, Jimmy Carter is obviously different. He apparently knows who he is; and he is the boss of his staff. In fact, though less extreme, his relations with his staff seem patterned after his own relationship as a young naval officer with Admiral Hyman Rickover. "He was unbelievably hard-working and competent," Carter wrote of Rickover in his autobiography, "and he demanded total dedication from his subordinates. We feared and respected him and strove to please him. I do not in that period remember his ever saying a complimentary word to me. The absence of a comment was his compliment. . . ." Carter is not so frugal with compliments. Jokes Jordan: "If my mother and father were here he'd walk in and say what a great guy I am."

Carter is also said to express his displeasure quietly. Jordan says he does "a kind of quiet burn." Aide-de-camp Greg Schneiders, who is with him more than anyone else, says, "He never yells. He almost never says anything to you in front of anybody else." Once, at least, he did. Carter, Jagoda, and Ed Rabel of CBS were in a car together after the Florida primary. Suddenly, according to Rabel, Carter erupted and yelled at Jagoda. He was upset with Powell over a scheduling matter. So Carter took it out on the startled Jagoda. Then, just as suddenly, the storm passed, and there was calm. The candidate, perhaps realizing a member of the press was catching him in an unguarded moment, began reassuring Jagoda that he knew it really wasn't his fault.

Despite the informality among the campaign staff, Jordan admits that Carter, like Rickover, "is a very difficult man to work for. He just sets such high standards. If he were in the next office, it would be hard as hell." The campaign manager remembers his days as executive secretary to the governor when Carter expected people to be in the office at 7 A.M. "That's one of the reasons," he quips, "we now schedule him so rigorously."

"I've noticed when they do speak to Carter, they play their aces," says one of the few staff members who requested anonymity. "People aren't fucking around with him. They don't waste his time. When Jody sits down he's got four or five points to make. If he's not sure of the fifth, he doesn't make it." The campaign's twenty-eight-year-old comptroller, St. Louis-born Paul Hemmann says, "I would not say he's an easy man to criticize."

But his people are proud of Jimmy Carter. "If we were all working for Lloyd Bentsen," half jokes Jordan, "his campaign probably would have lasted one week longer. You've got to have a candidate." It was Carter, not Jordan, who swept seventeen of thirty primaries. Carter made the ultimate decision to flaunt conventional wisdom and run in all the primaries (except West Virginia), to spend little time seeking endorsements, to stress personal qualities rather than issues, to challenge George Wallace in Florida. Hamilton Jordan may be able to overrule, but he probably can't fire Jody Powell. Jimmy Carter can.

Yet Carter's nomination victory is a shared one. It is shared not just with the handful of people he truly trusts, but with a national staff of 315 people, 240 of whom are based in Atlanta. Forty-one percent of the staff is female, according to Comptroller Hemmann, and 15 percent minority. The monthly campaign payroll is $160,000. Telephones run close to $60,000 per month. Salaries are often half those found in other campaigns. The highest salaries, $22,680, are paid to Powell and Jordan. Robert Keefe, Senator Jackson's former campaign manager, was paid $45,000. Surprisingly, most of the salaried positions in this campaign are held by people who never worked for Carter before. Hemmann, counting on his fingers, estimates that perhaps a dozen worked for Carter when he was governor.

The campaign began small and early, on December 2, 1974. It was first headquartered in a vacant second-floor wing of the law offices of Lipshutz, Zufmann, Sikes, Pritchard & Cohen, at 1795 Peachtree Street. The offices of Jordan and Powell, as well as the issues, scheduling, and most of the political coordination, remain there—hidden behind an unmarked door. When the campaign began to grow, it expanded and filled a single-story building across the street. There Hemmann oversees the personnel, bookkeeping, field support services, and many volunteers. Another building, alongside the original site, houses the chief delegate hunter, Rick Hutcheson, and his staff of twenty. Morris Dees's fund-raising operation shares the rest of the space.

It's not enough space. One of the problems ahead is to locate an adequate national campaign headquarters in Atlanta. Another problem is that the success of the candidate has outstripped his small staff. The staff is too thin. Unlike most front-runner campaigns, which have three or even four people

who travel with and can speak for the candidate, this campaign has one—
Jody Powell.

The staff, which is both very young and very good, can also be very
provincial. An aide to Andy Young once suggested he and Carter campaign
together in Harlem. They didn't. On the road in Trenton with one of
Carter's down-home field coordinators, I was struck by the way he talked
about New York as if it were a foreign country.

Who are these people who have been called robots like Haldeman and
Ehrlichman, "amateurs," or "the redneck Mafia"? Thirty-one-year-old
campaign manager Jordan moves around the office with a green wind-
breaker on his back, cowboy boots on his feet, and an omnipresent Coke
bottle in his hand. Occasionally he will wear a sports jacket. He began as
Carter's youth coordinator in a losing 1966 gubernatorial race. Today he is
the chief planner and strategist of the campaign.

Jordan is credited as the glue of the campaign, the person who contributes
most to its relaxed tone. Seated behind his desk, running a thick deck of
white phone slips through his fingers, Jordan describes himself as "a guy
who probably enjoys the sport of running and winning more than governing." He would like to go to Washington in a Carter administration. But
asked what might prompt him to resign such a position, he said he could
not think of any issue. "I don't know under what circumstances I would
resign other than that I became tired of it," he says. He claims it is "true"
that he is wedded more to Carter than to issues: "I'm beyond the point in
my relationship with Jimmy that I measure every statement he makes on
every issue and then reassess our relationship." Jordan says, "I'm not going
to spend my life in politics." Eventually? "I want to go back to school and
maybe write."

Jordan is not without his detractors. Comparing Jordan and press secretary Powell, an Atlanta reporter says, "Jody is capable of punching you in
the mouth. Jordan would wait until you turn around and slip a knife in
you." A former member of the staff says, "Hamilton has a good mind. What
I find hard to fathom is people saying he is a congenial person. I haven't
known anyone who thought that."

Robert Shrum did. The talented speechwriter who quit the campaign
after nine days, with a blast at Carter's character, told me Jordan "is very
gregarious, very smart. But he will say himself that he has no set views."

Press secretary Jody Powell, thirty-two, who looks like a young LBJ
without the ears, drove a car for Carter in his 1970 campaign while working
on his doctorate in political science. He lives not far from Plains, and served
as Carter's press secretary while governor. He is held in generally high
esteem by the traveling press corps because he knows his candidate well
enough to speak for him, yet is said not to lie for him. Speechwriter Patrick
Anderson, who once wrote an excellent book on presidential aides from the
Roosevelt through the Johnson administrations, thinks "Jody will become
the Bill Moyers of a Carter administration."

Powell will have to find his way to Washington to do that. "Jody is terribly disorganized," says David Nordan, political editor of the Atlanta *Journal.* "He forgets things. He never has cigarettes. He's always burning holes in his clothes." Powell is also a lousy returner of phone calls. That might be understandable, since he's always on the road. What's not understandable is that he doesn't delegate someone to return the calls for him.

Jody, explains assistant press secretary Betty Rainwater, is "totally disorganized. He works on whatever hits him at the moment. Totally the opposite of Hamilton." One of his great skills, she says, is that "He pulls Jimmy out of himself a bit . . . he gets Jimmy to relax a little bit." He can do that because he's got a sense of humor. When Carter promised an Oregon audience he would not permit the growth of an arrogant, powerful White House staff, Powell quipped, "He just lost my vote."

"He's a terrific press secretary," says Robert Shrum. But "he's so deferential and careful how he tells the guy he's wrong." That view is not shared by the Boston *Globe*'s Curtis Wilke, who has been on the bus from the beginning: "Jody's not afraid to correct Carter." But like Jordan, his commitment is to Carter, rather than to a classifiable set of issues.

If Hamilton Jordan is the chief executive of the campaign, the acknowledged chairman of the board is fifty-nine-year-old Charles Kirbo, senior partner of the prosperous law firm of King & Spalding. He is dubbed "the wise man" of the campaign by political director Butler, "the man who slows things down." He is addressed as "Mr. Kirbo" by most as he makes his daily one- or two-hour tour of campaign headquarters—visits which have become more frequent the last three months.

Like Carter, Kirbo has ice-blue eyes, grayish hair, red-blotched skin, speaks slowly, and looks older than his years. He met Carter in 1962 when he volunteered to be his attorney against an effort by the local Democratic machine to deprive Carter of a State Senate nomination. He went on to become state Democratic chairman while Carter was governor. Despite the slow drawl, his are often the homilies of Archie Bunker: "There's got to be some control over the size of the government." "Take the New York thing. . . . Woke up one morning and they're broke."

In addition to Harry Truman and Lyndon Johnson, the person Kirbo most admires is his father: "I find he was a greater man than I thought he was. He had eight children and educated all of them while making very little money. . . . When I was a little boy a good many of the people we knew were in the Ku Klux Klan. It was more a political organization. I remember when I was a boy they were constantly putting pressure on Papa to join the Ku Klux. He didn't, and I didn't understand it at the time. He shook hands with black people. . . . He was the only man I'd ever seen that shook hands with black people. The things that he told me when I was a boy about this racial thing—things have come to be the way he thought they should be."

Kirbo's view of the Vietnam war was less prescient. "I was in favor once they got in it," he told me in his slow, almost shy way. "I didn't know much of the reasons why we got in. Once in, I wanted to win it. I hated to lose. I thought the leavin' was worse than the comin'. I was ashamed of it. I think when the country gets in a war they need to support it. As long as the war was going on I didn't like to see people criticize their government. I'd have felt like hell when I was in Europe. I recognized then, and now, that we needed to do it without starting an atomic war. But I always felt we could have won it."

Kirbo says he usually talks to Carter once or twice a week, and writes regular memos to him. His role is "just sort of an adviser to the staff. . . . I just watch the overall operation, mainly to see they don't run up a debt, and to keep Jimmy aware how things are going financially, and otherwise." Would he like to go to Washington? He talks of his three school-age children, of his farm in South Georgia. "I would like to help Jimmy, and I probably would. I would have to take a substantial cut in salary. . . . I don't want to live up there. I hope I can maintain my help without having to go up there."

While Kirbo solemnizes, media adviser Gerald Rafshoon jokes. Asked whether he, like most of the others, called Carter "Governor," Rafshoon pleaded innocent. "I once called him governor," he exclaimed. "I said, 'Oh, fuck you, Governor!' " The forty-two-year-old Rafshoon, shirt open at the neck, sits behind a large, crowded desk in the eighth-floor offices of his ad agency. He looks like a cross between Norman Mailer and Richard Goodwin. His black hair is curly, with a clump of gray rising from the back. On his credenza rests a wooden statue of a hand with its middle finger upright. For ten years he has toiled for Jimmy Carter, and like the other members of this family, he is secure. "Jimmy Carter won't fire me because he doesn't like one of my television spots," he calmly predicts.

He does not feign modesty. "People ask me why we did so well in the media," he volunteers. "I say not having national campaign experience, not being taken seriously, was an advantage." He is particularly proud that they successfully pioneered—despite the naysayers—the five-minute TV spot. He is also most proud, he says, of Jimmy Carter's "guts. He just doesn't see any obstacles. When there are, he enjoys surmounting them." Charles Kirbo says, "Rafshoon is a very talented fella. He believes in Jimmy Carter. . . . He has a good eye for perceiving things about Jimmy that are capable of being portrayed on TV. He's kind of like Jody and Hamilton. They think about what they can do for Jimmy all the time."

If Rafshoon is a funny man, treasurer Robert Lipshutz is described by the departed Bebe Smith as "a terribly sweet man." The fifty-four-year-old lawyer, with the bulbous nose and subdued but friendly personality, controls the money in the campaign, attends what strategy meetings there are, and has stepped into both fund raising and Carter's troubled relations with the Jewish community. This takes "almost a hundred percent of my time," he claims. His first real involvement with Carter came in 1971 when the then governor asked him to co-chair an Ad Hoc Citizens Committee to reorganize the Georgia government. His relationship with Carter, like the others', is not a social one. "We've never gone fishing together or played tennis together," he says. "I don't think Jimmy has time for a normal social life."

A President Carter would, he says, "set a high moral standard in public life that we've gotten away from." When the Carter people say that they are not just referring to Richard Nixon or Wayne Hays. They are better described as traditionalists than conservatives. On domestic government programs they are, as Carter's autobiography clarifies, more the traditional populists, identifying with the little guy. To a Northern liberal ear, their traditional patriotism, sense of family, respect for institutions—like that of many working-class Americans—is often confused with conservatism.

"My own views about government and politics," explains Lipshutz, "are not too dissimilar to Jimmy's. I am, and always have been, a very liberal person on social programs—like integration." Now that his six children are grown, he says, "obviously I would consider" going to Washington.

The people who influence Jimmy Carter do not stop there. Rosalynn Carter—who wants to reintroduce square dancing to the White House and thinks premarital sex is sinful—commands her husband's attention. "If Jody and I strike out," Hamilton Jordan once told the Washington *Post,* "the best thing to do is to try to get Rosalynn on our side." The next best thing may be to get "Miz Lillian"—the candidate's seventy-eight-year-old mother—on your side. In addition to being more relaxed about life than her son (gathering a group of bleary-eyed, hungover reporters around her in Plains, she told us, "I'm older than any of you, yet I look better"), she is also the most liberal influence in his life.

The first person to formally urge Carter to run for President was Dr. Peter Bourne, in a memo dated July 25, 1972. Bourne, thirty-seven, moved to Atlanta from his native England when he was seventeen, met Carter in 1969, and joined his state administration in 1971. He moved again—to Washington—in early 1973. He remains close to Carter. He and his wife, Mary King, play host to Carter when he comes to town, and spend much of the rest of their time explaining to the natives that, no, Carter does not walk barefoot. A part of their time is also spent reassuring liberals—in and out of the campaign—that Jimmy is really one of them.

A picture of the campaign's youth, and its people who are new to Carter, could have been snapped on the night of the final primaries. There, at 2:30 A.M., in a hotel suite in downtown Atlanta, while a party was in full flower, Pat Caddell, twenty-six, and Rick Hutcheson, twenty-four, sat hunched in a corner studying election returns. Caddell is the campaign's influential pollster—he calls himself the "outsider's insider." Hutcheson, the politically neutral delegate hunter—he says he could "probably comfortably support any Democratic presidential candidate"—worked on a Ph.D. at Berkeley and met Jordan in 1974 while working at the Democratic National Committee. Greg Schneiders, the candidate's twenty-nine-year-old travel aide, is another "outsider" who's broken through. A small businessman in Washington, D.C., he volunteered last July and began traveling with Carter in November. He keeps the candidate moving, protects his schedule, does personal chores, and often controls the access of both people and memos to the candidate. "I pass a lot on and hold a lot back," he explains.

Among the people Carter has said he is most grateful to is Congressman Andrew Young. He has reason to be. Young has opened a lot of black and liberal Northern doors for Carter and stood by him throughout the "ethnic purity" flap. Aware that Carter has crafted a coalition of conservatives and liberals, Young says, "My only worry is that it stays a balanced coalition." He points with pride to those in the campaign who have worked for him. Stuart Eizenstat, thirty-three, the campaign's issues director, is a former Phi Beta Kappa and Atlanta attorney who volunteered to perform the same function in Young's 1972 congressional race and Maynard Jackson's successful 1974 mayoral run. It was Eizenstat, sitting alone with Carter at the Georgia Executive Mansion in 1974, who helped lay out the campaign's issue planning. He was Carter's representative to the recent platform hearings, and is now the issue person closest to him.

Do these people reflect what McGovern aide Alan Baron, in a front-page *New York Times* interview, condemned as "a staff committed to no ideals, like Haldeman and Ehrlichman"? Do they work for a man whose character former speechwriter Robert Shrum likened to Richard Nixon's? Both charges reflect common fears within the liberal community, and have certainly stung Carter's staff. Reactions vary from turning the other cheek (Hamilton Jordan) to "that bastard" (Charles Kirbo) to whoops of "bigotry" (Jerry Rafshoon).

"There are only two people you might say are vulnerable to the Baron charge—Hamilton and Jody," argued Andy Young, while munching on a hero sandwich in his D.C. office. "And that's because they're essentially technicians. In this office you could say the same thing about my staff. . . . I know Hamilton and Jody very well, and personally and privately I know they are not that way. The only similarity is their dedication to their boss. But I was dedicated that way to Martin Luther King." He calls many of the people in the campaign "idealists," and adds, "It is a program when a candidate promises that government will be open and honest."

"If Baron was talking about me, I'd like to talk to him," exclaims issues coordinator Eizenstat. "The guys like Alan Baron don't know what it's like to work for a black candidate in the South. It took guts for Carter to take a stand on civil rights. It's a lot harder to be liberal in the South than liberal in the North."

But there is a grain of truth to Baron's charge. Certainly many of the people around Carter slip into idolatry. Some—like many in the nation—acquiesced and were largely silent on the two great issues of the sixties, civil rights and the Vietnam war. It's instructive to ask many of Carter's people to identify his flaws. Kirbo, for instance, says Carter tries to do too much, but he really doesn't "know whether that's a fault or a virtue."

On balance, however, Baron's charge won't stand. It assumes that one of Carter's great campaign strengths—having people he could trust—is a weakness; it assumes that Carter's commitment to managing the government properly and better delivering services to the people who pay for them is not an idealistic or "liberal" end. That further assumes that Baron can clearly define what is a "liberal"—that there is a litmus test of, say, these six issues; if you're on one side you're good, on the other you're bad. Some of the dumbest people I know—who simply mouth platitudes—would pass Baron's test. Actually, many of the Carter people might qualify as idealists because they genuinely believe Carter will make a good President. This is distinct from many people who worked for Gene McCarthy or George McGovern, simply believing each had the right position on several important issues. For that matter, Carter people could use Baron's criteria and call him a "hired gun" for bouncing from the disparate campaigns of Harold Hughes to Ed Muskie to George McGovern to Birch Bayh.

Over breakfast in Washington's Mayflower Hotel two days after the climactic Ohio primary—Hubert Humphrey walked, alone, through the lobby to make a speech—Baron elaborated on his now famous remark. "I'd like to clarify my quote," he said. "It's a bad quote in the sense that Haldeman and Ehrlichman are considered felons, and since I was equating the Carter people with them, some people might assume I was calling them felons. . . . But the point I'm making is that many of Carter's people never worked for a cause other than Jimmy Carter, and if he's not elected, they don't expect to work for a cause or a candidate after Jimmy Carter. They see that as a strength. I see it as a weakness. I want some guys around my President—my candidate—who are ready to dissent when they disagree on issues, and are ready to say, 'I quit.' " Baron is a smart, likable guy; his argument would be more persuasive if he knew—as he admits he does not —most of the people he was blasting.

The Bob Shrum incident struck a similar Nixon chord, going more to the candidate than the people around him. After nine days as Carter's speechwriter, Shrum resigned. He said he found Carter lacking in character or a commitment to any set of issues. In a published memorandum, Shrum recounts many of the specific horrors at which he recoiled: Carter dismissing the Jewish vote as the preserve of Scoop Jackson; Carter toning down a prepared speech because it might alienate lobbyists; Carter, a driven, humorless, cynical man.

Humorless and driven he certainly appears to be. One morning, after an overnight stop at Newark's Holiday Inn, Carter emerged in the lobby at 7:30 A.M. He darted through an encampment of perhaps thirty journalists without moving his eyes or uttering a word. He looked straight ahead. And then, as if directed by radar, he banked left and zoomed toward *Times* correspondent Charles Mohr. Carter was unhappy about a front-page article Mohr had written two days before and quietly asked to talk about it later. Several seconds later he turned, made his way through a minefield of television equipment and luggage, went out the front door and into a waiting car. He greeted no one else. He had one piece of business to take care of, and he had done so.

Carter can also be, as Shrum charges, a cynical man. Though Carter's most notable campaign promise is that he will never lie, his basic stump speech is a consumer fraud. John Kennedy lied in 1960 about the missile gap. Lyndon Johnson lied in 1964 when he promised no wider war in Vietnam. Richard Nixon lied in 1968 about his secret plan to end the war. And Jimmy Carter is lying when he peddles himself to American voters as something he is not. "I'm just an average person like you are," he told a Cleveland fund-raising rally on May 27. Unlike Nixon, Carter doesn't compare the American people to children; he just talks to them as if they were.

A constant refrain in each of these speeches is that he knows that many of his listeners are brighter than he is, better executives than he is, more qualified to be President than he is. Repeatedly, he absolves the American people of blame for a war they supported, for a President, Richard Nixon, they voted for twice, and for many of the abuses of power we have all witnessed. Carter blames the government, not the people— *them,* not us— as if there were no connection between the two.

Naturally, his audiences like it. Carter's campaign has been brilliant in understanding that after the traumas of the last several years—Vietnam, Watergate, Agnew, assassinations—the American people needed reassurance. They didn't need to be told, in Tom Wicker's phrase, to "renounce yourselves," as Wicker says the 1972 McGovern effort suggested. They needed to have faith again not just in their government and their nation, but in themselves. But while the people need belief, they don't need bullshit. I have the impression that Carter as President will be more of an educator, a tougher leader, a more controversial and even more populist President, than his comforting stump sermon suggests.

Search his governorship: You discover a more principled and progressive leader than his platitudinous campaign has suggested. Read Carter's autobiography: It reveals a man who identifies himself as anti-establishment, committed to change. Look at his campaign: You find someone who knows how to be an executive, secure enough to delegate authority and concentrate on what is important. Listen to his staff: You hear respect and admiration, not contempt.

The point was obliquely made by Jerry Rafshoon. Asked what Carter's failings as President might be, his chief image adviser responded, "The failings might be that a lot of people who voted for him for their own reasons will be disappointed that he wasn't what they thought."

But Carter may not be what Bob Shrum thinks, either. Andrew Young is prepared to concede that many of Shrum's facts are right. Where he thinks Shrum wrong is in the conclusion he draws from them. "I can believe eighty-five to ninety percent of what he said—except I would give it a different interpretation. . . . If someone wanted to hang around here and do a real hatchet job and prove I was really callous and Machiavellian, they could probably do it. The only way to let off tensions in a campaign—you got to express them to somebody. I don't want to go home and take it out on my wife. I mean, you need an inner circle you can express it to."

Both Morris Dees and Stuart Eizenstat say that the specific cases Shrum cites in which they were allegedly involved are not accurate. "Shrum said Jimmy told me to bend over and be favorable to the motor carriers," says Eizenstat. "In fact, Jimmy Carter said just the opposite." Mary King, who coordinated work on a national health insurance paper for Carter, ironically complains that the draft Shrum did "was Nixonian in tone." Shrum wrote lines, according to her husband, Peter Bourne, like: "We can't throw dollars at problems."

Who's right? Probably both sides. Carter and his people are better than Shrum—who is used to working for more pliable and Northern liberal candidates—allows. And Carter, though I suspect he will make a good President, doesn't appear to be a very attractive human being. Can you imagine the number of magazine articles Shrum could have written about the manipulative Franklin Roosevelt? The most attractive human beings who ran for President—Stevenson, Goldwater, Udall—all lost.

One can draw some conclusions from the Carter effort. In many ways, Jimmy Carter resembles Bobby Kennedy. Yes, he lacks Kennedy's self-deprecating wit; his staff is not brimming with the anger or brilliance of Adam Walinsky or Peter Edelman; he does not excite an audience. Carter is more disciplined; Kennedy was more existential. One quotes Niebuhr; the other, Camus. But both evaded easy definition. Both appealed to blacks and blue-collar workers. Both were bad losers, and were outgrowing being their father's sons. Each could be tough yet gentle; compassionate liberals yet hard-headed executives. Both were surrounded by "conservative" and "liberal" advisers. And both attracted a staff that genuinely admired them, and never forgot who was boss.

Another conclusion drawn from both the Carter campaign and his governorship is that the people who are so important in his campaign will be less important in his government. As governor, Carter did not rely, as Nixon did, on a centralized staff. Instead, as in his campaign, he delegated—this time to his cabinet and budget office. "We all exercise more authority in the campaign than we will in the government," agrees Hamilton Jordan. He says, "There will be fifteen to thirty people" with key roles in a Carter administration. "Hamilton Jordan, if he were in the Haldeman job," notes Jerry Rafshoon, "could never call a Cabinet member and tell him what to do. Jimmy wouldn't allow it." Landon Butler, Jordan's deputy and a graduate of the Harvard Business School, predicts, "This staff will be the expediters and the appointment-makers. . . . The decision-making powers will get back out to the departments."

It is worth remembering that Richard Nixon promised to restore the Cabinet to a position of prominence. "I will bet you," warns Bebe Smith, "that at the beginning and end of each day as President, Jimmy Carter will have a closed-door meeting with those people." But then, several sentences later, she seems to suggest the closed-door meetings will not amount to much: "They don't care much about influencing him on substance. . . . Jimmy Carter will be a strong President surrounded by extremely loyal people."

Maybe they will be corrupted by power, but unlike Bebe Smith, I feel better about Jimmy Carter after meeting many of those "loyal people." I also feel a little better about America. It's hard not to while driving past the peach trees and bullet-pocked signs of Sumter County, Georgia. Thirteen years ago a white boy from the North would be scared to death on these back roads. Thirteen years ago, two hundred blacks were beaten and arrested in Americus, just ten miles from Plains, for trying to register to vote. Twenty girls, age nine to thirteen, were sealed in an eight-by-ten cell, without beds or toilet, for up to one month.

Today, Sumter County, home of Jimmy Carter, has produced the probable next President of the United States. The South has changed. The racial agony and ugliness within themselves that Southerners—unlike most of us in the North—have been compelled to confront make them better people. They, like Carter, emerge prouder, and more secure. Jimmy Carter, like many of his associates, has a greater sense of place, of roots, than most people in politics. That security and sense of inner calm could steer us clear of another Imperial Presidency.

New York City and its grinding decay distorts one's view of the rest of America. If you don't believe America is a growing rather than a dying nation, drive through Sumter County. The Civil War is over. Perhaps, with this election, America will be coming home.

SECOND THOUGHTS

In case you missed it, I did write: "I have the impression that Carter as President will be more of an educator, a tougher leader . . . than his comforting stump sermon suggests." In some respects—the Middle East, energy, the Panama Canal treaty—I still believe that. On balance, however, I was dead wrong. Jimmy Carter, partly because he lacks oratorical skills, has not been an educator or conveyed a sense of leadership. Actually, I had it upside down, thinking then that Carter was an unattractive human being who might be a forceful leader. Maybe it's because he strives to be a moral man that he failed in his first three years as President to do the distasteful things strong leaders must.

This profile of the people around Carter was wrong about Miz Lillian's enduring influence, and wrong in reporting that Carter's campaign team would be eclipsed once he took over the presidency. During one recent world crisis I saw a picture of good old boy Frank Moore counseling the President, and I became terrified. Had I known Hamilton Jordan would be running the country, I would have placed more emphasis on his admitted administrative incompetence. Finally, I wince as I reread the saccharine ending, though at the time I was genuinely moved by the changes in the South and the nation.

Is Jimmy Carter Weird?

The Village Voice, September 20, 1976

It was the week that should not have been for Jimmy Carter. As the challenger, he should have spent the first full week of the fall campaign chasing incumbent Gerald Ford. Instead, he spent the week chasing through ethnic neighborhoods to prove he was neither an *alien* nor one of them big-spending liberals.

Carter got hooted by small but noisy claques of right-to-lifers in most of the seventeen cities visited between Labor Day and Friday. On Tuesday his staff worried that Cardinal Krol might prevent his appearance in a Philadelphia church. He spent Wednesday denying a front-page *Times* story and explaining what he really meant in urging the ouster of FBI Director Clarence Kelley. Thursday, Carter called an airport press conference in Peoria, but for the first time in his campaign, refused to field questions. He just read a quick statement denying Ford's charge that Carter's election would cripple Western civilization. Returning home Friday night, Carter told reporters he was hopeful the five-day tour showed he was really a "moderate," not the "liberal" who picked Walter Mondale and had Ralph Nader as a houseguest.

Carter's advance work also contributed to the sense that the challenger had slipped into a defensive posture. On Tuesday, Carter was led to the wrong New York City subway stop (Columbus Circle rather than, say, Broadway and Seventy-second Street) and could find few hands to shake. His motorcade took the long way to Brooklyn College, where he had to chuck his prepared notes because there was no podium, and the microphone intermittently sputtered and died. He missed the morning shift of workers at the Haddon bookbinding factory in Scranton, an advance screw-up which left the probable next President of these United States to wander aimlessly and snap at an aide, "What do you suggest we do, stand here?" Upon arrival in Milwaukee on Thursday night, Carter was greeted by a bitter shoving match between local cops and his traveling press corps. His advance team had neglected to tell the cops it was okay for reporters to interview and record the candidate as he alighted from *Peanut One.*

Thus one of Carter's chief weapons—the presumption of a carefully plotted, skillfully executed campaign against a bumbling opponent—was blunted. Two planeloads of national correspondents were suddenly awake with talk of the weaknesses in the Carter, not the Ford, camp. A Carter victory no longer seemed as inevitable as a sunrise. Like sharks, reporters can scent blood.

Skipping from city to city with the Democratic nominee, I was struck by how different and perhaps unsettling he may appear to Northern voters. He comes from this *weird* section of the nation. Speaks in a *weird* accent, practices a *weird* religion, has this *weird* sister, smiles this *weird* smile. And he talks *weird*. Non-born-again Christians are unaccustomed to hearing presidential candidates say, as Carter did in Cleveland, "I want to be one of you, and I want you to be one of me." Those are the words of a preacher or a lover, not a politician, and sometimes they sound saccharine-sweet. As in Chicago the next night, where Carter delivered a low-key sermon to a frenzied mob of perhaps ten thousand of the Daley machine's finest. They wanted quick sex, while Carter talked of enduring love.

It didn't click. One reason Carter sometimes appears out of sync, particularly before larger audiences, is that there is a gap between what we know about the man and what we see. We know Carter is a hard, tough, brilliant politician; yet what we hear from the podium is often softly pious and platitudinous. This could lead to the public conclusion that Carter, who professes not to be one, is just another phony politician telling people what they want to hear. The point was made by an undecided worker and former Wallace supporter who listened to Carter outside the Caterpillar Tractor Company plant in Peoria. He wanted to vote against Ford, he said, but "I'm just afraid Carter will compromise too much."

It could be that Carter's acute sense of the people's mood is proving one-dimensional. Yes, they wish to be reassured and once again to trust their leaders. But they want to be led, not followed. The public is much more likely to believe a political figure who fearlessly says what he thinks, particularly one who is not easily classifiable as a liberal or conservative— as Jerry Brown proved in California. By carefully measuring his words, by blurring issue distinctions, Carter shapes a dangerously indefinite public image.

This partially explains the unusually large number of voters who are left uneasy. In the parlance of pollsters, Carter's support is said to be "soft." That's one reason he sought the boos of the American Legionnaires several weeks ago. And it's why he kicked off his campaign by invoking the memory of Franklin Roosevelt in Warm Springs, Georgia, and in each speech now places himself in the familiar Democratic tradition of FDR, Truman, Kennedy, and Johnson.

After the first full week of the campaign, it is somewhat easier to see how Carter could lose. True, he shouldn't. This ought to be a good year for a Democrat after eight years of Nixon and Ford, of confiscatory inflation and burgeoning unemployment. And Carter appears to be an impressive man —smart, tough, competent, thinking about how to govern as well as how to win an election, possessing a genuine feel for the outcasts of society.

But that may not be the way Carter comes across. His insistence on peddling verbal narcotics—softly telling people how good they are, appearing to smile his way through the campaign, deliberately tilting left one week (Mondale, tax reform, "big-shot crooks") and right the next (emphasizing the dangers of inflation and the need for a balanced budget)—could backfire. Perhaps more dangerous to Carter than appearing "weird" is the possibility that he'll come off as just another slick-talking pol.

Unmasking Hugh Carey

New York *Daily News,* June 19, 1977

"To me the guy is like a diamond, whichever way the light shines through, you see another reflection. He's a man nobody knows . . . The guy has more faces than Lon Chaney." That's the kind of thing usually said about California Governor Jerry Brown. It was said about New York's governor, Hugh Carey, who doesn't sleep on floor mattresses or mediate about Zen Buddhism, but is also becoming known as a strange, brooding Irishman.

The "diamond" watcher was David Garth, the media man who masterminded Carey's race for governor. Garth, like everyone else, is acutely aware that Carey is a jealously private man. One of Carey's prominent appointees who is considered close to the governor recalls the many hours spent alone, sipping wine with him at the Executive Mansion in Albany. They talked, sometimes into the wee hours of the morning, but this man cannot remember a single thing they talked about. What he does remember is that Carey never discussed anything personal. They talked about others, not about themselves. There seemed to be an invisible wall between them. Questions about the Carey family, about feelings or dreams crashed into the wall. Carey never asked about his companion's family.

Whatever his real face, Hugh Carey has a number of public faces. We glimpse *statesman* Hugh Carey, refusing to play politics with the fiscal crisis, speaking out against Abe Beame's reelection as mayor and capital punishment and the killing by both sides in Northern Ireland. Then there is *politician* Carey, playing coy games with the rent issue in Co-op City. Also we have *strategist* Carey, presenting a carefully thought-out state budget designed to reverse the trend of rising taxes and expenditures. And Carey the *bumbler*, clumsily barging into the New York City race for mayor in such a heavy-handed way as to make himself, not Beame, the issue. There is Carey the *Irish pol*, charming and witty, and Carey the *scold*, his humor more bitter than funny. There is former Congressman Hughie Carey, one of the boys, and Governor Hugh Carey, considered a recluse by most state legislators.

There is the secure Carey, delegating responsibility and credit to Big Mac Chairman Felix Rohatyn or former UDC Chairman Richard Ravitch; and the insecure Carey, who does not delegate well to his staff and goes through speechwriters the way women go through stockings. There is the happy Carey, campaigning hard and joyously to become governor, and the unhappy Carey, who many believe does not enjoy being governor. The anti-boss Carey, who aides say is committed to cleansing City Hall of "the clubhouse types"; and the clubhouse Carey, who annointed Patrick Cunningham, his state Democratic chairman, and huddles often with Beame confidant and Brooklyn clubhouse regular Harold Fischer.

There is the lace-curtain Carey, who frequents the "21" Club, and the barroom Carey, who hangs out at P. J. Clarke's.

As governor and as chairman of the Emergency Financial Control Board, Carey is perhaps this city's and state's most powerful figure. But he is also one of the least known. To understand the governor, one must understand, or at least try to understand, the man.

Hugh Carey is not comfortable with strangers. He has few friends. He prefers working closely with only a few members of a highly stratified staff. He has had four speechwriters in two and a half years. His controversial speech on the violence in Northern Ireland was crafted not by a speechwriter but by his chief of staff, secretary David Burke, a fellow Irishman. An aide explained, "That speech has a lot of his character," and "To say to Joe Jones, 'This is how I feel about death and Ireland'—that's a softness he would not stretch out to a stranger."

He plays things close to the vest, suggests a long-time friend, Tax Commissioner James Tully, because he is "on guard against giving information which may go against his interests. The nature of public life is to guard against people using you."

The private man is reflected in the way he is scheduled. The schedule has a limited circulation among the staff, as if it were a military secret. Press secretary James Vlasto admits it is "a real achievement" when he knows Carey's speech schedule in advance. Who does the schedule? "Carey does it himself," answers Vlasto.

By not delegating his scheduling, Carey creates political problems. Many speaking requests go unanswered. One former aide remembers St. Patrick's Day last year. The governor was the grand marshal of the parade. He was very proud to be the first Irish governor since Al Smith to be so asked. "All his kids were there," says the former aide. He was flooded with invitations from all over the city for the day.

Instead of letting a scheduling committee decide and organize his day or doing so himself, he had his assistant, Tom Regan, collect all the invitations. Tom was told not to answer. Just hold them. And so on the day of the parade, after it was over, the governor and Regan sat in the car and went through the invitations, deciding where to go. "We couldn't tell the press where he was going, and we couldn't tell people where he was not going," says the former aide.

"He is a black Irishman," says a well-known state official who admires Carey. "Everything is bad. A black Irishman is introspective and moody.

They can be surly or giddy. They have a damp, dark view of humanity, like a bad morning in Dublin with the fog rolling in. They have a sharp, piercing sense of humor that can destroy you. Their humor is destructive."

"He never shows his whole self to anybody. He shows as much as he wants you to see," adds David Garth.

"It's not my style to go around saying, 'Hi ya, fella,' " the governor said in response to such comments while lingering briefly in the doorway to his New York office.

A top state official thinks Carey deliberately hides himself—"Like an octopus, he puts up a smoke screen, usually with a barrage of words. Most people we know, the one thing that makes them human is that they exchange feelings. You don't exchange feelings with Hugh Carey. His feelings about people come out in little bon mots."

Usually. Sometimes they come out in other ways. When the wives of his communications director Harry O'Donnell and of writer-friend Peter Maas died, Carey lavished on them the compassionate concern of a lifelong friend, which he was not. More recently, Office of General Services Commissioner James O'Shea lost his wife to cancer. Suddenly in the course of an Albany speech proclaiming Women's Month, Carey interjected praise of O'Shea's "dear wife Kathleen," whom he barely knew. "He knows how it cuts," explains an associate, reflecting on the incident. "He knows this particular person at this particular time needs to be reached for."

"He was close to only one person—his wife," says a political associate. Helen Carey died of cancer in the spring of 1974.

Yet her memory apparently remains a central part of Hugh Carey's life. Her picture rests on the mantel of the Albany mansion's large living room, and in the family room. Her pretty face stares at Carey from the bookcase in his office. "He still loves his wife," says an old friend, recalling that Carey changed his position in support of the Vietnam war "after Helen kept telling him that the war was no good." The friend also recalls that he had often been in the same room with Carey's frequent date, Anne Ford Uzielli, and Carey never introduced them. Why? Because, he thinks, "I was a friend of Helen's."

Workers in his 1974 race for governor remember that even at low moments, when a primary victory seemed hopeless, Carey would reassure them by saying, "Things will be okay. We have a campaign manager. She is watching over us. She is always with us." A similar belief, suggests David Burke, explains Carey's principled positions in opposition to the death penalty, Abe Beame, and the bloodshed in Northern Ireland. "Carey is a very religious man," he says. "He believes he is being monitored. That there is a scorecard. That he is accountable." Not just to God, but to Helen.

Carey's circle of friends is small. The person closest to him is thought to be Dr. Kevin Cahill, his non-salaried health adviser and the doctor who treated Helen before she died. He spends time socially with Phyllis and Robert Wagner and Felix Rohatyn. Carey most often frequents P. J.

Clarke's, the "21," Elaine's, Jimmy Weston's and sometimes his favorite Chinese restaurant, the Shun Lee Palace. At these places, particularly at P. J.'s and Jimmy Weston's, he usually swaps bon mots and holds court with fellow Irishmen, including Tully, Thruway Commissioner Jerry Cummins, consulting engineer John Hennessee and writer Jimmy Breslin.

The *News*'s Liz Smith reported recently that Carey took Anne Ford Uzielli home at 2:30 A.M., and went back to Elaine's "to sit alone at a table." He did until Elaine encouraged a delegation of writers to join the governor, who traded jokes with them into the early hours.

Such tales fuel rumors that the governor likes his drink. Carey's associates dismiss these tales. "I've never seen him out of control," says a close aide.

A colleague who sees Carey socially adds, "There was a big rumor about that in the campaign. I have never seen the man drunk. Of course, for an Irishman the idea of drunk may be different than for an Italian." He believes the rumor chases Carey because of stereotypes about Irish politicians.

The other reason it chases Carey is because people are searching for explanations for his often erratic behavior. With the governor so secretive about his schedule, people begin to wonder when he comes in late to work. Why did he act so precipitously in firing Special Prosecutor Maurice Nadjari or endorsing Mario Cuomo? Why did he say in the text of his Northern Ireland speech, "I am somewhat reluctant to speak as an expert on the difficulties except on the broadest philosophical level"—and then in a press conference specifically denounce members of the Irish Republican Army as "killers" and "Marxists?"

Why did he refuse to state his position on capital punishment one week, and then threaten to veto a bill on it the next?

Whatever the truth about Carey's drinking, the speculation no doubt will go on as long as this brooding, distant man remains so unpredictable. "This guy can come off the wall at any moment," says municipal labor leader Victor Gotbaum, echoing a now-familiar refrain. "You never know what he's going to do."

What makes Carey tick? Who cares, responds Secretary of State Mario Cuomo, who has been known to puzzle over the question himself. "He's a good governor. Why not settle for that? Why do all this psychological probing?

"He saved the city from bankruptcy. He organized the Northeast governors. He came up with a good budget. He's helping restore business confidence. Who cares if he's happy or not?"

When Carey's not happy, it shows. A year ago he was an unhappy man. He was feuding with the legislature; bleeding from wounds inflicted by a then-credible Special State Prosecutor Maurice Nadjari and the indictments (since dismissed) of State Democratic Chairman Pat Cunningham; eclipsed by Mayor Beame, who rushed to Jimmy Carter first. Polls showed the governor as one of the state's least popular figures. Heady dreams of becoming the Democratic vice-presidential candidate were dashed. Carey sulked, lost his confidence, lost interest in state government.

Today he's a less unhappy man. His polls show he is popular, and many believe he has mellowed along with the polls. "I think he enjoys being governor now," says Burke. "He's very confident now."

"A year ago," says a leaner Carey, standing in the doorway to his office, "I had people around me saying I ought to go for the vice-presidency: 'This thing is going nowhere. There is no money.' Well, that's now been turned around. We did cut taxes. We do have some dollars to do things. *Now* I have a great sense of confidence in managing the state . . ."

The phone rang. His secretary announced that it was his son Thomas. ". . . The kids are enjoying it more," Carey continued. "The other day Thomas said to me, 'Daddy, we don't want to leave Albany. You have to run again." The governor wore his Mona Lisa smile as he turned and retreated into his office to speak to Thomas.

Remove Carey's contradictory masks—the statesman versus the slick politician, the strategist versus the tactical bumbler, the Irish pol versus the recluse, the bitter black Irishman versus the loving husband and father— and you are still left with a man who must be judged a good governor.

Carey seems to have an anchor, a sense of right and wrong. This is not to say he is trustworthy or pleasant, but it is to say that at the core of his person one finds hard principle. People can differ with his tactics or his choice of Mario Cuomo for mayor in 1977, but it's difficult to argue that his opposition to Beame's reelection was politically motivated. He didn't have to get involved. Just as he didn't have to press the legislature to resist popular howls to extend capital punishment.

Governor Carey is very different from candidate Carey. When he ran in 1974, Carey promised voters he would hold the city subway fare at thirty-five cents, subsidize Mitchell Lama rents, freeze electricity costs for senior citizens, pick up "at least fifty percent of the burden of local educational costs," insist on home rule because "a governor can exert strong leadership without forcing localities to abdicate power."

People didn't get what they voted for. Instead they got a governor who was smart enough to understand the depth of the fiscal crisis he inherited and wise enough not to spend his time blaming Republicans. Better to have a candidate who fibs than a governor who doesn't know what he's doing.

As a governor, Carey has also changed. "He's a lot surer and understands strategy more—how to get things done," observes a ranking state official who works closely with him. "He once rode passively with a state budget gap for ten months. He wouldn't do that now."

"Another difference in Carey from a year ago," says an aide, "is that he delegates more. When one of us makes a decision, he doesn't jump on us as quickly. He now understands you have to make decisions. Secondly, his involvement in this year's budget was superb. He must have spent 200 to

250 hours on the budget. And he spent it in the right way. He was less concerned with whether the Adirondack Park should have another hearing officer than he was on the big spending areas, like health. If this were 1967, a governor would have proposed a $1-billion tax increase. But Hugh Carey worked it through in a sustained way, as if he were shopping for a new thrust for the state."

A moment after describing this Carey, the same state official slipped back in his chair and moaned about another Carey, the one who that same week had embarrassed the legislature by vetoing a June primary bill to which he had previously given a green light.

Carey himself points to another change. His proudest accomplishment in the two and a half years he has been governor, he told me, is the 3.4 percent interest the state paid this month for the sale of $390 million in notes—"the smallest interest rate in five years." He talked of the money this saved the state to spend on other programs, of the $2.3 billion New York City would earmark for debt service in the coming fiscal year and how he couldn't get Abe Beame to focus on this problem. A similar complaint has often been aimed at Carey and his sidekick Felix Rohatyn, since many of their schemes to prevent bankruptcy have succeeded because they stretched—and enlarged—the city's overall debt burden. But Carey's pride in the state's low interest rate is justified. It reflects widespread confidence in Carey's fiscal stewardship.

"It may have been hell getting there," says a close aide, "but every time there were two outs in the ninth he put the ball over the wall."

Not every time. As chief executive, Carey also strikes out a lot. Asked why Carey has so little contact with his agency heads and has not immersed himself in the operations of most state agencies, a top state officer started to answer, then stopped himself and thought a moment. "The first words out of my mouth were going to be that he hasn't had to," he said. "That's the man. What has this governor done in two and a half years that he hasn't had to? That's his greatest weakness."

The weakness exists, he says, because the private Carey is still learning how to be an executive. "He doesn't know how to do things. How to take over a problem on a sustained basis. To define the problem. To pick people. That's the anti-manager Hugh Carey. That's where he's the prisoner of his own intelligence—he gets by on his wits. He's not a good manager of people. He doesn't manage us. He doesn't recognize the difference between a speech and a program." So, says this executive chamber official who admires but has no personal feelings for the governor, the great failure has been that "We haven't set an agenda for most state agencies. We do not look at the quality of how an agency executes its function. Instead we spend time on bills, legislative programs, annual messages. The dance of government, not the running or monitoring of it."

Carey is a crisis junkie. His support of the mayoral candidacy of Mario

Cuomo provides another diverting "crisis," providing an excuse for him not to hunker down to the glamorless task of managing a sprawling government.

Carey's style in governing is as different as his complex personality. One prominent state Republican wonders why "I've never seen him travel with a briefcase or a file. Rockefeller was always doing his homework. I take work home every night, every weekend. I get the feeling he doesn't do that . . . I don't think he's a guy who plans, who has an agenda. Rockefeller always came into a meeting with a pad. I've never seen Hugh Carey with a pad."

Working for Carey is not joyful. One of his four closest aides simply says, "He drives us crazy." On the eve of his own reelection effort, Carey is about to lose chief of staff Dave Burke, who will probably take a major media executive job; Budget Director Peter Goldmark, whom Carey regards as "a genius," is up for the post of executive director of the Port Authority, and counsel Judah Gribetz is often mentioned for a spot in the Carter government. They are three of Carey's four top aides. Each admires the governor and has a family to feed, but one senses they are worn out.

"The warmest he isn't. He yells," says one secretary in the executive chamber. A middle-level employee in the governor's city office expressed disgust when recalling this year's Christmas party at the mansion. The entire executive office staff was invited. Everyone was thrilled. They would have a chance to socialize with their boss, the man who had been too busy because of the pressing fiscal crisis. But instead of coming downstairs to mingle with the staff, Carey spent most of the time closeted upstairs, sipping wine with a few aides.

"You've got to provide your own rewards," says a now-wizened veteran. "He's not long on compliments or thank-you's." State Tax Commissioner James Tully, Jr., whose relationship goes way back to Carey's congressional days, agrees that "He's a tough man to work for. He can be demanding and sharp. He's the brightest man I know. His heart's in the right place, but you have to get to it."

A different perspective is provided by Steve Berger, executive director of the Emergency Financial Control Board. The morale problems which periodically plague Carey's staff, he thinks, are often self-inflicted: "The bitching comes from guys wanting to be stroked. Carey doesn't do that well. But he lets you do your job." David Garth makes a similar point: "You've got to be very secure to live with a guy like Hugh Carey."

Legislators, who must seek reelection every two years, are not terribly secure. A year ago Assembly Speaker Stanley Steingut's staff prepared what they called "The War Memo," sketching a secret strategy for waging war against the leader of their party. Hugh Carey was not very popular. For the first time in 104 years the legislature overrode a governor's veto (the Stavisky-Goodman bill); for the first time in 153 years, the State Senate rejected a gubernatorial nominee (Herman Schwartz as chairman of the Commission on Corrections).

In the last year both sides have pulled back from this precipice. The tone and texture of relations between Carey and the legislature are improved, if still shaky. Some of Carey's initial problems in dealing with them had to do with expectations. Most legislators believed former Congressman Carey was one of the boys, an Irish pol. Not without reason. Such an advertisement was a central thrust of Carey's campaign for governor. But, according to Representative Ed Koch, who served with Carey in the Congress and liked him, "He was a loner . . . While sitting on the floor of the House, I never saw Hughie move around and sit next to anyone. He had a reserve. But he was easy to talk to."

It bothers many legislators that the governor is not easy to talk to, and has yet to find a strong staff person whose primary job it is to talk to the legislature. Jim Tully explains Carey's distance by saying, "If he socializes with an assemblyman, they'll ask about a bill. It wasn't that way in the Congress. Now he's the recipient of the requests." Dave Garth offers another explanation: "It was a cultural shock for him. The difference between Washington, D.C., and Albany is like night and day. It took him a year to get over it. Now he plays the game more, but he's still not warm to it."

Assembly Democratic Majority Leader Stanley Fink praises Carey as "a good executive. He's loosened up a great deal and is exhibiting more trust and confidence in people." Yet he admits, "I find it tough to communicate with Hugh Carey. It may be me." No, Stanley, it's not.

How Carey is judged as a political leader depends on the audience. He would not, for instance, receive applause from most party and labor leaders. "He's a liar. His word means nothing" is the none-too-gentle proclamation of a city Democratic county leader. One reason labor leaders like Victor Gotbaum and teachers' union president Al Shanker have been so cool to the Cuomo candidacy is because Carey is its godfather.

There has been some very vague talk of a candidate to challenge Carey in a primary next year. There is resentment that Carey has not sufficiently rewarded the party faithful with patronage, that he too quickly abandoned the beleaguered State Chairman Pat Cunningham, that he deserts his own party when he pledges to support Cuomo as a Liberal if he loses the Democratic mayoral primary. Many reformers and liberals are upset to see Carey praised in William Buckley's *National Review* magazine, and feel he has been too quick to slash social spending programs. Irish-American leaders are steaming mad at what they take to be Carey's lace-curtain Irish blast at the IRA.

From their point of view, they are correct. From the public's point of view, Carey is doing just fine. Like Governor Jerry Brown of California, he does well in the polls because he is speaking out, because he is so unpredictable, because he has become something of a character. He's not another plastic politician. The more groups he angers, the better he does. Carey's closest advisers concede that in this time of instant communication what used to be bad politics is now good politics.

"I think he's a terrible political leader in the traditional sense," says Steve Berger. "But he's facing the right issues. No, he's not helping the party structure in the traditional sense. But he'll be a great guy to ride the coattails of in 1978." Gotbaum reluctantly agrees: "What makes him almost unbeatable is that he's gone almost to the extreme right. As a progressive, I hate to admit it, but he and Rockefeller have the formula: A Republican has to move to the left and a Democrat has to move somewhat to the right."

In this larger sense, Carey might be considered a very gifted political leader. As it took a conservative Republican to open doors to mainland China or to make détente respectable, so it may take "liberal" Democrats to teach that a budget is a set of limitations, that borrowing and inflation cost money. Fiscal conservatism is a key component of Carey's current popularity, in the style of Brown and Jimmy Carter.

"Carey can't be beaten by a Republican because he is a Republican," says a Democrat considered close to Carey. "He can only be beaten by a Democrat." Or maybe by himself.

Carey the Bull Artist

New York *Daily News,* September 30, 1979

"My brother Joe bought a fancy sixteen-cylinder Cadillac, second-hand, and Hughie borrowed the car one Saturday night without Joe's permission," Edward Carey once said of his younger brother, Hugh Carey. "Joe went out to get it, and the car was gone—Hughie had taken it off on one of his dates.

"He brought it back the next morning, and the car was just about demolished. Joe said, 'What did you do to my car?' Hughie said, 'What did I do to your car? That damn car of yours knocked down the Fulton Street el.' In other words, it wasn't his fault; it was the car's fault."

Grown up now, Governor Hugh Carey remains something of a bull artist, as recent events remind us. Carey aides privately concede he failed to properly apply for federal mass-transit funds—yet this week Carey screamed it was Washington's fault. He tried to hold the fifty-cent fare hostage to a November state bond issue—yet later denied this was true, claiming it wasn't his fault for saying it.

The governor has many sterling virtues. High regard for the truth and keeping his word don't happen to be among them. Back in August 1975 Carey said that Mayor Abe Beame, "faced with almost insurmountable economic problems, has shown himself to be tough and decisive. . . . I wish to commend him for his determination and strength."

Some months later Carey plotted to depose Beame. When this scheme surfaced, at first Carey denied it. Then, in August 1977, he called Beame "a weakling" who "showed lack of leadership" during the fiscal crisis. This came not long after he unceremoniously abandoned his hand-picked state Democratic chairman, Patrick Cunningham, when Cunningham was reeling from a torrent of vicious innuendo from the state special prosecutor.

When Carey's footprints were unearthed behind the candidacy of Mario Cuomo for mayor in 1977, he solemnly told reporters, "I'm not indicating a preference." Soon thereafter Carey endorsed Cuomo, vowing to support Cuomo on the Liberal line if he lost the Democratic primary.

When he was stumping for Cuomo in the Bronx that September, Beth Fallon of the *News* caught Carey pledging "a review" of the death penalty —but only if Cuomo were elected. Carey heatedly insisted that what was in Fallon's notebook wasn't his fault.

After Cuomo lost the Democratic primary run-off, Carey wiggled out of his commitment to Cuomo and endorsed Ed Koch, denying he had ever made a commitment to the Liberal party.

Two weeks ago, at a lunch with *Daily News* editors and reporters, Carey thundered that the fifty-cent subway fare would be jeopardized if voters rejected the $500-million bond issue on the November ballot. The next day, after being roundly attacked for retreating from a 1978 pledge to maintain the fare through 1982, Carey denied linking the fare to the bond issue.

Last week Leslie Maitland of the *Times* reported that Carey said he had "a firm commitment" from the Carter administration for "at least $60 million more than it would normally get" in transit aid, and for a total of $644 million. When federal officials expressed shock at what the governor's aides concede is a stretching of the truth, Carey launched an assault against unnamed federal officials.

"It was typical Hugh Carey," said one White House aide who journeyed with the President to New York last week. "He takes something that's ten-percent true, blows it up, and puts you on the defensive. By the time you've got your jaw back up, you're the bad guy. You stand there and say, 'He hit me!' while the public believes you hit him."

Equally typical is the dance Carey has performed around whether he will or will not support President Carter's reelection. At first the governor said he "expected" to support Carter. Then he said he would support Carter if Ted Kennedy did. This was amended to: I will support Carter if he runs for reelection. Later, at Camp David this summer, Carey joined a delegation of governors in flat-out endorsing Carter.

"He's endorsed us" is how Joel McCleary, Carter's state coordinator, described Carey's posture in midsummer. After Carter's transportation and energy speech at the New York Hilton on Tuesday, however, this is how Carey described his position in response to the question: Do you support Carter?

"After that energy speech? I think that was a fine speech."

Do you support Carter's reelection?

"I think we ought to have a political moratorium," Carey said, beginning a long response, a cascade of noise rushing from his mouth without punctuation, pause, or even paragraphs, drowning reporters in a waterfall of words.

But, Governor, do you support Carter?

"I have never announced for an unannounced candidate yet," he replied, wiggling away. "If Carter announced tomorrow," observed one of Carey's close government associates, mockingly, "Carey would tell the press, 'No, I never said I'd support him right after he announced. I said I'd support him *sometime* after he announced. Show me where I said the *next* day!' "
The rule: Always go on the offensive.

Ask David Garth, one of Carey's closest political counselors, to explain where the governor stands, and he says, "His current position is one of cemented neutrality."

Ask Lieutenant Governor Mario Cuomo, who is shepherding the Carter effort in the state, and he good-naturedly laughs. "How the hell do I know? It's all gas."

Ask White House agent Joel McCleary what Carey's position is, and he diplomatically sidesteps, saying, "The President feels Hugh Carey has endorsed him." Does McCleary feel that? "You can find statements where Carey has endorsed him," he says.

Admittedly, none of this may qualify Carey as a liar. "Carey is one of the best obfuscators in history," remarks Garth, mindful that slyness is an attribute of any skillful pol. Additionally, circumstances change. This summer Ted Kennedy had yet to announce his unannounced candidacy. This September, when Carey's "good friend" Kennedy shuffled the deck, the governor contracted his own case of presidential fever. "I think he thinks that by August he may be in the picture," observes Cuomo.

"There are two schools of thought among politicians," suggests an elected official. "One is the predictability school. It argues that in order to do business with the media, the legislature, other politicians, you have to have predictability or the system of trust breaks down. Your word is your bond, cementing relationships.

"The other school says that when you give your word, you lose options. To be pinned down or sometimes to live up to your word denies you flexibility, and flexibility is more important than predictability."

Mayor Koch and Mario Cuomo adhere to the first school. Correctly or not, they made a commitment to support Carter, and they will keep it. If either gave you his word, you could mortgage the house on it. Neither is a wiggler.

Most of the elected officials attending Mayor Koch's Hilton Hotel reception for Carter on Tuesday were wigglers. Few agreed to be pinned down. That's an acceptable part of the game. Like Carey, they were keeping their options open, perhaps waiting to gauge the mood of their constitutents, perhaps hoping to angle a federal grant for their community, perhaps waiting to glimpse who the winner might be.

So why is Carey different? Because most of the politicians sipping soft drinks and waiting to clasp Carter's hand as he circulated throughout the room had not made a commitment to support Carter; because they do not, regularly, deny the observable truth. They are coy, not mischievous. They had not crossed the line separating a skilled pol from a political opportunist.

Hugh Carey, once again, had crossed that line. He's been a pretty good governor; he's fairly popular among voters. But few colleagues, including Jimmy Carter, would dare turn their back on him.

SECOND THOUGHTS

A reader might wonder how the same reporter could write so differently about the same man. The 1977 Hugh Carey, despite his flaws, is presented as a good governor; the 1979 Cary as a bull artist. The disparity between the two says something about the subjectivity of columnists. At the time I wrote about Carey the bull artist, I was disturbed by his mischievous behavior, his unreliability. Cornered at a function for President Carter, the governor did more than evade press questions. He insulted reporters by assuming we would be pacified by his blather.

The second column zeroed in on the least attractive part of Carey. But it focused on only one part of a complex man. The column was a snapshot of a single side of a man at a single point in time. At other times, the negative qualities shine less bright than the positive.

Carey was angered by this column. He launched an attack on a Sunday-morning television program, charging that I was still resentful that he beat Howard Samuels, my candidate for governor in the 1974 Democratic primary. Ironically, while Carey thought I was bending over backward to wound him, in fact, over the years my interpretative pieces about him bent over backward to prove I held no grudges, to show how "fair" I was. I had always been self-conscious, fearing that the governor or his people might make that charge. Although I offered Carey no pillows, and was at times quite critical, I was inhibited. If I were too hard on him, I'd lose journalistic credibility. If I were too soft, I might not be serving the reader. This is the kind of dilemma common to public officials who feel they must choose from among the lesser evils. In a sense, I suspect this column represents my liberation. I no longer feel compelled to prove my impartiality. Hugh Carey has become just another guy I write about.

A Confused Director
Meets a Confused President

New York *Daily News*, June 10, 1979

The White House screening room was in use May 10. The President of the United States, several Cabinet secretaries and a flock of staff aides, perhaps fifty in all, were eager to see Francis Ford Coppola's unfinished epic *Apocalypse Now.*

The talented director of *Godfather* I and II paced nervously in front of the screen, biting his fingernails, scratching his beard, asking his distinguished audience to please keep one question in mind as they viewed the film: How should my movie end? While Coppola spoke, a market-research firm tabulated answers to the same question posed to three preview audiences in Westwood, California.

Several hours later, the movie over, the lights on, Coppola awaited suggestions. For fifteen minutes the President and his guests sat in stunned silence, saying nothing. Coppola departed without suggestions, and at least one White House aide departed in disgust.

The movie, which the aide thought flawed, disturbed him less than Coppola's groping insecurity. "Here's a major artist," said the aide, "a person from whom we expect vision, if nothing else. And what does he do? He passes out poll cards to find out how to end his greatest work, which is based on a novel by Joseph Conrad that already has an ending. It's unbelievable."

Not really. His boss, the President of the United States, is also known to take polls before deciding what to think. The Congress, with its ear to the ground, insists on a painless energy policy. New York City's Council and Board of Estimate, with their eyes on the next election, vie to add more cops to next year's budget. The mayor asks, "Hi, how'm I doing?" And when 70 percent respond favorably, Koch assumes he is doing fine.

Like television, our politics is a slave to rating points. How a performance is received often becomes the sole measure of effectiveness. In his superb new book *The Powers That Be,* David Halberstam recounts the time CBS invited celebrities to screen a Mary Martin special. When the lights went on, Truman Capote turned to CBS president Frank Stanton and exclaimed, "Isn't it wonderful!"

"Well, we really won't know until tomorrow when we get the ratings, will we?" Stanton blankly responded.

Like CBS, Jimmy Carter takes overnight samplings to measure his television performances. The *ME* decade has produced a generation of "other-directed" salesmen—politicians who feed the public what polls say they want, publishers who hawk how-to books and pulp novels, editors who demand more gossip and service. The Democratic voters of Kentucky recently purchased an empty package prettily labeled: John Y. Brown/Phyllis George.

An "inner-directed" leader like Woodrow Wilson would no doubt feel as if he were on another planet today. The former President began to school himself for public life at an early age. He studied the lives and thoughts of great British statesmen—Disraeli, Gladstone, John Bright. Just as Theodore Roosevelt struggled to prepare his body for more vigorous activity while at Harvard, Wilson struggled to learn to think and speak while at Princeton. He took lonely walks in the woods and practiced elocution to empty pews in his father's church. While still in his twenties, Wilson wrote *Congressional Government,* a seminal book exposing Congress's abuse of power and advancing the philosophy of a strong President.

As President, Wilson toiled for days on a single speech, much as presidential candidate Adlai Stevenson would in 1952. It may not have been time-efficient, but at least voters knew that they were not voting for the glib vision of an image-maker or speechwriter. Wilson spent less time hovering over his In box and more thinking about where he hoped to navigate the nation. And because he understood that leadership consisted of more than checking off the right policy option, his polished speeches, like FDR's practiced radio addresses, swayed people.

At the climax of his first campaign for President in 1912, Wilson addressed a packed Madison Square Garden. The speech was greeted by one hour and four minutes of sustained applause. The *New York Times* reported:

> Governor Wilson of New Jersey, who has spent many years of his life in studious paths and has been referred to by his opponents as a cold and bookish professor, last night turned a regular old-fashioned political meeting of 16,000 persons . . . into a wild, raving, cheering, yelling, roaring, stamping mob of enthusiasts that needed no songs and no hymns and no encouragement to keep it at a high pitch.

Like Wilson, Jimmy Carter is a good man. But unlike the first-term Wilson, he is not yet an effective President. One reason is his failure to project vision. Contrast Wilson with the Carter portrayed by his former speechwriter James Fallows in the *Atlantic Monthly*:

> I started to wonder about the difference between a good man and an inspiring one; about why Jimmy Carter, who would surely outshine most other leaders in the judgment of the Lord, had such trouble generating excitement, not only in the nation but even among the members of his own staff. One explanation is that Carter has not given us an idea to follow. The central idea

in the Carter administration is Carter himself. . . . I came to think that Carter believes fifty things, but no one thing. He holds explicit, thorough positions on every issue under the sun, but he has no large view of the relations between them, no line indicating which goals (reducing unemployment? human rights?) will take precedence over which (inflation control? a SALT treaty?) when the goals conflict. Spelling out these choices makes the difference between a position and a philosophy. . . .

The criticism that Carter lacked a philosophy or ideology was thrown at him in 1976 by liberal Democrats. Some of us thought the criticism unfair, believing instead that Hubert Humphrey was preaching an out-of-date old-time religion. Perhaps Jimmy Carter would eclectically redefine liberalism, shucking policies that didn't work, seeking to unscramble riddles ignored by most New Deal liberals: inflation, bureaucracy, big government, a musclebound civil service, mismanagement, dwindling budget and natural resources.

Maybe Carter couldn't turn on 16,000 people in Madison Square Garden the way a Humphrey or even a Ted Kennedy could, but at least he was thinking fresh, liberating the Democratic party of its New Deal crutches. He would fling open the windows of the Democratic church. He had a plan.

In fact, Carter had no plan or sense of priorities, no philosophy to bring order to his universe. He was eclectic—to a fault. And unlike a Wilson or FDR or LBJ, he lacks a sense of process, a feel for how government works. Instead of preparing himself to govern as Wilson did, Carter spent the two years prior to 1976 preparing to get elected—traveling, getting to know editors and reporters, meeting delegates, sleeping in local homes, boning up on geography rather than history.

How totally he misunderstood the process of governance is seen from the tire marks. At first Jimmy Carter revved his engine, driving over the Congress and the Washington establishment. He vowed to weaken the White House staff and rely on his Cabinet, raced to read every memo the day it came in, and approached tax reform and energy legislation as if they were technical rather than political problems.

Today Carter has gunned his engine into reverse, now seeking to mollify the Congress and the establishment, to strengthen the White House staff at the expense of his Cabinet, to better husband his own time, to become more political.

Admittedly, effective leadership is more difficult now than it was in Wilson's day. Multiple special-interest groups ambush Mayor Koch's civil-service-reform efforts and Carter's hospital cost containment legislation. To suggest, as Carter has, that Menachem Begin is a rigid ideologue, insensitive to the plight of the Palestinians, invites charges of anti-Semitism.

The growing dominance of television and the media also makes leadership more difficult. An omnipresent press induces politicians to become more "other-directed," to prize press notices. But more. The media robs our

Presidents of an aura of mystery, makes them too human. "We didn't live in Woodrow Wilson's bathroom," grouses a White House aide, mindful that the press's gluttonous appetite for something new—"news"—leads to overexposure.

Our Presidents, like old TV programs, become bores. "The President becomes one more talking head," says the White House aide. "He becomes the same size on the tube as all those other talking heads." He becomes too familiar. Giving low poll ratings to incumbents is the public's way of flicking to another channel.

To explain, however, is not to excuse. FDR employed radio to overcome the implacable hostility of Republican publishers. Eisenhower managed to communicate sincerity and retain public trust for the better part of eight years. George Washington, historian Hans J. Morgenthau reminds us, "proclaimed the neutrality of the United States in the War of the First Coalition against revolutionary France in 1793, while the popular consensus fervently wanted him to join France in that war. For weeks, crowds roamed the streets of Philadelphia clamoring for Washington's head, and John Marshall reports in his biography of Washington that if a motion for Washington's impeachment had not been tabled in Congress, it would have passed with an overwhelming majority. Yet if Washington had made consensus the ultimate yardstick of his policy, he would have gone down in history as the wrecker, not the father, of his country."

On some isues—SALT, the Middle East, energy—Carter has often exhibited courage and refused to pander. But, as an aide to the President admits, "Just being parental is not leadership. It doesn't motivate people." Governing, like directing movies, is an art, not a science. As is apparently true of Coppola's movie, Jimmy Carter doesn't seem to know where he's going. Or how to get there.

Carterizing Jerry Brown

New York *Daily News*, August 5, 1979

He is unpopular among voters, legislators, Washington insiders and the liberal wing of the Democratic party. Much of the press smirks at him. Critics lambaste his arrogance, complaining that he delegates poorly, is encircled by too many loyalists with Alamo mentalities, is a lousy politician, an incompetent leader, and is, well, strange.

Jimmy Carter? No, Jerry Brown.

After four and a half years as governor of California, Jerry Brown has been *Carterized.* Brown, who this week formed a committee to collect funds to challenge President Carter for the 1980 Democratic nomination, is in the peculiar position of opposing an incumbent whom he has been compared to rather than contrasted with.

At a time when Carter's poll ratings rival Richard Nixon's after Watergate, when leading Democrats in Congress warn that the clock is ticking and Carter has a few scarce months to reverse his political nose dive, when even such stalwarts as Attorney General Griffin Bell concede Carter may lose several primaries—Carter's only semi-declared Democratic foe is dismissed by those most eager to oust the President.

This is but one of several ironies haunting Brown. While some party pros believe Carter may be the first sitting President since Franklin Pierce to be denied his party's renomination, ironically, the chief beneficiary appears to be not Brown but Senator Edward Kennedy, who says he expects to support Carter.

A surprising number of Democrats don't take Brown seriously. This arouses anxiety among the Californian's advisers. Unwittingly, they fear, Brown may become a stalking horse for Kennedy, bloodying Carter in the early primaries and thus paving the way for Kennedy to be summoned to unify the Democratic party.

What creates still another irony is that polls and the record of the Democratic Congress suggest Carter and Brown are closer to the public's cautious mood on most issues than the more liberal Kennedy.

Though Brown runs almost abreast of Carter in national polls, in California his popularity sags. His 1976 approval rating of 85 percent has plummeted to below 50 percent, according to a recent survey. Matched against Kennedy and Carter in a hypothetical California primary, Brown attracts a measly 14 percent of the vote; Carter receives 17 percent, and Kennedy, 59 percent.

"It's obvious that he's at the bottom of the well," observes California Democratic State Chairman Richard O'Neill. Over the past thirty-three years, the California state legislature has overridden six gubernatorial vetoes. Four of these six came during Brown's tenure, three of them in the legislative session just completed. In a fit of spite and rage over her Vietnam views, the legislature recently rejected Brown's appointment of actress Jane Fonda to the state arts council.

Brown, who believes he has the vision Carter lacks and is less beholden to liberal ideology than Kennedy, may be a prophet without a party. "I agree with much of what Jerry says," explains a prominent elected California Democrat. "He addresses the economic issues—too little growth, too little productivity, too much inflation, too many federal deficits—our party tends to ignore. But he's an arrogant brat." Among politicians who know Brown and reporters who cover him, the suspicion is widespread that he has no anchor, no fixed convictions, no commitments— except to his own advancement.

A visit to the state capitol in Sacramento finds Brown surprisingly relaxed about all this. Greeting a reporter in the vestibule of his modernistic office, Brown is jacketless, the vest of his spacious Wall Street gray suit draping unbuttoned over a thin frame.

A few months ago Brown was shaped like a pear. He has since shed thirty-five pounds, eager to be combat-ready for a grueling campaign and, no doubt, to please singer Linda Ronstadt, whom he sees and phones regularly.

Inviting a reporter to wander with him in the botanical garden ringing the capitol building, Brown relaxes on a freshly painted white bench, waving to constituents who stroll by. He is bemused and perplexed by his unpopularity.

"I don't know why," he admits, one arm extended over the back of the bench, the other bracing his chin. "To most people it's become a cliché, a herd reaction. I am an indigestible element in the Democratic establishment. The contradiction is that some say I am a conventional politician, and others that I am unorthodox. Those things don't go together."

Echoing sentiments voiced by aides to Jimmy Carter, Gray Davis, Brown's chief of staff, claims the political establishment distrusts Brown "because he doesn't practice the politics of flattery. There is a College of Cardinals in this country that expects consultation. If you don't consult them frequently, they get upset."

Says Brown, "I really think that some of the ideas I'm trying to formulate are part of the tension. Some of it is personality. But a lot of it is due to ideas. I'm making their jobs harder by pushing against certain constituencies."

In recent months Brown has bucked his party by opposing huge hikes in pay for state employees and welfare recipients, by rushing to embrace Proposition 13, by zipping about the country preaching a constitutional amendment to mandate balanced federal budgets. Though Brown dubs himself a liberal, he believes liberal democracy is at the mercy of "the whole gang of people who are at the public fountain." Elected officials encounter political difficulty resisting what he calls the "guilt and greed coalition"— labor unions, welfare recipients, campaign contributors, doctors, corporations.

Boredom is another Brown affliction. The man who once boasted "The first rule of politics is to be different" is by now a familiar act. He admits, "Yeh, it does get boring. There's been a lot of drumbeat."

Although the head of the state government in California, Brown is an incessant critic of that government's bureaucratic institutions. However, he clearly realizes the public could hold him responsible for the things he's been hollering about. He sees that this is exactly what has happened to Jimmy Carter, and he is working on a strategy to see that it doesn't happen to him.

Brown is the first major candidate for President with views shaped not by the New Deal or World War II or the Cold War, but by the sixties. The skepticism this former Jesuit seminarian brings to many public issues, his sense of the limits of government action, are out of sync with the evangelical fervor of Kennedy and the liberals who dominate the Democratic party. His cool detachment is more common among journalists than politicians.

"Jerry Brown may be a transitional figure in American politics," says adviser Mickey Kantor, who managed Brown's belated 1976 primary challenge to Carter. It may be that someone else will piggyback and reap Brown's rewards.

Brown understands that he may be a transitional figure; not just a bridge over which Kennedy could gallop to the nomination, but a bridge connecting New Deal liberalism to something new. "We're on the verge of the collapse of traditional political rhetoric," he says, mindful the collapse could come after 1980. "I suppose the only way I can interpret myself in a positive light is to say I stand somewhat alone."

Brown's slogans—like "planetary realism"—seem as strange to a Northern ear as Jimmy Carter's Southern accent and Baptist piety. But as the following exchange with a hapless David Susskind reveals, Brown is no flake:

SUSSKIND: "You can't use phrases like that [planetary realism]. People can't understand it."

BROWN: "People use phrases like 'the New Deal' and 'the New Frontier.' "

SUSSKIND: "That's comprehensible."

BROWN: "The New Deal? What is it? A deck of cards? . . . Now I want to tell you planetary realism recognizes that this planet is finite. It is limited.

And we're all on it together. We're crew members of this limited point in the universe. We can destroy our own nest, with pollution, with an arms race, overpopulation, with greed, and as we sense that we are not just American, or Russian, or Mexican, we are human beings. . . . We know the earth is a small place, and that we are locked in an interdependent biosphere that can be degraded, and very much threatened, and the word 'planetary' symbolizes and points to that. The word 'realism' indicates that we're going to be realistic about these new concepts of man, and the nationalism, the egocentric . . . view of nations is our major problem."

As with Carter Brown's political problem is that the economic reality he glimpses is closer to Republican than traditional Democratic dogma. While most liberals focus on demand—redistributing income through government spending—Brown stresses the supply side—encouraging economic and thus government revenue growth. Liberals suffer from what Brown calls a "get-it-now philosophy," paying too little heed to the consequences of their actions.

Listen closely to Brown, however, and this theme parrots the shared sacrifice notions favored by the left: "The basic message is that as a people we're overcommitted to consumption rather than investment, and the time is at hand to redress the balance. In the short run, this means a period of fiscal stringency. In the longer term, it will lead to a strong, competitive economy." As many liberals did during the Vietnam war, Brown speaks often of "reordering our priorities."

The difference is that liberals usually want to take from the defense budget and allocate money for domestic needs, assuming almost infinite resources; Brown favors cuts in defense but believes Carter and the Democratic party are doing too little to reduce the proportion of national wealth spent by government. Aside from increasing federal funds earmarked for research and space and mass transportation and job training—all investments in the future—Brown says he would make deeper slashes in the budget, though he doesn't pinpoint them.

In his view, the great American economic machine has stalled. Personal income, which expanded 3 percent annually during the fifties and sixties, is almost static. American productivity, which once led the world, now trails that of Germany and Japan, and recently suffered its steepist plunge in five years. "America," he warns, "is living off its capital," robbing from the future to pay for the present.

"I would like to stand for the idea that it's necessary to build and sacrifice for the future, and to do so now," he says. "People used to save. Now it's get out the credit card, spend more money, tear down trees, get-it-now. That get-it-now philosophy worked when the country was still expanding, when we were pushing the frontiers."

Conceptually, Brown has probably thought more deeply about these issues than John Kennedy had about "getting America moving again" or "the missile gap." His call for a balanced federal budget is not at odds with his long-time view that the country has entered "an era of limits." In a lagging economy, borrowing to finance federal deficits unavoidably siphons the pool of savings available for new investment; enlarging the money supply without expanding the nation's wealth merely fuels inflation. Declining productivity balloons the cost of producing goods and services, also feeding inflation.

Aware that similar messages are being peddled at Republican dinners, Brown is groping to marry these heretical economic views with traditional liberal precepts. Brown says he differs from conservative Republicans in that "I envision a strong mediating role for the federal government. To believe that if we weaken government the market mechanism will solve the problem is an anachronism."

Brown is trying to string a thread stretching from balanced budgets to the need for more savings and investment to greater productivity to reduced inflation to the recognition that there are only so many whales to be killed. All are tied to Brown's concept of limits.

One can find the thread, but it is more compelling intellectually than it is politically. Brown's economic nostrums, like his conversion to Proposition 13 and a balanced federal budget, excite fears in Democratic circles that he is a sly opportunist chasing votes.

And certainly there is ample evidence that Brown has acrobatically flip-flopped on more than one issue. He bested Carter in five straight primary contests in 1976 as a stand-in for Hubert Humphrey, lurching to Carter's left, implicitly rejecting "limits" while embracing the Humphrey-Hawkins full-employment bill.

Back in 1976 Brown championed the "decentralization" of big cities. Today he says, "Given the energy problem, cities are going to be rebuilt. We just can't continue the sprawl. Greater density will be the order of the day." Special aid programs for cities, he says, fail to "achieve majority support. Now the energy crisis gives a real impetus to rebuilding cities. Now it's no longer a case of targeting aid for special cities. It's part of a vow to achieve greater energy self-sufficiency."

In the spring of 1978 Brown predicted Proposition 13 would be "expensive, unworkable and crazy. . . . I am convinced that there is a massive confusion that has been started and perpetrated by the demagoguery of Jarvis." The night Proposition 13 passed, Brown was magically transformed into a true believer.

When asked by Robert Scheer in a 1976 *Playboy* interview, "How do you feel about military spending?" Brown replied, "I'd be surprised if there were dramatic savings to be made." As for peaceful coexistence? "Well, I get the impression that we're being pushed around a lot and that America has become a big sap for the rest of the countries. And I don't like it. We have a lot of strength, so I don't see why we should have guilt feelings and act like we're always the fall guy."

Today Brown sings a different tune: "I would attempt to cut the military. I would cut the MX missile." He says he is vexed, as is George McGovern, that SALT II does not go far enough. Why did he appoint Edison Miller, a former POW who cooperated with Hanoi, to a vacancy on the Orange County Board of Supervisors? In response, Brown utters thoughts conventional liberals timidly shy away from: "The people who brought us into that war, who weakened America, we're not holding them up as pariahs. Many of them are doing well in America. We don't hold it against them. Why hold it against Miller?"

Still, a study of Brown's record suggests he has been more consistent than critics acknowledge. He was an early supporter in 1968 of Senator Eugene McCarthy's anti-war challenge to President Johnson. As governor, he has been an unswerving fiscal conservative, a consistent skeptic about big government, a steady foe of nuclear power, a persistent advocate of limits.

"His politics do not fall neatly into categories that have served political commentators most of this century," claims chief of staff Davis. "Maybe we have to invent a new category to describe Jerry Brown's politics." Since that new category is not at hand, liberal organizations such as Americans for Democratic Action mechanically pigeonhole Brown as a conservative. If one insists on labels, Brown qualifies as both a liberal and a conservative.

He is a liberal in that he opposes capital punishment, the expansion of nuclear power, increases in defense spending, and government prohibitions against abortions. California and Massachusetts have forged the most creative state urban policies in the nation, including anti-redlining legislation; consumer activists have been appointed to California regulatory boards, and his appointments of blacks, women, and Chicanos are unrivaled anywhere.

He is a conservative in that he rails against federal deficits and government bureaucracy, favors space exploration, improved productivity, more savings, more private initiative. In the short run, he is more concerned with inflation than employment.

Labeling can get rather silly. Is Ted Kennedy a conservative because he consorts with "war criminals" like former Defense Secretary Robert McNamara? Or because he supports the deregulation of airlines and trucking?

The notion that Brown is a conservative may say more about his critics, including the press, than it does about him. Not just about their partiality to cartoon labels, but their distrust of Brown. Dismissing someone as a conservative is easier than wrestling with his ideas.

"What is the other side of the argument?" asks Brown. "To print more money? To run bigger deficits? At what point do we bite the bullet and see that America is sliding and focus on a remedy?"

It is the ultimate irony that Brown is dismissed not because of what he says but because an important body of opinion doesn't believe he means it.

He seems to lack compassion. The self-proclaimed candidate of ideas is dismissed because of his personality. Carter's albatross may be competence; Brown's may be character. Carter is thought to be too naïve; Brown, too cynical.

Like Carter, Brown is currently stuck in a political groove. The governor of California's one consolation is that, at forty-one, if he fails, he still has Linda Ronstadt.

Jimmy's Foreign Policy
Ain't So Bad

New York *Daily News,* October 7, 1979

"The man on the street was no longer content to admire him as another 'ordinary guy.' From all over the country came a chorus of tired complaints: 'He means well but he don't do well.' "

—*Time,* March 15, 1948

As was true of Harry Truman, who went on to win reelection and is remembered as a tough guy, a mind-set has crystallized about Jimmy Carter. As *Time* said of Truman, Carter speaks in a "monotonous twang," is surrounded by too many "mediocrities," and has not proven he knows how to "lead." Unlike Truman, Carter seems to have learned politics from a Common Cause brochure.

And, yet, if you believe American foreign policy has at times been unrealistically reckless and you seek maturity rather than machismo from a President, Jimmy Carter's foreign policy ain't bad. In this arena, at least, he has meant well and done reasonably well.

In his speech to the nation Monday evening, Carter used his office as a bully pulpit. True, he and Secretary of State Cyrus Vance should never have allowed 2,600 Soviet troops, who may have been in Cuba for fifteen years anyway, to blossom into an international incident. Carter did not have to box himself in, as he did on September 8, by declaring, "This status quo is not acceptable."

Despite the missteps, however, on Monday evening Carter resisted the temptation to prove he was tough. He placed the overblown Cuban issue into a larger context. These troops were not a challenge to our security, he said, but "a challenge to our wisdom—a challenge to our ability to act in a firm, decisive way without destroying the basis for cooperation that helps to maintain world peace and control nuclear weapons."

Carter was mindful that some politicians behaved as if on the brink of a nervous breakdown. Senator Henry Jackson demanded an eyeball-to-eyeball confrontation, saying the brigade offered an "issue made-to-order" for Carter to prove his leadership. Senator Frank Church, who fears the wrath of Idaho voters in 1980, leaped to erase his reputation for sanity by linking SALT II and the hopes for further disarmament with the Cuban issue. Former President Ford and those who inhabit the right wing of the

Republican party chanted that only by risking war could we have peace.

And although Carter's poll ratings now rival a baseball score, he remained calm. Unlike Lyndon Johnson, he did not lie to the Congress and manufacture a Tonkin Gulf crisis. Unlike Nixon, Carter did not order a worldwide military alert on the eve of national elections. Unlike Ford, there was no phony *Mayaguez* crisis, which, incidentally, cost the lives of nearly a hundred American boys.

Without whooping or thumping his desk, Carter simply looked into the eye of the camera and declared, "I have concluded that the brigade issue is certainly no reason for a return to the Cold War. A confrontation might be emotionally satisfying for a few days or weeks for some people, but it would be destructive to the national interest and to the security of the United States."

Carter, who has been accused of failing to inspire hope, held aloft the hope of peace. Senator Jacob Javits, the ranking Republican on the Senate Foreign Relations Committee and a man, like Church, whose electoral contract is up for renewal next year, understood this. At seventy-five, Javits speaks as if he were more concerned with the permanent judgment of history than the transitory judgment of an electorate.

"It was a good speech," he told me. "It lifted the issue into the national realm of whether we should go forward with SALT or not. . . . I know press people like to be across-the-board. But you can't be in judging a President."

Javits faults Carter's international handling of the dollar, his inability to tame inflation or impose an energy policy. But he adds, "Because this guy is down, he gets a lot of gratuitous kicks. He's probably not gotten enough credit for the good things he's done." He cites Carter's successful handling of the Panama Canal treaties and his Camp David accord with Begin and Sadat.

Former Ambassador Averell Harriman, who has served the last five Democratic Presidents, says of Carter, "In foreign affairs and SALT and relations with the Russians, he's been very firm and decisive and definite." As for efforts to curb the spread of nuclear weapons, Harriman says, "Others have given up hope. He hasn't."

While a majority of the American people, according to the polls, think the President incompetent, the president of Egypt and prime minister of Israel did not come to the same conclusion at Camp David or in subsequent encounters.

As it took courage for a Republican to recognize China, so it took courage for a Democrat to recognize there could be no true peace in the Middle East if we ignored the Palestinians. Under Carter, relations with China have been strengthened; with the help of Andrew Young, America is no longer automatically bunched with the minority white governments of southern Africa. It's hardly an attack on Senator Kennedy to say that Carter did not "panic" when our ambassador to Afghanistan was murdered, when the governments of Mexico and Panama and Nicaragua let off steam at their huge northern neighbor.

The current vogue holds that America is on the defensive throughout the world. A helpless, pitiless giant. Put yourself in the place of a Soviet leader, however, and you might see an alarmingly different reality:

The bordering states of Iran and Afghanistan, which some say America "lost," are sources of instability for us. Soviet troops may be required in Afghanistan. Once-reliable Eastern Europe is restless, and making their own deals with the Americans. Pope John Paul II has journeyed deep within Poland and to the United States, giving dreaded Christianity a good name. We cannot send our ballet or musical companies overseas without fear of defections. Our economic system grows more dependent on American food and technology. Within a few years, we will be importing oil.

The damn government of Cuba costs us $8 million a day. We have "lost" several friendly governments in Africa. To the east, China menaces. To the west, NATO. In Southeast Asia the fleeing boat people have convinced many that Communism is not the wave of the future. Most socialist governments, including our own, have started experimenting with capitalist incentives to spur sluggish economies.

Because he has failed to master the symbols of his office and to convey a sense of strength, Carter, according to a senior aide to a Democratic senator, "doesn't get the benefit of the doubt on foreign policy." The Congress and the American people are not prepared to trust him, to defer to his judgment on, say, Cuba.

Still, Jimmy Carter has generally followed a sane foreign policy, and gotten too little credit for it. To date, no American soldiers have perished in foreign misadventures. No one can write of the Carter administration what the *Times*'s Sydney Schanberg so eloquently wrote from Phnom Penh in April 1975:

> After five years of helping a feudal government it scorned and fighting a war it knew was hopeless, the United States has nothing to show for it except a sad evacuation in which the ambassador carried out the American flag in one hand and his Samsonite suitcase in the other.
>
> There are, however, a million Cambodians killed or wounded (one-seventh of the population), hundreds of thousands of refugees living in shanties, a devastated countryside, children dying of starvation and carpenters turning out a steady stream of coffins made from ammunition crates.
>
> It's hard to declare that the Americans had good intentions in Cambodia —though some individual Americans did—because from the beginning, by Washington's own admission, its policy had nothing to do with Cambodians. It had to do with trying to distract and deflect the North Vietnamese long enough to remove American troops from Vietnam.

Think about that while reading Henry Kissinger's celebrated memoirs, or watching Washington reporters hail the former Secretary of State's "competent" handling of foreign policy.

SECOND THOUGHTS

American journalism suffers too many fools who call themselves columnists. Why are so many so boring? Four reasons. First, the columns have too little reporting behind them—they're what we call "pipe jobs." Second, they are pompous—"so I told the President . . ." Third, they write too often —few oracles have something important or interesting to say three to five times per week. And finally, they become utterly predictable. So why bother? Which brings me to the Carter column.

I believe what I wrote in this column, but I also knew the column went against the grain, against what the pack was then saying. In early October 1979—before Kennedy announced for President—journalists had fallen into a groove, complaining about Carter's incompetence, his dismal poll ratings, his inept handling of Cuba, and almost everything else. They had developed a mind-set. Part of me wanted to stand out and say, "Hey, wait a minute!" You get more attention that way.

The mind-set soon changed. Ted Kennedy, who it was widely believed would be nearly invincible if he ran for President, the next month announced he would do so. Overnight, the conventional wisdom shifted; the journalistic pack now pounced on Kennedy. Proving, I think, the correctness of former Senator Eugene McCarthy's wry observation: the press are "a little like blackbirds in the fall. One flies off the telephone line, and the others fly away; and the other one comes back and sits down, and they come down and sit in a row again."

As I write this, in February 1980, Kennedy and Carter have exchanged poll ratings, and my view of Carter's foreign policy is somewhat altered. The press now writes Kennedy off. And I worry that Carter has used the ruthless Soviet invasion of Afghanistan to steam nationalistic passions, which help him in an election year. To halt SALT and to call the invasion the most serious American crisis since World War II, as Carter has done, is imbecilic and inflammatory—precisely what he refused to do in Cuba. I'm not trying to imitate the lead blackbird, but today I'd fly off the telephone poll.

The Words of
Chairman Teddy

New York *Daily News,* October 14, 1979

Since Senator Edward Kennedy has (probably) answered the will-he-or-won't-he run for President question, the operative query becomes: How would his policies vary from those of President Carter?

The answer, one assumes, is to be found in Kennedy's new book *Our Day and Generation: The Words of Edward M. Kennedy.* The publisher imposed enough security measures—by midweek the only existent hardbound copy was squirreled away in Kennedy's Washington office—to justify a secret shipment of uranium. Or at least five explosive front-page stories.

After finally locating a copy, I think it is safe to report that if there's a substantive reason to publish this book, it's not to be found among its sixty-five pages of text, 159 pictures, and total of 158 pages. I am a soft touch for a Kennedy, but $12.95 strains loyalty. The book consists of what historian Henry Steele Commager, in a windy single-page preface, calls, "extracts from his public speeches."

The book does prove, conclusively, that Kennedy's speechwriters are better than Carter's. Or, perhaps, that the senator is more willing to indulge what John Marley called "the glory of words." At times they lift off the page and soar, in Sorensenian fashion, free of their moorings. They are designed to communicate feeling, not meaning; to inspire rather than to explain.

We are left with a bible of homilies, verities, incantations, occasional eloquence, and much twaddle. Some samples:

"We can light those beacon fires again. From the hilltops of America, we can . . ."

"I see a new America, an America in the sunlight . . ."

"Two hundred years of injustice is enough." (That's the entire paragraph.)

"The torch of leadership is passing to a new generation . . . these flaws in our society and in the world have been caused by human beings, and therefore can be resolved by human beings."

"If there is a more exciting and vigorous career for young people than in a revitalized fishing industry, I have not heard it."

The words of Chairman Teddy? From the book, one can glean only a handful of specifics: Kennedy supports the right to vote for eighteen-year-olds, national health insurance, gun control, the arms embargo against

Turkey, recognition of China and Cuba, and opposes capital punishment. I assume his call for an "end" to poverty, for programs to "make our cities citadels of the human spirit," to give Americans "safe streets" and "a decent education," to "insure that the heritage of old age is one of dignity," cannot be deemed "specific," since the senator does not share with readers *how* he will accomplish these ambitious goals, how much they will cost, nor how he would pay for them.

Somewhat confused, I requested an interview with the senator. No luck. So I interviewed one of his principal legislative aides, who asked not to be quoted by name. The senator says, on page 44, that it's a "dangerous myth" to believe inflation can only be cured by slowing and perhaps "ravaging the economy." Does this mean he opposes the high-interest policy promulgated by the Federal Reserve Bank?

"We don't reject the notion of high interest rates to slow the economy," conceded the aide. Nor does Kennedy reject Carter's notion to curb domestic spending or hold the federal budget deficit at $29 billion. The senator's position, the aide says, is to simultaneously attack inflation on many fronts —paring price and wage increases and government spending, freeing industries of excessive regulation, boosting interest charges. That happens to be Carter's current; ineffectual policy.

On page 48, Kennedy declares: "Tax reform can provide dollars to reduce the budget deficit; dollars for homes and jobs and schools and health; dollars for police and courts and drug control; dollars for the cities; dollars for capital formation; dollars for transportation and the environment; dollars to reduce the soaring burden of property and payroll taxes; dollars for revenue sharing with state and local governments—in short, dollars to meet all our urgent national priorities at home and around the world."

Does the senator still believe that? "Yes," responds the aide. "He still believes that. The votes are not there in the Congress." However, Kennedy's current tax-reform package, he concedes, would net just $5 billion to $6 billion—about one-fifth the claimed cost of Kennedy's proposed national health-insurance program.

Regarding foreign aid, on page 51 the senator says: "We must increase our efforts to help lift from mankind the most enduring curse of the ages —the curse of poverty." But the aide admits Kennedy does not propose "massive" increases in foreign aid: "He'd like to do more. He's concerned with the congressional cutbacks. We should at least hold the line on further cuts."

Does Kennedy still advocate the recognition of Cuba (page 60)? "I better double-check that one," said the aide. A moment later he returned to say, "We're not pushing steps towards normalization with Cuba."

One catches glimpses in this book of the Kennedy many of us find appealing. Alone among American leaders, Kennedy has proven a capacity to inspire hope and optimism. No other presidential candidate speaks so often or so hauntingly of the poor and the dispossessed: "We cannot ignore their faces pressed against our windows. We cannot ignore their silent cries for help." He spends less time congratulating America on its "progress," instead choosing to remind us of unfinished business.

He is clearly trying to evolve a coherent and intelligent position favoring increased competition and opposing "giantism" and "unaccountable" concentrations of power which are "inconsistent with democratic government." Thus, in the book's lengthiest section, he trenchantly (if too briefly) blasts the monopolistic health-care industry, which inflates prices, often with the active connivance of insurance companies; he understands that consumers pay for overregulated industries (trucks, airlines), and for underregulated ones (pharmaceuticals).

But Kennedy is shadowed with questions. Unlike John or Robert Kennedy, he does not face questions about his Roman Catholicism or about his father's influence or fears that he is not a liberal or that he is too ruthless. The concern is not that Kennedy is like his brothers, but that he is too much like Hubert Humphrey, a good man who recited the same New Deal litany until the day he died.

One of the exciting things about Robert Kennedy was the sense, particularly in the final months of his life, that he was growing, expanding, searching for fresh answers to old problems. Ted Kennedy does not convey that sense, certainly not in this new book.

He ignores the contradictions in modern liberalism, which he embraces. Kennedy is concerned about concentrations of power—yet supports concentrated national health insurance, more federal programs, more federal guidelines and planning. He says, "We are all beginning to realize that our resources are limited, that government money cannot be spread without end across the range of problems"—yet he holds out the promise of unlimited "dollars."

He urges greater private investment, in oil exploration, for instance—yet opposes tax incentives that might encourage the oil companies to do so. He favors more decentralized government—yet supports a stronger federal government. He advocates a government closer to the people—yet ignores taxpayer pleas to slash government spending and taxes.

Sandwiched between two hard covers, Senator Kennedy has come forth with a collection of placards for the faithful. In the tradition of *Why Not the Best?* (Carter) or *Conscience of a Conservative* (Goldwater), he has issued no road maps or diagrams for his presidency. We get a sense of Kennedy's prejudices, but not of his programs.

In the meantime, like Jimmy Carter in 1976, Kennedy's message seems to be: Trust Me.

Cowboy Connally Takes on the Middle East

New York *Daily News,* October 28, 1979

Henry Kissinger reckoned himself a cowboy. The reason for "my success," he blurted to Oriana Fallaci in 1972, is because "Americans like the cowboy who leads the wagon train by riding ahead alone on his horse. . . . All he needs is to be alone, to show others that he rides into the town and does everything by himself. This amazing, romantic character suits me precisely, because to be alone has always been part of my style or, if you like, my technique."

The pear-shaped Kissinger never looked the part. John Connally, the tall, forceful Texan chasing the Republican presidential nomination, does. He also talks the part. His recent speech on the Middle East auditioned Connally for the role of the lone cowboy.

"It was typically Texan," says a national Republican strategist who is neutral in the presidential contest. "The Texan mentality, or at least the stereotype of it, says that you do what is necessary to make a trade. You bluff. You shoot from the hip. You get out ahead of the pack. You stand alone and don't worry about touching bases."

Connally's October 11 speech to the National Press Club in Washington was strutted in full-page paid advertisements across the country. It was nothing if not audacious. Connally skipped the usual generalities and detailed a nine-point plan. Those seeking national office have an obligation, he declared, "to share one's views and thoughts and plans with the American people before—rather than after—they make their decisions about their national leadership."

He linked oil prices and peace, stating that the Middle East's oil "is and will continue to be the lifeblood of Western civilization," and that there can be no true peace or price stability until a treaty is reached between Israel and most of the Arab states. Fundamental to this peace, he said, was "a balanced agreement which will meet Israel's requirements for peace and security" and "Arab requirements for the evacuation of their territories occupied in the 1967 war, and some form of Palestinian self-determination."

He said America must make "a clear distinction . . . between support for Israel's security—which is a moral imperative—and support for Israel's broader territorial acquisitions." He warned that the passage of time worked against Israel's interest, that the Begin government was too inflexible, and that support for Israel in the United States "is eroding." Further, he said self-determination for Palestinians was "a moral imperative" and that a "strong" American "military presence" would be required.

The speech drew immediate hoots and hollers. Republicans and Democrats attacked Connally. Manhattan Republican leader Vince Albano "disinvited" Connally to his annual dinner in February. Several Connally supporters who are Jewish fled town. Concedes Connally fund-raiser William I. Spencer, president of Citibank, the effect has probably been "slightly negative" in New York.

And yet the speech was not as wild as the loud protests suggest. After all, Israel's foreign minister, Moshe Dayan, resigned this week because the Begin government rigidly refuses to confront the issue of Palestinian rights. Israel's highest court, also this week, unanimously rebuked the government for illegally permitting settlements on the West Bank. It is self-evident that if the last three American Presidents had not pressured Israel, particularly Jimmy Carter at Camp David, there would be no peace treaty between Israel and Egypt.

Jewish leaders agree that support for Israel is eroding both here and abroad. "In terms of world opinion, I don't see how Israel could be in worse shape," says Howard Squadron, president of the American Jewish Congress.

There are substantive arguments to be made against the Connally proposals. He assumed that oil prices would stabilize if there were peace, which naïvely assumes the reasons for the OPEC price hike are political rather than economic. He falsely assumed that more moderate Arab states can tame the zealots in Iran and Libya. The presence of American troops and ships, as Morris Abram, honorary president of the American Jewish Committee, observes, has "never been requested by Israel" and might "invite a Soviet presence."

To think that the United States can impose a settlement with a massive military presence in the area, as Connally proposed, ignores the lessons of American intervention in Vietnam. It is the policy of a macho cowboy, determined to make the U. S. of A. the world's sheriff. "I don't want that kind of a man as President," says a key national Republican operative who is unaligned with any candidate. "He's Johnsonian. I have visions of Connally as President holding up his shirt and showing off a tattoo of a map of the Middle East."

Having said that, however, one should also say that parts of the speech made sense. Connally boldly recognized certain realities, including the reality of the Palestinians. When I first read the speech, I applauded his courage, his specificity.

Then I figured out why the speech made me uneasy. Whatever the disagreements between America and Israel, I want to know that the President of the United States, in his marrow, understands that Israel's survival is more than a mere test of American will, more than a military alliance, more than the sum total of Arab oil. Israel—its history, its culture, its democracy—is special. That is not logic, it is love.

And there is none in Connally's speech. Briefly, too briefly, he announces that Israel's security "is a moral imperative." The only other time he uses that phrase is to say it is a "moral imperative" to end Israel's military occupation of Palestinian land. Absent is any passion, any attempt to embrace Israel, to convey special concern.

"It would have been a useful speech," says Squadron, "if he hadn't dumped on Israel so much" and seemed to equate Israel's security with Arab oil. "I think John Connally's thinking is affected by his oil background. He sees the Middle East as an oilman sees it. It's not anti-Semitic. He's so deep into the Arab world that he takes the Arab viewpoint. He's really a prisoner, as Begin is, as I am—as we all are—of his own history. And his history doesn't see Israel as *the* important ally of the United States in that part of the world."

Because Connally has no history as a friend of Israel, has made no real effort to reach out to that country or its supporters, he did not speak *to,* but *at,* Israel. Which, unavoidably, raises suspicions about his motives. Were they principled or political?

It should not go overlooked that Connally has raised more money so far than any presidential candidate, including the incumbent President, and much of it comes from the oil interests. His Houston law firm does represent Shell Oil, among others. A business partner is Saudi Arabian investor Ghaith Pharon, who last year purchased 85-percent control of the Main Bank of Houston, while Connally purchased 7.5 percent.

Despite the public controversy, the speech may have been coldly calculated rather than courageous. "It's a plus in terms of the nominating process," observes Ben Cotton, counsel to Republican National Chairman Howard Brock. "I'm not sure it's a plus in terms of the general election. We have little data on the question, but my popcorn poll of the man in the street suggests that Americans may now feel that Israel is asking too much or is going too far or is becoming the recalcitrant one."

Cotton explains that there are only seventeen cities or counties in America with significant numbers of Jewish voters. These, he said, are bunched in New York, California, and Michigan, where Connally is not strong anyway. "It's probably true that the speech appealed to most Republicans," says New York national Republican committeeman Richard Rosenbaum, who differs with Connally.

Robert Teeter, head of Market Opinion Research of Detroit, who conducts polls for moderate Republicans, says the controversy separates Connally from the pack and may help "create for Connally the sense that he is the general election candidate. He sets himself up against Carter and Kennedy."

If Republican delegates missed the Middle East speech, they could not miss his recent slashing attack on Ted Kennedy, nor its message: John Connally is one tough, mean cowboy. He offers "leadership," but where does it lead?

Exit Kissinger, Enter Peter Pan

New York *Daily News,* November 11, 1979

Henry Kissinger is out promoting his new book—*White House Years*—the way he bombed Cambodia. That is to say, secretly.

Unlike most authors, the former Secretary of State has consistently turned down requests for interviews. His book-promotion efforts have consisted so far of two appearances, both on NBC's *Today Show.* He is, not coincidentally, a paid consultant to that network.

Somehow, producer Robin Breed of the *Dick Cavett Show* got through. She offered him one hour of uninterrupted time, assuring him they would "do everything to make him comfortable." So it was that Kissinger showed up at WNET-TV's studio for a taping session.

Kissinger, slimmer now than when he was Secretary of State, looked splendid in a rich blue vested pin-striped suit. He sat in a rust-colored leather armchair just inches from Cavett. He seemed at ease. He carried no notes. Nor did Cavett, who, aides admit, did not have time to finish Kissinger's 1,500-page book.

Kissinger put on a really good show. He displayed the keen insight into people, himself excluded, that makes the book such a good read. "There are so many strands to his personality that almost anything you would say about Richard Nixon is true," he told Cavett. He humored the audience with tales of how Defense Secretary Melvin Laird set himself on fire during a papal audience by stashing a lit cigar in his suit pocket; how Haldeman and Ehrlichman impishly interrupted Kissinger's airborne conferences with President Nixon by handing him "top secret" folders, inside of which were pictures of beautiful actresses, signed, "Thanks for last night."

During the course of the one-hour taping, Cavett ad-libbed one terrific question: What would Kissinger say to the mother of a boy killed in Vietnam who asked him to cite a single result of that war that made her son's death worthwhile?

Kissinger thought a moment, locking his knuckles together, and in his grave, gravelly voice, reminded the audience that the Nixon administration inherited the war. When they came to office in 1969, he said, 32,000 Americans already had been killed. Another 14,000 would die, but 9,000 of these perished in the first year, before any new administration could reverse course, he added.

"I go back to 1965," Kissinger stated. "Was it worth it to put 550,000 troops there? I say, probably not." But by 1973, he noted, all American soldiers were withdrawn. "I thought this would lead to a period of national reconciliation," he said. He thought hawks would be satisfied that America had honored its commitment to an ally; that doves would be relieved that the war was over. If Watergate had not intervened to open new divisions and weaken the government, he said, the worth of his and Nixon's Indochina policy would be seen by all.

Cavett might have pointed out that Kissinger's response suggested that the young man's life had been wasted. Unfortunately, unlike David Frost in his October 11 hour-long TV interrogation of Kissinger, Cavett seemed intent to fish for anecdotes, not information. This strategy led Cavett to ask:

"Has your accent changed appreciably over the last forty years?"

Who would you want to play former Defense Secretary Laird in a movie of your book?

"How much did your parents suffer in Germany?"

Why did you change your first name from Heinz to Henry?

"Did you wear glasses at the time?"

Cavett did not ask the former national security adviser and Secretary of State why he authorized the illegal wiretaps of subordinates. Frost, on the other hand, forced Kissinger to concede that "seven or eight" of these wiretaps "emanated" from his office.

Kissinger was not asked about the 539,129 tons of bombs—three times the tonnage rained on Japan in World War II—that the U.S. secretly deposited on Cambodia. William Shawcross, in his compelling book on Cambodia—*Sideshow: Kissinger, Nixon and the Destruction of Cambodia*—claims Kissinger and others falsified documents to camouflage the bombing and deliberately deceived the Congress, which under the Constitution is supposed to retain sole power to recruit armies and declare wars.

Kissinger was not asked about his role in scheming to overthrow the elected government of Chile. To Frost, Kissinger was forced to concede his role, offering as a defense the fact that Salvatore Allende won with a minority of the vote—"Some 36.3 percent of the votes, " Kissinger said. Frost had the wit to counter that this was "about the same as President Thieu got elected with in South Vietnam." Richard Nixon was also a minority President, capturing just 43 percent of the vote in 1968.

Finally, Kissinger was not asked about the report in the November issue of *The Nation* that he "volunteered information to the FBI that he had obtained by opening another person's mail when he was a member of the Harvard University faculty in the 1950s." The author of the article, Sigmund Diamond, reproduced a July 15, 1953, memo from the FBI agent in charge of the Boston office detailing how Kissinger willingly spied on his students.

The interview over, Kissinger and Cavett enjoyed a generous round of applause. Entertainment-wise, the show was a hit. News-wise, it drew a blank. As soon as the lights dimmed, members of the press surrounded the still-seated Kissinger. The questions centered on the fifty American hostages held by the crazed zealots who rule Iran. Reporters wanted to know how Dr. Kissinger, were he still Secretary of State, would handle the crisis.

Clearly enjoying the attention, the microphones pressed close to the flesh, the reporters clinging to his every word, Kissinger leaned back in his soft chair and, measuring his words carefully, insinuated that he differed with the Carter administration's handling of the situation without telling how. Suffice it to say, he noted, that no Soviet embassies have been overrun. Why? Because adversaries understand "the risks are too grave," he said.

After a while a reporter asked about the FBI memo. "That's totally ridiculous," Kissinger shot back, his round, impassive face slightly red now. "I said then it was not true."

But *The Nation* magazine reproduced the complete text of the memorandum from the FBI agent, countered the reporter. "Are you saying you never offered information to the FBI?"

"I never offered, nor was I ever an informant of the FBI," said Kissinger. (The FBI refuses to either confirm or deny even the existence of the memo.) Kissinger, looking about, seemed anxious to return to current events, to place someone else on the defensive, to share his wisdom and hint at how Super K would save the lives of fifty American hostages.

Outside, on West Fifty-fifth Street, Kissinger's midnight-blue Mercedes and driver waited. As reporters lingered in the cold to ask one last question of Kissinger, a sleek black Cadillac pulled up. Out leaped actress Sandy Duncan, star of Broadway's *Peter Pan,* who hurried through the side door to tape an installment of *The Dick Cavett Show.*

One entertainer departs as another enters. In her portrayal of Peter Pan, Ms. Duncan magically soars above the stage. In real life, Super K soars above a full accounting of his public record.

A "Respectable" Bigot

New York *Daily News,* April 3, 1977

A bigot is on the loose in Queens, pursuing scapegoats, arousing passions, gathering support from frustrated, frightened citizens. If only we can purge *"them,"* he comforts pleased audiences, our problems would cease.

"Them" is a code word for politicians, and the man running against *"them"* is Maurice Nadjari, the Republican candidate for Queens district attorney. "I'm not a politician," the former state special prosecutor told several hundred members of the Corona Preservation Senior Citizens Center on Wednesday. "I'm not one of *them.* I'm one of *you* . . . I'm unconcerned with *them.* I'm concerned with *you.*"

The people cheered. In Queens, Nadjari is hailed as a hero because he preaches the one remaining fashionable form of bigotry—he's against *all* politicians.

"Why is it that the city is going downhill?" Nadjari asked his listeners. "Why is it that people of your age group seem to be the butt of the violent criminal offender? *We* know the answers, but unfortunately there are not many public servants who wish to deal with them."

Like the rest of us, Nadjari doesn't know the answers. It doesn't matter. Like the people, he knows the villains. "The politicians are ruining the country," exclaimed Mrs. Elsa Zimmerman as the candidate shook his way through a thicket of outstretched hands. "I don't believe *them.* They're only looking to make money," shouted a white-haired lady who said she had been mugged three times and believes Nadjari will make her neighborhood safe again.

Nadjari is counting on the public's rage, and his own high name recognition, to win. He has little else. There is no campaign organization, no headquarters, no literature, no budget. He claims "the establishment" and "the power brokers" are against him, as are the Democratic, Liberal and Conservative parties. Each has endorsed the incumbent, John Santucci.

The Queens Bar Association has, in effect, declared Nadjari unqualified. And in recent months the courts have dismissed seven cases Nadjari brought as special prosecutor.

Despite all this, Nadjari remains formidable. "He's the people's candidate," worries Queens councilman and former Democratic county chairman Matthew Troy. "Remember how Huey Long got started," blurts a close political adviser to Governor Carey. "He's going to win, and win big. And if he does, nothing can stop him. He'll be a candidate for state office in 1978."

Queens Republican county leader Jack Muratori is jubilant. "I get phone calls every day from people in the county who want to know what they can do for his campaign," he says. "That's never happened before." A less jubilant Queens Democrat predicts, "He's gonna win. What counts is an issue. A great issue, like a great horse, makes a winner. And Nadjari has the perfect issue. The issue is that politicians and lawyers and judges are no good. Unfortunately, that's what the people believe."

That's certainly what Nadjari seemed to believe as special prosecutor. A tenacious prosecutor, he pursued corruption with great and commendable zeal. But Nadjari became a zealot, seizing any weapon he could to hunt and destroy *them.*

Instead, he destroyed the office's good name. In four years as special prosecutor, Nadjari won lasting convictions of not one major politician, prosecutor or judge. In recent months the courts have declared he employed "inaccurate testimony" to indict former state Democratic chairman Pat Cunningham, used illegal wiretaps to indict Manhattan Supreme Court Justice Irving Saypol, stacked grand jury proceedings to indict Bronx Supreme Court Justice Joseph Brust, and exceeded his authority to indict Carmine De Sapio and Irving Goldman. In November the State Investigations Commission issued a 112-page report concluding that Nadjari tried to get politicians by unethically leaking information to the press.

Corruption takes many forms. A prosecutor, Justice Sutherland wrote in a landmark 1934 opinion, "may prosecute with earnestness and vigor—indeed, he should do so. But while he may strike hard blows, he is not at liberty to strike foul ones."

Because he did not love justice so much as he hated politicians, Nadjari lost his sense of proportion. As all blacks are alike to a redneck, so all politicians became alike to Nadjari. Even his friends concede that. "Maury is a smart, sweet guy," observes someone who worked for him in the special prosecutor's office. "But there's no question that from the word go, he believed politicians are no good. He sees things one way." Them versus Us. Good Guys versus Bad Guys.

"We hope to dissuade him," says someone who works with him now, Joe Fristachi, executive assistant to the state attorney general and a Republican candidate for City Council in Queens. "Now, for the first time in his life, he's mingling with politicians and I hope he realizes now that all politicians are not crooks."

After speaking in Corona, Nadjari stopped in a Flushing diner for a cup of coffee. He was asked to name one good politician. He paused for a long while. Then he talked of *them* as if they were Martians: "You have me, really, at a disadvantage because I know no politicians up close." Could he name anyone, even at a distance? "You're asking me to endorse somebody," he said warily. Okay, name anyone in the country, Democrat or Republican? He picked Brendan Byrne of New Jersey, an honest man, and a lousy governor.

Byrne is no longer an abstraction. Nadjari has been retained to do some legal work for the state of New Jersey. But his current opponent remains an abstraction. "I don't know John Santucci from a hole in the wall," confessed Nadjari. A moment later he declared, "I think he's more interested in John Santucci, who has gone from assistant district attorney to councilman to state senator to district attorney, and possibly to judge. I think that's John Santucci's main interest. Not violence, not the people."

Why was Nadjari different? "Because," he responded softly, "I've been a subway strap-hanger all my life, and I pay taxes, and I feel the same frustration most of us feel." Presumably, politicians do not ride subways, pay taxes, feel frustration.

They are different. Only *they* seek publicity or run for office or make wild charges. Only *they* cheat on their income taxes. Only *they* compromise or dirty the streets or steal Medicaid funds. Only *they* play "politics."

Next we will be told *they* smell different. Maurice Nadjari probably won't be the only one to believe that. Which is why he stands a good chance of winning.

SECOND THOUGHTS

Nadjari lost.

David (The Boss) Garth

New York *Daily News,* February 12, 1978

A rather large gray computer console with rows of white buttons is planted on Dave Garth's immense desk. Press a button—there are twenty or so—and a phone rings in the office of Mayor Koch, Governor Carey, New Jersey Governor Byrne, Connecticut Governor Grasso, City Council President Bellamy, or some New York political or journalistic figure.

No secretary need dial when Dave Garth calls. The master political (and media) wizard gets right through.

When he's on the phone, Garth is either chewing an endless supply of thin Brazilian cigars or staring toward Niccolò Machiavelli's admonition, which hangs from his Fifth Avenue office wall: "Whatever causes another to become powerful is ruined because he creates such power either with skill or with force; both of these factors are viewed with suspicion by the one who has become powerful."

The warning remains on the cork wall, though Garth is currently proving it false. Even after they're elected, Garth's princes continue seeking his advice, and not just about politics. "I don't believe that just because someone was doing media, they necessarily know nothing about government," Garth says. "During the transition, members of Koch's police task force said, 'What right does Garth have to interview candidates for police commissioner? He's only a P.R. man!' *Bullshit!*"

Garth says he rarely presses the white buttons of government officials, preferring to await their calls. "There's a certain protocol," he says. "I watched Clark Clifford operate—on a different level, obviously. He went and helped only when he was called. And then he went over to the White House and advised how to do something."

The phone rings often. On Wednesday, Carey called, a frequent occurrence. "Hugh Carey is convinced he cannot win reelection without Garth," explains a key state official, recalling how important the media man was to Carey's 1974 campaign. Garth has told the governor he wouldn't work for his reelection unless state aid to the city was increased. "I only have one contract as far as Carey is concerned," says Garth. "The city's got to be helped."

This past Monday, Koch and Carey announced agreement on a state aid package. Garth volunteered that he was pleased. He didn't volunteer information about his behind-the-scenes role. Garth attended several fiscal meetings, claim two state officials, because Koch was using him as "a wedge" against Carey. One negotiating session between Deputy Mayor for Finance Phil Toia and secretary to the governor Robert Morgado was convened in Garth's office. Just three principals attended: one representing the city, one representing the state, and Garth—representing both.

"Garth didn't play any role in the state aid package. Not directly, anyway," exclaims Morgado. "He was present at one meeting. But I had a series of ten meetings with Toia." Morgado said it was "a lot of crap" to think the nuts and bolts of government, or a budget, were "influenced by so-called advisers." To his knowledge, Garth and the governor never talked about it.

To John Lo Cicero's knowledge, "Garth sits in on many financial meetings." Koch's special adviser explains: "They need someone who's not here every day to look at it from a disinterested point of view." Garth also sat in on the selection of some key city officials. "I never knew McGuire's name until the day I sat down and interviewed five people turned over to Koch by his selection committee," says Garth of the city's new police commissioner. "Ed wanted to have an outside judgment. I was very impressed."

Garth also promoted the appointment of Deputy Mayors Herman Badillo and Basil Paterson, press secretary Maureen Connelly, Planning Commission Chairman Robert Wagner, Jr., the decision for seven co-equal deputies, rather than one preeminent deputy mayor, the dismissal of several Beame holdovers. When Carey assumed control of the state government, three of his top aides—Secretary David Burke, Budget Director Peter Goldmark, planning chief Steve Berger—were recommended by Garth.

If access to important people is power, Garth has it. He is known and deservedly trusted by most editors and reporters. In the closing days of the mayoral runoff primary, Garth arranged meetings with Koch and labor leaders. And just last week Senator George McGovern, who is talking about running for President again, called and asked to meet some people when next in New York. He and Garth lunched and—presto!—conclaves were arranged with Felix Rohatyn, Jack Bigel, Steve Berger, editorial writers. With a measure of pride, Garth notes, "McGovern went off to make a speech in Lexington, Kentucky, supporting the city."

Garth is currently plotting a campaign to win more federal support for the city. The mayor asked him to serve on the executive committee of the Mayor's Coalition on Long-Term Financing. The committee is going to put the arm on Washington, as Garth is now putting the arm on President Carter by shopping for a Democratic challenger.

"Garth is the Mel Brooks of our political system—he produces, directs, writes the script, sings the song, sometimes plays the lead character," complains one Carey adviser, who probably feels Garth is edging him out of the campaign. "I'd rather have a David Garth in there than former

Mayor Wagner," says a Garth admirer who worries about his lack of government experience. "David's at least doing what he believes is right."

There is irony in all this. For years Garth has been dubbed a mercenary —yet here he is prodding Carey over an issue of principle. He gets no money to help the city, and has turned down some lucrative P.R. accounts to avoid taking advantage of his political friends. "If I have any power," he says, "I want to use it to do two things: put the city back on its feet, and see that Koch does a good job."

The other irony is that Garth—the political expert—now passes as the government expert. For instance, he opposes city tax cuts. And we are treated to the spectacle of Ed Koch, who knows next to nothing about management, seeking solace from David Garth, who knows even less. Push aside Garth's good intentions. What if Bronx Democratic Chairman Patrick Cunningham demanded the governor bend government policy in return for political support?

If a party leader made such a threat, Carey or Koch would probably howl and make a public issue of it. But political parties don't count for much, as they did in the old days. They no longer serve as the intermediary between candidates and voters. "Today the media is the party," observes a Carey strategist. Which explains why talented media experts like Dave Garth have become our new political bosses.

In a television age, public opinions are formed—and changed—so quickly that an elected official would be nuts not to consult a media whiz. A leader who blows his public support is probably blowing his governmental program. Which is why the President consults his media guru, Gerry Rafshoon, about wearing cardigan sweaters on TV, the mayor talks to Garth about cracking down on city limousines, and the governor once consulted him about dyeing his hair.

None of this was true in fifteenth- and sixteenth-century Italy. Which is why our new princes can ignore at least one of Machiavelli's admonitions; and the public should ignore nothing.

Lonely Is the Loser

New York *Daily News*, November 12, 1978

For the losers, politics is a cruel business. While we journalists flocked Wednesday morning to the Sixth Avenue offices of a victorious Governor Carey, the East Forty-second Street offices of the loser, Perry Duryea, were nearly deserted. Reporters weren't clamoring for interviews. Perry Duryea was yesterday's news.

It showed. The walls of the large bullpen area, which the night before were dressed with sprightly banners and posters of the candidate, were now bare. The phones did not clang. The campaign manager was out. The press secretary was out. The New York City coordinator was out. One of the few Duryea people in early that morning was Peggy Wilson, the office manager, and she was worried about selling the furniture, shutting off the phones, planning an orderly evacuation by Friday.

At his desk in the large open room, Carmine Guadagnino was preparing to leave. The twenty-eight-year-old Con Ed engineer had decided "to gamble," so he took a leave from his job and joined Duryea as an advance man. He loved it. He got to spend time with the candidate, and to know the Duryea family. He thought of maybe moving from his home in Brooklyn to Albany. He began to dream.

But in the closing days of the campaign Carmine began to sense they were going to lose. The polls were predicting *Carey.* The pundits were predicting *Carey.* Even Republicans were whispering *Carey.* That great invisible glacier we call momentum was moving the other way. Nothing—not press releases, not TV ads, not help from the Rockefeller wing of the party—could stop it. Carmine felt helpless.

Now it was over, and he had time to think as he alternately filled out his final expense report and searched for people to talk to. "It's getting me, sitting here," he said. "It's a feeling of emptiness." The feeling that a cannonball has rammed through your stomach, spilling no blood but leaving this enormous void.

I know the feeling. Four years ago I masterminded Howard Samuels' resounding primary loss to Hugh Carey. The day before the voters spoke I received more than a hundred phone calls. The day after, the only calls were from bill collectors. It took a day or two for the bleeding to start. At first you don't want to appear bitter, you wish to comfort others. It is a self-conscious hurt. "Perry Duryea was a brave champion" is how Manhattan Republican leader Vince Albano described his friend's behavior in the privacy of the New York Hilton's State Suite on election night. "When everybody was sort of depressed, Perry was running around with a big smile." By now, Duryea has probably relived the campaign a thousand times. *What did I do wrong? Would it have made a difference? What if . . . ?*

You start imagining that everyone is talking about you. In fact, no one is. After losing a campaign, writer Jeff Greenfield said on WNET-TV election night, you feel as if you have "moral leprosy." So you spend a lot of time in safe places where people don't intrude—like home. After a while, the bleeding stops, the wound heals.

Carmine Guadagnino will rejoin Con Edison. John Berner, after driving his defeated gladiator home one last time to Montauk Wednesday afternoon, will re-retire. Al Hambsch, the kindly receptionist, logged in only three visitors that morning but will always remember the Duryeas: "They were nice people. Every time they came in the office they would shake hands. Mrs. Duryea would sit down and talk. She was a very friendly person." Carol Pavacic, who worked with Carmine after graduating from Vassar in May, first thought of Duryea: "It hurts more for him than for us. I saw it in his eyes. His eyes can be cold. But yesterday, before his concession speech, they had a twinkle. Afterward, the twinkle was gone. Resignation had taken over. I think he couldn't wait to get home. He needs a few days to walk the beach."

Then she thought of herself. Like most campaign workers, she was out of a job: "I don't need a few days. I need the money."

The phone rang. "Duryea for Governor," reflexively answered Carmine.

To most of us, Perry Duryea was just another loser. There are two kinds of losers. Duryea was the gracious kind, making a simple and generous concession speech to Carey early Tuesday night, and fading from view. His much-touted media adviser, John Deardourff, was the other kind. The kind who heaves children out of lifeboats. Duryea's defeat, he declared the next day, was ordained because "I was never listened to . . ." and because "inexperienced people" counseled Duryea. A real sweetheart, that Deardourff. He advises his candidate to hibernate for the entire summer, concocts a series of negative TV ads, reminds voters that his candidate for governor is a lobster fisherman. . . . At least Duryea lost without acting like a loser.

Yet, in the end, he deserved to lose. Perry Duryea happens to be a nicer man than Hugh Carey. He looks people in the eye; every conversation is not a contest; he is loyal to friends. But the public correctly perceived, as one prominent state Republican observed days before the election, "Carey is sharper and smarter than Perry. The governor's job is too big for him." Carey communicated a loyalty to a set of beliefs; Duryea to a set of friends.

• • •

As was true in the 1977 mayoral race, voters once again demonstrated their instinctive intelligence. At first the governor wallowed in the polls because voters were smart enough to see that he could be a nasty man. But they were also smart enough to remember he has been a pretty good governor. They were smart enough to discard the petulant candidacies of his two primary foes; smart enough to realize, perhaps, that though they differed with Carey's opposition to capital punishment, the electric chair would not extinguish crime. Forty-two percent of those favoring capital punishment, a WNBC-TV Election Day poll revealed, voted for Hugh Carey.

Upstate voters were smart enough to purge their traditional antipathy to New York City. Despite being hailed as "the man who saved the city," Carey ran almost even with Duryea among traditionally Republican upstate voters.

Statewide voters were smart enough to pierce City Comptroller Jay Goldin's slick veneer, preferring Republican Ned Regan for state comptroller. Where they excused Carey's personality, they would not excuse Goldin's. Goldin is the kind of man who would campaign for votes in a funeral home. In contrast to Duryea, the question about Goldin concerned not brains—he's brilliant—but character.

And in New York and across the nation, voters were smart enough to register their protest against government waste and spiraling taxes. They declared the New Deal dead. But just as their support can no longer easily be purchased with the promise of more spending and programs, so it couldn't be purchased with the glib Kemp-Roth promise of massive tax reductions for all.

In the wake of this election, it remains for all of us to figure out what replaces the New Deal. It remains for Governor Carey to discount campaign rhetoric and prove he understands that though he saved the city from bankruptcy in 1975, the city has not yet been saved. Can Carey meet his promise to cut taxes while increasing aid to close the city's widening budget gap? Will the beneficient partnership between Carey and Mayor Koch survive when federal aid shrinks and Koch has nowhere to turn but Albany? Can both walk that fine line between inspiring hope in the Big Apple's future while telling the public the truth about the hard fiscal years ahead? Will State Comptroller Ned Regan, the new member of the Emergency Financial Control Board, remain outside the city establishment and prod colleagues to reassume their original role as cop rather than cheerleader?

These are more important questions than whether the governor will marry the lovely Anne Ford. The questions remain to be resolved. Just as it remains for Perry Duryea, Carmine Guadagnino, and the other losers to get some sleep, permitting the passage of time to heal their wounds.

SECOND THOUGHTS

In response to a journalistic insult, many politicians give reporters a cold shoulder. Occasionally a public official will call your editor to lodge a complaint, which is invariably counterproductive. Good editors have a mother's instinct about protecting one of their own. Back in the early 1970s Mayor John Lindsay visited the editor of the *New York Times* to complain about Marty Tolchin, then City Hall bureau chief for the *Times*. The mayor thought Tolchin was being too hard on him, and came to the meeting armed with a stack of documents. The managing editor, A.M. Rosenthal, was very courteous, offering Lindsay coffee or tea and a comfortable seat. As Lindsay was about to proceed, Rosenthal excused himself, saying, "There's someone else I want to sit in on this." A moment later he returned, trailed by Tolchin, who lugged his own set of documents. Rosenthal, seated, began, "Well, tell me what's on your mind?" Lindsay stiffly, and sometimes incoherently, stammered through the remainder of the session.

It has been my experience that the wounds of politicians heal quickly, at least on the outside. Lindsay had to cooperate with Tolchin and the *Times,* and he knew it. Politicians can be tougher-minded about this than journalists who hedge their copy for fear of alienating their sources or in the hope of keeping their lines of communication open. Reporters sometimes neglect a truth: our sources usually need us more than we need them. Public figures forget insults because it is good business to forget, and also because they believe in themselves and are convinced that with a little effort, so will you. Politics is a game of seduction—wooing voters, organizations, legislators, reporters—and too much pride or shame can get in the way. It always amazed me that Mayor Abraham Beame continued to talk to me when I was covering him. I had written some tough, even cruel things about him. Although Beame did not go out of his way to be helpful, he was always courteous and polite. Talking to me was business.

Occasionally, after you've written something nasty, a pol will go to the other extreme and pretend he never saw it, though, of course, he did. One example: after my column asserted that City Comptroller Goldin was the type of man "who would campaign for votes in a funeral home," I ran into Goldin at City Hall. Effusively, he greeted me, going out of his way to be pleasant. I was pleased that he spared me a scene. But I suspect most reporters, like myself, would have respected him more if he had simply ignored me, as one of his aides did. Besides, it might have made me feel guilty. Maybe I would have felt I owed him one.

The Last Liberal

New York *Daily News,* December 3, 1978

Ten years ago most liberals looked at a fourteen-year-old armed robber and saw a kid. Today we see a monster.

Most of us have changed. The change is reflected in our attitude toward crime. When Robert Kennedy extolled "law and order" in the 1968 Indiana presidential primary, liberals winced. They worried he was using code words to reach racists. The fashion was to talk about the causes of crime; about rehabilitation, not punishment; defendants' rights rather than victims' rights; societal, not individual, responsibility.

Ten years later the contagious optimism is gone. We are more skeptical about most things, including human nature; less sure of the answers, more into ourselves and families, more afraid, more aware that dreams cost money.

Somehow Peter Edelman has managed to escape the last ten years. He remains a liberal. In the late sixties he was composing eloquent speeches for Senator Robert Kennedy, blowing the whistle on hunger, poverty, racism, injustice. Robert Kennedy was killed, but Peter kept going. He and a brilliant black civil-rights activist, Marian E. Wright, were married reading Walt Whitman poems to each other as the Reverend William Sloane Coffin, Jr., pronounced them man and wife. Both remained independent activists, kept the torch burning.

Today, at forty, Edelman gives the speeches. He still talks about the causes of crime, about joblessness, hopelessness. "I won't accept the idea that fiscal constraints make it impossible" to transform prisons into rehabilitation centers, cities "into livable communities," he declares. "To say that we can't afford to create a decent environment for a relatively small minority in this country that is in worse shape than it was ten years ago is to say that government has no purpose and no function. I think we can find the money. We're in a deep trough in America in terms of the poor and minorities. . . . I guess I do sound as if I'm in a time warp. But we're not going to stay in that trough. There will be better leadership. There are people around who believe this stuff. But it isn't fashionable. It's a measure of how deep our trough is. I'm not suggesting that we reinvent model cities. But let's prove we can do it somewhere."

• • •

For the past three and a half years Peter has tried to prove that the State Division for Youth could make a difference. As its director, he was in charge of 2,400 employees and a $60-million budget. His task: to provide direct care for about 2,000 delinquents, most between the ages of fourteen and seventeen, in state institutions, and to provide after-care services for 3,000 released delinquents.

Peter approached the task with the same intensity he once offered Mississippi's rural poor. "The responsibility that goes with the job," he said at the time, "is to be an advocate for every kind of progressive program for kids. Sometimes that makes trouble." So he became a troublemaker. He wanted to craft what he called a "children's bill of rights," struggled to avoid mixing youngsters with hard-core, adult criminals, labored to humanize the institutional warehouses he inherited, to push for amendments in the criminal law. He believed his constituents were primarily the kids inside his institutions, not the public outside.

He tried to view the juveniles as individuals, neither all monsters nor all innocents. He knew that half of the 2,000 youngsters under his custody were PINS—persons in need of supervision—who came voluntarily. Most were not violent, some were psychotic, all required a variety of treatments. He knew some needed punishment, others love. He learned how to manage his bureaucracy. "Whenever I was asked who the top-flight commissioners were," recalls former state Budget Director Peter Goldmark, "I always put him in the top three or four in the Carey administration."

Most of all, Peter Edelman remained the Pied Piper of the possibilities of rehabilitation.

But the tune he was strumming ran smack into the gubernatorial campaign. The thrust of his concern was for rehabilitation and prevention. The thrust of the public's concern is safety and punishment. One violent delinquent escaped from an Edelman facility. Several who were home on furlough, or recently released, committed heinous crimes. By July, State Senator Ralph Marino, chairman of the Select Committee on Crime, urged Governor Carey to fire Edelman. He had, the Republican senator charged, "adhered to a policy of going easy on chronically assaultive youths because he does not want to make them 'angry or bitter.'" Soon, Carey's gubernatorial opponent, Perry Duryea, chimed in with a call for Edelman's scalp.

Carey, concerned that he was vulnerable as "soft" on crime because of his veto of the death penalty, rushed to proclaim authorship of a draconian piece of legislation. From now on, the law declared, any thirteen-, fourteen-, or fifteen-year-old charged with a felony could have his case tried in Criminal rather than Family Court. The sentencing provisions were stiffened. Youths of thirteen could now be grouped, photographed, and incarcerated with men of thirty. Robbers with murderers. They were all declared monsters.

Many are. But just as liberals were often guilty of throwing money at problems, law-and-order types are often guilty of throwing tough-sounding laws or cops at problems. Lock up someone and the problem disappears. Which explains why we focus 80 percent of our criminal-justice dollar on cops, leaving the courts unable to process those arrested, the district attorneys without the staff to prosecute, the Legal Aid Society lacking resources to offer a defense, the prisons overcrowded and undermanned, the probation officers swamped. By November the Criminal Court was overloaded. Three of every four teen-aged defendants in New York City had their cases either dismissed or transferred back to the Family Court.

In campaigns, reason is the first casualty. Logic counts for little. Posturing, press releases, passing tough legislation is what counts. Even Governor Carey, who bravely opposed the death penalty, partly because he believes in human redemption, saw nothing inconsistent about vigorously supporting mandatory lifetime sentences without parole for murderers, denying them at least the chance for rehabilitation or redemption.

Nevertheless, his State Division for Youth director knew enough to keep his mouth shut, to try and minimize the liability a faithful liberal would have been in that campaign. Peter Edelman is perceived as a coddler of criminals. Even some of his admirers believe he has spent too much time promulgating his views on rehabilitation and too little addressing the need for punishment.

Peter made an easy target. He still refers to juvenile delinquents, many of whom commit monstrous crimes, as "more victims than anything else." Presumably, society is to blame. He promulgated policies, later amended, instructing his staff not to file criminal charges against those who escaped detention because "it subjects a youth (over sixteen) under the care and custody of the Division of Youth to an adult criminal record." When a juvenile fled, the new policy permitted his escape to be credited toward his time served. Deep down, he believes a fourteen-year-old murderer is a kid, not a monster.

No matter. Peter Edelman is escaping, quietly. In January he will go and practice law in Washington, D.C. "I finally decided," he says softly, pausing often, his horn-rimmed glasses and cropped, curly hair no different than they were ten years ago, "that even though we did make things better for hundreds of kids a year, I was continually picking up the pieces, and the agency was. I was just seeing an avalanche of broken kids. Kids whose lives were destroyed by society . . . You can only pick up pieces so long. You begin to wonder why somebody doesn't make an effort. You just see kid after kid coming at you. . . ."

So Peter Edelman, one of the last of the liberals, is getting out, presumably to be replaced by someone tougher. Before he departs it's well to remember what Peter represented. Sure he made mistakes. He is probably naïve, too devoted to the liberal faith. But he believed individuals should not be lumped and herded and automatically called monsters. He reminded us that all criminals are not alike, and some are reachable. Peter Edelman didn't give up, didn't cave in to the corrosive cynicism of the day, didn't lose hope.

Most of the rest of us have.

PART II

The Press

Dorothy Schiff:
"Maybe I Am a Silly Person"

[MORE] Magazine, January 1977

People who have worked for publisher Dolly Schiff usually resent her. I don't. Had she been nicer to me, I might still be working at the New York *Post*.

Mrs. Schiff, as any employee of the liberal *Post* would tell you, was not a liberal when it came to spending her own money. The catered lunches in her gymnasium-size office overlooking the East River were indeed special. Each victim was allowed two slices of rye bread and a choice: two thin, cold pieces of beef or a smattering of tuna salad. Lunch was inevitably preceded by a pre-mixed Bloody Mary. As far as I can tell, this was the menu for special guests. As the strategist responsible for masterminding Howard Samuels's come-from-twenty-points-ahead gubernatorial defeat, twice I was invited to this feast.

The third time we met was in October 1974, when the publisher interviewed me for the job of chief political correspondent and every-Monday columnist. Instead of eating, Mrs. Schiff alternately smacked or stroked her yelping Yorkie into momentary submission. She had some questions. "Tell me," she inquired, her passive face transformed into wide-eyed wonder, "what was Howard Samuels' first wife *really* like?" The small dog darted about the room, breaking Mrs. Schiff's concentration. "Tell me," Mrs. Schiff blurted her second question, forgetting the first, "what was Howard Samuels' second wife *really* like?"

I started work in mid-November. On day three, almost half the newsroom converged and listened to Mrs. Schiff's recorded voice. Their stomachs ached from laughter. They heard a taped debate between the two gubernatorial candidates staged in Mrs. Schiff's upstairs office. The gladiators had been carefully prepared for combat, honing their positions on housing, crime, unemployment, and aid to private schools. Each of these issues bored the publisher, but she gamely feigned interest. Quite suddenly, after dutifully asking the necessary questions, Mrs. Schiff leaned forward and delivered the question uppermost in her mind. "Tell me," she inquired of Hugh Carey, "what do you *really* think of Teddy Kennedy?"

I found out what Mrs. Schiff *really* thought of my inaugural column through very subtle means. No one shouted, growled, or bitched. Monday's paper came and the column was simply not there. It had pleased my editor, but apparently not my publisher. Don't dare ask why, was the solemn advice proffered. Just quietly prepare another column the next week, close your eyes, and pray she will forget to read it until it was already in print.

I requested an audience. My God, I was warned, *you don't really want to see her!* The game was to avoid her, not to risk exciting her. *What if she ever came down to the newsroom and noticed the missing strawberries?*

At 5 P.M. the next day the three of us (counting the dog) met for nearly two hours. I was intent on discovering, specifically, what it was Mrs. Schiff found objectionable in the first column before I would write the second. She wanted to know when we ever agreed I would write a column. Or be called chief political correspondent. Or be paid such a large sum of her money. Besides, what did I really think of Samuels' second wife, anyway.

For more than an hour this wrestling match continued. Each time I advanced one question she pummeled with ten. Then she tired. *Tell me, precisely, Mrs. Schiff, what was it that troubled you about the first column?* She stammered, rose to fetch the copy, returned to her soft chair, fixed her glasses, and read silently. Ah, she now remembered, the word "likely" appeared twice in the same paragraph. That, as far as I could tell, was one of her weightier complaints.

Downstairs, my colleagues were waiting to find out what happened up there. One editor hustled me into executive editor Paul Sann's office and locked the door. He listened to my tale, phoned Sann at home and warned that Mrs. Schiff would probably be calling him at any moment. Terrified, Sann announced he was evacuating his home immediately. The next day, after two full weeks on the job, the paper's chief political correspondent also evacuated.

Mrs. Schiff and I next spoke in May 1976. An article I had written in *The Village Voice* drew parallels between the behavior of politicians and journalists. There was a brief mention that Mrs. Schiff sought to manage the news by insisting on approving each word of a magazine profile prior to publication. She phoned my editor to complain, requesting a retraction. I called her. No, she denied having word-for-word approval; yes, it was true that a precondition of all her personal interviews was that she possess, in her words, "the right to see the manuscript to correct factual errors and debate conclusions." She conceded reporters at the *Post* did not grant similar "rights" to their sources.

Suddenly our conversation veered. Mrs. Schiff warmly apologized for the way "my editors handled you." I said it really wasn't their fault. She said she was sorry. I said I was grateful it happened. She said, "I'm so glad we're now friends." Her newest friend told her she was too isolated, her employees too often reduced to craven fools or robbed of their fire.

Dolly agreed. Dolly said she was getting old, and tired. Maybe she had not done a good job. Nora Ephron, she remembered, had written that her former boss was essentially "a silly person." God, that angered her. "But maybe," the publisher who might have been a gossip columnist sighed sadly, "Nora was right. Maybe I am a silly person."

The Boys on the Bus—1976

[MORE] Magazine, October 1976

Leo Tolstoy and Tim Crouse have something in common: Jimmy Carter has read a book by each man. When Carter was twelve, Julia Coleman, his teacher, gave him *War and Peace.* When Carter was forty-eight, Gerald Rafshoon, his media adviser, lent him *The Boys on the Bus.* From Tolstoy, Carter learned how common people shape history. From Crouse, he learned how journalists shape a presidential campaign.

But the eager student did not stop with Crouse. He went about his mission with the thoroughness of Napoleon preparing to conquer Russia. Frank Mankiewicz, press secretary to Robert Kennedy in 1968 and chief spokesman for George McGovern in 1972, recalls a visit the former governor of Georgia paid him in early 1975. He remembers being dazzled by Carter's extensive knowledge of the press. Carter already knew, remembers Mankiewicz, "that the press would cover him like a blanket in Iowa," the first contested state. "He knew Iowa was this year's New Hampshire" and that the contest "was unlike the National Football League, where game fourteen can count as much as game one."

Senator Henry Jackson's managers believed they could horde their money and wait until April and the New York and Pennsylvania primaries. Carter knew better. One of the key lessons learned from the Crouse book, says Rafshoon, was "that what you do early the media gives it a hype . . . a domino effect." Knowing that the press was sensitive about how late they were to understand Gene McCarthy's emergence in 1968 and McGovern's in 1972, Carter knew early victories would generate attention, which in turn would generate momentum.

Carter also knew about the element of surprise. Yes, Ed Muskie won the New Hampshire primary in 1972, but because the margin of victory was smaller than he had predicted, McGovern "won." So Carter lowered expectations, transforming his 28 percent in Iowa into an unexpected triumph. Just as he later minimized a string of spring primary setbacks by first predicting them. The rule: feign surprise with your victories and let no one be surprised by your losses.

Carter knew about the melodramatic biases of television, too. Paul H. Weaver, in a perceptive piece in the *New York Times Magazine,* wrote: "Carter also understood and derived benefit from television's myth of the politician. In running against Washington, he was in fact running against a political image that television helps to perpetuate."

Because he studied the press as carefully as he did the electorate—not only did the candidate read Crouse's book twice, but, according to deputy press secretary Betty Rainwater, "everyone who worked with us in early 1974 and 1975 read Crouse's book." Carter was prepared for his long march. "The strategy was to get to know the press," recalls Rafshoon. "We knew your names, even if you didn't know ours." The Carter camp studied the names in *The Boys on the Bus* and those in other campaign books, and throughout 1974 invited reporters out to breakfast and for dinner at the Governor's Mansion.

By July of 1976 Carter's people had a sense of how the press would play their vice-presidential choice. Campaign manager Hamilton Jordan says he sounded out fifteen or so Washington reporters about prospective nominees, concluding that Walter Mondale was the press favorite. They learned that the press, in general, thought Senator Frank Church "was a lightweight," Senator Ed Muskie "hot-tempered" and "lazy"; and they feared reporters would pick apart Senator John Glenn's income-tax returns. Two days before Mondale was selected, Carter's pollster, Pat Caddell, predicted that "the press reaction is a factor" (in the choice).

Sometimes the solicitation of a reporter's views is quite innocent. How comfortable a source feels with a journalist—their personal chemistry— often determines how much of a story the reporter gets. Two weeks before the convention I was fishing for Carter's VP choice. After I had asked one Carter intimate perhaps fifteen questions, suddenly he asked me one: Had I ever had any exposure to Senator Abe Ribicoff? I said yes. He asked me what I thought of him. Does the journalist at this point say, "I'm sorry, but I ask the questions"? The aide wasn't exactly asking me to give away state secrets. So I quipped that I thought Ribicoff might be the single most pompous politician in America. We laughed, and I was able to add another name to the list of Carter's prospective Vice-Presidents.

In its new role as political power broker, the press played a role in the selection of Carter's vice-presidential candidate. Even the hard-nosed boys on the bus seemed pleased by it. The Boston *Globe*'s Curtis Wilkie wasn't consulted, but he congratulated Carter for "picking a good man." The *New York Times*'s Charlie Mohr glowed: "Mr. Carter, whose physical stature is modest, seemed to have assumed a larger personal presence after his nomination Wednesday night."

"The press is an ever-present consideration," explains Carter's television adviser Barry Jagoda. "A lot of things Carter would like to do he can't do. He'd like to play tennis with someone on the staff, but he can't because the press would want to come."

The candidate is thus both victim and victor. He loses his privacy, but gains politically. Just prior to the final round of June primaries, the boys on the bus were grumbling about Carter's Nixon-like isolation in the plane's first-class compartment. A "them" versus "us" attitude was beginning to form. Shortly thereafter Carter became more accessible, resuming his strolls to the rear of the plane, permitting brief peeks into one of the multitudinous trap doors that comprise his complex personality.

At the end of his first full campaign week in September, Carter had another back-of-the-plane tryst with the press. It was a kind of confessional. Yes, he told the reporters, he had deliberately tried to manipulate his image in that first week—he'd tried to change it from spendthrift liberal to budget-conscious management-expert in response to Republican attacks. The practical result of this was to produce end-of-the-week round-up stories by David Broder and others in which Carter came off as disarmingly honest about his campaign strategy, rather than cynically manipulative—almost as if the press were being protective about someone who seemed to trust them with his confidences.

It may have been just this kind of effect Carter was seeking when he made his famous "I have committed adultery in my heart" confession to *Playboy* interviewer Robert Scheer. Again, that remark left the press with two conflicting interpretations: either Carter was deliberately seeking approbation for the candor of his confession and deliberately trying to remake what he thought was a too-moralistic image, or he was just Jimmy Carter speaking from his heart.

Surprisingly, Carter does not spend a lot of time following what those on the back of the bus are saying and writing about him. According to administrative assistant Greg Schneiders, who spends more time with Carter than the candidate's wife, when on the road Carter reads the local press, the *New York Times* "when he can get it" (usually two or three times a week), *Time* and *Newsweek*. When in Plains, he reads the two Atlanta papers, the *Constitution* and the *Journal*, and has the *Times* flown in. He no longer reads it as carefully, but his press office provides daily clippings from eight to ten newspapers (usually, in addition to the two Atlanta papers, the first edition of the *Times* and the Washington *Post*, the Washington *Star*, the Philadelphia *Inquirer*, the Baltimore *Sun*, the Chicago *Tribune*, the Los Angeles *Times*, and the St. Louis *Post-Dispatch*). At home, Carter watches television news. On the road, Schneiders guesses he watches the morning news maybe twice a week, the evening news rarely.

Carter's press secretary, Jody Powell, says his press office in Atlanta transcribes the television news for him most nights, and that "I try to keep up with what the people on the plane are writing." According to his deputy, Rex Granum, they don't succeed: "We see a limited number of clips."

This could account for the rarity of complaints about press coverage. A simpler, and more likely, explanation is that Carter's people genuinely like the reporters who cover the campaign and are respectful of the adversary process. When the candidate is upset about a story, he usually keeps it to himself. "He'll just say privately that something is bullshit," says an aide.

Does he use that word? "Yes, sometimes." Occasionally he will complain aloud. Eleanor Clift says Carter once gently berated her for a *Newsweek* article favorable to Morris Udall that was juxtaposed with an unflattering look at Carter. At a recent *Time* luncheon Carter made one of his infrequent journeys off-the-record to say some unappetizing things about *Newsweek*'s failure to check facts as carefully as *Time* does. Carter was particularly incensed by a *Newsweek* story that wrongly claimed Joseph Califano and Ted Sorensen were masterminding his transition government plans. Eleanor Randolph of the Chicago *Tribune* recalls how he snapped at her during a Florida press conference: "I've answered that question a thousand times. Why do I have to answer it again?" Standing in the lobby of Newark's Holiday Inn one early morning in late May, reporters were startled to see the candidate, as if directed by radar, zoom toward Charlie Mohr. He asked to see Mohr later to take issue with the veteran reporter's incisive story comparing Governor Carter with candidate Carter on the subject of Lieutenant William Calley.

Recently Powell made one of his few complaints of this long campaign. He walked up to the *Times*'s Jim Wooten, whose September 8 front-page story was headlined "Carter 'Would Have' Ousted Kelley, But Won't Say He Will If President," and said, "I have a bone to pick with you, doctor." They picked away, leaving each other's position unchanged. Wooten is also left with the impression that "Jody is the best I've ever seen at it. He had a point to make. He did it with a maximum of civility, and, I may say, a minimum of logic."

The Carter people have other means of expressing their anger, though they rarely use them. They can take their time tracking down press-requested information, stick reporters on the second campaign plane (the "zoo plane"), be pleasant but uncooperative in answering background questions, follow Secret Service advice and restrict access to the candidate, not return phone calls.

One of the few reporters who feels she has received the treatment is Kandy Stroud, who is writing a book and is a plane regular. "They have never bitched to me," she says, "but they have punished me." The Carter people have sometimes bitched that Stroud was a pushy pain in the ass. During the Democratic Convention, Powell rudely kept her on hold for almost two hours. And once, she says, she had clearance to fly to Plains to interview Carter during the Republican National Convention. Before departing Washington, she phoned Powell, who said everything was fine, come on down. She arrived in Plains but never got her interview with Carter. Sorry, just a screw-up, Powell said.

It is a wonder there are not more. Because press secretary Powell spends so much of his time advising Carter, is so informal and oblivious of details and has trouble delegating authority to his staff, the Carter press operation is hardly a model for its candidate's government-efficiency proclamations. Though Carter wanted no less than forty-five press releases put out after

Labor Day, to meet this goal Powell will have to distribute five a day during the campaign's last week. There are few meetings to plot strategy or determine how to make news. Though respectful of Powell, several staff members complain that, in the words of one, "the trains don't run on time."

Powell feels the press has been "generally, pretty good." His greatest frustration: "I think that because of the press's experience with Nixon, where they feel they were had, and because for the first time in their life the press is faced with a candidate they didn't know—at times he is subjected to overinterpretation and analysis. If he went from one side of the street and walked across to shake hands on the other, some reporter would find symbolism that he was working both sides of the street."

The press does sometimes behave like Kremlinologists, searching for arcane clues and hidden meanings. Charlie Mohr is the press's most respected Carterologist. He can pick up the subtlest shadings and tricks in Carter's repertoire. Sometimes he goes overboard. Over drinks with several reporters in downtown Chicago in early September, Mohr announced his latest discovery. Did anyone notice that earlier that day Carter referred to a "national health *system*" rather than "national health *insurance.*" Later that night, before ten thousand of the Daley machine's finest, Carter made Mohr's point seem frivolous by urging "national comprehensive health insurance."

Of course, what the Carter camp considers nitpicking is often the press just doing its job. Carter is, after all, the candidate who once said, "Oregon is the most important primary—perhaps."

The Wooten incident is a useful case study of nuance. Carter had said, in response to a question, that based on what he knew about FBI Director Clarence Kelley and the gifts and carpentry done in his home by Bureau personnel, he would fire Kelley. But, Wooten's second paragraph noted, Carter "declined to say whether, if he became President, he would dismiss Mr. Kelley." Paragraph three advertised this "apparent contradiction," as did the headline. Though Carter publicly said he hedged because he may not have had access to information that was available to President Ford, Wooten thought he was trying to have it both ways, a not uncommon Carter trait.

Powell argued that Carter was trying to be responsible in allowing that there might be information unavailable to him. Powell's view was implicitly supported by most of the traveling press corps. A sampling of what they filed that day reveals: the AP led with Carter saying "he would have fired" Kelley "knowing what I know now." The *Daily News* gave the story only three paragraphs. None of the three networks gave major prominence to the Kelley story on the evening news. The Atlanta *Constitution* spotted no contradiction, granting just three paragraphs to Kelley in a twenty-eight-paragraph story. David Broder's Washington *Post* lead read, "Jimmy Carter said today that based on what he knows, he would have fired . . ."

Carl Leubsdorf of the Baltimore *Sun* disagreed with the way Wooten played the story. "I think we have a tendency to seize on half sentences," he said. "I didn't play it that way because my reading of it—granted Carter gives some grounds for ambiguity, but we've got to use our brains—is that he doesn't want to say something that assumes he's President."

Wooten, because he assumed Carter is so crafty and careful with words, concluded that Carter was being cute. Leubsdorf, because he assumes Carter is so crafty and careful with words, concluded that Carter was too smart to be cute. Both reporters shared the same facts and assumptions about Carter. Yet both wrote very different stories.

Powell's mild storm over the Wooten story passed quickly. What lingers among many of those on the front of the plane is a deeper resentment toward those "big shot" Washington journalists who disparaged Jimmy Carter as if he were some barefoot backwoodsman. This resentment of certain "commentators" mirrors the Carter camp's feelings about "incestuous" Washington—the leaking of stories, the self-promotion, the fancy dinner parties, the favored few.

When the *Times*'s James Reston wrote a column early this summer scolding Carter for ignoring a new generation of Harvard professors whose expertise the Plains primitive surely would need to govern, Carter's staff exploded. "Plenty of people at Harvard are good," said Rafshoon. "But we got good people in Atlanta. We don't generalize about Harvard and we don't want them to generalize about Southerners." Part of the problem, issues director Stuart Eizenstat said at the time, is that the Washington press is "dealing with someone who won't give them his private phone numbers and talk on a background basis."

"Carter has never understood why David Broder is so highly regarded," laments one Carter intimate, acknowledging, "Obviously he's influenced by the way he feels Broder treated him." (Not taking Carter seriously.) In addition to Reston and perhaps Broder, a Carter shit list, according to one aide, would probably include columnists Joseph Kraft, Evans and Novak, and Reg Murphy, now the editor of the San Francisco *Examiner* and formerly editor of the Atlanta *Constitution.* (Murphy dubs Carter "one of the four phoniest men I've ever met.") The Carter people take great pride not just in waging a brilliant campaign to capture the nomination but in having flaunted conventional wisdom and leaving many of these opinion makers embarrassed.

The other side of this resentment is respect for those reporters they feel spotted Carter early. Johnny Apple of the *Times* trekked to Iowa last December and wrote an influential front-page story accurately predicting Carter's strength. "He always praises Apple as the best political journalist in the country," says one of Carter's top aides. The candidate is said to harbor real respect for the Washington *Star*'s Jack Germond and the St. Louis *Post-Dispatch*'s Tom Ottenad, who made a trip with Carter in January 1975 and wrote that he was a candidate to watch. Carter has thanked *Time* magazine for what he called its "fair coverage." Tom Wicker and

William Shannon of the *Times* are perceived as two columnists who took him seriously early. Elizabeth Drew in *The New Yorker* and Richard Reeves in *New York* wrote pieces that are praised for their perceptiveness. And an aide says Carter thinks that John Wall, editor of *Christian Century,* is "one of the finest people he knows." Indicative of the respect—and appreciation—is that Carter aides can remember specific pieces, and sometimes whole sentences, which comforted them many months ago when they were lonely.

The people in the front of the plane truly like those in the back. This is meant figuratively; some Carter staffers do have seats in the rear of the plane. But there is some feeling, particularly among the "little people" in the campaign, that the press can act like prima donnas. One rider to whom the press rarely talks put it this way: "Sam Donaldson [ABC] is the biggest asshole that ever walked the earth. There was no meal on this flight and he went after the staff and the stewardesses. It was explained to him that it was United Airlines' fault. He wouldn't buy it. He insisted it was somebody on the plane's fault. . . . The film crews and the cameramen are good all the time. The correspondents and the producers become piranhas on the plane."

The press doesn't always get the last word. One lowly staffer recalls Linda Charlton of the *New York Times,* since departed to cover Mondale: "Linda Charlton I hated. One time in August in Plains, she was wearing sandals and walking toward this red ant hill. There are these really big red ants in Plains that bite and really sting. I thought I should warn her. She kept walking toward it. I got ready to, but I said no, this is my shot back. She got some real nice bites. They itched for a good week."

For the first time in recent memory, the journalists are in the unaccustomed position of fearing that the candidate is smarter than they are. They are always on guard, watchful of his every move. It's like playing chess with Bobby Fischer.

Most of the regulars respect but do not like Carter. They suspect he will make a good President because he is smart and able and tough; but they feel he is always on, always working, always measuring his time, his words, what he can extract from any encounter. Unlike John or Robert Kennedy, Jimmy Carter isn't seen as a charming man by most reporters. Asked how he felt about Carter, the Cox Newspapers' Andy Glass laughed: "It's like asking me if I like an IBM 45. I like to watch the lights, the switches."

Jim Wooten, who has covered Carter full time since January and before that as Atlanta bureau chief for the *Times,* is both fascinated and repelled: "I think I can speak for everyone here. A lot of us were surprised to be covering a presidential candidate whose intellectuality was a part of his campaign equipment. Christ, he used his brains." But: "I would like to have written that there are very few things the man wouldn't do to promote his candidacy. I couldn't. I tried to." Eleanor Randolph thinks Carter "has trouble dealing with women reporters. He likes the loud, robust camaraderie with the men in the press. That's true of a lot of politicians. He's a Southern politician and can't treat us like ladies." Did she like him? "Personally, no. But I respect him the more I'm around him." Curtis Wilkie, who has run hot and cold on Carter, calls him "the most intelligent guy I've ever covered."

With a straight face, Jimmy Carter promises never to lie. That absurd claim gives the press their potential advantage in the chess game. So they spend a fair amount of their time searching for evidence Carter is lying—or at least fudging. When they score—as when Wooten caught him omitting Martin Luther King's name from the litany of those he admired before a white Florida audience, or "ethnic purity" or Mohr's Calley report—they await some acknowledgment of their point. Instead, they usually get the flash of Carter's steel-blue eyes. He has "a slight messianic complex," believes David Nordan, the Atlanta *Journal* reporter who covered Governor and candidate Carter. "I don't think he can be corrupted by power, but he could be corrupted by his own belief in himself. He's not easily dissuaded."

The only time Wilkie can remember Carter admitting he was wrong was over "ethnic purity," and then it took him two days to apologize. Wooten says Carter apologized immediately for the omission of King's name. At Brooklyn College, on September 7, Carter was asked why he was silent for so many years about the Vietnam war. He stiffly answered that he was not a public figure from 1965 to 1970. Nor were most of the protesters.

What saves Carter from a potentially fractious relationship with the press is his staff. "The one thing that makes me feel better about him is his people," Wilkie once told me. "The guy's an automaton, but not his people."

The most visible member of the staff is the thirty-two-year-old Powell, who lives near Carter in south Georgia. Though columnist William Safire has compared him to Ron Ziegler, the analogy is inoperative. Unlike Ziegler, Powell had four years' experience as press secretary to Governer Carter before joining the campaign. Unlike the pre-1974 White House robot, he is close to his candidate, has a sense of humor, and seems to understand he has obligations to the press as well as to his candidate.

Jack Germond of the Washington *Star,* no stranger to campaigns, thinks Powell is one of the "best press secretaries I've ever seen. He's a remarkably cool cat . . . The key thing in any press operation is, does the press secretary know what the hell he's talking about? When you talk to Jody Powell you don't get a guy who's blowing himself up. He knows what his candidate is doing." And thinking.

Not that Powell qualifies for sainthood. He is in the business of peddling his candidate, which means he doesn't volunteer harmful information. Wooten, who is very fond of Powell, also thinks he is very manipulative—"Southern-style. Jody and Hamilton will say, 'Come in and have a drink.'

They are naturally gregarious. And genuinely hail-fellows well met." Though reporters can recall few instances when Powell lied to them, Stan Cloud remembers Powell standing up to announce that speechwriter Robert Shrum, who had just resigned, was never on the campaign payroll. "That," says Cloud, "was literally true. But it was false" because a bookkeeping error had kept Shrum off the payroll but not off salary.

A major difference between Powell and Ziegler is that Powell is as disorganized as Ziegler was orderly. "Powell forgets things," Dave Nordan once mused. "He never has cigarettes. He's always burning holes in his clothes. He never has any money. Every time he's ever taken an airline trip, he's lost his luggage. He's always losing notes to himself." Kandy Stroud says that in nine months he's never returned one of her phone calls. He once returned one of mine.

Powell's disorganization, and unwillingness or inability to delegate authority to the people who work for him, drives the press up the wall. Powell's press office, laments Wilkie, is composed of "nice people, but they're not informed. They're constantly forwarding to Jody your questions. I don't know why Jody just doesn't give it up and let someone else do it." According to Stan Cloud, "If we had fifteen Jody Powells it would be all right. It's an abysmal press operation when you get below Jody Powell." In a rare but naturally back-handed tribute to McGovern, Bob Novak observes, "The Carter people are much more poorly organized than the McGovern press operation." Eleanor Randolph says, "The only real problem we've had with Jody is that he's an adviser, too. Sometimes you can't find him."

When Powell can't be found, the only other person some reporters on the plane feel they can turn to for authoritative answers is Greg Schneiders. Carter's twenty-nine-year-old aide-de-camp, who once ran two restaurants in Washington and joined the campaign full time in November 1975, gets little publicity. Visiting reporters tend to dismiss him as a functionary because he is sometimes spotted carrying Carter's bag and because he doesn't hover in the rear of the plane eagerly awaiting a summons for information.

The real problem for Powell is that he doesn't know he has a problem. "I've been accustomed to doing things myself," he admits. "My impression is that they [the press staff] are assuming more and more responsibility. Frankly, reporters don't have to get to me as much as they do."

The favorable but somewhat mixed feelings reporters have about the Carter press operation is matched by the mixed feelings they express about their own work this past year. In general, they take pride in their output. David Broder believes the press has done a good job "up to a point. I think the Carter phenomenon was spotted relatively early—earlier in other people's papers than ours. The press did a pretty good job on two things. One, analyzing how his strategy accounted for his success. Two, analyzing what Carter was saying and where he was coming from. . . . I think the press has done about as much as we can to raise the relevant questions about Carter's policies in terms of consistency and operative clauses."

Frank Mankiewicz, among others, thinks the press "ignored Carter" early, the way they ignored McGovern and McCarthy. But Carl Leubsdorf, Andy Glass, Jack Germond, Chris Lydon, Johnny Apple, Stan Cloud, and some others have reason to dispute that judgment.

Another somewhat sensitive subject is Plains. Charles Seib, press ombudsman for the Washington *Post,* wrote on August 20: "All in all, the reporting from Plains was soft and sleepy, like a Southern afternoon." One Carter campaign secretary, originally fearful "of the animals from the press," as she then called them, says she grew fond of the boys on the bus. We used to joke, she said, somewhat wistfully, and call it "Camp Carter. As camp counselors we arranged softball games and barbecues. We got to know these people. We stayed at the same motel. We all ate at Faye's. Sat by the pool. Swatted the same gnats. Some of the guys went off to Kansas City for the Republican Convention and called and asked, 'Are you playing softball tonight?' They were nostalgic."

Curtis Wilkie credits some real benefits, if not exactly an adversary relationship, from the Plains stay. There was a "rare intimacy" there, he says. The press got to "see where the guy came from, his family, his environment." It may be worth noting that Wilkie, who is admired for his tough questioning of Carter and a brilliant story on Carter's black neighbor losing his home, started the summer not liking Carter and ended it with better feelings toward him.

Another justification for the stay is that it inspired Eleanor Randolph of the Chicago *Tribune* to write a terrific and hilarious article about "summer camp," as she called it. She introduced her readers to ABC's Sam Donaldson as he was being chased by CBS producer Rick Kaplan, who "was trying to add highlights to Donaldson's carefully sprayed hair with a can of Reddi-wip instant topping." She told of the nine injuries incurred by the press in pursuit of athletic prowess, the battles with Georgia wood chiggers and red ants, the plan to sneak uncooked gelatin under the sheets of one TV correspondent, the red eyes of reporters—from the pool's chlorine. Most of the press corps laughed, wishing they had written the piece themselves. But not Sam Donaldson or Rick Kaplan. For a long while Kaplan did not speak to Eleanor. Now he nods.

It's hard not to be impressed by the Carter press corps. Sure, there are some real clunks. But there are a lot of serious, talented people on that plane. Funny ones, too. Jim Wooten filed this pool report on Carter's September 7 pilgrimage to the Rotten Apple: "Commentary on his moments there seems superfluous since it was more or less adequately covered by every single member of the New York City press corps except Geraldo Rivera, who is in Cuba exposing Fidel Castro as an agrarian reformer, and Barbara Walters, who is practicing getting from her apartment to the ABC studios and back without getting lost. It seems at least of passing interest, nevertheless, to point out that the governor's egalitarian efforts this morning resulted in a total number of eight contacts with common people, a lovely rose from the swishy proprietor of a subterranean florist, one broken escalator, and an uncharacteristic show of temper from Zorba the Great [head of the Secret Service detail], who was punched in the eye with a microphone."

How subjective is campaign press coverage? Not just in what we put in or leave out of a story, or what we lead with, but in impressions as well. In Springfield, Illinois, for instance, Jim Klurfeld of *Newsday* was struck by the meager size of the Carter rally. Jack Germond was impressed by the size of the crowd. The press played down Scoop Jackson's 40-some-odd percent in the New York primary; emphasized Carter's win in the June 8 Ohio primary, while deemphasizing his huge losses in that day's New Jersey and California races. Too few reporters suggested that Carter's nearly unbroken string of late primary losses raised a fair question of whether he really did capture the mood of the country.

Reporters say much about the potential interest conflicts of politicians, but little about their own. Ask a journalist who has been a regular on the Carter bus whether his own career advancement is tied up with Carter's, and he sounds like a politician. Watch:

Stanley Cloud: "That's a good question. I have had no promises from anyone at *Time*. I suppose if Carter wins, I will become White House correspondent. I view that with mixed emotions. I suppose I wouldn't turn it down. Obviously, the thrust of the question is does it affect one's coverage? I think not, because I'm not all that enthusiastic about going to the White House in the first place." Trust me.

Jim Wooten: "There is a distinct possibility I may be asked to go to Washington. My inclination at the moment is no, I don't want to go to Washington. On the other hand, there are strong arguments. I'm forty years old. Maybe it's time to stop running around the country." Headline: "Wooten Would Turn Down White House Now, But Won't Say Flatly He Will."

Curtis Wilkie says flatly he doesn't want to go to Washington. But he acknowledges other rewards: "I'm going to be in a position to actually know a President and a Vice-President and be able to say to my kids, if they win, that I covered probably the most remarkable political story of this century. The political thing to do is say it doesn't matter. Shit, it does . . . If he sees me he'll know who I am. No President ever knew who Curtis Wilkie was."

There are benefits in having reporters cover one candidate regularly. They gather an encyclopedic knowledge of the candidate, being much more sensitive to a candidate's changing mood and the nuances of his words. They develop valuable sources within the campaign. But Andy Glass makes a better argument for the rotation of reporters: "It's a bad system. It gives the correspondent a conflict of interest with the candidate. It doesn't serve the interest of the viewer or the reader. The relationship ought to be an arms-length one. It should be a disinterested one . . . The reader is as well served by a fresh eye." Jack Germond recalls that many of the boys on McGovern's bus, as if locked in a time capsule, actually thought he would win.

Like politicians, reporters are also interested in headlines. "You're competing and want to be on the front page," observes Klurfeld. You're moving fast, swept from one speech to the next, city to city, plane to plane. You have a daily deadline and there is no space or time to think, to add some perspective. Besides, you've heard the speech before. So the right-to-life demonstrators get more coverage than they deserve. The boos of the American Legionnaires are amplified.

Take Carter's August speech before the Legion in Seattle. It was a seven-page address, just several paragraphs devoted to the pardon proposal which attracted hoots of "No, no, no" from the audience. The bulk of the speech contained a good outline of the candidate's rather hawkish views on national defense. A search of ten newspapers and the networks revealed that the explanation of his defense policies was downplayed in favor of the drama of the boos. The day before, in Los Angeles, Carter gave what speechwriter Patrick Anderson considered one of the campaign's most important—and eloquent—speeches. The candidate sketched his vision of the country. The press focused most of its attention on the few sentences that attacked Ford.

Getting caught in the swirl of conflict happens to reporters covering reporters as well as those covering candidates. Late one night in Milwaukee, a wild melee suddenly erupted in front of *Peanut One*. The local sheriffs and Secret Service men began struggling to keep first the TV crews and then the rest of the press contingent from the ramp of the plane. The TV people tried to pry themselves loose and get near the candidate. Sam Donaldson was shouting above the roar of the jet engines, "Tell these people to get the fuck out of here . . . I'll do my job and you won't lecture me." Ed Bradley of CBS, who covered the Vietnam war and never got into a scrap there, was engaged in his second fight of the week. Andy Glass and many of my colleagues were screaming about the press's rights, supporting Ed and Sam. But not me. I was taking notes. Hell, it was a good story.

The three principal actors—candidate, public, and press—are each seeking to manipulate the other. The candidate carefully picks his spots, hoping to maximize the media impact—the sense of crowds surging and pressing in upon him. The public performs—"Hey, take my picture"—hoping to see their pusses on the tube. And the press, as several network correspondents bitched in Philadelphia on September 7, have a hard time covering a good visual event after 3 P.M. and still get it on the nightly news. In Columbus, Ohio, CBS and ABC complained when the candidate's staff tried to make a corridor so the public could reach Carter. By being forced to walk ten feet in front of the candidate, they protested, they were deprived of right-angle shots of the candidate. In most cities there are three station wagons lined up behind the candidate's car in the caravan. On the back of each jumps a network film crew, the cameraman risking his life by aiming his machine at the candidate's car as it reaches speeds of seventy miles per hour. The TV people have coined a word for this madness, "protective coverage"— which means your ass is on the line if a bullet rips through Carter's head and it isn't filmed in living color.

What to do about the press?

It's not an easy problem. "When a guy gets to be nominated for President," sighs Powell, "almost all the forces work toward his isolation. Accessibility comes to mean accessibility to the press, even if the candidate is not accessible to the public."

Many of these issues were again raised at 30,000 feet, as Carter's chartered plane streaked from Milwaukee to Hollywood, Florida, in early September. Clustered in the back of the plane were Powell, his shirt collar open, his jacket lost, his legs draped over an aisle seat facing Sam Donaldson, who was sporting a gray suit and buttoned vest. Behind them crouched Don Oliver of NBC and Sharon Lovejoy of CBS radio and an assortment of television people. It was the morning after the airport altercation, and Powell was attempting to mold a policy to ensure television access to the candidate as he disembarked from his plane, without denying access to the public.

Donaldson, who speaks the same on or off the air, bellowed, "I'm prepared to work with you on the ramp problem." He gave Powell a choice of a) all three network cameras at the ramp but no questions, or b) a press conference each time Carter got off the plane. Powell's eyes grew wide, and he shook his head.

"What about radio?" Sharon Lovejoy interjected. "What about the First Amendment?" huffed Donaldson, adding, "We don't want to give up access to the candidate." Powell responded that to end the crush at the ramp of the plane, "we're going to have to go to more set-up press conferences" away from the plane.

Now Oliver rolled his eyes, shrugging. "You talk to my desk." Powell asked how he could give special consideration to just the electronic media when he had as many as 150 other journalists to worry about. Donaldson said that print reporters had the same access as TV.

They moved into a discussion of what constitutes press coverage. Donaldson asked Powell to define what he considered fair press access. One press conference a week, Powell answered. Joining the conversation, Stan Cloud reminded him that his candidate conducted two or three press conferences a day during the primaries. But the "scrutiny is more intense," responded Powell.

"It's the impromptu statements that best reveal the man rather than the rehearsed statements," said Donaldson.

Powell: "We have to be sure we don't react to what the press says Ford said. If it's false and Carter responds to false information, the question evaporates and only Carter's statement will remain."

Oliver suggested that one solution to the ramp problem would be to block the local press's access to the ramp.

"No," said Powell.

"Let them do a pool report," said Oliver.

Still no.

Donaldson explained that the need for the cameras to be at the ramp is "a protective thing," and protected himself by once again invoking the First Amendment.

"What I need, Sam," said Powell, "is not statements about fundamental human rights, but what you really need."

As I thought about this colloquy, I recalled Sam Donaldson's thoughts on the candidate's handshaking tour in downtown Columbus. Seeking a compromise to protect his interests and Powell's, Donaldson exclaimed that there were some things representatives of the media and the candidate could agree were news and worth covering. *"When Mickey Mouse is there, we all want the shot,"* he said.

SECOND THOUGHTS

Three years later, much had changed. A once-relaxed relationship between the Carter staff and the press had turned ugly. The President's entourage wails about the cynicism of reporters who treat minor stories as major scandals, and private rumors as public facts. In turn, the White House press corps bristles at what it sees as the Carter staff's bunker mentality, inaccessibility, and incompetence. It can no longer be said that either side "truly likes" the other. By mid 1979 Carter announced he would hold fewer White House press conferences, preferring to escape the White House and to be interrogated by local reporters who ask more issue-oriented questions (softer ones, too). By fall, Carter adopted Nixon and Ford's Rose Garden strategy, rarely venturing from the White House and forcing the press to rely on handouts and photo opportunities.

Whatever their flaws or prevarications, Ron Nessen and Ron Ziegler can probably take comfort from the fact that the poisonous relations between them and the press were institutional, as well as personal. Being herded together in the White House basement, waiting for the public-address system or the lights to flash on announcing the start or close of the day's press business, can grate on a reporter's nerves. Just as being pummeled by question after question, some of them rude or irrelevant, gets on the nerves of the White House press staff.

Little wonder, then, that during a September 1979 trip to New York City, White House press regulars openly snickered as the President spoke, scoffed at his pedestrian prose, his incessant monotone, his "second-rate" staff. A gruffer Jody Powell, searching for an ashtray, slipped his unlit cigarette stub into the baggy suit pocket of a press regular. Had Powell been caught, perhaps the headline would have read: WHITE HOUSE STEPS UP AT-TACK ON PRESS; TRIES TO SET REPORTER ON FIRE. As in some marriages that go on too long, the partners were now irritable and bored with each other.

President Carter also proved not to be the word wizard that many of us thought he was. Recall his tendency to plant one foot in his mouth when inviting, then abruptly disinviting, the Russians or Palestinians into the Middle East peace negotiations, or making human rights and the Soviet brigade in Cuba first a central issue, then a non-issue.

Several Washington columnists whom the Carter people deeply resented during the campaign—James Reston of the *New York Times,* for instance —became presidential insiders, invited, on a background basis, to regularly glimpse the awful burdens borne by the leader of the Free World, solemnly informing readers: "The President is known to believe . . . " Others— syndicated columnist Joe Kraft, for instance—were kept at a distance. During the 1976 campaign I believed Kraft's hostility to Carter came from his annoyance at not being invited to dine with the Carter people. In retrospect, Kraft seems prescient, not hungry. He has consistently criticized Carter's inability or unwillingness to understand the domestic governmen-tal and political process. David Broder, who had an off year (for him) in 1976, is now widely (and justly) admired for his thoughtful coverage of politics and government.

Finally, some things didn't change. As I write this in the autumn of 1979, coverage of the 1980 presidential contest has already commenced. And, so far at least, there is scant evidence that this campaign will be covered differently. The will-he-or-won't-he-run questions this year centered on Ted Kennedy, not Hubert Humphrey. Once again we overplay the importance of small state contests (Carter's win in the Florida straw poll, Bush's in the Iowa caucuses), handicap the campaign as if it were a horse race, reminding readers or viewers who's ahead at the sixteenth and quarter poles. Once again we see the tendency of the press to play up conflict and play down issues and character and executive ability. In 1968 Richard Nixon was allowed to get away with his vague *bring-us-together* campaign; in 1976 Carter got away with a smile and *trust-me.* This year, so far at least, Ted Kennedy got a free ride on the *leadership* slogan and, more recently, Carter got one with his Rose Garden strategy.

Television news, which I paid too little attention to in my 1976 piece, is a major culprit. For television, as Paul Weaver has noted, "is not primarily information but narrative; it does not so much record events as evoke a world. It is governed not by a political bias but by a melodramatic one."

Candidates often become national soap opera performers—*Dallas*, without the jiggles.

The problem is not exclusively television's, nor even an individual reporter's. Journalism's form often dictates the content. Racing around the country after a candidate, compelled to file daily reports, does not encourage thoughtfulness, a broader perspective and ability to sift the important from the unimportant. The sealed "metal envelope," as T.R. Reid of the Washington *Post* referred to the Kennedy press plane, unavoidably distorts a reporter's perspective. Just as too many sedentary Washington dinner parties distort.

The daily press form does not lend itself to discussions of complex issues. "You can't make inflation comprehensible," says Theodore H. White, the godfather of modern presidential coverage. "Some things can't be simplified. Nor can racial conflict in our cities. Yet those are the big issues." The average newspaper story is perhaps 500 words; on television, about 200 words. That space constraint, and the need to compress news into headlines and lead paragraphs and summaries, invites unintentional distortions.

Stymied—perhaps personally bored or convinced readers or viewers will be—by the bigger issues, journalists tend to concentrate on what we know best: politics and narrative. We search for conflict, for winners and losers, for liberals versus conservatives, for something that is new, and thus, we often wrongly assume, *news*.

Covering the Campaign, Cynically

The Village Voice, November 8, 1976

It's okay to malign politicians. The press does it. The public does it. Common Cause does it. Sometimes politicians do it.

Even Panasonic does it. Their latest thirty-second television commercial features a bombastic caricature of a politician doing what all pols do—making promises. From behind a lectern a chunky fellow exclaims, "I promise . . ." And he does—just about everything save free bicycles. The point of the advertisement is that a Panasonic tape recorder enables you to preserve the words and trap the lying lout.

Looking back on this long, weary campaign, one recalls a lot of trapping. Also a lot of lying. But the lies and obfuscations of presidential candidates are not new. The cynicism rampant among the press and the public is new. During this marathon campaign we slipped into the habit of blaming politicians for most everything—including our boredom.

This was the year of *cynical chic.*

When we could get near the candidates, we traveling journalists—like the *paparazzi*—scrambled for something "new." Some new slip, some new controversy, some new shot or angle that *we* had not heard before. So Jimmy Carter shaking hands with Mickey Mouse in Columbus, Ohio, became something *new* for television in early September. Just as we seized on and amplified the boos of the American Legionnaires, Ford banging his head or putting his foot in his mouth on Eastern Europe, or Carter's "lusts." The three debates were generally dismissed as "dull" and "issueless"—even though the candidates took differing positions on whether combating inflation or unemployment would be their first priority, whether they would cut the defense budget, grant amnesty to Vietnam draft resisters, support national health insurance, take further steps to stem nuclear proliferation, increase aid to our beleaguered cities, adopt new environmental policies.

The public, unsurprisingly, adopted the same disdainful pose as the press. People boasted of planning not to vote. "I voted last time. I wouldn't want it to happen again," boasted a Mr. Black of Culpepper, Virginia, on PBS after the final debate. Polls repeatedly warned that perhaps less than 50 percent of all eligible Americans would vote. And if one wandered through the crowd while traveling with either of the presidential candidates, it was stunning how often one heard people casually denounce all politicians as "corrupt" or "liars" or people "who will promise anything to get elected."

Not that our politicians don't deserve ridicule. Johnson lied to us about the war. Nixon about Watergate. Agnew about taking money. Ford about the pardon. The CIA and FBI lied about spying. Carter has conducted one of the most unfocused presidential campaigns in history, tumbling almost thirty points in the polls since his nomination; Ford has mounted what appears to be one of the shrewdest, using taxpayers' money and the White House as a prop.

Yet the degree of our cynicism seems excessive. Perhaps journalists, as well as politicans, have some answering to do when this protracted campaign ends. Take John Chancellor. Addressing the New York Civil Liberties annual dinner in mid-October, NBC's anchorman intoned, "I appear before you this evening as one who feels that his civil liberties have been violated" because "I have been deprived of my right to a decent election." Adopting the favored snide posture of journalism, Chancellor proceeded to focus the blame on candidates—not NBC, not journalism, certainly not his viewers—for the campaign's "demagoguery, brainwashing, cardiac lust, freedom in Poland, shacking up, how to get along in Congress on five dollars a week, ethnic purity, and the wit and wisdom of Earl Butz." Presumably, these stories dominated and lingered in the news over the objections of Mr. Chancellor.

The *New York Times*'s respected R. W. Apple, quoting that noted expert George McGovern, dispatched an influential October 20 front-page story about this "petty" campaign. He wrote that the contest was "unusually barren of serious dialogue on the issues." After the first debate, CBS's Roger Mudd complained that it was "dull" and "no new positions were taken. No new ground was broken." On the next evening's news, Mudd called the encounter "a letdown"—presumably because the candidates did not entertain by scratching each other's eyes out.

Personally, I found the third presidential debate the most illuminating. It helped spotlight the stated differences between Carter and Ford on the economy, the role of the federal government, gun control, the cities. But like most observers, Bill Moyers did not agree. On CBS that night he put it down thus: "I think there's all the more reason to be undecided after tonight's debate, because the differences seemed to narrow instead of to become more distinctive." Moyers, who had read most of their speeches, even if the public had not, complained that the candidates broke no new ground. Walter Cronkite mildly demurred, but Moyers continued that "the undecided voters" were "looking for some breakthrough in vision or imagination or in concept or in program that will enable them to do something about these generalities they've been espousing. . . ." But Moyers wasn't through: "Neither one of them has come out with any intelligent, comprehensible way to propose that he's going to do something about unemployment and hold down inflation at the same time." The person who comes up with that will no doubt win the Nobel Prize.

This glib cynicism—even from thoughtful men like Mudd and Moyers —is contagious. After the third debate, the New York *Post* offered what the writer called "the postyawn analysis." Sandy Vanocur of the Washington *Post* declared on PBS that it was "a disaster." Even Jimmy Carter, pandering to his audience's sensibilities as he did to *Playboy*'s, afterward thanked and congratulated several thousand students "for staying awake."

It is nitwitted for the press to say that no "new" things were said in the debates. The point is not for candidates to say new things, but to say substantive things. It is insane to expect a candidate, after more than a year of campaigning and a lifetime's public record, to have new things to say.

Of course politicians will try to blur distinctions, broaden their support, get by on a smile. They're in the business of trying to get elected. But that's not exactly a revelation, and it shouldn't be treated as if it were. The major role of journalists in a political campaign is to compel politicians to discuss and define their stance, to cut through the evasions and the vagueness. We don't always succeed; Nixon, like Ford to a lesser extent this year, hid in the White House in 1972—and the press let both men get away with it. Every time Mudd or Chancellor or Moyers or their colleagues bleated about this "issueless campaign" they were, unintentionally, criticizing themselves.

The purpose of the debates was not, as Sandy Vanocur suggested, to determine the candidates' "character," but to define what it is they proposed to do as President. Too often, television and print reporting in this campaign said that the two presidential candidates were the same—what else is the implication behind the incessant complaint that there were "no issues" between the candidates?

The press has altered the fundamental nature of political campaigns. One reason candidates don't espouse serious positions is because we don't take their positions seriously. You can't in a forty-five-second TV film clip for the evening news. And too many print reporters are not interested, or fear they would put their readers to sleep if they did.

When he wasn't performing on PBS, Vanocur wisely said, "Let's start covering campaigns according to the candidates' propensities to do what they think is important, rather than have them form their statements to fit the evening news or the nightly leads. In today's coverage, you could not get the kind of a speech that Adlai Stevenson made to the Los Angeles City Forum in 1952, which was a magnificent blueprint of democracy. We are not covering these people; they are crazy if they give us anything substantive, because the press will distort it or tear it apart."

The press intrudes on the campaign process in many ways. Our intrusion is visible to any citizen trying to shake hands with the candidate as he walks down the street surrounded by an impenetrable fortress of reporters and television equipment. But the most intrusive aspects are far more subtle. We have a need to label and simplify things, if for no other reason than space. So Morris Udall and Fred Harris were judged to be "liberals" or "outspoken" because, for instance, they flatly advocated breaking up large oil companies. Carter was labeled a "moderate" or "cautiously vague" because he refused to make a similar flat statement. That Udall and Harris were never "specific" or "outspoken" in detailing exactly how they would accomplish this, or in telling the public of its consequences, really didn't matter. During the Democratic National Convention, Carter's press secretary, Jody Powell, reflecting back on the reportage, complained that Carter's position "on divestiture was long and complicated" and couldn't be explained "in thirty-eight seconds."

He made the point another way: "I remember, in 1975, Carter was delivering a laundry list of all his recommendations to prevent another Watergate. No one paid any attention. If instead of that he had said, 'We can't afford to have this country governed by a man who pardoned Nixon'—that would have been picked up. The press would have said he was specific. Why? Because he was sharp."

The insulting television spots of the two presidential candidates say as much about their audience—and about this campaign—as they do about the candidates. They got by on a smile. Ford's exhibited a McDonald's-like jingle, crediting him with the Bicentennial, being a nice man—"like my father"—and being a former Rotarian and football player. Carter's also had a snappy upbeat jingle and advertised the candidate's boyhood on the farm, his wife, his kids. Thankfully, he didn't have a dog.

Harrison Schmitt is the Republican candidate for U.S. senator from New Mexico. His slogan—"Honesty for a change"—caters to the public's notion that those in office are "crooks." Prodded by Watergate's aftermath and Common Cause, the new federal campaign finance law is also predicated on that notion. In their panic to calm an aroused public—and protect their own incumbency—Congress passed this law limiting each candidate in the general election to a ceiling of $21.8 million. The legislation also banished all private fund-raising for the two candidates. It was a fine theory—except that it screwed minority candidates. And, in practice, it has often reduced this campaign to a buttonless, bumper-stickerless, bloodless bore. Lacking sufficient money to spend, the campaigns are absent the normal rallies, literature, and excitement, much of it contrived by money. In the name of opening the political process, the campaign finance law and its strict limits help close it by inducing further apathy.

As fewer people vote—"nonvoting is becoming the norm," laments pollster Peter Hart, after an extensive study—the nature of democratic government changes. Elections become more susceptible to highly organized special-interest groups who can tip the balance. Assuming that half those eligible vote, the next President will be elected by roughly 25 percent of the electorate. Aided by public apathy, our politicians become more, not less, beholden to special interests; more, not less, "crooked."

All of this is not meant to make you feel sorry for our poor, beleaguered politicians. Many are making out just fine. The *Times* reported last Thursday that the South Korean government paid money to influence at least ninety members of Congress. Bernard Bergman's nursing-home thievery would not have been possible without the connivance of politicians. The press did not invent the gifts from Gulf Oil that were received by Republican Senate Minority Leader Hugh Scott and a bipartisan claque of government officials. We should write more about Jerry Ford's free golf trips and Jimmy Carter's free airplane rides.

But maybe, looking back on this long campaign, we have demanded the wrong things. Maybe we nitpick too much, pouncing on each slip, each nuance, as if it were a new Cuban missile crisis. Maybe we shouldn't blame Ford and Carter for conducting "dull" debates, instead blaming our own lack of interest in issues, our own taste not for the clash of ideas but for the more colorful clash of personalities. Instead of just dismissing candidates for encouraging apathy, perhaps we should also say the public is lazy, and that much of what they're offered as news, particularly on television, amounts to brain candy. Maybe we are the new *paparazzi*—the boys on the bus could teach Ron Gallela a few tricks. Maybe, like too many politicians, journalists are feeding the public what it wants to hear, wanting to grab attention, titillate, entertain.

Everybody's doing it.

Tom Brokaw Becomes
a Press Victim

New York *Daily News,* January 7, 1979

Most reporters don't know what it's like to be a press victim. Like B-52 pilots, we unload our bombs and fly away. Rarely do we see, much less sense, the punishment we inflict.

Usually it's no fun being on the other side, as Tom Brokaw of NBC found out. The bombs began to rain on Brokaw on Wednesday, November 15. On that day the front-page headline of the Washington *Star* exploded: "TV Star Gets SBA 'Minority' Aid." Brokaw, host of the *Today Show,* received a $345,000 Small Business Administration federal loan guarantee to buy a radio station back home in Rapid City, South Dakota. Since the SBA program was originally designed to encourage minority ownership, Brokaw had reason to stay in bed on November 15, unless you count rich, handsome, thirty-eight-year-old white males as a minority.

He felt as if he were in a bunker. Headlines from newspapers across the country crashed about him. Columnists and cartoonists lobbed missives. Irate letters flailed NBC. There were printed rumors of a Senate investigation, gossip that he was no longer heir apparent to John Chancellor as anchor of the nightly news.

"It made me more paranoid than I should be," Brokaw admits. Indeed. "What have you written about me?" was his greeting when we met for the first time at a Christmas party. At first, says Brokaw, "It was like a death in the family. I entered a room and everyone got quiet. Even friends were afraid to say anything." He broke the ice by posting an explanation on NBC's bulletin board.

It was difficult to adjust. As a White House correspondent for NBC, Brokaw asked the questions. He made members of the Nixon and Ford administrations squirm. He enjoyed a reputation as a good reporter, no small feat for a TV journalist. And, unlike his predecessors on the *Today Show,* Brokaw refused to hawk products on the air, claiming he was a reporter, not a salesman.

Today, almost two months after becoming a victim, Brokaw searches for lessons from his travail. Seated at his desk in a cramped seventh-floor Rockefeller Center office, soft classical music from a Japanese-made radio filling the room, the shaggy-haired, boyish-looking newsman thumbs through a folder of press clippings. *His* press clippings.

He pauses and half laughs at a Los Angeles *Times* cartoon from Paul Conrad, a once close friend. It's a drawing of a desolate Indian reservation occupied by a single radio tower and tepee—"Owned and operated by Tom Brokaw." It is very clever. Also, very painful.

"I know what happens," says Brokaw, talking about journalists. "We pick up a scent, we get on the trail of something. Here's a guy, Conrad, who's got to turn out a cartoon. It's a dull day. Along comes a name—*Brokaw.* Then—*minorities.* Both good buzz words. The story has appeal. I think that the constraints come off. Sometimes we journalists lose a little perspective.

"I don't think I was oblivious to this problem, to the kind of treatment people sometimes receive in the news. But I don't think I had a full appreciation of the effect of a strong strain of negative news coverage. There's a real ripple effect. It happens even with a story that is written quite accurately and with great care."

Journalism is the business of sorting through and simplifying mounds of information, contradictory statements, allegations, sometimes lies. We do not record, we report. And what we report is a condensation of what is, in our judgment, the story. We select facts, quotes, the lead paragraph, which telegraphs what we think the news is. Editors further compress our story into terse headlines. If you're a columnist or cartoonist, you take greater liberties. In all cases, readers or viewers are more at the mercy of individual judgment than of "objective" journalistic rules and standards.

The people we write about are more aware of this than journalists. Tom Brokaw, today, is more aware of it. He fingers a clipping from the *New York Times* and complains that the reporter did not aggressively seek to contact him. The Washington *Star* reporter tracked him down in New Haven. The *Times* reporter simply wrote that Mr. Brokaw "could not be reached at his New York office." Thus the story contained no refutation of the implication that Brokaw's $345,000 loan guarantee was a direct grant of federal dollars.

This gift implication was common. The Baltimore *News American* headline dubbed it a "loan," as did the Philadelphia *Daily News,* the Topeka *Daily Capital,* and the New York *Post.* The difference between a loan and a loan guarantee is significant, as New York City successfully argued when it captured a $1.6-billion federal loan guarantee.

A loan is a direct appropriation of federal monies. A loan guarantee means that a bank makes the loan and the federal government agrees to pay up to 90 percent if the creditor defaults. Since the government demanded that Brokaw take out a second mortgage on an expensive Washington home, and since he admits to earning more than $250,000, SBA officials concede there is little risk.

Press accounts tended to ignore another fact: the loan was made by a local South Dakota bank. "I had given the name and phone number of the banker, David Gross, to everybody," laments Brokaw. "As far as I know, no one outside of a Sioux Falls, South Dakota, reporter called him." Gross told them: "The loan was above our legal lending limit, which is 10 percent of our capital accounts. We went to the SBA to guarantee the loan."

Many headlines and stories suggested Brokaw was stealing food from the mouths of poor people. "TV Star Gets Aid Meant for Minorities" blazed the Miami *Herald.* Of the first thirty-two loan guarantees "aimed at helping disadvantaged Americans buy broadcasting stations," said the *Times,* only seven went to minorities. While it is true that the SBA does a miserable job aiding minorities, its program to secure financial assistance to acquire or expand broadcast facilities was amended a year ago to include non-minorities.

And, finally, Brokaw comes to the clippings from the *Daily News.* "And now we hear that Sen. Gaylord Nelson (D. Wis.), who heads the Senate Select Small Business Committee, has decided to take a really deep look into the Brokaw affair," teased the "People" page. Presumably, citizens were left in suspense as to whether Brokaw would be carted off to jail. One week later, their "deep look" completed, the *News* reported the Senate Committee found "There was nothing wrong with NBC *Today Show* anchorman Tom Brokaw . . . obtaining a $345,000 federal loan guarantee."

"Should I have gotten the guarantee?" asks Brokaw. "No. I made a minor mistake in judgment."

The federal government also made a mistake. The loan guarantee program is supposed to be for those who cannot arrange financing without government assistance. Tom Brokaw admits he could have gone to any New York bank and paid perhaps a quarter percent more in interest, but he preferred doing business with a hometown bank.

Brokaw made a mistake. Because he is something of a celebrity, he paid for it more than the rest of us.

There are, thankfully, no formal checks on the power of the press. Except self-restraint and good judgment. Perhaps an occasional article or broadcast press criticism. We possess incredible power to destroy reputations, to deprive people of a living, to wound. Tom Brokaw didn't fully appreciate that until he got hurt.

"It will change me a little bit," he says. The other day he visited a producer and reporter at NBC about one of their stories. "I told them," he says, " 'No doubt you were on the right road, but you didn't have your facts nailed down. You made it seem bigger than it was and gave it bigger play because of the names involved.' It was celebrity journalism. We have to be careful not just how we treat the people involved. But also whether the public will continue to believe what we're reporting."

Now that he has been a victim, Tom Brokaw will probably become a better reporter.

Would You Lie, Steal or Cheat to Get a Story?

[MORE] Magazine, March 1977

Two months after Jimmy Carter made Robert Scheer a journalistic celebrity by telling him about the lust in his heart, Scheer created further controversy with some heartfelt remarks of his own delivered at [MORE]'s A. J. Liebling Convention last November.

He participated in a panel discussion on "The Art of the Interview," and when asked how far a reporter should go to get the facts behind a public official's statements, Scheer told the audience that "politicians try to prevent you from knowing what's going on because that's how they survive. And they have lots of people employed to help them. The journalist's job is to get the story by breaking into their offices, by bribing, by seducing people, by lying, by anything else to break through that palace guard."

As for giving his word to a source, Scheer said, "Maybe if there was somebody I really wanted to interview and they said, 'I've got to have some control,' I can't say now I wouldn't lie. I think the most important thing to a journalist is to get the story . . . maybe I would promise anything, as long as I could get out of the country on time." As to whether he would break his word after promising something was off the record, Scheer said, "Even if I had [promised] and they said something that I thought was important for the public to know, I would print it. I can't imagine not printing it."

Now forty, Scheer comes from a tradition of journalistic controversy that he describes as "counter-journalism." As a graduate student at Berkeley, he published a book on the Cuban revolution and, soon after, one called *How the U.S. Got Involved in Vietnam,* one of the first critical books on the war. He led anti-war marches in Berkeley and Oakland in the mid-sixties, then went on to anti-war, anti-establishment journalism for *Ramparts* in its heyday. He participated in *Ramparts'* exposé of secret CIA funding of U.S. student organizations, and in 1966 briefly entered politics with an unsuccessful run for Congress on an anti-war platform, attracting a surprising 45 percent of the vote. After editing *Ramparts* for five years he wrote *America After Nixon,* a study of the power of multinational corporations.

In the past year Scheer has written a regular political column for *New Times,* co-authored the exclusive jailhouse interviews with SLA members Bill and Emily Harris for *New Times*, and produced a series of interviews and profiles of presidential aspirants Jackson, Rockefeller, Brown, and Carter for *Playboy, New Times,* and *Esquire.*

Scheer has lately given up free-lancing for a reporting job with the Los Angeles *Times,* guest commentaries on ABC's *Good Morning, America* and a book on the Carter administration.

Recently Scheer spent almost five hours being interviewed himself. In the edited text that follows, one of America's "hottest" reporters talks about journalism and journalists, ends and means.

At the [MORE] convention you said that "politicians try to prevent you from knowing what's going on." Therefore, you said, a journalist's job is to find out "by breaking into their offices, by bribing, by seducing people, by lying, by anything else to break through that palace guard." Do you stand by those words?

Yeah, I would stick by them—if that's the only way. I'm not talking about trying to find out who Jacqueline Kennedy was sleeping with, by hook or by crook. But it seems to me that in the case of the Pentagon Papers —the example I used at the convention—that the public had a right to see those papers. And that is true, too, of the committee report on the CIA that Daniel Schorr leaked, and it's true of the CIA documents we printed in *Ramparts.* At *Ramparts,* we printed plenty of documents that had been pilfered. When you feel a story is important and there is no other way to get it, yes, then you use certain means. For example, we were going after the National Student Association–CIA connection in the sixties. We could not prove that the international organization they belonged to had received funds from the San Jacinto Foundation, which we knew was a CIA front. So I went to Leyden, Holland, to the offices of the San Jacinto Foundation, and I got into that office by cajoling and by flattering and by everything else.

How else? How'd you get into that office?

I stayed longer than I was supposed to stay. I hung around rooms that I wasn't supposed to be hanging around in. And I ended up in possession of a document that made the connection that allowed us to go with the story.

Did you break in?

I don't want to get into the specifics of it. But certainly it was in a gray area of activity. And I would do it again. Getting that document allowed *Ramparts* to expose the whole use of foundations as conduits for the CIA, a terribly important thing to reveal.

In what other instances would you do it again?

I will be very glad to get any serious government documents of any government in the world that shows it screwing people and misusing power. There are other examples. In 1963 I took some of Yevtushenko's poetry out of Russia, and it was considered a crime to do that. So what? Another example, one I also used at the [MORE] convention, concerns a tax-supported project of the Rockefeller Foundation. I spent a hell of a lot of time making all the right requests for interviews and information and still couldn't crack it. Finally some guy's secretary was willing to let me in on some of the data, and it was just terrific. I didn't inquire about whether she was violating the code of her employment.

Did you seduce her to do that?

No. She was a radical who had been overly educated for her job. There was no seduction. She felt her boss ought to have talked to me. When he went out to lunch she said, "Look, come in here." And I'm sure that's happening in a hell of a lot of offices in this country because we've got people working there now.

If the foundation was not tax-supported, would you have had less of a right to do that?

If there's not a public interest, sure.

So you determine the public interest?

I think you have to stand behind your judgment of it, but I think any time you do that you have to be prepared publicly to defend what you've done. You may have penalties as a result.

But you haven't been willing to tell me whether you broke into the office in Holland to get the CIA documents?

I would say, technically not. Someone in that office would say I exceeded the bounds of my invitation.

Where do you draw the line between what is permissible and what is not permissible?

Well, I look at situations where that question has come up. I don't know where Deep Throat got his information. I don't know what laws he violated. But it seems to me it was very useful that that story was cracked. A hell of a lot of the investigative journalism of the last five years has come from such information. Files that are lifted, people who are violating the conditions of their jobs, and so forth. What I was trying to say at the convention is that I think that's basically a good thing. If that's the only way you can get that story, it should be done that way. I didn't invent the situation, nor am I one of its main practitioners. I'm not a second-story man, you know. I'm only talking about situations of serious public misuse.

Isn't that what Ehrlichman said, that "national security" dictated breaking into Ellsberg's psychiatrist's office?

But John Ehrlichman had the White House. He had state power. What do I have—a chance to write an article for *Playboy*? I was addressing myself to extreme situations where there was something important that the public had a right to know. At least, that the journalist felt the public had a right to know. That was important to the formulation of public policy. And there was no other way to get it. I guess in retrospect that would have been a wiser statement to make than the unqualified one that you're using here.

If I were Dan Schorr, I would not break into the House Committee's office to get their CIA report. I have a sense, from a literal interpretation of your statement at the [MORE] convention, that you would?

What if some people had broken in and they'd given it to you?

Tough question.

I've faced this. I've got transcripts of Bilderberg meetings which everyone knows were pilfered by European radicals. The same with a number of other things—FBI documents stolen from Pennsylvania, and so forth. I don't see the great distinction between some kids out there stealing stuff and using it and what the *New York Times* did with Ellsberg, even though the *Times* took the position that they were just printing the stuff, and those other guys Xeroxed it. I don't see the distinction.

What about breaking your word? You said at the [MORE] convention that if some powerful person said something to you off the record, you would break your word and print it if you thought it was an important story.

I think that "off the record" has been misused. It has no legal standing.

But you sometimes use it, don't you?

I was trying to think about that. And it's not a normal thing for me to do. Very few people ever say "off the record" to me.

But there was an incident in your Carter *Playboy* piece where two of his aides were on an elevator and were obviously carrying on extramarital affairs. Carter was also on the elevator. You didn't name the aides. You used your discretion.

Sure, but that wasn't because anyone said that it was off the record.

Yes, but you also talked to Carter aides and did not use information they told you. If they said to you, "Listen, I'll tell you this and you can use the quote but don't use my name," you wouldn't use their name on it, right?

I would make that judgment.

Would you say to them, "Okay, I won't use your name," and then use their name?

As I said, if they told me something that I thought was important and that people had a right to know, even though they had said that this was off the record, I would use it.

Even if you had agreed not to?

Yes. Here's a good example. Hubert Humphrey—I am not sure if it was off the record—Hubert Humphrey told a couple of us who were brought in to see him, sort of a co-option scene, something about the fact that the Vietnamese had been willing to negotiate and the United States hadn't taken them up on their offer. We ran it in *Ramparts.* And we ran it with his name because he was the Vice-President of the United States and it was important. The statement had a different meaning with his name on it. And I thought that I had been co-opted by this "off the record" business. A politician can misuse that. If something is important, your highest obligation is to print it.

What about your obligation to keep your word to the person who trusted you with the information?

I think it's more important not to break your word to your readers. There's an implicit understanding when a writer writes for a reader that you're telling the reader what you know. And I'm saying that my bond to myself is that I'm not going to withhold information from my readers.

Let me ask you this, Ken. If you were with General Brown and he said that he would tell you what he thinks about Jews—off the record—would you print it?

First off, I might not grant him "off the record." But if I agreed it was off, I wouldn't print it.

Don't you think you're playing God in a way?

Of course, and that's the whole point of the interview: Where do we draw the line?

Well, you've made a judgment about this. You said you would honor "off the record" no matter what. Even if it means that a war continues or funds are stolen.

Wait a second. If you make the argument you made at the [MORE] convention that if someone told you he was going to blow up the world in three weeks—off the record—I presume that in that case I would violate "off the record" because if I didn't, I wouldn't be around in three weeks.

So we can agree that my position is no more arbitrary and no more playing God than yours.

No.

You just happen to think that your decisions about "off the record" are correct and that mine are incorrect.

No, there is one difference. I am not breaking my word and you are.

Well, as I've said, I think that you're breaking your word to your readers. And what you're saying, for example, is that you'd rather not identify General Brown than break your word to him.

No, not to General Brown. Maybe my bond to myself.

And what I'm saying is that my bond to myself is that I am not going to withhold information from my readers. And what's happened here is that you've denied the *moral* basis of what I am saying, implying that my position is cynical and arbitrary and that yours is somehow dignified.

No. We all make individual judgments.

Well, let's talk about burglary again. You told me that you thought it was correct that Ellsberg took the Pentagon Papers. Now, if Ellsberg gave those papers to you and he told you that he stole them from the Rand Corporation, would you print them?

Yes.

What if Ellsberg only knew of the papers' existence, hadn't read them, thought they were probably important and then stole them and gave them to you? Would you have accepted them then?

That's one of the questions that we have to answer, and I think you, me, and all of us, haven't given enough thought to these questions.

Clearly. But what I resent is your assumption that somehow I just stated various positions at the convention without having given them any thought at all. What I was responding to at the convention was the reality of journalism: the fact that some of the most important stories of recent years have involved theft, burglary, seduction, and conning people. And I believe that those means are justified if the stories are terribly important. I don't mean to say that I've got some little calculus that allows you to make these judgments, a measuring stick that will tell you where it's right or wrong. I think these are tough questions and I think you are going to fuck up a lot.

The problem is that there are a lot of journalists who aren't interested in national security but are interested in getting the story. And if they start saying that they can do anything to get a story, then they're on pretty dangerous ground.

That's why it must be put in the context of politicians engaging in major wrongdoing, as was the case with the Pentagon Papers and the Pike Committee report Daniel Schorr leaked.

In fairness to you, I thought most everyone on the [MORE] panel was troubling. Dick Reeves talked about doing just about everything, like calling accident victims' families to get stories and cloaking his identity as a reporter. Nora Ephron talked about the faking of taking notes or lulling the subject by not taking notes during interviews and then running to the bathroom to write things down. All the panelists talked about their techniques, including some rather sly ones like reading memos off people's desks, and then they reacted with such horror to some of the things you said. As I thought about what they said and compared it to what you said, the difference was not so much one of kind but of degree.

What developed in the sixties—of necessity—was a guerrilla journalism that came about because we did not want to be part of access journalism. And what we did was break through in all kinds of ways. We hung out at parties and eavesdropped and stole memos and every other damn thing to crash through. I wish we'd never had to do any of it. They are not wonderful things to do. Obviously it would be better to live in a world where you don't burrow and seduce. Obviously it would be nice to always honor "off the record." And I don't find that the way I conduct my own life, my own behavior, involves seduction, bribery, burglary. If I gave that impression, I think that that was a mistake. I apologize for that.

But what if you attend a Georgetown dinner party as a guest and you hear what is assumed to be a confidence?

I will violate that civilized behavior and maybe not get invited to anymore parties. Absolutely. I went to my first Georgetown party the other night with some journalists. I couldn't believe the conversation. These people are hearing conversations the rest of us never hear. Access journalists are constantly in possession of information that the rest of us never get.

I think that's absolutely right. But there's a difference between hearing the stuff and not using it because you're afraid of offending your sources —which is the case of too many access journalists—and entering into an agreement with someone and refusing to break your word.

Almost all of these conversations were off the record. In fact, they don't even have to say "off the record." I'll give you an example. At this dinner party, I heard something that I thought was interesting. I said, "My God, nobody knows that!" A guy looked at me horror-stricken. This is a dinner party in Georgetown. You just don't. So their idea of "off the record" is that just the act of going to a dinner party means you don't ever report that, see? Now, what that means is that most journalists of power in this country are part of a culture that is almost all "off the record." Tom Braden, Henry Brandon, James Reston are constantly swimming in a sea of information the rest of us don't get to see. But it's all very ethical, it's all very civilized.

What I've done throughout my career in journalism is react to that. In a way I overreacted. Maybe counter-journalism overstated the case. I would say now it is time to establish certain codes of behavior. But I would not be willing to sacrifice my right to be irreverent and uncivilized unless they sacrificed their right to play that game. There's one reason why a counter-journalist has to use tricks. It's that we aren't part of that business. Take the Jimmy Carter quote. I could have played a fifth assistant press secretary, and said hey, we better go over this and make it make Jimmy look better, right? Which plenty of journalists do. If I'd done that, I'd be in that club. The Rockefeller story is the perfect example. You know that whole Helms part. Here were the Vice-President and Richard Helms and all these people at a party. They're supposed to be in an adversary relationship. Rockefeller's investigating the CIA, which Helms once headed. It was an "off the record" dinner party. I got one of the participants in that party, Joan Braden, off the record, to tell me what the hell went on and I printed it.

Why would you give me her name?

'Cause you're not gonna use it, are you?

Is it off the record?

I don't give a shit. She's the only one who could have done it. She's blasted me for doing it. But I mean I'm sorry, you know? I don't think I became a lousy human being when I printed that story even if I had used Joan Braden's name. Because I think that exposing what the hell was going on there makes you a *better* human being.

Did she say you couldn't use anything she told you? That it was off the record?

I'm not real good on these technicalities but she said yeah, you should print it. And you're saying that you wouldn't have?

That's right. If it was off the record, I would not have. One of the things that is interesting is that here we are, political journalists, judging politicians harshly for doing things that in some cases we do ourselves.

That's not what I judge politicians for. My real basis of judgment is whether they want to blow up people, keep them impoverished, or whether they want to rip off their money, and that stuff. I am much more concerned with journalists building an empire or forgetting what they're supposed to be about than whether they're uncovering important stories by dubious means. All this emphasis on the question of dubious means bothers me a lot, because phone-calling and getting down there and talking to people and trying to confirm stories and library work are more important. The best thing about the goddamn Carter interview is that I was able to use the library down there. I went down there and talked to the people in that town, and that's the most important thing about it.

I don't want to emerge from all this that my main contribution to journalism is to advocate going through the second story. I mean, if I had to make a choice, I'd say give up burglary, seduction, and all that for the library. So if I had to make a rough choice between a young journalist going to the library or breaking into an office, I'd pick the library. But, unfortunately, I've somehow gotten mousetrapped into becoming the major advocate of using dubious means, and one of the ironies of celebrity is that you can probably advance your career by taking outrageous positions.

It seems to me that's what you were doing at the [MORE] convention.

Well, if I was doing it at [MORE], I regret it. Basically, I was trying to get at establishment journalism. I was trying to present a raunchier view.

But there is something exhibitionistic about that, isn't there? Especially since you now say you really don't believe that.

I give a shit about these questions and I do believe that.

You do give a shit about it?

Yeah. I care a lot about these questions. And I have great doubt about when to do what, you know. As to being a celebrity, well, I was wearing a suit the other day and someone said, "Boy you're really making it, look at that suit." Well, I've been wearing it for seven years or something, that particular suit. It's the same with this position on breaking in to get a story —a position really coming out of *Ramparts.* There were all those years of being an illegitimate journalist, and the thing that's confusing to me now about it is that all of a sudden it's possible to believe that maybe you don't need to do all that, that maybe there's another way to do it.

At *Ramparts* there was no other way to do it. I got into journalism doing that Vietnam stuff in 1962, '63, when all the editors who now offer me contracts told me there was no sense doing a book on Vietnam because the war would be over before the book came out—Kennedy was going to end it. It was a whole different experience. We were kind of guerrilla-kamikaze journalists. Maybe the times have changed, because now I have personal access. But maybe times haven't changed. That's another question. If I was responding to anything at that panel, it was as if I was again the editor of *Ramparts* and there I was stating our position vis-à-vis the *New York Times.*

Why?

I was trying to explain why there is such a thing as counter-journalism. That's the tradition I come out of and respect.

But hasn't "counter-journalism" become accepted journalism?

It's quite possible, it's tempting to think that, but on the other hand, it may be totally wrong. Maybe someone like myself has just mellowed. I'm not prepared to tell a group of young journalists to do this and that, because I see too many people working for regular papers that don't have real freedom. Someone at the convention who works for the Atlanta *Constitution* asked where the counter-press is. I said there are lots of young people working, and she said, "What's that got to do with where I work? Maybe we have one investigative journalist in the house, because that's fashionable now." So let's not exaggerate the amount of change.

You've spoken of how you work, of preparing before you meet the subject of your interview and of then going back to the typewriter and "waiting for that moment when you're going to kill him."

Well, I think that was an exaggeration. I believe that if you're going after some powerful person, a person in a position where he can make a lot of decisions that affect people's lives, then you have an obligation to unravel him in some way. And after you've spent time with him and gotten your information, then your job is to sock it to him, in a way—which is not the same as doing a hatchet job.

But one of the things you pride yourself on is being a tough guy.

No, I don't think that's true. In fact, I find that the opposite pressures apply. I find that I have to remember what I'm there for. It's easy to end up liking these people. I don't get to the typewriter and figure out ways to hate them. But I do have to remember that these people are very good at getting you to like them. They are very charming. It's easy to be lulled.

What about your own personal political beliefs and how they affect your work? You are a self-proclaimed Marxist. Is Bob Scheer an ideologue or a journalist?

Well, is James Reston an ideologue or a journalist? Is Clay Felker? I mean, just because you embrace the establishment's dominant ideology doesn't make you any less of an ideologue.

Well, you once wrote a piece for *New Times* in which you criticized Tom Hayden for using his father-in-law, Henry Fonda, in campaign commercials when he ran for the U.S. Senate in California. You wrote of it as a cheap kind of trick. And yet you talk openly of employing tricks yourself in getting stories. Why is it different for Hayden to get elected than for you to get a story?

Well, what I said in the piece on Tom was that his victory would have meant a hell of a lot more if he had run a campaign that was more clear in its radicalism. I would have understood if his goal was to get elected, but I thought his campaign started out as an educational thing. And I didn't think getting Tom Hayden elected senator was a really critical thing to do.

In talking about getting a story, you've mentioned employing different techniques. Do you consciously decide, when interviewing someone, whether at some point to appear to be sympathetic—either by nodding your head or saying "yes" or smiling—or at some point deciding to act contentious with the subject of your interview? Does the person you're interviewing know how Bob Scheer really feels?

Well, I don't think there was ever a time when Jerry Brown didn't know how I felt. He knows me. Our paths have crossed. We have friends in common. And certainly, in the case of Nelson Rockefeller, he had a Secret Service print-out on me.

One of Rockefeller's aides said that the Secret Service let you in to interview Rockefeller but they thought they had to accompany you wherever you went in the Executive Office Building.

Hell, they wouldn't let me go to the bathroom by myself.

When interviewing, is it more effective to make your subject think you know more than maybe even he does about his position, or to make him think you don't know very much?

The second, for sure.

So the "dumb question" does fit into that?

If that's what you mean by a dumb question, sure. There's no doubt that it's better to be less threatening. But you need the killer instinct, too. You ask the dumb question, but at some point you have to spring back with the contradictions. Otherwise you'll just end up with little lectures.

Do you allow your interviewees to read transcripts and omit parts they object to?

Well, I'll let them tell me why they think something should be changed, and then if I still want to go ahead with it, and they then denounce me, that's fine. Then I have the data and they have the data and we can have it out. I did change some things that Jerry Brown wanted cut out. He had taken a couple of swipes at his father and he didn't want them printed, so sure, we cut them out.

Why?

They didn't seem to really reflect his feelings about his father. But maybe it was wrong to accept that cut. As for Carter, if the interview had been done on the run, maybe we would have changed some things. But the interview was done in a controlled setting. His press secretary was there, it was in his house, it was quiet. He knew the tape recorder was on and I felt, "All right, you're a grown man, you're a politician, you know what you're doing." And I offered to show the interview to him.

What would have happened if Carter had objected to the "lust" quote?

Well, I don't know what *Playboy*'s position is; mine is that I would not have changed the "lust" quote because I felt it was an important statement on how he felt about things. If he had wanted to say "living in sin" instead of "shacking up," or he had wanted to say "making love" instead of "screwing," I think I would have argued for letting him make that kind of change.

How does your perspective change now that you're making a reported $40,000 from your new job at the Los Angeles *Times*? Is that an accurate figure, by the way?

I really don't want to get into too great detail about the L.A. *Times*. It has already caused some tension in my trying to get along with everybody. My salary isn't out of line with what well-paid reporters are making at the

L.A. *Times,* and that's how the salary was chosen. There are other people at the L.A. *Times* who make more, and certainly all the executives make more. . . . But I am making a lot more money than I have made before.

I understand that your Carter book advance is a big one.

I don't know, maybe the right thing to do is to give it away or something. I don't know—give it to the Fund for Investigative Journalism—these are things I'm thinking about. It's not a simple question. I know I'm thinking about this more already. I went out and bought an electric typewriter and a tape transcribing machine. I bought the first bed that I have ever had. Before, I always had this foam-mattress wood thing, the way most people in Berkeley do. Now I've got a real bed with a spring. And I bought my mother a couch. I've noticed that all of a sudden you do more consumer stuff than you would otherwise be doing. I could send my mother down to L.A. to where her sister is for two months, not that my mother is particularly willing to let me do things like that. But you know, you have to know the lean years that I had. Most years it was more like six, seven, eight thousand dollars. So obviously this is really a different thing. I live collectively with people, you know. It's not the high life. The money will change things. It's a fucking big change.

You spend a lot of time at Elaine's when you're in New York. Do you think there's something wrong with a place like Elaine's where journalists are treated like movie stars?

I started going to Elaine's when I was with *Ramparts.* In the sixties it was our way of plugging into New York. We needed to meet people. I can go to Elaine's and see half the people I'm trying to see during the course of the day. I didn't have a credit card until two months ago, and Elaine's is the only place in New York where I can cash a check.

The one thing I will grant you—off the record—is that you don't have to talk about Elaine. Because I know if you talk about her, you won't get back in there.

I'm willing to talk about Elaine. . . . Maybe Elaine is the problem. I don't know.

Is that rarefied atmosphere, of people coming in and gawking at you as a celebrity, healthy for a journalist?

I haven't seen that. The time I like it best there is at four or five in the morning. I stay up late. I like bullshitting with Elaine. The thing I like about Elaine is that she's always been real friendly to me, and to the people I know. I'm sure people will read this and say, "God, you're so full of shit. You're so naïve." But I don't feel that.

But Elaine sits at that front door, determining who gets tables and who doesn't. Which table they get in which room.

Jesus, eighty-sixed at the one place I like and can cash a check. I'll defend her. I like Elaine's. I like Elaine. I like the place. If that's going to be a sell-out. . . .

My question is more fundamental than whether one likes Elaine personally. Elaine's in New York City is a useful symbol. Is there something potentially distorting for a journalist who exposes power becoming caught up in some of the same things politicians become caught up in?

Well, I think your basic point is valid. Writers, journalists, obviously have become something more than they should be.

SECOND THOUGHTS

Journalism can be very inbred. To be a good reporter requires humility— asking questions without fear of looking stupid, keeping an open mind, remembering how little you know. And yet, as an institution, journalism is insufficiently humble about what we do, as the Scheer interview illustrates. Insufficient thought is given to important ethical questions about means and ends. We tend to become defensive at suggestions that our First Amendment rights may be in conflict with a defendant's Sixth Amendment right to a fair trial. Most publications—unlike the Washington *Post,* which prints its own press ombudsman, or the Los Angeles *Times,* which last July ran a series of front-page stories critical of its own coverage of major stories— don't criticize themselves in public. Society's whistle-blowers prefer not to have the whistle blown on them; prefer not to be reminded of the rude, dumb questions many TV colleagues ask, of our sometimes mad scramble for headlines and entertainment.

During its too-short life [MORE] magazine tried to police the press. Most of the time, at least. The Scheer interview ran during the reign of the magazine's next-to-last editor, Michael Kramer. It was tape-recorded over five hours, then transcribed and edited to space. To certify that nothing was taken out of context, the transcript was forwarded to Bob Scheer in advance.

Word came back through Kramer that Scheer was unhappy, not with the editing but with some of his answers. He requested an additional interview, which was refused. Or so I thought. I soon learned that editor Kramer promised Scheer another interview, permitting him to alter previous answers. Moreover, Kramer planned to do the interview himself, inserting the fresh answers under my by-line. Kramer agreed because he was a too-eager-to-please mouse. Naturally, when I threatened to strangle him, he backed down. The interview ran as originally edited. It is no small irony, however, that the editor of a major journalism publication was himself willing to cheat to get a story.

Rockefeller's Death:
Where Do You Draw the Line?

New York *Daily News,* February 18, 1979

Fred Friendly plays a Socratic game with editors and reporters who visit his class at the Columbia University Graduate School, where he is Edward R. Morrow Professor of Journalism. He subjects them to a hypothetical test. Imagine, he coyly asks, you learned that J. Fearless Fosdick, retired head of the FBI, had a homosexual liaison, was a compulsive gambler, and was treated for a nervous disability while in office. Imagine, also, that J. Wesley Prince, presumed family man and prominent civil-rights leader, chased good-looking women. Would you print either story? Should you?

With the death of Nelson Rockefeller, Friendly's intramural and hypothetical question has been thrown open to the public. Should the press have reported as much as we have about Megan Marshack and Nelson Rockefeller? I suspect the public, like me, devours every morsel of titillating gossip, and feels somewhat vulgar for liking it so.

I felt a twinge of guilt and anger when the *New York Times* first raised questions about the circumstances of Rockefeller's death. Recall that Hugh Morrow, the Rockefeller spokesman, announced that death came on the fifty-sixth floor of Rockefeller Center and only a personal security aide was present. Within hours, Morrow's story began crumbling. Under the pressure of diligent reporting, it turned out that Rockefeller had died while alone in a West Fifty-fourth Street apartment with a female aide, Megan Marshack.

As the Morrow lies were exposed—and new titillating details tumbled into the press—I read every damn word. But I felt queasy. Did the public have a right to know the social schedule of a retired politician? Did his bereaved family not have a right to privacy? Had the press altered Jack Anderson's rule of what was newsworthy—Sex plus X equals a story? Was the new rule: Sex equals a story? Would this episode receive such prolonged attention had Morrow, rather than an attractive young woman, been alone with Rockefeller when he was stricken?

At the *News, Times,* and *Post,* editors said the main question that concerned them was finding out whether Rockefeller's life could have been saved if Marshack had not delayed calling for help. But they published dozens of juicy details that didn't bear on this issue at all. There was the suspicion that the press, like the politicians we criticize, was out shopping for votes—circulation.

As the line between gossip and news blurs, so does the line between privacy and the public interest. "I think the press has gone too far," says a First Amendment attorney for one newspaper, who requested anonymity. "I think in terms of three hypotheticals: Would the press print it if Rockefeller were alive? My answer is no, for reasons of taste. Suppose Rockefeller died in her arms and there was no one-hour delay. Would the press print it? I don't think so. The press would say it was private. The third question is: What happened? There is no question there was a cover-up. It's not a legal question of what the press can print. The press has the right to print what they have. But, for myself, the question is whether they should have printed it. I just don't think covering it is that important. On balance, there is more of a claim to privacy than any legitimate public interest."

I agreed. Until I thought about it. When the lawyer thought about it, he added, "I don't think the press should be in complicity with duplicity." There's the rub. He said, "The story's been overplayed." True. But that is different from saying the story should not have played. On Saturday, January 27, the press innocently reported Hugh Morrow's lies. When reporters unearthed the truth, they were obligated to correct the record.

Once you correct the record, the can of worms opens. Some facts beg explanation. How much time elapsed between the heart attack and the call for medical help? Why did Ponchita Pierce, who made the call, slip out before help arrived? Why was there no autopsy? "Could he have been saved?" asks Syd Schanberg, metropolitan editor of the *Times*, which broke the story, and with one or two exceptions, covered it tastefully. "Were the people involved more concerned with saving their own reputations or saving his life?" asks Sam Roberts, city editor of the *News*.

Fred Friendly raises another angle: "It seems to me this is strictly a case of the media's need to establish the fact that it is not in the cover-up business. I'm an old fan of Rockefeller's. But when his aides lied, it was no longer possible not to write that story. We live in an age when most of our kids believe in conspiracy theories. They believe there was a conspiracy involved in the death of Martin Luther King, John Kennedy, and Bobby Kennedy.

"Everything gets covered up. I respect privacy. But far more important than privacy is the credibility of the news media. When I put on the scales the right of privacy versus the credibility of the news media, I come out on the side of the press. What I don't want to see is a story in a magazine with pictures and headlines: THE STORY THE *DAILY NEWS* AND *TIMES* AND *POST* SUPPRESSED. Once the country believes they are not being told the truth by newspapers and broadcasters, then we've lost one thing that distinguishes this country: We know what's going on."

Or are supposed to. But are we supposed to know *everything*? On this story, the press strayed and described the gifts Rocky made to Megan, giving them more prominence than the turmoil in Iran. Did we need to know that? Yes, answered an editor. "It is important that we know as much about their relationship as we can find, so that we can establish what happened in that fatal hour."

The editor is standing on a banana peel, not a principle. Follow that logic and every nook and cranny of Megan Marshack's life is open to inspection and disclosure. Logically, we should ask Happy Rockefeller what she knew and when she knew it. And what about the Rockefeller kids? Shouldn't we report on what the chauffeur and butlers knew? Where does it stop? Digging through garbage cans, like the *National Enquirer*?

"Public figures," says Friendly, "give up all privacy. Period." That, too, is a banana peel. Because it is important to find out what kind of people we elect, does the press therefore have the right to interview children to learn if they like their father? Was the Washington *Post* correct, in the course of exposing former Congressman Wayne Hays, to eavesdrop on his lurid phone conversations with Elizabeth Ray? Should journalists, while trailing candidates, follow them to their motel rooms, and demand to know whom they're sleeping with? And who is a public figure? Friendly says the definition should include editors, TV executives, even working journalists. Ho, ho.

Where do journalists draw the line? Just a few years ago, it was easy. We tended to print the handouts of politicians, acting as if we were one of the boys. Vietnam and Watergate and a hurricane of lies changed that. We applied a new test to Wayne Hays when he abused the public payroll to employ a harem; to former Congressman Wilbur Mills, chairman of the Ways and Means Committee, who was tipsy on public time. In both cases, the line was clear: their private acts impinged on the public.

Some of the reporting on Rockefeller's death does not meet that test, and that raises anxiety about where we're going. Journalism is a business of quick decisions and deadlines. There is little time to reflect.

Without some sense of the borders beyond which we should not go, the privacy we should not invade, the means we should not use, the higher ethic could become just getting a story. Any story of interest. On deadline, without time for adequate discussion, preoccupied with beating competitors or boosting circulation, we inadvertently stretch the boundary.

"When you fill your news columns with stuff that is only ten-percent news," the late A. J. Liebling wrote, "I suppose you create in the reader's mind a doubt that any of it is news."

SECOND THOUGHTS

I made my own mistake with Nelson Rockefeller. Back in late 1978 I suggested to news executives at WNET-TV that a one-hour conversation with the former Vice-President could be fascinating. I had just completed my book on New York City's travails and had questions to ask the former governor about his own complicity in the city's mess. What's more, we could discuss his new career as an art dealer, the famous people he had known, glance back on his own life, his party, his state, his nation. Great idea, said the news executives. I called Rockefeller's press secretary, Hugh Morrow. He was interested, but made no commitment.

He did, however, want to meet the producer, Isabel Dane, to review where and how the conversation would be conducted. After their meeting, Morrow said he'd like to hold off until late spring. Fine.

On the first Monday in February, Isabel phoned to say that Morrow had just phoned her. Rockefeller was prepared to conduct the interview that Friday afternoon. Impossible, I said. I had another deadline. Besides, more than four days were needed to research and prepare questions for Nelson Rockefeller. Isabel concurred, adding that her crew was committed elsewhere on Friday. Like me, she preferred to put it off until spring. It could wait, we both agreed. That Friday evening Nelson Rockefeller died.

That Queasy Feeling

New York *Daily News,* September 9, 1979

When newspapers blared that the owners of Studio 54 accused Hamilton Jordan, President Carter's chief of staff, of snorting cocaine, the first thing I thought of was Megan Marshack and the reporting of Nelson Rockefeller's death. Both stories produced this queasy feeling.

Oh, my God, I thought, *do we have the right to know everything?* Does a press pass grant the right to peek into bedrooms and the back seat of limousines, as the New York *Post* did on Thursday by splashing on page three a chauffeur's tale of Jordan's date with a buxom blonde?

On the other hand, snorting coke is against the law. So why feel queasy? First, the allegation against Jordan was played on page one. Anytime a public official's name appears on page one and he is said to be under investigation, say good-by to the presumption of innocence.

The story also didn't pass the sniffer test—it didn't smell right. The number-two man in the federal government, President Carter's surrogate son, wouldn't—couldn't—be so stupid. Could he? Besides, Studio 54's owners were desperately singing as part of a plea-bargaining scheme to escape December 1978 indictments for federal income-tax evasion.

As a friend of mine said, "Here are these guys who are, in effect, dealers —no matter what they do on the side, like run a disco—who don't believe there should be penalties for using drugs. Yet they're screaming to the government."

The more stories I read, the more doubts I had. At first Ian Schrager and Steve Rubell, co-owners of Studio 54, claimed Jordan committed his crime during an April 1978 visit to their gilded palace. Then they amended this to June 1978. First they alleged that Jordan was accompanied by White House press secretary Jody Powell. Then they retracted this, presumably on the theory, ya know, that all Southerners look alike.

They claimed there were two witnesses to Jordan's escapade, one a drug dealer, the other a publicist. Then the drug dealer denied to the FBI that he saw anything. And the publicist, owner Steve Rubell admits, "is a flake."

The story reeked of something else: Roy Cohn. Throughout his celebrated career, first as a young prosecutor, then as an aide to Senator Joseph McCarthy, later as a defendant in three criminal and numerous civil trials,

Cohn has been a master at leaking innuendo. And Cohn is Studio 54's attorney.

Cohn goes right for the throat. His legal theory has always been that a good offense is the best defense. Once, in the early seventies, Cohn was accused by a Florida judge of tricking a dying eighty-four-year-old client into changing his will to make Cohn a trustee and executor of his $75-million estate. Instead of retreating into a righteous defense of his ethics, Cohn immediately counterattacked, charging that the opposing lawyer snuck into Lewis Rosenstiel's hospital room, and while he "was in a coma put a pen in his hand and had him sign an X to a piece of paper, which divested him of substantial assets out of his estate."

Cohn did not defend his own ethics; instead he disparaged those of his opponent. When Vice-President Spiro Agnew was forced to resign for accepting bribes, Cohn wrote an open letter to Agnew: "How could one of this decade's shrewdest leaders make a dumb mistake such as you did in quitting and accepting a criminal conviction. Alger Hiss and Daniel Ellsberg can still argue their innocence. You no longer can."

It did not offend Cohn that the Vice-President was a thief. What troubled him was that Agnew admitted it. The same preoccupation with form, not content, surfaced in a book Cohn wrote about Senator McCarthy. "His staff was aware," he writes, "that McCarthy was not going over well, but at the time it was not our main concern—although hindsight tells me it should have been."

As for his own behavior during the Army-McCarthy hearings, Cohn only admits he appeared "arrogant" and "smart-alecky." That he trifled with people's reputations and lives by making reckless charges that they were "Communists" or "Communist dupes" merits no apology.

The problem with my theory that Cohn masterminded the Jordan leak is that Cohn denies it. "Absolutely not," he says when asked if he leaked the story. "I have been totally against this thing from the beginning. I heard the Jordan story way back. Frankly, it didn't hit me." He says he disagreed with the decision of Studio 54's criminal attorneys to bring the cocaine charge to the federal prosecutors: "One doesn't make Brownie points with an administration that is prosecuting you by supplying derogatory information about the number-two man in that administration."

Don't misunderstand. Cohn is not opposed, in principle, to innuendo. "There is still someone who is unidentified and was there with Jordan that night," he mischievously hints.

Nor does Cohn have anything against leaks, according to two journalists at different publications who have covered this saga. Early on, they claim, Cohn leaked like a sieve. "He was talking openly to reporters, peddling stuff —not for quotation, of course," says one reporter, not for quotation. The other says Cohn was "jubilant" on Saturday, August 25, the day the story broke.

One journalist who should know flatly declares that Cohn was the original source of the story, leaking it to *Times* columnist William Safire, an old friend. The *Times* reportedly held the story for four days for fear of being used, prompting an exasperated Cohn to phone a *Times* editor with more juicy information.

Cohn flatly denies both these assertions.

Knowing Cohn, I believe the journalists. Still, questions about Cohn do not eclipse those about the responsibility of the press. Do we employ a double standard when smugly reporting the use of drugs by public officials but not the use of drugs by the media? Does the press trifle too freely with public reputations, and thus livelihoods and the presumption of innocence, by jumping to report that someone is "under investigation"? What rights to privacy does a public figure enjoy?

"Some days I feel like I'm working for the *National Enquirer,*" confesses one sensitive reporter who is spending most of his time sleuthing rumors about Hamilton Jordan. "It's unpleasant reporting. I find myself talking to people about parties and drug use—essentially private matters."

Yet, this reporter knows he has no choice. For the press not to have printed the charges against such a prominent official, particularly when the Justice Department is, by law, obligated to investigate any such allegation of wrongdoing, would invite charges of a press cover-up. Plea-bargainers may sound like "canaries"—as Cohn once called them—but their testimony is admissible in court.

There are three additional reasons he has to continue digging into Hamilton Jordan's life, says the reporter. First, there is the question of "judgment." Were he under the influence of drugs, could a presidential aide be counted on to offer clear-headed advice?

Second, people sworn to uphold the law must be held to a high standard. If a White House aide snorted cocaine, he broke the law. And, finally, there is the question of truthfulness; Jordan flatly told the *Times* he has never used drugs of any kind.

If he can prove Jordan lied, the reporter knows he might topple the Carter presidency. There might even be a Pulitzer Prize in it for him. Yet, like a lot of us, he hopes this is one story he can't pin down. He, too, is queasy.

The Proper Etiquette to Seduce the Press

Esquire, December 1977

Like dogs, good politicians have instincts. When it comes to correct political manners—which may differ from good manners—the pros know how to behave. For ambitious male beginners, here are some useful tricks.

In Social Situations
- Outside Washington, D.C., you should not be seen alone with a woman.
- Inside Washington, you should not be seen alone with your wife.
- Don't carry luggage unless a photographer is nearby.
- If people are watching, jump in the *front* seat of the limousine.
- To greet people, quickly thrust your hand as far as possible into the hand you are shaking. People will think you have a firm handshake, even if your hand is limp. This will also protect fingers from being crushed.
- Everyone is a sucker for flattery. I once hated my job working with Democratic party officials, until Robert Kennedy draped an arm over my shoulder and whispered how important my work was.
- Everyone is a sucker (as Jimmy Carter reminded us) for personal notes, even if dictated by an aide and printed by an IBM machine.
- Know that every other politician is a competitor, but never show it. Address them with respect, defer to them when entering a room—but never when the camera blinks.
- Always point your finger at the chest of the person with whom you are being photographed. You will appear dynamic. Besides, then no photo editor can crop you from the picture.
- Do not have your picture taken with unpopular colleagues.
- If a camera is near, put down the glass.
- In pictures with other people, always smile—unless you are at a funeral or busy denouncing some evil that only *you* can end.

Political Piety
- Proclaim you are married to the greatest woman in the world. Former California Senator John Tunney did—right up until his divorce.
- Have lots of children and mention them often. They're like wives: you don't have to spend much time with them and they're great for brochures.

- Thanks to Carter, you're again obliged to mention your deep religious commitment.

Campaigning

- Always arrive at least a few minutes late. The crowd will then be assembled and relieved that you could make it. Apologize profusely. They will be flattered, and you will have something to talk about.
- Pause at the entrance before entering a crowded room. The audience will turn to notice you, and you will have a moment to case the joint and maybe remember a few names.
- When hiring a room for a function, choose one that's slightly too small. The gathering in your honor will appear larger.
- The same principle applies when predicting election results. Always understate how well you expect to do. Remember, Ed Muskie won the 1972 New Hampshire presidential primary but was considered to have lost because he said he expected a majority.
- Don't eat at political dinners. There are hands to shake and three or four more dinners to attend anyway, and people feel slighted if you eat and don't talk to them. Considering the food, it's no big sacrifice.
- If you can't remember a name, just substitute "friend," "buddy," "son," "honey."
- Don't be like other people and brood. If opponents or the press suspect you are bleeding, they will move in for the kill like vultures.
- Always publicly flatter the public's intelligence while basing your campaign on its stupidity. You'll never air an important thirty-second TV spot if you don't believe that. Remember Abe Beame: he ran for reelection as mayor of New York by proclaiming "He made the tough decisions."
- Always say, "I am taking my campaign to the people," even while investing 90 percent of your budget on advertising.
- Always say, "The only poll that counts is the one on election day," even while earmarking huge sums for polls.
- In a jam, seize the smallest piece of positive news and go on the offensive. Nixon did this with his Checkers speech. Carter did it with Bert Lance.
- If you lose, be gracious. An early concession speech will attract more media coverage.

The Press

- Politics is an arena where the important audience is the press, not the public. A solitary reporter or photographer, even if an absolute jerk, is worth more attention and reaches more people than any Rotary luncheon.
- The press will complain that you are conducting an issueless campaign unless you bombard them with position papers, which they will not read.

- Act warm and solicitous, but never trust a reporter. His job is to get a story. Sometimes that means getting you.
- Nothing is ever off the record.
- Journalists will tolerate fibs—inflating polls, exaggerating support—but lie blatantly, and they'll get you.
- If you don't like a story, say you were misquoted—unless the reporter used a tape recorder.
- Don't go over the reporter's head to complain to the editor. You will make an enemy of the reporter, and the editor, like a mother, will always defend his own.
- Remember that a campaign is a contest, not a forum. Unless you are a secure incumbent, use colorful language in denouncing opponents. You want to make page one; so does the reporter.
- Reporters, like you, just want to be loved. It's okay to complain, but do it gently. They'll feel they owe you one. Contrary to myth, reporters like a compliment, as long as it is not sappy.
- Most important, unless you're really unpopular—like New York's Mayor Lindsay or New Jersey's Governor Brendan Byrne—never, ever, accept blame for anything. Your job is to take credit, not blame. If you get in trouble, blame your predecessor. Or Communists. If that doesn't work, blame your staff. Abe Beame understood. When New York hovered on the brink of bankruptcy in the spring of 1975, his press secretary joked about preparing a press release in case the city defaulted. It was to have begun: "City Comptroller Harrison Goldin announced today that the city of New York was unable to pay its bills and . . ."
- Unless you have a fat book contract, you should enter prison protesting your innocence.

PART III

New York

El Cid's Final Campaign

New York *Daily News,* May 22, 1977

As Abe Beame bounced on his toes and parried gentle questions about his candidacy for reelection, First Deputy Mayor John Zuccotti glumly stood off to the side, behind the rows of Beame adherents who visited Gracie Mansion to politely clap. This was not so much celebration as ceremony, and the deputy mayor seemed sad.

He had reason to be. On June 24, just one day after reaching the age of forty, Zuccotti will depart city government to hide in Europe for the critical final two months of the campaign—leaving behind six years of city service, a dedicated staff, and a dream of running for mayor. He also leaves behind the eighteen months he has now graced the deputy mayor's chair. It was these eighteen months Beame emphasized in his three-page announcement speech, ignoring his first two dismal years.

Since Zuccotti announced he would return to the practice of law, his phone rings less often, there are fewer pieces of mail, fewer meetings, fewer requests from those seeking favor. So it was this day. As Abe Beame lingered in the warm sun and proclaimed, "I want to finish the job, and I'm the only one who can do it," John Zuccotti loitered in the shade and watched. What he witnessed was a funeral, one that buried, probably forever, the hope that most of the city's diverse forces—Beame and Carey, regulars and reformers, business and labor, bankers and neighborhood leaders—could unite behind a common candidate: John Zuccotti.

Also buried, as least temporarily, was another political corpse—the real Abe Beame, the cautious accountant, the meek survivor, the man who follows but does not lead. Instead we were told that the timid man we observed throughout 1974 and 1975 had really acted "decisively"—"I brought this city out of the problems it had." Beame took credit for having "weathered the storm" that has not yet passed. He again blamed John Lindsay for leaving him "a billion-and-a-half dollar deficit"—ignoring the incriminating evidence that as city comptroller, Beame approved Lindsay's last four budgets, even certifying, in a joint June 18, 1973, statement with Lindsay, that the worst of all Lindsay's budgets was "balanced."

None of this mattered today. To his supporters, Abe Beame is El Cid. Like the ninth-century Spanish warrior who, though dead, was propped up by his army to lead one last battle, Beame's army gathered on the expansive

Gracie Mansion lawn to spread tales of their El Cid. Howard Rubinstein, who is sufficiently skilled at the art of public relations to peddle dung as deodorant, claimed Beame's announcement statement meant "He's calling it as he sees it rather than rewriting history." Campaign manager Tim Hanan said of the man that polls suggest is a polarizing figure, "His appeal, if anything, is stability and noncontroversial themes. Others yell and are vitriolic."

Shortly after Hanan spoke, a man who does not yell and claimed to be Abe Beame spryly stepped before the microphones to read his statement of candidacy and flick aside questions whose answers he had obviously rehearsed. It was a skillful performance.

Those who had reason to be grateful smiled. Harry Van Arsdale and Peter Brennan, labor leaders who have more access to Beame than they deserve, looked pleased. As did Jack Bigel and the presidents of the Patrolmen's and the Sergeants' Benevolent Associations, labor leaders with some cushy benefits Mayor Beame dares not challenge.

Stationed beside them were other beneficiaries of the status quo—attorney Bunny Lindenbaum, William Shea, and Harold Fisher. Each has amassed fortunes and power from their political relationships. As have such Democratic county leaders as Brooklyn's Meade Esposito and the Bronx's Pat Cunningham, who also support Beame and chose not to attend only so Beame could claim, as he did, "I haven't seen any politicians around here."

Hovering on the fringes were the younger wolves, those who often work hard at playing politics the way others play the stock market. Sid Davidoff, who five years ago toiled for Lindsay and disparaged Beame, now wants back in and has invested his services. A week ago Jay Fisher served as campaign manager for Ed Costikyan, the candidate most specifically critical of Beame's don't-rock-the-boat approach to governance. With Costikyan out of the race, Fisher jumped aboard. As did Zuccotti's future law partner, Peter Tufo, who used to privately snicker at Beame but now, no doubt, hopes to serve as his ambassador to Elaine's.

Abe Beame wears down everyone, including those of us in the press. What we take to be humiliation his announcement speech dubs "perseverance"; what we remember as indecisiveness his speech claims is an unwillingness to move "precipitously." Most of us know there is no way to pierce Abe Beame's armor, to make him bleed, because inside he is dead.

That is why few of us flinched when Beame simply responded, "No," when asked whether he had just once thought of *not* running for reelection. Nothing wounded him. Not the adverse polls or newspaper editorials or friends who told him he owed it to the city and Zuccotti to step aside and retire at the age of seventy-one.

He hasn't retired because Beame really believes he is El Cid, really believes he has done more, as he said, to reform city management than any previous mayor. It doesn't matter that the state or the federal government or the new city charter or events were needed to prod an ever-reluctant

Beame. Nor does it matter, of course, that what's been accomplished pales in comparison with what remains to be done.

Abe Beame knows a secret shared only by other survivors: he is utterly without shame. That is why, at the ceremony's conclusion, Abe Beame and his courtiers walked back into Gracie Mansion, and John Zuccotti walked, alone, to his car. El Cid lives, at least for one last campaign.

Simple Simon:
The Dumbest City Pol

New York *Daily News,* June 17, 1979

The circus came to City Hall on Wednesday. It was a glorious day, the sun bright, the air crisp, a day for watching, not working. And our politicians, bless them, were out of their cages performing for the press.

Off in the Blue Room, Mayor Koch honored Justo Barreiro, the motorman who rescued Renee Katz. In the marble rotunda separating the mayor's west wing from the City Council's east wing, Councilman Henry Stern solemnly vowed for the 700th time to tame Westway; Manhattan Borough President Andrew Stein squinted and paraded his 998th call for a grand jury investigation, this time of the Transit Authority.

On the steps outside, Deputy Mayor Peter Solomon displayed polished electric-driven buses and cars. Mayoral press secretary Maureen Connelly morosely wandered about distributing a three-paragraph letter announcing the death of civil-service reform. In just two hours reporter Mike Eisgrau caught six acts for WNEW Radio.

"Isn't this a circus?" joked publicist Howard Rubenstein, waiting for Stein to finish so he could hook reporters. Stanley Simon was about to announce his candidacy for Bronx borough president. "Step into our tent," Rubenstein beckoned.

Several of us did. While we wondered if this was the second time this year Simon had announced his candidacy, the candidate was consulting his media guru: "Howard, Howard. How do I start?" he whispered.

"You just say," tutored Rubenstein, an experienced hand, "I'm here to announce my candidacy for a full term . . .' "

"I'm here to announce my candidacy for borough president of the Bronx," began the stolid Simon, clutching with both hands a rolled-up map of the Bronx. Flanked by his wife, two daughters, campaign managers Congressman Mario Biaggi and Councilwoman Aileen Ryan, Simon was clearly less nervous about his three opponents in the Democratic primary than he was about his appearance. It's no big deal for a Stanley Simon to speak before a local club or planning board. That's the minor leagues. But today, surrounded by City Hall reporters, it was the big time.

A gold Big Apple pin was carefully placed in the lapel of his glittering chocolate-brown suit, the jacket buttoned to cover a mid-life bulge. His dark hair was fastidiously starched and ironed.

Keeping his head down as he read a prepared statement, Simon occasion-ally flashed mechanical smiles and gestures that were out of sync with his words. When Simon finished, his tiny eyes raced toward Rubenstein, who nodded approval. A brief, drowsy silence followed, which was finally inter-rupted by Rubenstein, who barked, "Congressman, would you like to say something?" Biaggi said something about Simon—the man who served five years on the City Council, the man who brought unity to the Bronx, the man who . . .

Simon says: "Together in unity we can succeed . . . People today are sick and tired of party labels . . . I know there are problems in the Bronx. I know those problems. I share those problems." To his credit, Simon did not say, "I am the problem."

Everywhere Simon went, aides hovered and sometimes cringed. It is normal in politics for aides to contract ulcers worrying whether their candi-date will stumble, or say the wrong thing, or pick the wrong fight. But working for a candidate like Simon could induce heart attacks. Aides tremble not that he will say the wrong thing, but that he will have nothing to say.

Simon says, when asked about the South Bronx, "In the South Bronx we have been getting many empty promises. My plan would include the entire Bronx."

Simon says, when asked if he agrees with Koch that some municipal hospitals should be closed to reduce the city's deficit, "I don't know."

What does that mean?

Simon says, "That's my personal thought."

Simon says there is no inconsistency between his advertisement of "Dem-ocratic unity" and his support of Ted Kennedy for President. Simon says, "The people of the Bronx need the best unity."

"Can I interrupt one second for a photograph?" says Rubenstein, in-structing his horse to gallop across the street to City Hall Park with Biaggi and Ryan for a "photo opportunity." Trailing a few steps behind, Ruben-stein urges him to appear relaxed by smiling more, to appear forceful by jabbing at the air, to appear warm by clasping an arm around Biaggi.

Rubenstein, a good P.R. man with a roster of blue-chip commercial clients, doesn't need this account. He has counseled Mayor Beame and presidential candidate Jimmy Carter. He seems rather embarrassed to be waving his arms and racing across the grass while choreographing the movements of a local candidate, something he was doing fifteen years ago.

But this race is all about loyalty. Rubenstein is doing a favor for his friend Bronx County Democratic chairman Stanley Friedman. In turn, Friedman is doing a favor for his friend Stanley Simon. When Friedman ran for county leader in May 1978, Simon, then a councilman, withdrew from the contest, throwing his support to Friedman. The new county leader, in January 1979, needed a borough president to fill the remainder of Robert Abrams' term. His long search somehow led him and the council to Stanley Simon. Simon met the twin requirements: He was loyal. And he was Jewish.

Six months later Simon boasts of some accomplishments. He has, he says, brought "unity" to the Bronx. And money to construct a precinct house in Pelham, to modernize twenty schools, to build several ramps for the handicapped, to plant trees. To spur economic development, Simon says, "I appointed the best brains I could think of to a committee."

Those are not Simon's only accomplishments. Were it not for him, Andrew Stein could lay claim to being the dumbest member of the Board of Estimate. Among colleagues, Simon wins that contest hands down. But there is still some debate. "I can't believe he's that stupid," declares an aide to Council President Carol Bellamy, who watched him loll silently through the recent budget deliberations. "No one could be."

"He ain't so dumb," counters an aide to a borough president. "He's a nice man." The middle position is expressed by an elected official: "He's a nice dummy."

These are cruel things to say. They overlook Stanley Simon's other parts. His word is more reliable than Comptroller Goldin's. Unlike Stein, Goldin and Bellamy, he pants for no higher office. He is less uptight with colleagues than Bellamy and doesn't growl and carry a chip on his shoulder like Brooklyn Borough President Howard Golden. He is probably a devoted father—at least, one notices him embracing the hand of his nervous daughter.

Brains have never been a requirement for public office, certainly not for membership on the Board of Estimate. The Bronx declined under two brainier borough presidents—Herman Badillo and Robert Abrams.

Stanley Simon is no different from many who rise from the clubhouse to district leader, to councilman, to the borough presidency. He is a survivor. Staunch, dependable, loyal. As such, he matches Ambrose Bierce's definition of perseverance: "A lowly virtue whereby mediocrity achieves an inglorious success." Voters could do worse. It's hard to believe they can't do better.

SECOND THOUGHTS

Abe Beame and Stanley Simon had a right to want to punch me in the nose. What I wrote was, I think, accurate; but also cruel. It had a sharp point of view (which editors generally like), but it was also snide. I considered the idea of Beame's or Simon's candidacy ridiculous, and treated it as such. The killer in me has no regrets, even savors a few of the lines. Another part of me agrees with Mrs. Meyer H. Bagun, who wrote: "What makes *you* so smart? . . . You don't have to like Stanley Simon. You don't even have to vote for him. But you can be a 'person' if you are informed and if you practice a little humility by voicing your opinion without being so insulting."

Falling Out of Love
with Mario

New York *Daily News,* September 18, 1977

For me, the real conflict in this campaign is not between Mario Cuomo and Ed Koch, but between the memory of Mario Cuomo the man and the reality of his candidacy for mayor. The contest has been about many things. For me, it has been about falling out of love.

I first fell in love with Mario in the early seventies. Here was a role model for Italo-Americans. Mario understood neighborhoods as well as ideas. He was witty, sensitive, decent—Adlai Stevenson with a vowel at the end of his name. And he was tough.

But no one knew him. I remember two editorial lunches with Mario in late 1976 and early this spring. The assembled journalists were skeptical, and a little tense. *My God, would he eat with his hands?*

After mocking the embossed silverware and pretension in the room, including my own, he took us on a journey through the canyons of government and his subtle mind. He had a distance on everything, including himself. What a journalist he would make! Journalists are schooled to see two sides of everything. Mario saw five.

My colleagues fell in love, too. "He's terrific," they exclaimed as soon as he left. "That's the kind of person we need in politics." I was very pleased.

At the beginning of this campaign I thought the people of New York would also fall in love with Mario. But a campaign tests a public man. We learn whether the candidate knows how to delegate authority, whether he surrounds himself with substantive people and listens to them, whether he is disciplined, decisive, calm under pressure, whether he understands management and has done his homework. Each are qualities demanded of a good mayor.

By this test, Mario has failed. He has not proved a good delegator of authority. Cuomo may charge that Ed Koch is a "puppet" of adviser David Garth, but at least Koch delegated responsibility. Just as a mayor cannot run a city alone, so a candidate for major office cannot be his own campaign manager. Mario never understood this. His campaign is run by a committee, with decisions backing up to steal precious candidate time. Most routine scheduling choices are made by Mario, not his staff. He must have twelve press secretaries.

Nor, with some exceptions, has Cuomo built a first-rate campaign team.

He has run a confused, ad hoc campaign. Before the PBA convention last weekend, he spoke off the cuff, without prepared notes. He admits some members of his staff are weak, but says he did not want to hurt them by making a change. By comparison, Koch relied on Garth and Maureen Connelly, the talented research director responsible for much of the campaign's specificity, and on campaign co-chairman Edward Costikyan, who will become first deputy mayor if Koch wins.

Mario has also failed to demonstrate great self-discipline. Unlike Koch, he is usually late. He missed Monday night's WPIX-TV debate because he lingered too long at an *Amsterdam News* interview. Not only did he agonize over whether to run, but he has agonized, aloud, over whether his TV commercials were right, good, demeaning.

Mario seems different. Sure, there are still flashes of humor, intelligence, decency. But he often seems ill at ease. When he talks, his eyes stare at the floor, like Hugh Carey's. He seems to have lost that distance on himself, that sense of comedy. His new TV ads snarl. At Wednesday evening's Channel 13 debate, he sat facing a calm Ed Koch. The cameras rolled and Mario snapped and played cute lawyer tricks. Neither distinguished himself, but Cuomo persisted in ignoring questions so that he could pummel Koch for favoring capital punishment. It was almost as if Mario were running not to win the runoff but to win an excuse for losing. Perhaps to prove his moral superiority.

In that, he may have succeeded, though not by much. Koch told a roomful of journalists on Monday that his campaign had not issued a piece of literature that left out jobs or the economy as the most important issue. Yet his "Voter's Scorecard" literature made no mention of either. Instead, it cited five issues—his support of the death penalty, stiffer sentences for those assaulting senior citizens, a residency law for city employees, a call-up of the National Guard during the recent blackout, and his opposition to strikes by cops and firemen. Koch panders on capital punishment; Cuomo panders with TV ads accusing Koch of being another John Lindsay.

In this past week Cuomo has virtuously refused to cut deals in order to woo endorsements. That is probably not true of Ed Koch, nor of Dave Garth. The tempestuous media magician is easily the most brilliant political strategist in the race. But like his candidate, he sometimes believes in killing. Garth wages campaigns as if they were wars, not contests.

But where Mario has not succeeded is in living up to his own May 10 declaration of candidacy. "The people of this city have a right to know, in the most precise detail," he said then, "what their candidates intend to do." Yet detail has been absent from Mario's campaign. In contrast to Koch, his TV ads feature platitudes set to music; his positions tend to be vague. Ask Mario about excessive fringe benefits—the $4,640 fringes' cost per city employee, the twenty "sick days" granted City University professors, the up to twenty-eight "chart days" off given police sergeants, the five weeks' paid vacation starting sanitationmen get, the two days off given cops and the one day given firemen who donate blood—and he vaguely says this is a subject for "negotiation." Ask about rent control, decentralization, or Westway, and he promises studies. Ask Ed Koch about future layoffs, and he says they are unavoidable. Ask Mario, and he says they are "undesirable."

After hiding in Europe all summer, former Deputy Mayor John Zuccotti missed most of the campaign. But since returning, he's tried to observe the candidates. The other day he debriefed a reporter, and when finished, puzzled out loud, "Did Mario take time to learn the issues?"

The answer is no. And the problem is that there is little time to learn. By January 1 Mayor Beame must submit a financial plan to the state's Emergency Financial Control Board and the Federal Treasury. Presumably, the new mayor will wish input. By April 15 the new mayor's budget must be submitted. Next year's city deficit, a ranking city official said the other day, would be $300 to $600 million. MAC chairman Felix Rohatyn says it will be $400 million, not counting the cost of labor contracts which expire this spring. Control Board executive director Steve Berger pegs the deficit over the next three years at $1.5 billion.

Only drastic surgery—not Band-Aids—will keep the patient alive, or convince Washington this city is worthy of being saved. The key question then becomes: Which Democratic candidate better understands the radical budget and management changes needed?

Koch wins that contest. Throughout the campaign his emphasis has been on the word "leadership"; Mario's has been on the word "conciliation." Obviously, a mayor has to be a leader and a conciliator, as well as a manager. But considering the task ahead, leadership is the key.

"What the city needs is a mayor who is a leader," says Deputy Mayor Don Kummerfeld, who is neutral. "A mayor who can go before the people, state the issues clearly and succinctly, and then persuade them to accept solutions that may not be popular or easy to accept. Koch has, I think, been trying to focus on that. Whether he will do it, I don't know. . . . Mario is right, you can't negotiate all details in public. On the other hand, in order to build public and press support, you have to make the outlines clear. The big important demands should be made public."

Last Saturday, before a foot-stomping, cheering PBA convention, Mario did not make his big demands public. Without explaining how, he said "politicians" were to blame for police frustrations. He promised "I will be a tough negotiator" but—instead of lowering their expectations by telling them one or two things he would be "tough" about—he soothed them with "you are still the best in the whole country." Mario's emphasis was on conciliation.

By contrast, just moments before, Republican mayoral candidate Roy Goodman's emphasis was on leadership. "I feel it's my duty to level with you," he said. "Shut up, you creep!" shouted some cops. Goodman kept talking: "I'm not here looking for your endorsement. But if New York City is going to avoid bankruptcy, we'll all have to tighten our belts, and that includes the police." As Ed Koch has done throughout the campaign, Goodman then ticked off some specific belt-tighteners.

Mario shuddered and thought Goodman was seeking confrontation. But how do you build public support or shrink appetites without plainly telling the truth? Several weeks ago Mario told me that, when mayor, he would convince the public and municipal unions of the need for change by using a blackboard. He would simply lay out the facts, showing just how tight the budget was. "I think reasonable people can settle on issues," he said.

That may be naïve. One man's fact becomes another's opinion. Mayor Beame's Temporary Commission on City Finances reported that city employees rank first in the nation in total compensation. The unions claim they rank sixteenth. Lyndon Johnson thought he only had to place his hand on Ho's knee and the Vietnam war would cease.

Unlike Forest Hills or Co-op City, where Mario served as mediator, many city issues no longer have a middle ground because there is no money to pay for it. Mario concludes his sensitive book *Forest Hills Diary* by extolling this middle ground: ". . . the only safe route past Scylla and Charybdis is somewhere between them." But the next mayor can no longer act like a third party to negotiations.

Mario Cuomo and Ed Koch are both good, often courageous, men. Like the rest of us, they have flaws. Neither has extensive management experience. Repeatedly, both have forfeited their dignity in debates, pouting like children. With Koch, there is worry that he will conciliate too little; with Cuomo, that he will conciliate too much. But with Cuomo, there is an additional worry that his latent personal virtues—sensitivity, reflection, solitude, personal honor—will become his public vices.

It's a mean job being mayor. It's very difficult to succeed as mayor and succeed as a human being. That's what Mario means when he says, "Maybe I'm miscast." Forgetting last week's performance, Mario, like Plantagenet Palliser, cares more about success as a human being. And like the failed Prime Minister in Trollope's novel, you worry that he would be immobilized by:

> . . . the feeling that so many people blame him for so many things, and the doubt in his own mind whether he may not deserve it. And then he becomes fretful, and conscious that such fretfulness is beneath him and injurious to his honour. He condemns men in his mind, and condemns himself for condescending to condemn them. He spends one quarter of an hour in thinking that as he is Prime Minister he will be Prime Minister down to his fingers' ends, and the next in resolving that he never ought to have been Prime Minister at all.

Learning to Govern

New York *Daily News,* December 4, 1977

Jewelle Bickford burst through the door, nearly colliding with David Brown. The scene of their near-accident was Ed Koch's transition offices in the basement of 345 Park Avenue. Jewelle is the youthful coordinator of Mayor-elect Koch's Study Group on Community Planning Boards. David is the deputy mayor-designate for planning.

"David," she exclaimed, braking suddenly. "We're inside talking about your responsibilities. Could you tell us what they are? We're working in a vacuum. In forty-eight hours we have to decide what to recommend to Ed."

In one sense, Jewelle Bickford was not operating in a vacuum. The office was full of young aides scampering about, shaking their heads, hollering instructions, squinting and sporting that burdened look that goes with youth and unaccustomed power.

Our new centurions are much like the old. To visit Ed Koch's headquarters is not unlike entering a time capsule, returning to 1965 and the bright, eager young Lindsay team. Koch's people smile more, and seem less brash and arrogant. But one thing is unchanged: a handful of aides with little city government experience is directing the transition to power.

The Koch transition is elaborately organized. Twelve "independent panels" have been appointed, says the November 17 press release, "to search for highly qualified people to fill key administrative posts" in the new administration. The panels feature an impressive array of names.

In addition, three task forces—budget, finance, and community development—have been formed and are working with Beame administration officials in these critical areas. Finally, fifteen study groups—like Jewelle Bickford's—are functioning. Their purpose, according to staff aide Jim Capalino, twenty-seven, is "to get a little head start so when the commissioner comes in, he can go in running."

It sounds pretty good. Take a closer look and you find more motion than movement. The search panels don't seem to have received clear direction. Aside from one over-all meeting with all of the search panels, Koch has only spoken on the phone with several of the chairmen. The panels work mostly through Capalino, who is very competent, and very inexperienced. Working by his side is Victor Botnick, twenty-five.

A chairperson and members of five different panels concede they have received no definition of Koch's criteria to select a commissioner, aside from a vague one- or two-page memo. Former Deputy Mayor John Zuccotti was asked to lead the search in intergovernmental relations—though Koch had independently decided to choose his longtime and capable aide Ronay Menschel. Arthur Liman, a prominent attorney, was originally drafted to search for a corporation counsel—though Koch had already determined to cede this post to former law partner Allen Schwartz.

The three task forces have been meeting independently. Tomorrow the budget group, which is under the expert care of First Deputy City Comptroller Martin Ives, will present to Koch their analysis of the looming budget gap.

The fifteen study groups operate under less expert care. Their official coordinator is former City Administrator Maxwell Lehman, a professorial gentleman who drew disdainful snickers even before his mentor, Ed Costikyan, fell from grace. The actual coordinator is Capalino. He says most of the fifteen coordinators worked in the Koch campaign and their task is to talk to experts and help Koch focus on critical questions. Beginning this week, these coordinators—not the experts—will accompany Koch when he meets with current city agency chiefs.

It's all very democratic. Judith Friedlander, twenty-eight, co-chairs the transportation study group. She is a warm, outgoing person, on assignment to the campaign from media adviser David Garth. Does she have a background in transportation? "Not in particular," she admits.

Judith is not alone. The fire study group is coordinated by Lorraine Koziatek, twenty-four, who worked with community newspapers in the campaign; consumer affairs is guided by Larry Weinberg, in his mid-twenties, who worked in the scheduling office; human resources is supervised by Dianna Chapin, thirty-five, the Queens campaign coordinator; economic development is staffed by the scholarly Lehman and Fritz Favorule, a young former P.R. man for the Association for a Better New York, who also worked in the campaign. These and several other inexperienced coordinators may perform brilliantly.

Then again, they may not. Some of Koch's advisers are worried. "The transition committee is a joke," says one well-known adviser. "Most of the kids there are kids. There is no mature leadership around. There has been too much suspicion. There has been some drawing of the wagons around to keep people out. You've got some people on task forces whom I wouldn't let in the building. On the other hand, Ed hasn't had a team until this past week."

The embryonic Koch governmental team—four deputy mayors and three aides—does not tell us whether Koch will effectively utilize the month remaining before he takes office. Nor does Koch tell us much when he says his transition is moving faster than that of most previous mayors. Circumstances are very different in the city—that is to say, worse.

The federal government is demanding a three-year fiscal plan in three weeks. On the recommendation of the new mayor, the state legislature must decide what oversight mechanism will replace the Emergency Financial Control Board. The budget gap must be gauged. There are critical labor negotiations, decisions on tax cuts, new lobbying stratagems for Washington and Albany, and critical appointments to make. "Everybody has to be allowed to make some mistakes," says a former deputy mayor. "Koch's problem is that he has less room for mistakes than previous mayors."

For the city's sake, Ed Koch better get off to a flying start. "The fiscal crisis has shaken a lot of us up," municipal labor leader Victor Gotbaum told a City Club conference this week. In this sense, the fiscal crisis is an opportunity. Koch can transform the way this city is managed—cleaning house, introducing performance standards for managers and workers alike, pushing for civil-service reforms, experimenting with competition, or gain-sharing and worker cooperatives to improve services.

There are reasons to feel good about our new mayor. He has a clear grasp of the radical changes required. By daring to appoint the aggressive Herman Badillo as deputy mayor for operations, Koch revealed, in the words of one adviser, he was "emotionally secure." The appointment of the experienced Basil Paterson as deputy mayor for labor relations calmed nervous union leaders. With Koch's concurrence, Badillo wisely asked Lee Oberst to remain as director of operations; Paterson induced Anthony Russo to stay as director of labor relations.

Koch has also moved to shore up his inexperienced transition team. Deputy Mayor-designate Brown admits zero experience with city neighborhoods and lacks Costikyan's brilliance, but he is an expert on Ed Koch. For five years he ran his congressional office. Costikyan worried about policing problems; Brown will know how to police Koch. Brown is destined to become the chief of staff of the staff. This week Koch placed him in charge of the transition effort.

And though Koch does not bring charisma, he does bring enthusiasm to his task. "My special expertise is being able to get people to work together and carry out my policy," he says. Koch promises to be a "hands-on" mayor, as his easy accessibility suggests.

The problem is that Koch only has two hands, which he sometimes forgets. "We don't have a first deputy mayor who does everything," he announced the other day, flanked by his four "co-equal" deputies. "We'll have a mayor who does everything."

Those are the words, I fear, of a man whose enthusiasm for the job exceeds his knowledge of it. In the campaign Koch not only promised to appoint Costikyan, he also promised to expand "the management responsibilities" of the first deputy. Why did he change his mind? Because, one of his seven new appointees explained, "Ed never thought about the first deputy's job until he saw the drafts of organizational charts with all the lines leading to the first deputy mayor. Then he began to feel like the Queen of England, a ceremonial leader." It's incredible that Koch never thought of this before.

Perhaps Costikyan lacked the humility to make Koch feel that Eddie was working for Ed. But his absence from the new administration makes one wonder who will be the thinker, the strategist, in the Koch administration. Brown is supposed to be, but he is an unknown quantity. Badillo could be, but operations leave him little time to reflect. Koch will need a strategist, since that's not his strength. "Ed works off an oral tradition," claims an old friend. "He learns from conversation, not reading."

Koch's egalitarian habits leave little time to think, much less read. "Everything, every staff person, goes to Ed," admits a worried key adviser. Koch has even proposed to hold a "lottery" to determine which deputy mayor will sit in the office next door to the mayor. If Brown is going to serve as the all-important sheriff of Koch's staff and the mayor's valuable time, it makes sense he should have that office. That's what Koch really wants, suggests a principal adviser. But, then, all deputy mayors are "equal," even if they don't require equal access.

"A lot of the mayor's time goes into being a leader," says a Koch strategist. "Ed has never done that before. That's why he needs a chief of staff. The most precious thing Koch has is his time."

Right now, the only time Koch has is one month before becoming mayor. He's yet to husband that time well. Which could lead us all to an accident.

To Be Heard, Commit Suicide

New York *Daily News,* April 29, 1979

You wouldn't want Herbert Bauch's job. The sixty-six-year-old secretary-treasurer of the New York City Civil Service Retired Employes Association can't get city or state officials on the phone and can't escape calls from widows pleading for increases in their $100-a-month city pensions.

Bauch represents 11,000 such widows whose husbands retired before pensions skyrocketed. Few are eligible for Social Security payments. None received cost-of-living adjustments. Many threaten suicide. "No one cares," he complains.

In total, Bauch represents 98,000 retired city employees or their widows. Of these, 18,000 struggle to survive on less than $3,000 a year. It's easy to overlook these victims. Those of us weaned on memories of sweatshops, of Upton Sinclair and *The Grapes of Wrath*, find it more difficult to square memories of yesterday's downtrodden workers with today's reality of organized labor's power. Pistol-toting prison guards on strike hardly qualify as candidates for sympathy. Many union leaders have a lot more power than most of the legislators their stuffed union treasuries help elect.

But some gods have not failed. There are 11,000 widows of cops and firemen who were hired prior to 1940 and of "street cleaners" hired prior to 1929. Living only on city pensions of about $1,300 annually, widows of cops and firemen receive but $106.66 a month and widows of street cleaners $98.66.

Another 7,000 city employes who retired prior to 1957—when New York joined the Social Security system—survive on annual pensions of about $3,000. That, too, is below the federal poverty standard.

Others, like Ethel Mirin of Forest Hills, Queens, retired before city pensions became as lucrative as they are today. After teaching thirty-three years in city schools, she exited in 1965. Over the last fourteen years Ethel Mirin has watched transit workers and sanitationmen win the right to retire after twenty years at half pay; watched state employees win three supplemental pension benefits; watched last month as the state legislature gifted itself and judges and commissioners 40-percent raises.

Yet Ethel Mirin struggles with a pension less than that provided a welfare family. "At this point," she nearly cries, "sixty percent of my city pension goes to pay the landlord each month."

These are not typical cases. The bulk of city retirees do relatively well. Those retiring after 1957 receive Social Security payments of about $500 a month, which are tax-free and adjusted as the cost of living climbs. Social Security is paid on top of their city pensions. Career employees retiring after 1968 gained the right to retire at half their final year's salary. Before 1968 employees retired on the average salary of their final five years.

Counting the final year's overtime payments, most career employees who left after 1968, claims Jonathan Schwartz, chief actuary for the New York City Retirement Systems, retire at about 70 percent of pay. Yet those retiring prior to 1968 receive only about one-third their final year's pay, which was then meager.

"No city retiree who gets Social Security in addition to their pension is hurting," claims Schwartz. The average city retiree, he calculates, receives a pension of $7,800 and Social Security payments of about $5,000, or a total of $12,800. Since they pay no taxes on the Social Security and no state or city taxes on their pension, that's not bad. Counting the tax forgiveness, many earn more in retirement than they did working.

But averages are misleading. They exclude inflation. Unlike federal employees, city retirees get no cost-of-living escalator clause. If double-digit inflation continues, today's lush benefits could be wiped out. And averages don't distinguish the pensioner receiving $25,000 from the widow receiving $1,300.

The widows get overlooked. They become, in Michael Harrington's still apt phase, our "invisible poor." There are few votes in helping them. Occasionally, as happened in 1978 when the plight of 400 widows of police and firemen killed in the line of duty seized public attention, the governor and mayor and state legislature will act. Displaying a compassion that is most evident in election years, the governor and legislature then agreed to virtually double their pensions.

Because 18,000 other widows and poor pensioners lacked similar clout, they were ignored. "It was a big political deal," charges Herbert Bauch. "We were the only ones against it. To me a widow is a widow." Bauch favored an increase for all widows.

He could as well have been screaming to himself in an empty room. Among politicians, these retirees mean few votes. "Everybody says, 'They'll die off,' says former city Labor Relations director Anthony Russo.

What of the unions who represented them when they worked for the city? "It's a good question," answers Bauch. Established union leaders act like politicians, suggests Russo: "They sell them out. Retirees don't pay dues or vote in union elections."

It comes down to power. Widows don't have it; striking OTB clerks do. Flexing their power to shutter OTB's 160 offices, and thus potentially deprive the city of $60 million in OTB revenues, the 1,300 clerks demanded —and won—a new contract exceeding those granted other city employees. They got the same 8-percent two-year raise, the same $1,500 cost-of-living adjustment. But they also got their titles reclassified from *cashier* to *betting clerk*. The new title brought a $2,000 hike in base pay, pushing their total two-year raise near 40 percent.

OTB officials and City Hall rushed to defend the raise. A new title justified a fat bonus, they argued. Using that logic, sanitationmen could demand to be reclassified as *hygenic workers* and merit $2,000 raises.

When the United Federation of Teachers and Board of Education agreed to reclassify paraprofessionals as full-time employees, City Hall—rightly, I think—rejected their contract. The agreement, City Hall said, exceeded that granted other workers.

Why give to OTB clerks what you would not give to teachers' aides? Power. Or as city Labor Relations director Bruce McIver candidly concedes, "You wouldn't go on strike if you were a paraprofessional because you couldn't harm us as much as the OTB clerks."

City government is no stranger to double standards. There is no money for widows; yet Ed Koch's 1980 budget proposes to swell the mayor's staff by twenty-seven people, the city comptroller's by fifty-seven, the borough presidents' by thirty, the district attorneys' by seventy-five. There is no money for 18,000 poor pensioners; but there is to pay a tax-free disability pension to 55 percent of all police officials retiring since 1970 with the rank of captain or above.

Admittedly, a single standard is easier claimed than applied. City Hall cannot afford to right all wrongs. To boost the pensions of 11,000 widows by, say, $1,000 a year would cost $11 million. How does City Hall address the needs of widows without unleashing me-too demands from all workers?

That's one of the problems with bigness. A sense of responsibility breaks down. Constituents, be they city executives, workers, or taxpayers, assume there is money. With a $13-billion budget, what's a few more dollars? *Gimme gimme.*

Over the years, City Hall surrendered to the loudest and most powerful complainants. Herbert Bauch's Retired Employes Association was not among them. But Bauch is learning. He plans a Madison Square Garden rally on May 9 and a picket line to circle City Hall on May 15. Maybe those he represents will not have to commit suicide to be heard.

A Tale of Two Cities

New York *Daily News,* January 21, 1979

"It was the best of times, it was the worst of times, it was the age of wisdom, it was the age of foolishness, it was the epoch of belief, it was the epoch of incredulity, it was the season of Light, it was the season of Darkness, it was the spring of hope, it was the winter of despair, we had everything before us, we had nothing before us . . ."

—Charles Dickens, *A Tale of Two Cities*

For Eli Ginzberg, A. Barton Hepburn Professor of Economics at Columbia University, it is "the spring of hope." New York City, he told the fortieth-anniversary conference of the City Planning Commission in a keynote address on Thursday, is experiencing "a turn of the wheel." Its economy is rebounding, middle-income families are retracing their steps back to the city, foreign investment is flourishing—soon "it should be clear that New York City will be number one both in the United States and in the world."

Eli Ginzberg's city radiated from the cover of a recent *New York Times Sunday Magazine.* Echoing Mayor Koch and the Association for a Better New York, the magazine flaunted New York's "renaissance." The January 15 issue of *Newsweek* devoted several pages to what they implied was the "revival" of older cities. The December cover story in *Harper's* swaggered that the urban crisis was over.

Professor Ginzberg and the others behold one city: a bustling downtown city sparkling with new towers and stores, brimming with hotels, plays, concerts, nightlife, wealth. That city "of Light" is Manhattan, or at least that part of Manhattan south of Ninety-sixth Street.

For Al Sinrod, however, this is "the winter of despair." He lives in another city, Coney Island, on Brooklyn's southern border. As a boy, I shopped for shirts and pants at Al Sinrod's clothing store near West Twenty-fifth Street and Mermaid Avenue. Today that store has vanished; Sinrod the haberdasher is now Sinrod the tailor, on West Twenty-fourth Street.

The entire front of his store is covered with red paint, including the solid planks of wood that blanket the two windows and door. A solid wall, except for a tiny wire-mesh window peephole. The sturdy door is locked. After two knocks, a familiar face peers to inspect the visitor, before unlocking his fortress.

At first, Sinrod's voice is faint, like Dickens' shoemaker—"the faintness of solitude and disuse." He brightens at the recognition of a former customer, inviting me into a windowless dungeon. The only clues that it is a tailor shop are two irons, an ironing board, and a small sewing machine. There are no racks for clothing, no customer tickets. Across the rear of the room juts the big sign that used to hang over Al Sinrod's clothing store.

"In the blackout of 1977 the store was destroyed," explains Sinrod, now sixty-three and sporting a goatee. For Sinrod, it was the last of many fires. He sold the property. The new tenants rebuilt and opened a store. Four months later it was torched, a final time.

"I'm retired," says Sinrod softly. "This store is sort of to keep busy. I do tailoring—alterations, cuffs, that sort of thing. And I watch my five buildings. If people know you're not an absentee landlord, they don't look to hurt you." Sinrod struggles to remain an optimist. "Four of my five stores are rented," he says. "You know what I'd like you to do, Kenny—I'd like you to be a little up about Coney Island. All the rentable stores on Mermaid Avenue are rented."

The problem is the unrentable stores—ones that are charred skeletons, steel-shuttered, or vacant lots. Mermaid Avenue, from Stillwell Avenue to Thirty-seventh Street, used to be a boulevard of shops, the commercial hub of Coney Island. Today, close to 90 percent are gone. Empty rubble-strewn lots multiply, sprouting weeds as tall as wheat fields.

A block from Sinrod, between West Twenty-fourth and Twenty-fifth streets, there were once twenty-four stores, the top floors housing families. Today two stores and no apartments remain. Across from Sinrod, nine of the eleven stores are gone. A young boy carting cardboard boxes strolls across the street toward the former Tel Star Cleaners, on the corner of Twenty-third Street, and tosses the boxes through the open window. This is his dump. Next door, where a dirty seat cushion is propped against a bare brick wall surrounded by beer cans and whiskey bottles, is home to a collection of derelicts.

Neptune and Surf Avenues, which border Coney Island on the north and south, have also lost much of their commerce and multiple dwellings— replaced by $750-million worth of public housing, cinder blocks instead of stoops and porches. Three of five banks fled, the four movie theaters closed, the luncheonettes and bakeries and Pete's Fish Market and Weepy's pool hall and Panarella's Italian grocery store—all memories.

"So many people go to Italy to see the ruins of Pompeii," says Mike Russo, who with his three brothers owns Garguilo's on West Fifteenth Street, one of New York's best Italian restaurants. "All they need is money for a subway ride to Coney Island and they can see the same thing they see in Pompeii."

For years Coney Island's population, like the rest of New York's, has been shrinking. Unlike mid-Manhattan, however, it was left with too many poor people and too few middle- and upper-income people to support them. Professor Ginzberg sees hope. "The city's population decline," he told the Planning Commission Conference, "makes it somewhat easier for people and jobs to balance out."

Al Sinrod, who lacks a Ph.D. in economics, sees it differently. "A business depends on customers," he says with a sigh. "But in the process of urban renewal, the city tore down the houses behind the stores in Coney Island. They took away our customers. Business died." The owner of a gas station on West Seventeenth Street, who asked not to be quoted, says he now employs four fewer mechanics and does one-third the business he did ten years ago. A private economy was replaced by a public one; private homeowners by a city government that now owns most of the land and cannot provide heat.

"Everybody pays premium prices to live by the water," intoned Eli Ginzberg, presumably speaking of the city of Manhattan, where he admits to having "lived my entire life within forty square blocks." Yet Coney Island, whose water cascades on once-white sandy beaches, "can't sell its land at auctions," declares Planning Commission Chairman Robert Wagner, Jr.

The growth of service jobs cheers Eli Ginzberg. The mismatch between these white-collar jobs and the dominant blue-collar population of Brooklyn and the Bronx drives others to despair. Ginzberg toots the "large inflow of capital and competence from abroad." Yet neither boats nor capital have yet visited Coney Island. Ginzberg sees the return of white middle-class families; others see poor people without the means to move up into the middle class.

Dr. John Keith, president of the Regional Plan Association, prodded the conference, urging "comprehensive planning" and government intervention. Yet Coney Island still bleeds from the abstract arrogance of planners and intrusive government. "The fact that Coney Island became a slum," says Wagner, who seems to have more humility than is fashionable within his profession, "is even more depressing than what happened to the South Bronx, because we spent money on Coney Island."

And we planned. In July 1958 Housing Chairman Robert Moses promised to rebuild it as a residential rather than amusement capital. The bulldozers came. Fourteen years later the Board of Estimate had another vision: Coney Island would be rezoned to prevent residential development and be revived as an amusement and recreational center.

Every couple of years a since-forgotten city official journeyed to promise some neighborhood improvement. It must be twenty years since the city pledged to construct a promenade along the waterfront in Kaiser Park. Today a large green sign squats outside the park—"Coming Rehabilitation Bulkhead and Promenade." Over the name of Abraham D. Beame is stripped and pasted the name Edward I. Koch. Parks Commissioner Gordon J. Davis is substituted for Joseph Davidson.

If you lived in Coney Island, as my family still does, you'd be depressed. Eli Ginzberg might be depressed. But Al Sinrod, who looks depressed, claims he hasn't abandoned hope. "Throw in a little bit about casino gambling," he says, waxing enthusiastically about how city-owned land in Coney Island could be sold "for knockdown prices" to hotels and casino operators. So Sinrod hangs on and waits, like residents of Far Rockaway, the Catskills, and Niagara Falls.

Logic suggests they will be disappointed. But neighborhoods—cities—cling to life with a grit and hope that can defy literal logic. New York's other cities—Coney Island, Bushwick, South Jamaica, to name a few—would be wise to ignore Professor Ginzberg, as his narrow vision ignores them. Professors are supposed to think with their heads. Hopefully, people like Al Sinrod will continue to think with their hearts.

If New York Went Bankrupt?

New York *Daily News,* February 25, 1979

The New York State Urban Development Corporation careened toward default in February 1975. Eager to learn his options, Governor Hugh Carey nastily invited Lewis Kruger, a bankruptcy expert, to Albany. Suppose the UDC filed for bankruptcy? the governor asked. One hour later Kruger was still talking, still explaining the labyrinthine federal bankruptcy law. Horrified, Carey decided bankruptcy was not a viable option for the UDC or, later, for the city of New York.

Now, four years later, the option again surfaces. Since Kruger's conversation with Carey, the Congress has twice amended Chapter IX of the federal bankruptcy law. And as a December 20, 1978, memorandum to President Carter from three of his top domestic advisers warned, with New York City's expanding budget deficit, "serious discussion of the bankruptcy option is possible."

Such a discussion occurred over scrambled eggs and bacon at the Waldorf this past Thursday. Sponsored by the Council on Municipal Performance (COMP), the breakfast featured three speakers: Kruger, an attorney and former chairman of the New York Bar Association subcommittee on municipal bankruptcy; Professor Lawrence King of the New York University School of Law and one of the authors of the amended statute; and James Ring Adams, an editorial writer with *The Wall Street Journal,* which has advocated bankruptcy.

The law, it seems, was created by lawyers for lawyers. Professor King, a diminutive man with a full goatee and mustache, began by explaining why Chapter IX differed from a business bankruptcy: "Obviously, New York City cannot be sold" or liquidated to satisfy creditors. Kruger, however, wasn't certain Central Park couldn't be sold. King said one clause was clear: creditors could not force New York to declare bankruptcy. Only the city government could voluntarily do so.

Procedurally, the city can simply file for bankruptcy by alleging that it is insolvent and cannot pay debts as they mature. Until October 1, 1979, a bankruptcy petition would be filed with the U.S. District Court. After October 1 the amended Chapter IX specifies that the filing would be deposited with the U.S. Bankruptcy Court. The judge would be selected by the chief judge of the Circuit Court, based on his or her availability. The lawyers in the Penn Central bankruptcy case, for instance, have kept one poor judge occupied nearly full time for almost nine years. The bankruptcy of New York, King and Kruger say, would take at least that long to resolve.

After the selection of a judge, the next requirement is that a meeting of "impaired creditors"—those owed money—be summoned. The lawyers would litigate who could attend—note and bondholders? City suppliers? City workers? Welfare recipients? Citizens deprived of services? "Where are they going to meet?" Professor King asked rhetorically. "Yankee Stadium?" When they meet, their lawyers would negotiate and strive to agree on a common plan of who should get paid first and how much. Approval would require support from those attending and holding two-thirds of the dollar value of the debts outstanding and from 51 percent of all creditors. Their plan would then be submitted to the mayor's lawyers. If they concurred, it would be forwarded to the judge.

Even the best lawyers might find it difficult to reach agreement. Not that they would suffer, since their meters are always running. But could the city, despite state legislation, agree to pay MAC bondholders before employee pension funds or a Queens printer? Would city workers take precedence over welfare recipients? Would investors receive eighty cents on the dollar while small businessmen received sixty? Would unpaid suppliers of medicine continue to service city hospitals?

Failing agreement, Kruger says the statute contains a "cram-down mechanism"—the mayor could ask the judge to resolve disputes. But there is a catch-22: the court must first determine that the plan is "fair and equitable." Which means further litigation. If the court dismisses the city plan? Kruger suspects the state would be required to step in, but he concedes, "I haven't the faintest idea." The legislation is murky.

What about the argument that bankruptcy would relieve the city of the $2 billion paid each year for debt service? That is almost 30 percent of all locally raised revenues and four times the sum appropriated by the city for welfare. King and Kruger say it is not clear if bankruptcy would offer relief. Would note and bondholders—perhaps a majority of the creditors—agree to slash their own payments? In a private bankruptcy, explains Kruger, a moratorium on interest payments is invoked. But, he admits, "none of us know" whether this would be permitted in a municipal bankruptcy.

There are no precedents. No small or large city, he says, has ever sued for bankruptcy. Like the city of Detroit, many governments defaulted and failed to meet their obligations during the Depression. But they did not appear before a court and formally file for bankruptcy. They were just slow to pay bills. Only fifty or so jurisdictions entered bankruptcy proceedings, and most of these were small water or sewer districts.

The second major argument for bankruptcy—that expensive municipal labor contracts could be renegotiated—runs smack into three catch-22s. King and Kruger believe the courts would probably allow the abrogation of certain contracts. However, City Hall must convince the court the contracts are "onerous and burdensome." That's the first catch: the unions will deny this, and enter protracted litigation. Which brings us to the second catch: there are provisions in all contracts requiring that the terms of the old contract remain in effect during any renegotiation. Thus there is no immediate budgetary relief. The final catch: "I'm leaving open the question," says Kruger, "of whether employees would work."

While rejecting two major arguments advanced by those pushing bankruptcy, King and Kruger also undermined a central argument pushed by its foes. They did not believe a non-elected judge would wantonly quash the power of elected officials and anoint himself mayor. Besides, the mayor must agree to the creditors' plan. In the absence of agreement, City Hall decides who gets paid and what services are reduced. The judge, says Kruger, would "play as minimal a role in determining how the city functions as he can. It is clear the judge would not supersede elected officials." If anything, the judge would turn to the state and its Control Board, something the city has already done.

But, James Ring Adams countered, bankruptcy may be "inevitable." The size of city deficits is increasing; the city has successfully sold two small issues of notes but has yet to sell long-term bonds to public investors; the city's overall debt, and thus its future debt-service payments, has swelled since 1975. If you assume, as Adams does, that bankruptcy is inevitable, better to voluntarily declare it now before undertaking new debt obligations.

Is it inevitable? Jim Adams and others believe it is without much deeper sacrifices from the banks, unions, city, state and federal governments. The threat of bankruptcy is seen as an artillery attack, softening, perhaps scaring the opposition. Will the banks agree to drastically reduce usurious interest rates? Will the unions give up some padded fringes and inefficient work rules? Will citizens volunteer to perform functions previously expected of government? Will the state and the federal government do more?

It has been four years since the "fiscal crisis" invaded our vocabulary. Over that period, New York has successfully avoided bankruptcy. But we have failed to balance the budget, failed to reenter the bond market, failed to improve city services, failed to restore the economy.

As Thursday's breakfast made abundantly clear, bankruptcy does not offer salvation. "Chapter IX of the bankruptcy act provides a mechanism," Professor King cautioned. "It does not provide a solution." There are lots of arguments against bankruptcy. The most potent is a simple explanation of how the law wouldn't work for anyone but the lawyers.

Passing the Reality Test

New York *Daily News*, April 15, 1979

Both have drooping eyelids and thinning hair, are essentially shy, and served as chairmen of the City Planning Commission while in their mid-thirties. Former Mayor Wagner and his son, Robert F. Wagner, Jr., are very devoted to each other.

They are also very different. The former mayor is a thick-skinned, anecdotal, and wily *how are ya?* pol who believed that if you ignored problems long enough, they would go away. While limousining through Harlem in the early sixties, an idealistic young aide spoke of the visible poverty and blight. He was shocked. "What should we do? *What should we do, Mr. Mayor?*" he pleaded.

"Turn right at the next corner," Wagner calmly told the driver.

The father quotes Frank Sinatra; the son, George Orwell. The son is sensitive, intellectual, eager to peel the onion of public problems. All of which suggests he's in the wrong business. When he ran for Manhattan borough president and lost in 1977, friends thought he should become a professor. Ed Koch disagreed, appointing Wagner chairman of the City Planning Commission. Those who knew young Wagner knew he had the brains. But was he tough enough? Would he risk angering the mayor and family friends by aggressively speaking out? Would he pass the reality test, coming down on the side of the do-able as opposed to the desirable?

Wagner passed the test. In his first year Wagner prodded City Hall to shift the thrust of capital spending away from new construction and toward rehabilitating existing structures. He persisted in reminding City Hall that the available resources to "rebuild" the South Bronx did not match the public promises made. And, in the past week, Wagner's office has issued two more tough-minded reports—each transcending the narrow "liberal" versus "conservative," pro- or anti-landlord labels our politics and journalism consign most development issues to.

On Sunday the commission released a 104-page report scolding city government and urging New York to "adjust our capital spending and priorities to facts." The overriding *facts* were that the city's population was shrinking, its economy and budget contracting. This reality, declared the commission, evaded the Board of Education. Despite a 24-percent drop in elementary school enrollment and 40 percent in high schools over the next decade, the board still requested $299 million for forty-seven new projects. Instead of closing schools, they wanted to build them.

Ditto higher education: "The City University faces the loss of 41 percent of its senior college students and 20 percent of its junior college students by 1992 from the 1975 peak enrollment, yet remains committed to eighteen separate campuses and plans for a $681-million construction program."

Ditto the city's municipal hospitals: "New York created its municipal hospital system to serve its poor residents; however, the development of Medicaid and Medicare has meant that hospital care for the poor has become available outside of the municipal hospital system. Clearly, this change undercuts the logic behind the city's ownership and operation of seventeen hospitals."

Ditto Mayor Koch's sunny optimism about a city "renaissance": "Dramatic improvement in the city's economy is not likely in the near future."

The failure to confront reality, said the commission, induced the Transit Authority to leap and build a Second Avenue subway—"with four giant underground caverns its only monument." We constructed new libraries as we were cutting funds for libraries, new pollution-control plants as we sliced the staff to operate them. Woodhull Hospital, a new edifice in Brooklyn, stands empty. The commission could have lodged a similar complaint against the city's Westway plan, but didn't. Instead of spending more than $1 billion on this highway and development project, to be consistent the commision might suggest that City Hall spend these funds to replenish its 6,700 subway cars or repair its 232 miles of tracks.

But the report did say: "Even today, to a remarkable extent, the city remains committed to a reality which no longer applies."

On Wednesday, Wagner and the commission plunged into another thicket—the spread of abandoned housing. Sadly, they noted that City Hall has become the landlord for 10,000 multiple dwellings—8 percent of all such city buildings. By September 1980 the city will own 16,000, or 13 percent. Abandoned by private landlords, these buildings no longer pay property taxes, robbing city revenues of several hundred million dollars annually and costing $35 million for fuel and electricity.

Unlike the Beame administration, which essentially ignored the cancer, Koch has vainly tried to curb it. Housing Commissioner Nat Leventhal has beefed up the management of these buildings, aggressively sought to convert buildings to tenant ownership. Almost 53 percent—$128 million—of federal Community Development funds, which are supposed to be earmarked for construction and rehabilitation, are siphoned off to maintain these buildings.

Yet the cancer multiplies. Next year 82 percent of these federal funds is projected to be diverted. By August 1981 almost 400,000 New Yorkers will collect in these buildings, most of them poor. A population larger than the state of Wyoming. And, Wagner laments, only 31 percent of these tenants currently pay the rent.

The city has tried to contain a flame within a paper bag; struggled to calm the smoke but not remove the fire's fuel. Despite the fiscal crisis and the obvious limits on its budget, City Hall has inadvertently backed into a new welfare spending program.

Enter Wagner. Seated at a large round conference table in a bright corner office behind City Hall, Wagner declared, "The city of New York cannot be the landlord of last resort. Just as we learned the city could not be the employer of last resort." The commission, he announced, will undertake a study and shape a strategy to prevent future abandonment and return already abandoned buildings to private or tenant ownership.

The nub of the problem, said a twenty-five-page commission report, is economic: "Property owners are unlikely to invest in capital improvements or basic maintenance when the economics of ownership are leading them to forfeit their properties rather than pay real-estate taxes."

Wagner feels he already knows some answers. He believes rent control and rent stabilization, which blanket 125,000 multiple dwellings, are too rigid. Since landlords are not in the charity business, he embraces the view that rents must rise and taxes on these "overassessed" dwellings must drop. Some might consider that "pro-landlord." But one could also say it is "pro-tenant" and "pro-city" to prevent abandonment and rundown neighborhoods and guarantee that poor tenants get heat. This past winter seven citizens froze to death.

Wagner believes these steps must be coupled with new strictures against bank and insurance company redlining, which strangles communities; the city, with one-third of these buildings less than 30-percent occupied, needs to consolidate tenants in partially occupied buildings. If these and other steps don't reverse the trend, Mayor Koch is prepared to abandon the abandoned buildings and, some will charge, the people in them.

"If we cannot restructure the whole business and get out of the rent business and we're still left next year with these large numbers of properties," Koch told me, "we're going to vastly reduce our commitment to providing services to these buildings. No other city does. What they do is simply tell tenants, 'You don't like it, get another apartment.'" Koch says he will decide on or about July 1, 1980.

Confronting a similar problem, many of us might prefer to remain in bed. If there is a solution, it will not be painless. Because of high costs and rent regulations, New York City is uneconomic for many landlords. They cannot charge an economic rent. Yet, tragically, their poor residents cannot afford to pay an economic rent, a point the commission overlooked. This gap between rent and income could be bridged with a government subsidy, but the city and state lack the resources and the federal government is curbing its Section 8 subsidies.

The politics are volatile, and just as depressing. To lower the tax assessment on New York's multiple dwellings—40 percent of them constructed prior to 1901—might require higher taxes on one- and two-family homes. Any effort to ease rent regulations would undoubtedly fan a fever among city residents, 75 percent of whom are renters.

There is considerable evidence that powerful constituencies would resist rent hikes, anti-redlining legislation, the closing of some municipal hospitals. There is less evidence that long-term planning has a constituency. Wagner disagrees. "There is a constituency out there for being as accurate as we can in describing reality," he said. "That's the constituency that elected Ed Koch. Obviously, self-interest is a powerful political motive. But people can be persuaded that their immediate self-interest is not in their interest five years from now."

Under Wagner, the seven-member commission seeks to carve a more independent role. "There is a role of serving the administration," Wagner says. "But the commission should be dealing with issues that maybe the administration cannot. Otherwise, there's no reason for our existence."

To Wagner's credit, he sounds like neither his father nor like a meek college professor.

SECOND THOUGHTS

The most frequent complaint public officials register against the press is that we are guilty of oversimplification. Stark headlines or sharp leads or too-brief news reports or opinionated columns, they say, often do not capture the competing realities they must balance, the absence of good versus evil choices they face. In this sense, they accuse the press of flunking a reality test.

Unlike columnists, a mayor has the responsibility not just to tell the truth (as he sees it), but also to inspire confidence and faith. I can go around yelling *The-end-of-the-world-is-coming;* a mayor cannot, unless he wishes to encourage more businesses and middle-income people to flee New York. A city, like a bond market, requires confidence to thrive.

True, some realities are simple. No matter the number of excuses, city streets are filthy, city services are declining, the special interests are too powerful, Governor Carey can be a bull artist, Mayor Beame was in over his head. Once in a while, however, it's useful to remember that people like me sometimes denounce the motivations of people who are merely wrong, not venal. Hugh Carey doesn't think of himself as a bull-artist, as Abe Beame didn't think he was in over his head.

For a moment, imagine you were the mayor of New York. You pick up the paper and read that too many sanitationmen have lost the work ethic, which is true. Talk to citizens and they complain of lousy sanitation service. Yet talk to sanitationmen and they complain that citizens are slobs. The forces of good government prod you to crack down on malingerers, yet your sanitation commissioner cautions that worker morale is low and no new productivity scheme will work without the cooperation of his men. The men complain about faulty equipment. Impatient, you berate the commissioner, who reminds you it takes twenty-four months to order and receive new equipment.

Mayor Beame refused to confront the sanitation union, and the press accused him of being co-opted by it. Mayor Koch attacks the union, and is accused of being a confrontationalist. Editorial writers or columnists usually address a single issue, a single column, at any one time. But a mayor cannot. He must make connections between issues. If he takes on the unions and publicly demands two-man rather than three-man sanitation trucks, for instance, will he lose the unions' cooperation to ease civil-service strictures and improve management by removing more supervisors from the union? If during labor negotiations he persistently demands give-backs from the unions and a modest pay hike, will he harden union demands and thus guarantee a more expensive settlement? A mayor can ask: Is it better to be honest or to be effective? That is a dilemna foreign to many reporters, a reality we sometimes skate over.

Babes in Bureaucracyland

New York *Daily News,* March 11, 1979

A sure cure for a bad case of skepticism is to visit B.J.'s Kids. No, it's not a new Burt Reynolds movie. Or a fast-food shop. Rather it's the name of a child-care center at 331 West Eighty-fourth Street, conceived and operated by B.J. Richards, a young woman who could be locked up for her contagious good cheer.

By conventional standards, the center—which occupies the entire ground floor of a brownstone—is a flop. It does not earn a profit. It receives no government grants, has no consultants, and has only a skeleton staff, which parades in jeans. It does not advertise. It does not have a license. But for twenty-six children, age eighteen months to three years old, B.J.'s works.

It also works for the kids' black and white working-class families, who can afford neither the luxury of not working nor the $110 or more per week charged by most child-care centers. Frightened of baby-sitters who treat children like products on warehouse shelves, noticing only when they fall off, parents scoured the city, hoping to find someone, someplace, who cares. Since she opened for business last June, B.J. Richards has become their surrogate mother.

A happy ending? It was until the big bad wolf—the city Department of Health—threatened to shut B.J.'s Kids in April. The department refused to grant B.J. a license, as it has eight hundred other centers. The four rooms, it claims, are too small. The regulations say each child under three must be provided forty square feet of space. There are too many children under three.

The small saga of B.J.'s Kids spotlights the perils of burdensome bureaucracy. "Hello, I'm from the government, and I'm here to help you" has become a nightmare of the seventies. As has the neglected need for reasonably priced child care in a nation of eighty-four million mothers, one-half of whom work or are seeking to. And, finally, B.J.'s Kids spotlights wondrously naïve people who care about others.

B.J. Richards is an unlikely candidate for martyrdom. Two years ago this chunky thirty-one-year-old woman with a Buster Brown haircut was a secretary. She was bored. Frustrated. She began baby-sitting, taking neighbors' children to nearby Riverside Park. "For the first time I loved what I was doing," she recalled the other day, sitting in the kitchen of her center as her brood sang songs. "So I read every book I could get. I started using space in my bedroom for play space. But I had two roommates, and they were going nuts."

Encouraged by neighborhood parents, B.J. quit her job. Together they searched for space, finding an entire ground floor filled with junk on West Eighty-fourth Street. The building was owned by the United Farmworkers Union, received as a gift when they were headquartered in New York. B.J. wrote them, pleading to rent the space. They agreed, charging her but $200 a month.

The parents—struggling secretaries, nurses, actors, writers, bakers, hospital workers, divorced mothers—pitched in to help clear the debris, paint the walls sprightly yellows, blues, and greens, repair doors, hang plants, donate workbenches and bookcases. No one thought to apply for a government grant. Nor did B.J. think of profits. This was to be their commune.

When the center opened in June, they didn't know what to call it. A cold-sounding title wouldn't do, so they christened it B.J.'s Kids. They didn't know enough to apply for a license, as such centers are supposed to. B.J., who doesn't know the difference between net and gross income, and couldn't care less, didn't prepare a budget. She had no idea how many children the four-room apartment could accommodate.

No matter. Applications poured in. Within days twenty-five families signed up and more crowded the waiting list. There are few places in New York that welcome pre-three-year-olds. For only $55 a week, parents could enroll their child from 8:30 A.M. to 5:45 P.M., five days a week; for two mornings, the fee is only $15; for three days, $30. The center brings in $800 a week and spends $800 a week. B.J. takes a weekly salary of $175; Tony Lee, a former baker and longshoreman whose wife is a waitress, quit his job to take care of "Z," his twenty-two-month-old son, and to work full time with B.J. He, too, earns $175. Both voluntarily reduced their salary to hire a trained teacher, Denise Prince, a handsome black woman. Because the center is more concerned with kids who receive their service than with the middlemen who provide it, none of the parents feel ripped off.

At B.J.'s, the children paint or bake or play on the slide or have stories read to them until 9:30 A.M. Then B.J., Denise, Tony, along with two to four aides who are paid $3 an hour, gather them in a circle to sing, "Good morning, it's Wednesday. Happy Wednesday today." Each child gets serenaded, "Good morning, Julia. How are you today?" At ten o'clock homemade snacks are provided by the center. They play, visit the park to feed the pigeons, and recite and read until lunch, which they bring from home. Nap time is from twelve-thirty to two-thirty, followed by songs, a snack, and more play and instruction until their parents arrive.

Everyone seems happy, except the Department of Health. The Department first heard of B.J.'s Kids in September and sent her an application, which she filled out. Three months later inspectors descended from the Fire, Buildings and Sanitation Departments. Then, on January 5, a Health Department official, Ms. Eva Wolfson, paid a surprise visit and warned she would close the place. "She said, 'Get rid of those eighteen-month-olds and just have three-year-olds,'" recalls B.J. "But the need is for those three and under. Once you're a three-year-old, there are a thousand options."

Wolfson told B.J. they could agree if only ten children were in attendance at any one time. "But she knew that if we just had ten children, we couldn't make it financially," says B.J. "I understand the need for licensing. I have seen some places that shouldn't be in existence. But rules can be interpreted in many different ways." B.J. and Tony remained optimistic. They traveled downtown several times to meet with four different officials. After their last meeting, on February 23, their optimism was drained.

They were desperate, angry, scared. So they decided to call upon the only weapon a large bureaucracy usually understands: publicity and political pressure. B.J. and the parents reached out for Councilwoman Ruth Messinger, inviting her for coffee. She came. So did a lone TV crew from WNEW. On March 1 Robert J. Sullivan, a parent, wrote to Mayor Koch: "My family needs B.J.'s Kids, for our careers, for the social and educational benefit to our daughter. It's embarrassing to find that in a city that prides itself on innovation and creativity, there seems to be a system that appears bent on destroying initiative and hard work."

The heat was now on the Health Department, which was being bombarded by calls, letters. On Wednesday, when I phoned Eva Wolfson's office, her secretary answered, "Is it about B.J.'s Kids?" Martin Fox, the chief of licensing, was "in a meeting." It was suggested I call the public-relations office, which suggested I call Dr. Bernard Bihari, deputy commissioner for Departmental Operations. Clearly B.J. and her tiny army had broken through to the top of the Health Department.

That afternoon Dr. Bihari returned the call. The only remaining obstacle, he softly said, was "a complex issue involving space." But he spoke of "compromise," of having "no intention of immediately closing them. We plan further discussions." B.J.'s Kids was no longer an address on a licensing application. It was real people. "One of the things working for them is the reputation of the person running it, and the good atmosphere there," he said. "We're willing to negotiate. But rather than come back to us, they've gone outside to open discussions with the media and politicians."

Because they went "outside," these little people are probably going to conquer big government, at least this once. Congratulations, B.J.

Hard Feelings

New York *Daily News,* November 18, 1979

With the aid of a razor strap, my father was very persuasive. "Don't go near the mobsters who hang out on Mermaid Avenue," he warned me at an age when I still looked up to tough guys. "You see them, you walk across the street."

I listened. In the late sixties, when the Justice Department reported that Anthony Scotto was a *capo* in the mob, when the press printed tales of Scotto's alleged waterfront perfidies, I walked across the street. I worked in politics, where Scotto was important, but I kept my distance.

In 1971, when I worked for OTB, one of Scotto's close friends was recommended for a job. I took the application to an expert on organized crime. He said he did not know whether it was true or false that Scotto was a *capo,* or even whether he worked for the mob. "But I'm sure of one thing," he said. "The mob controls the waterfront, and Tony Scotto would not have been made head of the longshoremen's union at such a young age unless he at least played ball with them."

It may have been unfair, but Scotto's friend did not get the job.

I didn't know Scotto, but I was always struck by the gap between his appearance and his reputation. He dressed and talked like a banker, not a racketeer. Since I also sported a vowel at the end of my name, I sometimes wondered whether he was not a victim of vicious innuendo, of ethnic stereotyping.

Still, I stayed across the street. We shook hands once in an elevator on the way to a press conference I was covering. Last Christmas I talked with Scotto and his wife, Marion, at a party. She wore a bright smile and asked to be remembered to my dad, whom she knew from her work in the Brooklyn borough president's office. A nice gesture, I thought.

At a friend's wedding this spring I again ran into Marion and Anthony Scotto. We talked briefly, exchanging a few jokes and pleasantries. "How's your father?" Marion asked, aware that cancer had recently plundered our family. I noticed that when the Scottos talked to you, they didn't look around the room. They seemed like nice, sincere people.

I stayed away from Scotto's trial, although I followed every word of it in the newspapers. Scotto sounded guilty. The prosecutors' evidence—the tape-recorded conversations of Scotto retreating to bathrooms to accept cash-filled envelopes, his whispering to an associate of a "kitty" that "we'll split up"—seemed devastating.

I remembered the advice of my dad and of the OTB crime adviser, thought not of the good deeds Anthony Scotto performed for the port of New York but of the workers and businesses and consumers who have been bled or bludgeoned by the mob's control of the waterfront. Once again I became stern. Anger swelled as I read some of our favorite columnists. If Scotto was guilty, they said, then all blue-collar workers—indeed, society, the system, the world—were guilty. They blamed the prosecution for using tapes, not Scotto for what he said on those tapes.

They sounded mushy-minded, too emotionally involved. To excuse Scotto by claiming that everyone who lives in a blue-collar world practices a little extortion is not only insulting to honest men and women but is akin to saying the law should apply only to those we don't care for. Like the Gulf executive who makes illegal cash contributions to win foreign contracts, for instance.

Suffused with more than my usual high quotient of self-righteousness, I went to the federal courthouse early Wednesday. Once in the seventh-floor courtroom, I briskly asked, "Could I please have the complete transcript of the trial summations?" Heading toward a rear bench, several pounds of paper in tow, I was stopped by a pretty blonde with a rainbow for a smile who asked, "How's your father?"

Marion Scotto's shower of kindness momentarily washed away my journalistic edge. Here, on the fourth day of this wake, waiting nervously for the jury to return with a verdict that could send one father to jail for twenty years, Marion Scotto asked about another father. I didn't think it was an act. Torn between what I felt and what I thought, I wanted to offer sympathy, a word of encouragement. Coolly, I kept my distance.

Escaping to the rear of the courtroom, I busied myself reading the final arguments of the defense and prosecution. James LaRossa, Scotto's able attorney, stuck to two basic themes. Instead of laboring over a detailed factual rebuttal to the charge that his client extorted and pocketed $300,000 from waterfront firms, he went on the offensive, attacking the credibility of the prosecution's principal witnesses. They were people who had pleaded guilty to crimes, LaRossa said, and in a desperate attempt to bargain for leniency, had offered Scotto's head.

The second major defense thrust was one of innocence by association. "The sitting governor of the state of New York doesn't walk into a criminal trial and testify for everybody," LaRossa said. "Two prior mayors, a future president of the AFL-CIO, and on and on and on. Could have brought a hundred of them in . . . This whole town would have come in for Anthony Scotto."

"You know, a lot of lawyers will do all kinds of sympathetic things and suggest that his family is sitting in a certain place in the courtroom, that he has four children, or anything like that," he declared. "Let me tell you something, folks. I am not doing that, and I'm not getting on my knees to you. He doesn't need it."

This seemed very clever of LaRossa, especially since Marion and her four children—Elaina, Rosanna, John and Anthony Jr.—appeared daily in the first two rows to the right of the jury. Each day as the jurors filed in or out, they brushed past the Scotto family. LaRossa ended by asking the jurors to say, "Anthony Scotto, go home. Keep up the work."

Looking up, I saw Marion Scotto embrace one of their many friends and relatives who joined her daily vigil. Anthony Scotto, hands in his pocket, glided in and out of the courtroom, good-naturedly joked with reporters, studied the caricatures of his family drawn by the press artists, instinctively touched friends, refusing to permit their pity.

A friend of the Scotto family, Marion's gynecologist, introduced himself. "Isn't it terrible what the prosecution has done," he told me. "I reread *1984* the other day. The police state that George Orwell wrote about we're seeing here in this courtroom." He complained of how Scotto was bugged, tailed, how his kids saw planes swoop so low overhead to snap pictures they feared the planes would crash into the house. To the good doctor, Scotto was a victim.

To U.S. Attorney Robert Fiske, the prosecutor, he was a villain. Relying on tape recordings, Fiske peppered the jury with alleged facts—Scotto's collecting regular envelopes, Scotto's telling an associate to burn the books if the federal government subpoenaed them.

He dismissed Scotto's impressive character witnesses because "they were not there when any of those things happened." The issue, Fiske stated, was not whether Scotto was a good labor leader or a friend of the famous. Nor whether he served his city and state well. The issue was extortion for personal gain.

I glared at Scotto. Even if the jury found him innocent of the legal charges, surely the moral basis of Scotto's defense was weak. LaRossa conceded that Scotto took $75,000 in cash from the waterfront firms (not the $300,000 charged). He said he took it for political campaigns, not personal gain. The cash went to Mario Cuomo's 1977 mayoral effort and Hugh Carey's 1978 reelection, he said. Since such cash contributions are illegal, LaRossa was implicitly pleading guilty to a state misdemeanor in order to avoid a federal felony charge.

Scotto admitted he gave expensive dinner tickets to the city commissioner of ports and terminals, the agency that supervises the waterfront; that an employee of the Waterfront Commission, which polices the port, was encouraged to smuggle to Scotto confidential information concerning investigations; that he knowingly approved "phony disability" payments to his workers. Above all, Scotto used reported political contributions, totaling $1.3 million in 1977 and 1978, to purchase political power.

Scotto dealt from one reality, the prosecutors from another. Scotto's world is peopled by practical "business" transactions. I walked over and asked Scotto about this. Raising funds from waterfront businesses is not extortion, he said evenly, looking me squarely in the eye and leaning back against the rail behind the defendant's table, his arms folded. "It is no different than what the AFL-CIO or maritime interests do nationally. The maritime industry puts together maritime funds. You see it on the state level where contractors get together with the building trade unions . . . There's no question that unless you're strong in the state legislatures and the Congress, you can lose what you won at the bargaining table."

A moment later, just a few feet away from Scotto, a prosecutor spoke of another reality. "If I accepted Scotto's own testimony as the truth—which I don't," he said, "it's one hell of an indictment of the political process." Cash contributions to campaigns may be *normal,* as politicians suggested all last week, but they are not legal.

Privately, many reporters covering this trial believed the facts eclipsed Scotto's able defense. However, several admitted they were secretly rooting for Marion and Tony Scotto. The facts collided with their feelings.

Glancing quickly at Marion Scotto as I left the courtroom, I was determined not to let that happen. After a while the elevator came. The Scotto children got on first, trailed by relatives, friends, and Marion and Tony Scotto.

The last place in the world I wanted to be was on that elevator, but the Scottos insisted on squeezing the rest of us on. Part of me wanted to reach out and wish them luck; another insisted I keep a journalistic distance. I stared at the floor lights: 6 . . . 5 . . . 4 . . . 3 . . . 2 . . . 1.

The doors finally parted. As we walked out, a hand touched my arm. "Remember us to your father," Marion said. "And, Ken," she added, smiling but sad, "be good to us."

On Thursday the jury was not good to Marion and Anthony Scotto. I thought the jury probably made the only decision they could. Excuse me for sounding mushy-minded, but when I heard the news I felt sick.

ABOUT THE AUTHOR

KEN AULETTA was brought up in Coney Island, attended New York City public schools and the State University of New York at Oswego, and received an M.A. from the Maxwell School of Citizenship and Public Affairs at Syracuse University. He worked for the federal and city governments and participated in national and state political campaigns. A former contributing editor of *New York* magazine and staff writer for *The Village Voice,* he is now a writer for *The New Yorker* and a columnist for the New York *Daily News.* His work has also appeared in the *New York Review of Books* and the *New York Times,* and he appears regularly on New York public television. He is the author of *The Streets Were Paved with Gold,* a widely acclaimed study of New York's governmental and financial crisis.